THE RA EXPEDITIONS

BY THOR HEYERDAHL

The Kon-Tiki Expedition
Aku-Aku
American Indians in the Pacific
Sea Routes to Polynesia

WITH EDWIN N. FERDON

The Archaeology of Easter Island

THE RA EXPEDITIONS

Thor Heyerdahl

TRANSLATED BY PATRICIA CRAMPTON

London
GEORGE ALLEN & UNWIN LTD
RUSKIN HOUSE MUSEUM STREET

FIRST PUBLISHED IN 1971

This translation © George Allen & Unwin Ltd, 1971

Translated from the Norwegian
© Thor Heyerdahl, 1970

ISBN: 0 04 572020 7

PRINTED IN GREAT BRITAIN
in 12 point Bembo type
BY BILLING & SONS LTD
GUILDFORD AND LONDON

To Yvonne

CONTENTS

20°   0°   20°   40°

SARDINIA

MEDITERRANEAN

Larache
Safi
MOROCCO
Cape Juby

CANARY
ISLANDS

Canary current

CAPE VERDE
ISLANDS

Byblos
Giza
EGYPT

Tigris
Mesopotamia
Euphrates

R. Nile

RED SEA

TROPIC OF CANCER

CHAD
Lake Chad   Bol
Fort Lamy

Lake Tana

Lake Zwai

ETHIOPIA

EQUATOR

TROPIC OF CAPRICORN

0   1000   2000 km

0   500   1000 nautical miles

20°   0°   20°   40°

ILLUSTRATIONS

11

Illustrations

One Riddle, Two Answers and No Solution

A REED flutters in the wind.

We break it off.

It floats. It can bear a frog.

Two hundred thousand reeds flutter in the wind. A whole meadow billows like a green cornfield along the shore.

We cut it down. We tie it into sheaves, like great corn dollies. The bundles float. We go on board. A Russian, an African, a Mexican, an Egyptian, an American, an Italian, and myself, a Norwegian, with a monkey and a lot of clucking hens. We are off to America. We are in Egypt. It's blowing sand, it's dry and hot, it's the Sahara.

Abdullah assures me that the reeds will float. I tell him that America is a long way off. He does not think people like black skins in America, but I assure him he is wrong. He does not know where America is, but we will get there in any case, if the wind is blowing that way. We will be safe on the reeds as long as the ropes hold. As long as the ropes hold, he says. Will the ropes hold?

I felt someone shaking me by the shoulder and woke up. It was Abdullah. 'It's three o'clock,' he said. 'We are starting work again.' The sun was baking inside the hot tent canvas. I sat up and peered through a gap in the door opening. The dry heat and blinding sunshine of the Sahara thrust at me from outside. Sun, sun, sun. A sun-soaked expanse of sand met the bluest thing God has created, a cloudless desert sky unfolding in the afternoon sunshine above a world of golden-grey sand.

A row of three large and two small pyramids were set like shark's teeth against the arch of sky. They had stood so, motionless and unchanging, since the time when men were part of nature and built in accord with nature. And in front of them, down in the shallow depression, lay something timeless, built yesterday, built ten thousand years ago, a boat in the desert sand, a sort of Noah's Ark stranded in the wilderness of the Sahara, far from surf and seaweed. Two camels stood beside it, chewing. What were they chewing? Trimmings from the boat itself perhaps, the 'paper boat'. It was built of papyrus. The golden reeds were lashed together in bundles, taking the form of a ship with prow and sternpost which stood out against the blue sky like a recumbent crescent moon.

Abdullah was already on his way down there. And two coal-black Buduma Negroes in fluttering white robes were clambering on board, while Egyptians in colourful garments dragged up fresh bundles of papyrus reed. There was work to be done. '*Bot! Bot!*' shouted Abdullah. 'More reeds!' I staggered out on to the hot sand as if I had awakened from a thousand-year sleep. After all, they were working for me; it was I who had conceived the absurd idea of reviving a boat-builder's art which the Pharaoh Cheops and his generation were already beginning to abandon at the time when they ordered the building of those mighty pyramids which now stood there like a solid mountain range, hiding our timeless shipyard from the twentieth century maelstrom whirling in Cairo's hectic city streets down in the green Nile valley on the other side.

Our world, outside the tents, was bare sand. Hot sand, pyramids, more sand, and huge stacks of sun-dried reeds, brittle, combustible papyrus reeds, which the men were now dragging over to the liquorice-skinned Negroes who sat on the crescent moon, tightening rope lashings with the aid of hands, teeth and naked feet. They were building a boat – a papyrus boat. A *kaday* they called it in their Buduma tongue, and they knew what they were building. Busy fingers and teeth strapped the loops round the reeds as only experts could. 'A paper-boat,' said the people at the Papyrus Institute down in the Nile Valley. For there they soaked these reeds in water and beat them into a crisp paper, to show tourists and scientists what the world's most ancient scholars had used to paint their hieroglyphic memoirs on.

A papyrus reed is a soft, sappy flower stem which a child can bend and crush. When it is dry it snaps like a matchstick and burns like paper. On the ground in front of me lay a tinder-dry papyrus reed, savagely screwed and fractured into a zigzag tangle. It had been thrown there in the morning by an indignant old Arab who mangled it between his fingers before flinging it away from him on the sand, spitting after it and pointing scornfully. 'That thing,' he said, 'that wouldn't even hold a nail; and how could you fix masts to a thing like that?' The old man was a canny boat-builder who had taken the bus up from Port Said to conclude a contract for masts and rigging for the vessel we were building. He was so outraged that he took the next bus back to the coast. Were we trying to make fun of an honest craftsman, or were the men of today completely ignorant of what was needed to build a decent craft? It was no good explaining to him that similar boats were painted in large numbers on the walls of the burial chambers of the ancient pyramid-builders out here in the desert. After all, these tombs also contain paintings of men with the heads of birds and serpents with wings. Anyone could see that a reed was a soft stalk in which neither nails nor screws could find a grip. Material for a haystack. A paper boat. Thanks for the return ticket.

What now? Boats must have masts. Our three black friends from Lake Chad in the heart of Africa declared that the boat-builder was an idiot; he could never have seen a proper *kaday*, because they were always made from these reeds. On the other hand, they had never seen masts on a *kaday*, and what did we want with one? If people wanted to cross the water they used paddles. Lake Chad was large, the sea could not be larger, they claimed. Stoically unperturbed, they continued to lash the bundles of papyrus together. That was their speciality. The Arab from Port Said was an ignorant bluffer who had never seen a *kaday*.

I went up to the tent again and dug out of the portfolio the sketches and photographs of ancient Egyptian boat models and wall-paintings. There were no spikes in the papyrus boats. A thick, wide footplate was made fast with rope on top of the reed bundles where the mast was to stand, and then the bottom of the mast was stepped into the solid block of wood and secured with rope. I pushed the drawings aside and lay down on my back on a heap of ropes and canvas stacked along one wall of the tent. It was cooler here and I could think. What was I really taking on, and what reason had I to think that such a craft could be used outside the Nile Delta? I admitted to myself that the suspicion was based as much on intuition as on concrete facts.

At the time when I decided to build the *Kon-Tiki* raft of balsa logs, my grounds had been quite different. True enough, I had never seen a piece of balsa wood then and never sailed a boat, let alone a raft, but I had had a theory, solid scientific evidence and a logical conclusion. This time I had none. Before I ventured to set sail with

B   17

Kon-Tiki, I had already accumulated enough material to fill a very bulky manuscript with evidence proving to my own satisfaction that an offshoot of the oldest civilization in Peru had reached the Polynesian Islands before any voyagers had reached the East Pacific out of Asia. The balsa raft was considered the nearest thing to a boat known in ancient Peru, and I therefore concluded that it had to be seaworthy. How else could the ancient Peruvians have come across to Polynesia? I had no other reason to trust the abilities of a balsa raft. But the conclusion held good.

This time things were different. I had no theory that the ancient Egyptians had carried their civilization to distant islands or continents. There *were* many others who believed so and argued that the Egyptian pyramid-builders had brought cultural inspiration to tropical America long before Columbus. I had no such theory: I had never found any conclusive evidence favouring it, but neither had I found any evidence to the contrary. I was fascinated by the problem, but in no position to see any tenable solution. Science lacked too many pieces of the jigsaw puzzle. Anyone seriously looking for a possible connection between the ancient cultures of Egypt and Mexico could not avoid finding wide gaps in the chronology, inexplicable contradictions, and an ocean gap ten thousand times wider than the Nile.

For water travel the ancient Egyptians originally had only bundle-boats made of papyrus reed. Later they made themselves long wooden ships of planks, dovetailed and sewn together, vulnerable in a heavy sea, but eminently suited to all kinds of transport and trading on the calm waters of the Nile. A few hundred yards from the tent where I lay, at the foot of the Pyramid of Cheops, my Egyptian friend Ahmed Joseph was busy piecing together one of the magnificent wooden ships of the Pharaoh Cheops. Archaeologists had recently discovered that a large ship lay buried on each side of this large pyramid: four ships in all were lying there, hermetically preserved. They lay in deep, airtight chambers, covered with enormous stone slabs. Only one pit had been opened so far, revealing hundreds of thick sections of cedar-wood planking piled in stacks, as fresh as when they were buried over 4,600 years ago – some 2,700 years before Christ. Now, Egypt's chief curator, Ahmed Joseph, was busy threading new rope through all the thousands of small holes where the ship had once been held together by hempen rope. The result was a ship over 140 feet long, so perfectly streamlined and elegant that the Vikings had not built anything more graceful or larger when some millennia later they began to sail the high seas.

There was only one essential difference between the two types of ship: the Viking ships were built to bear the brunt of the ocean rollers, while Cheops's ship was built for pomp and ceremony on the placid Nile. Wear and tear on the wood, where the ropes had chafed furrows, showed that Cheops's ship had been in proper use, and had not been just a 'solar ship' built solely for the Pharaoh's last voyage. Yet the streamlined hull would have collapsed on its first encounter with ocean waves. This was truly amazing. The exquisite lines of the ship were specialized to perfection for true ocean voyaging. Its gracefully curved hull, with elegantly upthrust and very high bow and stern, had all the characteristic features found only in sea-going vessels, specially designed to ride breakers and towering waves. Here was something to puzzle over. Perhaps the real key to an unsolved mystery. A pharaoh, living on the calm shores of the Nile nearly five thousand years ago, had built a boat which in practice could only stand up to the peaceful ripples of the river, yet he had built it on architectonic lines which the world's leading seafaring nations never surpassed. He had built his frail river-boat to a pattern created by shipbuilders from a people with a long, solid tradition of sailing on the open sea.

Then one could begin to guess. There were only two possibilities. Either this sea-going, streamlined shape had been developed by Egyptian seafarers of the same brilliant generations which had already evolved writing and pyramid-building, mummies, brain surgery and astronomy; or the pharaoh's shipwrights had been trained abroad. There are facts which point to the latter. No cedars grow in Egypt; the material of which Cheops's ship was built came from the cedar forests of Lebanon. The Lebanon was the home of the Phoenicians, experienced shipbuilders who sailed the whole of the Mediterranean and part of the Atlantic with their ships. Their principal port, Byblos, the oldest known city in the world, imported papyrus from Egypt because Byblos was a centre of book production in ancient times, hence the word *Byblos*, or Bible, which means book. There were lively trade relations between Egypt and Byblos at the time when the Pyramid of Cheops was built, so Cheops's shipbuilders might have copied their specialized design here. Maybe.

The trouble is, we know little or nothing about the appearance of the Phoenician wooden ships. All we can say with certainty is that they can scarcely have been papyriform, that is, built on the lines of a papyrus boat, since the Phoenicians imported papyrus from Egypt because it did not grow in Lebanon. And here the problem arises. The Pharaoh Cheops's ship was papyriform. All the other large wooden ships depicted from Pharaonic times in Egypt were also papyriform; they all had the papyrus boat as their direct model. And here we come to the nub of the problem. The papyrus boat was the model for Cheops's boat. And it was precisely this model, built of papyrus, which had all the sea-going ship's characteristic properties, with prow and stern soaring upward, higher than in a Viking ship, to ride out breakers and high seas, not to contend with little ripples on the Nile. It was the papyrus ship which had been the model for the wooden ship, not the other way round. And the design of the papyrus ship was already fully developed when the first pharaohs had their mythical ancestors, the gods, painted on the walls of their tombs. Sun-god and bird-men, the legendary forefathers of the first pharaoh, are not portrayed as passengers on Phoenician wooden ships, nor on rafts or river barges, but on upswept papyrus ships of precisely the same style which the Pharaoh Cheops's boat-builders copied in every minute detail, even to the sharply incurved stern, with the calyx shape of the papyrus flower at its tip.

In order to build a ship as the Egyptians did, at the time when the Mediterranean culture was finding its feet along the banks of the Nile, one needs neither an axe nor a carpenter's skill, but a knife to cut reeds, and some rope. That was what my African friends Mussa, Omar and Abdullah were now doing, down there near the foot of the pyramids of Cheops, Chephren and Menkaure. They were building a papyrus boat of the same design as the ancient ships painted on the walls of the tombs about us, where we had chosen our building site in the desert sand.

Why? What was I trying to prove? Nothing. I did not want to prove anything. I wanted to find out something. I wanted to find out if a boat like this could be used at sea. I wanted to find out if it was true, as the experts believed, that the Phoenicians had to come to the Nile to gather the papyrus, because the Egyptians themselves were unable to sail their reed boats outside the Nile Delta. I wanted to find out if the ancient Egyptians themselves had originally been seafarers, before they settled down to become sculptors, pharaohs and mummies. I wanted to find out if a reed boat could withstand a sea voyage of 250 miles, the distance from Egypt to Lebanon. I wanted to find out if a reed boat would be able to sail still further, even from one continent to another. I wanted to find out if a reed boat could make the journey to America.

Why? Because no one knows who was the first person to reach America. Columbus, the school books say. But Columbus did not discover America. He rediscovered America. Columbus was an extremely intelligent and courageous man, who sailed out into the unknown because he knew in his own mind that the world was round, and that he would not tumble over the edge. Columbus marks a turning-point in history; he changed the way of life of a whole world, gave birth to mighty nations and was responsible for the growth of skyscrapers where only bushes and scrub had grown before. But he did not discover America. He was the first to show the rest of the world the way to America, but he only arrived there in the year AD 1492.

When was America discovered? Nobody knows. The first man to set foot on American soil had no method of calculating time. He had no calendar. He could not write. His geographical concepts were too limited for him to realize that he had reached a new continent hitherto untrodden by man.

The first representative of *homo sapiens* to go ashore in America was a homeless, nomadic hunter and fisherman who spent his life, like his forefathers, roaming the frozen coasts of Arctic Siberia, until one fine day he found himself on the eastern shore of the ice-covered Bering Strait, without suspecting that only the wild beasts had roved here before him. We do not know if the discoverer of America came walking across frozen water, or paddling with his crude fishing tackle in a frail craft along the naked shore of tundra and snowdrifts. All we know is that the first man to die on American soil was born in Arctic Asia. We also know that the discoverer of America was ignorant of agriculture and architecture, metal and weaving; that he clothed himself in the skin of wild animals or pounded bark; his weapons and tools were of bones and stone, because he was still a pure Stone Age man.

Science does not yet know for certain when the descendants of the first discoverers of America began to spread southward through Alaska and down through the whole of North, Central and South America. Some believe that the settlement of the New World began about 15,000 years before Christ, while others maintain with equal conviction that this time-span should be doubled at least. All agree, however, that that first step into America was taken in the Arctic North, and that only the simplest Stone Age tools were in use among the unorganized flocks of savages whose numerous descendants were to become known to the present world as the wide variety of aboriginal American Indians.

The narrow gap between Arctic Asia and Alaska was always open for man to cross, and many recent discoveries indicate that primitive family groups continued to move back and forth in both directions between Siberia and Alaska. The Aleutian chain of islands and the Japan current to the south also provided a bridge for those who had seagoing vessels. Inside America, from Alaska in the north to Tierra del Fuego in the south, the rising generations settled in igloos, in wigwams, in leaf huts and in caves, for as man moved southward he was to encounter every variety of climate and nature. Through inter-marriage in isolated groups and through new migrations and mixing, a long chain of highly distinct Indian tribes began to develop inside America. Not only did they differ strikingly from one another in facial type and body build, but they spoke quite unrelated languages and evolved completely different ways of life.

Then came Columbus. On October 12, 1492, he landed on San Salvador in the West Indies with his standard and his Cross, and in his wake followed Cortés, Pizarro and all the other Spanish *conquistadores*. No one can ever deprive Columbus of the glory of having flung open the doors of America to all those peoples who had not already struggled in across the Arctic ice. But we Europeans easily forget that there were thousands of non-European people waiting to receive him on land. And on the mainland, behind the islands where he had landed, great empires with high cultural achievement were seemingly prepared for a visit from across the sea. Their scholars told the Spaniards that white-skinned, bearded men had come over the sea once before, bringing with them all the secrets of civilization. The arrival of the Spaniards caused surprise neither in Mexico nor in Peru; they were not received as 'discoverers' but as voyagers repeating an ocean crossing held to have been achieved long before by culture-bearers who had come to their forefathers at the dawn of traditional history.

And it was certainly true that this part of America was no longer inhabited by primitive hunters and fishermen, like those who had originally made their way down from the ice-fields of Siberia. On the contrary, in those far from stimulating tropical zones, just where the trade winds and the mighty ocean current from Africa had carried the Spaniards themselves ashore, they were met by learned men who themselves produced paper books and studied history, astronomy and medicine. They could read and write, with a system of their own. They had organized schools and scientific observatories. Their astronomical and geographical knowledge was so astonishing that they had worked out the movements of important celestial bodies with maximum accuracy, calculated the positions of the equator, the ecliptic and the tropics, and were able to distinguish between the fixed stars and the planets. Their complicated calendar system was more accurate than the one used in Europe in Columbus's day and they began their precise chronology, the Mayan year 0, with the year 3113 BC by our calendar. Their physicians mummified eminent people with professional skill where the climate allowed preservation, and like the ancient Egyptians they performed trepanning, or true cranial surgery, without killing the patient, an operation unknown to European surgeons until long after Columbus.

Scribe and layman lived together in planned urban societies, with paved roads, aqueducts and sewers, market places, sports grounds, schools and palaces. The urban population lived neither in tents, nor in leaf huts; they manufactured brick-shaped adobe blocks of sun-dried clay mixed with straw, made according to the same formula as in Mesopotamia and Egypt, and built proper houses of two or more stories arranged in regular city streets. The grander structures had halls with colonnades to support the roof, and the walls were decorated with reliefs and artistic frescoes painted in beautiful and durable colours. The loom was in common use and spinning and weaving had reached such perfection that the Spaniards were shown tapestries and cloaks which in technical accomplishment and skilful composition surpassed anything to be seen in Europe. Professional potters made jars and dishes, jugs and mugs and ceramic models of people and animals involved in all sorts of activities, with an expertise equal to, if not surpassing, the best that the classical cultures of the Old World had been able to produce. And the gold and silver work of the local jewellers, with filigree and inlay, was so highly developed, both technically and artistically, that the Spaniards drew their swords, losing all self-control and conscience in their ecstasy at what they had 'discovered'. Stepped pyramids of breathtaking magnitude, pillared temples, and the gigantic monolithic monuments of priest-kings towered over the adobe roofs, while regular roads, man-made waterways and large suspension-bridges set their stamp on the landscape. Countless artificially irrigated and terraced fields bulged with different varieties of root crops, cereals, vegetables, fruit, medicinal herbs and other cultivated plants. Even the cotton plant had been refined from its unusable wild state and was professionally cultivated in huge quantities as a lint-bearing species. Both wool and cotton were spun, dyed and woven, and sometimes with thinner thread and finer mesh than any fabric ever produced in Europe prior to the twentieth century.

The Spaniards at first thought they had circumnavigated the world and reached some of the amazing civilizations of distant India. All the people who received them, irrespective of physical type or cultural standing, were therefore termed 'Indians', a name to survive for ever in European languages even when the Spaniards knew the mistake they had made and realized they had run into a new world.

Who discovered whom? Those who were standing on the shore watching the ships arrive from beyond the eastern horizon, or those who were standing on the decks spotting people ashore as land emerged from the western haze? Informed of the Spaniards' arrival by his organized scouts and messengers, the priest-king was carried to receive the newcomers in his elegant litter with fan and parasol. He too, like the arriving Spaniards, had bewildered preconceived ideas as to whom he was to meet. The mighty priest-king, like his entire people, was convinced that he himself was descended from the sun through bearded white men, just like those who were now repeating their visit to his country. The occasion called for celebration. His musicians played on flute and trumpet, beat drums and rang silver bells. He came with his bodyguard and a standing army of many thousands of men. His scouts had found a handful of Spaniards coming ashore and making their way across country towards the capital.

1. *Reed boat off Easter Island,* where the author's interest in reed boats began. The island's enigmatic giant statues were carved by seafarers who planted the South American freshwater reed in the crater lakes and built reed boats of the type found in Peru.
2, 3. 4, 4a. *Reed boats* were once in use from Mesopotamia to the Atlantic coast of Morocco. They have survived to the present day on Lake Chad in the African interior (2) on Lake Zwai in Ethiopia (3) on Lake Tana at the source of the Nile (4) and in Sardinia in the Mediterranean (4a).

Precisely the same thing happened in the Aztecs' mighty kingdom of Mexico as in the gigantic empire of the Incas in South America. A small handful of Spaniards with white skins and beards vanquished those huge empires virtually without firing a shot, simply because the scribes and priests on the shores where they landed had either hieroglyphic records or verbal religious traditions which stated that white men with beards had brought the gifts of civilization to their forefathers before they eventually passed on to foreign regions with their teaching, promising to return. All American Indian tribes were completely beardless. This peculiar feature was common to all descendants of the golden-brown stock which had filtered in from the Arctic north. But the Spaniards, when they were 'discovered' by the Indians on land, were bearded and white-skinned; a mere handful, they were warmly welcomed back to Mexico and Peru by the mightiest absolute monarchs of their time.

The rest of the world caught only a brief glimpse of the New World's great civilizations before they disappeared almost as abruptly as they had become known. Great cultural centres had once been strung like a row of beads from the Aztec and Mayan kingdoms in the north to the Inca kingdom in the south, yet never outside this central area. Aboriginal American civilization never spread beyond the tropic zones to those parts of America where the climate has stimulated men in our day to great enterprise and industry. The curtain which Christopher Columbus drew aside for his contemporaries was quickly pulled across again by his successors. Only a few decades passed before America's pulsating civilizations crumbled in ruins, ceased to function, and partly by annihilation, partly by integration, took new forms which make it easy for us Europeans to believe that everything positive, everything which smacks of culture, is due to ourselves, while any exotic, murky aspects are the heritage of the pre-Columbus era. We gained this impression because the gold-hungry conquistadors, with the Cross for alibi, were so quick to draw the curtain again, before anyone had

5. *In Mexico* reed boats were once in use both at sea and on inland lakes. The last to survive were used by the Seris Indians in the Gulf of California.
6. *Lake Titicaca* in Bolivia and Peru has the world's best reed boats today. Large reed ships used to sail along the shores of the Inca kingdom.

fully realized what had been found on the other side of the globe.

What had really happened in Mexico and Peru before Columbus and his followers turned up in America? Was the ignorant Stone Age man from the Arctic tundra alone responsible for planting the seeds of all that the Spaniards found? Or had his descendants stood on the beach and received some unknown voyagers who came sailing over the Atlantic without a return ticket, perhaps in the morning of time, long before civilization had spread from Africa and Asia Minor up to the coasts of barbaric Europe?

This was precisely the question. And the answer was no. Obviously no. Possibly no. Possibly . . . I felt a coil of rope grinding into my back and sat up a little uneasily in the tent. Possibly . . . The question tormented me. I settled myself more comfortably on the ropes. I could see no solution, It was no use brooding. I was simply thinking the same thoughts all over again. If the ancient civilizations of America had developed locally in Mexico or Peru, the archaeologists should be able to trace the sites where gradual development had taken place. But wherever a centre of civilization was found in Mexico or Peru, excavations proved that it had arrived in fully mature form, developing local variants later on. There was no clear beginning to be found any-where. So the answer should be obvious: importation. If civilization began suddenly without local evolution, it must have been imported. Infiltration from overseas. Obviously. The only trouble was that at the time when the great civilizations were beginning to flourish in the New World, some centuries before Christ perhaps, a couple of thousand years had passed since corresponding cultures had ceased to exist in the relevant areas of the Old World. In Egypt, for instance. So the answer was not obvious at all. We were stuck.

Then why build a papyrus boat? My thoughts floated away again, via America, right out into the Pacific. There I was on my home ground. It was there that I had devoted all my time to research and field work. I had been visiting Egypt simply as a tourist when I first saw the wall-paintings of reed boats in the Valley of Kings four years earlier. I had recognized the type of boat at once. It was of the same general type as the pyramid-builders in North Peru had painted on their ceramic pots when their civilization flourished in South America, long before Polynesia was inhabited. The largest reed boats in Peru were depicted as two-deckers. Quantities of water jars and other cargo were painted in on the lower deck, as well as rows of little people, and on the upper deck the earthly representative of the sun-god usually stood, the priest-king, larger than all his companions, surrounded by bird-headed men who were often hauling on ropes to help the reed boat through the water. The tomb paintings in Egypt also portrayed the sun-god's earthly representative, the priest-king known as the pharaoh, like an imposing giant on his reed boat, surrounded by miniature people, while the same mythical men with bird heads towed the reed boat through the water.

Reed boats and bird-headed men seemed to go together, for some inexplicable reason. For we had found them far out in the Pacific Ocean too, on Easter Island, where the sun-god's mask, the reed boats with sails, and men with bird heads formed an inseparable trio among the wall-paintings and reliefs in the ancient ceremonial village of Orongo, with its solar observatory. Easter Island, Peru, Egypt. These strange parallels could hardly have been found farther apart. They could hardly furnish better proof that men must have arrived independently at the same things in widely separated places. What was even more strange was that the aboriginal people of Easter Island called the sun *Ra*. *Ra* was the name for the sun on all the hundreds of Polynesian islands, so it could be no mere accident. *Ra* was also the name for the sun in ancient Egypt. No word was more important to the ancient Egyptian religion than *Ra*, the sun, the sun-god, ancestor of the pharaohs. The one who sailed reed boats, with an entourage of bird-headed men. Giant monolithic statues as high as houses had been erected in honour of the sun-god's earthly priest-kings on Easter Island, in Peru and in ancient Egypt. And in all three places, stone blocks as big as railway trucks had been sliced up like cheese and fitted together in stepped pyramids designed on an astronomical basis according to the movements of the sun. All in honour of the common ancestor, the sun, *Ra*. Was there some connection, or was it just coincidence?

Centuries ago, when sail still ruled the sea, it was usual to assume that the ancient civilized people were capable of almost unlimited movement. After all, Magellan, Captain Cook and many others had sailed round the world once or twice with only the wind to help them, so why not? But then we invented the propeller and the jet, and as the world grew smaller and smaller for rising generations, we began to get the idea that it must have been larger and larger, going back through the ages, until in the days before Columbus it must have been endless, and the oceans impassable.

The year 1492 had a magical effect on us all. It was then that Columbus discovered America. It was then that the world first became round. Before that time, the earth had been flat and the sea had been flat, so that everything which floated on the currents and winds must necessarily have tumbled off the edge. Actually, we know today that the world was round also before Columbus, but it was somehow not completely round, more like an egg-shell. In any case, anything which went far enough out on the ocean currents would fall off.

Nothing could float over the abyss and into the unknown before 1492, not even a reed. After Columbus had rounded our planet, nothing tumbled over the edge. Anything which could float across the Atlantic would land on the other side, on the new coasts which had turned up, either on the islands where Columbus himself had landed, or on the long tropical coast just behind them. Columbus sailed over like a sort of St Peter, with the keys to the New World. After him came caravels and other small sailing vessels in their thousands, and twentieth-century adventurers have even crossed the Atlantic in droves by dinghy, rubber raft, amphibian and kayak.

Columbus patented the Atlantic. Before him, America could only be reached on bare feet, or in moccasins, across the snow-covered ice which stretches interminably along the Siberian wasteland in the bitter cold of the Arctic. Up there no one could plant cotton or build towns of brick houses. On that point everyone agreed. But how did the fur-clad migrants get the idea of cultivating cotton which could be spun into thread and woven into garments when they moved down into the drowsy, sedative climate of the tropics, where palm-leaves would have served this need? And how did they hit on the idea, down in the torrid zone, that they should mix straw with clay and mould regular building bricks so that they could live in proper houses? Here agreement ends. Here the schism begins among those who have been looking for the answers.

One of the last to have unreservedly allowed the peoples of antiquity to sail round the world was the Englishman, Percy Smith. He observed that the ancient cultures of Mexico and Peru had so many special features in common with the civilization of ancient Egypt that he thought there must have been some form of trans-oceanic contact. When he also discovered the same remarkable similarities on Easter Island and other Polynesian groups nearest to the Peruvian coast, he reached for his ruler and his flat world map and drew a line from

Egypt via the Red Sea, the Indian Ocean and the Pacific, all the way to Polynesia and South America. That, he wrote, was how the sun-worshippers reached America. Via Easter Island.

Others consulted a round globe and shook their heads. A voyage from Egypt to Easter Island was meaningless. Easter Island was closer to Egypt by way of America than by way of India. The round globe shows the Pacific as a complete hemisphere which extends over half the circumference of the world. If Egyptians had sailed 2,500 miles eastward, they would barely have reached India, and would still have exactly half the world left in order to reach Easter Island. On the other hand, if ancient South Americans had sailed 2,500 miles westward from their coast, they would already have by-passed Easter Island. With the *Kon-Tiki* raft built on the ancient Inca model, we travelled 4,300 miles westward from the coast of South America and passed Easter Island half-way through our voyage.

Easter Island. The world's loneliest inhabited island. It lies off the open coast of Peru, not off the Nile delta. Easter Island. On this sea-girt lump of lava almost a thousand abandoned stone colossi in human shape raised their heads mutely to the sky when Europeans eventually reached those shores and 'discovered' the island in 1722. 'Easter Island' we call it, because a Dutchman sailing from South America stumbled upon it on Easter Sunday. 'The Navel of the World' was what the Polynesians called it when they landed there in dugout canoes a few centuries earlier and found the little island already inhabited by still older seafarers who carved large representations of reed boats with masts and sails on the chests of some of their stone giants. These sickle-shaped reed boats were also painted on the stone walls of Easter Island's oldest ceremonial village together with sun symbols and mythical men with bird heads. It was at the same ceremonial site that the sun, locally known as *Ra*, was observed and worshipped, and the entire population of the island was united in an annual bird-man cult, swimming to offshore bird islets, supported by small reed boats. This custom survived until missionaries put a stop to it with the introduction of Christianity in 1868.

Reed boats on Easter Island. At this my thoughts stopped revolving. One thing was quite clear. It was there that reed boats began for me. Yet perhaps it was there, geographically speaking, that the history of reed boats had finally come to an end.

I had indeed seen reed boats long before I came to Easter Island. I had used them on Lake Titicaca in the high Andes when I was there studying South American stone monoliths of human form which had been abandoned in the plains around the great inland sea. I had been impressed by the carrying capacity of these vessels, which had actually been used to ferry huge blocks weighing many tons across the lake to the ruined city of Tiahuanaco. But I had regarded this peculiar type of bundle-boat mainly as a curiosity. Like everyone else who had read the history of the Inca empire, I knew that these reed boats on Lake Titicaca were simply the surviving remnants of a pre-Columbus water-craft which had been in general use all along the Pacific coast of Peru when the Spaniards landed. In fact, at that time they were still seen as far north as Mexico and California. The smallest of these reed vessels was shaped like a curved elephant tusk and could bear no more than one man, supporting his chest on it while swimming. The biggest the Spaniards saw had a crew of twelve; tied together in pairs, such vessels were strong enough to help the colonists carry cattle and horses by sea. In Peru the reed boat went back as far as the balsa log raft; as far, in fact, as the earliest pre-Inca civilization, because the first pyramid-builders on the coast of Peru, the Mochica people, seldom failed to include sea-going reed boats in their versatile pictorial art.

When I decided to build the *Kon-Tiki* raft I had a choice. Three types of sea-going vessel had been used in the ancient Inca empire. Rafts of balsa logs usually brought from the jungles of Ecuador; reed boats made of *totora*, a reed which grew wild in the mountain lakes and was cultivated by irrigation along the entire Pacific desert coast; and pontoon floats made of two big inflated sealskin bags joined together with cross-bars in the form of a plough.

I had no difficulty in making my choice. The air was inclined to escape from the inflated sealskin pontoons when they had been at sea for days on end, and the Indians had to swim alongside and blow them up at regular intervals. They did not tempt me very much. I had no particular faith in the reed boats, either. One usually thinks of reeds and straw as exceptionally fragile, delicate things. One clings to them, figuratively, when all else has failed. One does not put to sea on reeds or other flower stalks of one's own free will. So I thought then. And everyone else agreed. If we were to go, then we were to go on the balsa-wood raft, a solid platform of light, untrimmed timber. And so we did. The balsa-log raft was tried and found amazingly seaworthy. And so the reed boat was discarded and forgotten – for the time being.

CHAPTER 2

Why a Reed Boat?

IT WAS on Easter Island. The surf was breaking on the eastern shore. Four old brothers, their skin wrinkled like tobacco leaves, jog-trotted down the beach and into the breakers, carrying a small, banana-shaped craft between them. The sun was dancing on the blue ocean waves and painting the banana-boat with gold. The four nimble old men pushed the vessel out between the foaming crests and jumped on board, paddles whirling, just in time to send the boat through the froth of a retreating breaker. Hoop-la! Like a see-saw it rocked over the next rising breaker, and the next, and then it was out among the rollers on the open sea. It was just as dry inside as before the breakers had surged over it. All the water which had showered on board had run out again in the same instant through a thousand fissures in the bottom. There were no sides to the boat, no hollow hull; the four men sitting on the flat deck were sitting right on the thick bottom. Only fore and aft the raft-boat curved up in snout-shaped points, the better to ride the seas. It rode them like a golden swan.

This was the first time for a hundred years that a reed boat of this type had put out to sea from Easter Island. It had been made by the elders of the island, who wanted to show us a type of boat made by their ancestors for sea-fishing. It was a miniature of the larger vessels in the illustrations from the island's bygone golden age; but it was impressively large by comparison with the tusk-shaped one-man boats, *pora*, which the islanders had used in their bird-man contests, until Christianity was introduced at the end of the last century. It was a solemn moment for the natives of Easter Island when they saw the four old fishermen paddling out of the open inlet in a boat which they all knew so well from their fathers' tales, a boat which meant to them what the *Mayflower* means to the average American, or the Viking ship to us in the north. The little craft slithered over the wave like an air-bed with the crew perched dry on top, up and down, over and round the waves, no matter which side they came from. As the four brown bodies in the golden boat rounded the point where we were busy re-erecting the first of all Easter Island's overthrown giant statues, more than one of the old people on land whispered with eyes shining that the island's dead past was about to be resurrected.

To me, however, what had been resurrected was a vessel once used far beyond the eastern horizon. There was a striking similarity here to the boats I had seen on Lake Titicaca, and a still greater similarity to the crescent-shaped reed boats of pre-Inca times which the old Mochica people had so often portrayed in their realistic ceramic art, on the Pacific coast of South America. The water flowing round our legs on this beach came straight from the coast of South America. I myself had drifted past here by raft with these eternally circulating masses of water. The suspicion was born.

Up in the crater of the extinct volcano Rano Raraku, six men were sinking a 25-foot steel bore into the edge of the marsh. Round about us, high in the crater walls, lay large numbers of unfinished stone giants, bearing witness to the sculptors' suddenly interrupted work. Some of them were completed in every detail apart from the back, which was still firmly embedded in the rock as part of the crater wall itself. They lay with closed eyes and hands curved on their stomachs, petrified in a giant's version of the Sleeping Beauty. Others had been hacked free and raised on end to give the sculptors a chance to complete the rugged back which was to be made arched, slim and elegant like the rest of the giant. These standing giants were scattered at random round about the rock galleries, some covered up to the chin by land-

7. *The world's oldest reed boat models* from Egyptian mummy tombs, examined by the author in Cairo Museum.
8. *Tomb reliefs in Egypt* show that the custom of gathering papyrus reeds to build boats goes back to the earliest dawn of civilization.
9. *Boat-builders in ancient Egypt* bound papyrus reed together with strong hemp rope. Some were black-haired, others fair.
10. *Naval action on the Nile*. The papyrus boats were loaded with cages of ducks, baskets of food and jars of drink.

slips. Thin lips compressed, they craned in all directions, as if critically appraising what these six little dwarfs of flesh and blood were up to, with their steel bore, down there on the brink of the crater lake.

The long steel spike sank inch by inch into the soggy mud. Rain and a thousand years of sludge had changed the bottom of the deep, dead crater into a glassy blue lake where the sky was mirrored so that small, white trade-wind clouds seemed to be drifting across the surface and disappearing into the green reeds in an eternal procession from east to west. Three such rain-filled crater lakes, encircled by tall reeds, were the only water supply available on Easter Island. Here the islanders had fetched their drinking water since the days when they had burned down the primeval forest and changed the wooded landscape into one of open grass and bracken slopes, where all the brooks gradually seeped down into the porous lava floor and vanished.

The mud we extracted with the long bore had much to tell us about this early destruction. At the tip of the long steel rod was a revolving blade and a small cavity with a lid which opened to allow the chamber to fill with mud, clay or sand, according to what lay in the depths we wanted to study. The deeper we bored, the further we delved into the past. The swamp edge was like a closed book, with the first page at the bottom and the last on top. At the lowest level there was nothing but solidified lava and volcanic fall-out from the days when Easter Island rose fire-spitting from the ocean floor. Above this sterile bottom layer, clay and mud had begun to ooze down from the weathered crater rim of the dead volcano, and as time passed, the layers of mud further up began to contain more and more hermetically preserved flower dust, pollen. By studying the stratification of different kinds of pollen, a professional pollen expert could tell us the order in which different species of grass, fern, bush or tree had spread to the new-born island, carried by the current, the wind, birds and finally man. Every

11. *Pharaoh and his wife* in the cabin on board a papyrus boat, served by a royal butler, while an ordinary seaman, portrayed normal size, steers with the double steering oar.
12. *Cattle freighting on the Nile.* The herdsman's rolled-up papyrus tent made an effective lifebelt.
13. *Sailing skills* were extraordinarily advanced in Egypt almost 5,000 years ago. The mast was straddled, with steps.

plant has its own characteristic form of pollen. Seen under the micro-scope they resemble fantastic fruits and berries of the most extraordinary shapes and patterns.

A detective hides behind many names: some call themselves palaeo-botanists and thus escape other people's curiosity. They are the ones who sort out pollen grains with the same thoroughness as others identify fingerprints. We tamped our small pats of soil down in numbered tubes of glass, for delivery to just such a vegetable detective bureau in Stockholm. That was how we came to know a little about things that had happened in Easter Island's forgotten past, a little about where they had come from, those first, mysterious sculptors who raised their gigantic monuments on the island, unobserved under cover of the darkness of history.

The pollen borings revealed that this island – which the European 'discoverers' found barren and naked, with mere savages living amidst fields of sweet potatoes, abandoned quarries and giant monuments from a forgotten past – had originally been wooded, and that swaying palms had covered what are now arid cones and crater walls. In the midst of this virgin greenery skilled stonemasons landed long before the Europeans knew the Pacific. These masons set fire to the woods. Smoke and particles of soot from their burnings rained down upon the lakes in the dead volcanoes, and were deposited at the bottom together with the last pollen from palms and forest trees which now suddenly began to vanish. The newcomers burnt down the forest to clear space for large fields of the American sweet potato, which was their staple diet. They wanted clearings for their houses, which were built of stone, and for large temple plazas with stepped platforms of giant dressed blocks resembling the religious structures of ancient Peru and the mastabas of Egypt. They destroyed the palms and tore turf and earth away from the volcanic slopes to gain access to the solid rock which their expert sculptors converted into smooth building blocks and monolithic statues of deceased priest-kings. The trees that fell were ignored as building material, for the first settlers of Easter Island were accustomed to working with rock and not timber. Stone was their traditional raw material. Blocks as heavy as railway trucks and as high as houses were transported from one end of the island to the other, raised on end as monoliths, or hoisted on top of one another and meticulously fitted into solar-oriented megalithic walls, the like of which the world has never seen except in Peru and

Mexico and among the ancient Mediterranean sun-worshippers on the opposite side of the globe.

The detectives digging into our pats of soil had more to tell. Not only had the early settlers destroyed Easter Island's natural vegetation, but they had partly replaced the exterminated species with cultivated plants that could only have travelled across the ocean through human agency. The strictly American sweet potato had been brought to Easter Island and neighbouring Polynesia from Peru before Columbus reached America. We had known this before, because until our day this plant had been the staple food of the Easter Islanders, who call it *kumara*, the name given to the same plant throughout Polynesia and among the aboriginal population in vast areas of the ancient Inca empire. But in our pats of earth there were remnants of another plant which was of greater importance to a seafaring nation.

The reed. The *totora* reed.

The uppermost layers of mud, after the forest had been burned down, were yellow with destroyed pollen from *totora* reeds, mingled with a network of tough shreds from the reed stalks. Huge quantities of decayed reed fibres formed a floating mat over most of the crater lake. The pollen of only one other water plant was mingled with this sludge right down to the mud layers containing the rain of ash which marked the coming of man. Before man's arrival there was no pollen from fresh-water plants. Before the stone sculptors came, nothing grew in Easter Island's crater lakes; they lay open, the extinct volcanoes filled with clear rain-water.

Here were clues for a detective: fingerprints in the mud. That the two fresh-water plants had been brought by men across the sea was easy to understand. Both were useful species; one a principal building material, the other a medicinal plant, and neither was a species which could transplant by means of the ocean currents, birds or wind – only by means of its suckers. In order to become established in three fresh-water lakes inside deep volcanoes on lonely Easter Island, they must have been planted as living bulbs brought dry across the salt ocean. And now we were right on the trail. For both plants belonged to species which grew nowhere else in the world but on the American continent. The *totora* reed, *Scirpus totora*, was one of the most important of the plants in use among the aboriginal population all along the desert coast of the Inca empire. The coastal peoples of Peru cultivated it in irrigated swamps and used it to make large and small reed boats, house roofs, mats, baskets and rope. The other water plant, *Polygonum acuminatum*, was used by the South American Indians as a medicine. Both plants served precisely the same purpose among the inhabitants of Easter Island.

With a piece of the light, sun-dried *totora* reed in my hand I stood watching the four old Polynesians bobbing about on the wave-tops out on the open sea, as nonchalantly as they would trot round on horse-back ashore on their rocky island. I had known for a long time that one of the great mysteries of Pacific botany was to understand how this American fresh-water plant came to grow down in the three crater lakes hidden away on the world's loneliest inhabited island. Here was the simple solution. Perhaps those old voyagers from Peru had not reached the Pacific islands with balsa rafts alone. Perhaps at least two of their three old forms of water craft had followed them across the ocean. Perhaps they had imported the practice of building reed boats as well, and even living tubers, so that they could continue the old tradition with identical material.

As we dragged the crescent-shaped reed boat up the beach I was no longer in any doubt that Easter Island's oldest population had inherited the art of building these remarkable vessels from the old pyramid-builders in Peru, the homeland of their reeds.

Five years later I was sitting round a large table with the leading Pacific archaeologists gathered for a world congress at Hawaii University. Five years had passed before all the diversified material from the excavations on Easter Island had been analysed by colleagues who were all specialists in different branches of science. Skeletons and stone tools, blood samples, pollen and carbon from bonfires, all had their tale to tell to the scientific detectives whose task it was to find out what had happened on Easter Island: who had come, when, and from where, long before those following in Columbus's wake had shown our own race the way to these remote Pacific islands via America.

Our results from the Easter Island expedition had been presented by my collaborators at the congress. Those of us seated around the large table were ready to sign a scientific document, a so-called congress resolution. The text declared that, together with South-East Asia and adjacent islands, South America represented the main homeland of the ancient peoples and cultures on the Pacific islands. I had nothing against signing. It was indeed to the feasibility of this mixed settlement that I had wanted to call attention by sailing to the islands from Peru on a

balsa raft. This bilateral origin of Polynesian culture was what I had
suspected, long before the *Kon-Tiki* voyage, when I was living for a
year as a Polynesian among Polynesians on the lonely island of Fatuhiva
in the Marquesas group, where the surf pounded on the east coasts,
and clouds and seas, day and night, came scudding and rolling in the
same direction from South America. The resolution was read out to
the 3,000 Pacific scholars participating in the plenary meeting
and unanimously approved. I left the Tenth Pacific Science Congress
with a mandate to promote further excavations on the Pacific islands
directly facing South America, and the South American coast was
included for the first time in the archaeological areas of concern to
oceanic archaeology. The gateway between Peru and Polynesia was
left open, the Pacific had acquired two sides.

The reed boat, however, sank into oblivion once more. Then
came the moment when it was dragged back into the limelight in a
totally unexpected way and from a totally unexpected quarter. A well-
known anthropologist at the University of California pointed out in
the professional journal *American Antiquity* (January 1966) that the reed
boats of ancient Peru resembled the reed boats of ancient Egypt. And,
he said, the reed boat was not the only peculiar feature in which the
two ancient cultures bore a striking resemblance to each other. The
article contained a list of no less than sixty special features, of a quite
unusual nature, which were characteristic of the ancient cultures of
Egypt and the eastern Mediterranean, and could at the same time be
found mustered together among the pre-Columbus civilizations of
Peru. The reed boat was only one of sixty different items on the list.

Now it is usual in science to interpret a single cultural feature, or
even two or three, which crop up in the same form in widely separate
areas as a matter of coincidence, a result of independent evolution
along parallel lines. Human beings are so alike all over the world that
it is natural for them to have similar notions. But if a really varied
and numerous array of similarities or identities occurs and these are of
such a specialized nature that no equivalents are found outside two
clearly defined geographical areas, then one must be aware of the possibility of contact between these two cultural centres. The list of sixty
specific cultural parallels was a textbook example of the latter category.
It accordingly sounded the alarm: tread warily. So I was not alone
in my astonishment. Not because the list was impressive and thought-
provoking. It certainly was. But because it had been drawn up by an

isolationist. The author was known as one of the most zealous advocates of the theory defending a total isolation of America before Columbus: only the ice in the north could have provided a passage for human beings. Nevertheless, he it was who had now produced a list which Percy Smith and his old school of diffusionists would have envied him: sixty specialized cultural parallels between ancient Peru and Egypt.

This list could provoke conclusions. It was in fact intended to do so. The author of the article concluded that, since Egypt is in Africa and Peru in America, there are two continents and a whole Atlantic Ocean between them. Two cultures both of which used reeds for boat-building could not have had contact across the open sea as a reed boat cannot traverse an ocean. Accordingly, the sixty cultural parallels must have arisen independently of each other without being the result of mutual contact. The lesson to the reader: diffusionists, those who believe that America received inspiration from across the sea before 1492, must stop nosing around after cultural parallels, because it is hereby demonstrated that such parallels prove nothing.

The diffusionists reacted vigorously. They could not swallow the reasoning. They remained convinced that Mexico and Peru had received some early impetus from across the sea. But which sea? And in what ships? Although they could not agree, the waves of discussion refused to subside. The answer had not yet been given.

In the same year the organizers of the Thirty-seventh International Americanist Congress decided to summon representatives of the two contending doctrines to a scientific duel. Every other year this congress assembles scholars from all over the world, specializing in America's aboriginal population. This time it was to be held in Argentina and I had been asked to invite speakers to a symposium for and against trans-oceanic contact with America before Columbus.

The meeting was in session. The doors were closed. The author of the sixty points of resemblance was invited, but did not show up. But the diffusionists who believed in contact attended in strength, with speakers from four continents. The isolationists were also present in strength, but only in the audience. Their tactics were to let the others speak and then shoot down their arguments. They had always stayed on the defensive, deliberately leaving the burden of proof on those who believed that the ocean had been crossed before Columbus. The diffusionists never lacked arguments, but they always lacked proof. Therefore, said the isolationists, the oceans had not been crossed.

The Icelandic sagas, written down in detail by Viking historians long before Columbus, were one of the themes for discussion. No one could deny that Norwegian Vikings had settled Iceland and later the whole south-western coast of Greenland, where they had lived continuously for nearly 500 years before Columbus hoisted sail. They had left behind the ruins of countless farmsteads, graveyards, sixteen churches, two monasteries, and an episcopal residence which kept in touch with the papal throne via regular sea communications with Norway. This pre-Columbus colony on Greenland paid taxes to the king of Norway.

The distance across the North Atlantic from Norway to the Norse settlements in Greenland was as great as across the South Atlantic from Africa to Brazil. It was only a negligible jump of some 200 miles from Greenland to the coast of the American mainland, but it was this last hop which had not been made, said the isolationists.

It had been made, said the written text in the ancient Viking sagas. Bjarni Herjolfsson was recorded as the first to make the full Atlantic crossing, because his ship went astray in a fog. But instead of landing on the long, unknown coastline he had discovered, he put about and returned to nearby Greenland. His ship was bought by Leif Ericsson, the son of Greenland's discoverer, Eric the Red, who in about the year 1002 set sail for the south-west from the colony in Greenland with thirty-five men. Leif and his men were the first to set foot on the new coast, which they named Vinland, and there they built houses and spent the winter before returning home to Greenland. His brother, Thorvald Ericsson, made the crossing next year and settled in Leif's deserted houses with his people. Two years later, on a voyage of discovery along the wooded coasts of the new continent, he was killed by an arrow in a fight with the natives. His thirty men buried him in Vinland and sailed home to Greenland.

Thorfinn Karlsefni and his wife Gudrid were the next to make the journey, with two ships and a large number of people. Eric the Red's daughter Freydis was with them, and this time the emigrants took cattle for their settlement. Gudrid gave birth to her son Snorri in their newly-built home in Vinland, but steadily increasing attacks by large numbers of Indians, *Skraelings*, made life in the new land intolerable, so that in the end the colonists left their farms, after bloody losses, and went home to Greenland and Europe. The handwritten sagas were crammed with prosaic facts. Coasts and travel routes were described in detail. There could be no doubt about it. The Vikings really had discovered Vinland and tried to settle the new country, in the first ten or fifteen years after the year 1000.

But where was Vinland? How can we know that Vinland was America? This is what the isolationists had been asking for years. And then came the sensation. The congress was given proof.

At Lanse aux Meadows on the northern tip of Newfoundland evidence had been found proving beyond doubt that the Vikings had landed and attempted a brief settlement about the year 1000. The earth embankments from a cluster of house foundations in typical style had been discovered, well preserved under the turf. The charred fragments of wood had been dated and the results checked ten times over by radiocarbon analysis. The houses had been inhabited at the very period, about A.D. 1000, referred to in the Viking sagas. The Indians had known nothing of iron. And here were remnants of iron nails from doors, and bog-iron from a primitive smithy. The Indians up here in the north could not weave. And here under the turf lay a typical Norse spinning-wheel of soap-stone.

The discovery was made by the noted Norwegian Greenland expert Helge Ingstad, who had hit upon the site through a practical geographical appraisal of the old Icelandic records; and the excavations were conducted by his wife, the archaeologist Anne Stinge Ingstad, with the aid of leading American archaeologists. These were sober scientific facts. No one could protest. No one tried to raise any more objections. The Vikings had been in Newfoundland. They had reached America by crossing the Atlantic, and recorded the events before anyone else. But, said the isolationists, they had come and gone without leaving any traces other than a few grassy mounds. Their visit had had no bearing on the course of history. The savage Indians here in the north had driven them out and their own ancestral way of life had not been influenced. According to the sagas the Vikings had given them no more than a few strips of red cloth before fights and slaughter put a stop to further trading.

The Vikings never gained a lasting foothold in America. But America had at least been reached, both from east and west, in the Arctic north, before Columbus crossed in the tropical latitudes.

In the tropical belt the isolationists won the battle. And this was the main battlefield. No one could present tangible proof of landings in Mexico before the Spaniards. The written and verbal records to this effect made by Mexico's aboriginal people were taken even less seriously than the sagas of the Vikings. The diffusionists' mustering of ever more cultural parallels was as easily repulsed as before. Cultural affinities on two sides of an ocean were interesting observations but not proofs. The isolationists remained unshattered on their sea-girt island when the duel in the tropical belt was over. Two large oceans defended their position. One important argument seemed clearly in their favour. An ocean crossing required a seaworthy craft. If anybody had sailed across from Africa and acquired such a strong foothold in America that they could have taught the Indians to build with bricks and write on paper, then the least one could expect was that they should also have taught them how to build sea-going vessels. No mariners could cross the Atlantic with architects and astronomers capable of building pyramids without also bringing their own ship-building traditions with them. At least 2,700 years before Christ, the Egyptians had learned to build proper wooden ships, with hollow hulls and decks and cabins of trimmed planks, but the idea of a ship's hull built of planks had never reached the Indians. In the whole of America before Columbus, no one had learned to build vessels other than reed boats, various kinds of pontoon floats or rafts and canoes made of skin or dug-out tree-trunks. That was a fact which could not be disputed.

Reed boats, rafts and dug-out canoes were all that ancient America possessed. Here they were again. The balsa raft had been proven seaworthy, but it could only have set sail from America, for before the Spaniards came the balsa tree had grown in no other part of the world. But the reed, reeds of different types, grew everywhere, not least on the Nile.

'Yvonne, we must return to the Andes and take a second look at the Indian reed boats,' I said to my wife. The Ingstads came with us, to be shown that the Vikings were not the only ones who could build elegant vessels. On the day the congress closed, we climbed into an aircraft for La Paz in Bolivia, and next day we were up by sky-blue Lake Titicaca on the roof of the world, 12,500 feet above sea level, surrounded by snow-covered peaks which soared yet another 6,000 to 9,000 feet higher into the empty blue. Behind us on the plateau lay the ruins of South America's mightiest pre-Inca capital, the old cultural centre of Tiahuanaco, with the devastated Akapana pyramid, megalithic walls and gigantic statues of unknown priest-kings carved in stone.

In the strong breeze out on the lake some Aymara Indians manoeuvred to and fro as they fished. At a distance one could see only the wind-filled sails. Tattered canvas had been hoisted on most of the boats, but a few had stuck to tradition and hoisted a big mat of golden *totora* reed on two straddling masts joined at the top. Three of them steered straight for us, sailing flat out, and soon we could see the Indians in their rainbow-striped stocking-caps looking out from behind the sail, while the shape of the boat itself appeared above the waves. Glorious. They were expertly built. Each straw was placed with maximum precision to achieve perfect symmetry and streamlined elegance, while the bundles were so tightly lashed that they looked like inflated pontoons or gilded logs bent into a clog-shaped peak fore and aft. They cut through the water at high speed and ran right up to the shore in a clearing between the reeds, where they were driven firmly aground in the mud while the Indians waded ashore with their catch of fish.

Boats of this distinctive type are still built in their hundreds on every side of this enormous inland sea. They were built exactly in this way by the Aymara and Quechua Indians' fathers and grandfathers. This, too, is exactly how they had looked 400 years ago when the Spaniards came here and discovered Tiahuanaco's deserted ruins with their stepped platforms, pyramid and stone colossi, abandoned vestiges which the primitive Aymara Indians believed to have been left since the morning of time by the Viracocha people. These were described as white men with beards, whose king was Con-Tici-Viracocha, the sun's representative on earth. The Viracocha people had first settled on the Island of the Sun out in Lake Titicaca. Legend has it that it was they who built the first reed boats. The white and bearded men were specifically claimed to have come forth in an entire flotilla of reed boats when first appearing to the local Indians, who at the time were ignorant of sun-worship, architecture and agriculture. These legends, which the Spaniards wrote down 400 years ago, are still alive among the lake-side Indians. Many times I was addressed as 'Viracocha', which is still the word for 'white man'.

I did not know what to believe. Again, I was filled with admiration as I gazed at the enormous blocks, weighing fifty to a hundred tons, carved to perfection and fitted together to a fraction of a millimetre, and down on the lake the elegant, reed boats which still plied the waves today as they had when ferrying the giant blocks from Kapia, the extinct volcano over on the opposite shore. There was no reason to doubt that this vanished civilization was somehow connected with the other ancient American cultural centres which European discoverers found abandoned and overgrown, strung through the tropical jungles from Mexico all the way down to this wind-blown plateau, shared today between Peru and Bolivia. Before the giant pre-Inca structures of Tiahuanaco tumbled into ruins, this had been the capital of one of the world's mightiest empires, with an influence extending all over Peru and adjacent parts of Ecuador, Bolivia, Chile, Brazil and the Argentine. A coastline of at least 1,500 miles was under the influence of the art and religion radiating from its inland capital by the mountain lake, and ceramic sherds of coastal Tiahuanaco origin have been excavated on the Galapagos Islands, 600 miles off shore. Our findings on Easter Island had made it clear to me that this was the culture that had sent an offshoot to Easter Island in pre-Polynesian times.

But where were the roots? Here in America? Or on the other side of the Atlantic? Who were right, the isolationists or the diffusionists? At the congress none of them had seemed convincing. As leader of the symposium I had taken a neutral stand. But I was certain of one thing. Both isolationists and diffusionists underestimated the qualities of the ancient type of boat, surviving to modern times on the blue waves of Lake Titicaca. The reed boat would not have held its own against 400 years of European cultural contact had it been an inferior craft.

Admittedly, plank-built ships were known on only one side of the Atlantic. But reed vessels were known on both sides. After all, this was one of the sixty points of resemblance. The art of building reed boats was an ancient heritage both in Egypt and Peru. Only in those two places? No. And this was where I had discovered a tiny crack in the logic, because reed boats were not quite as isolated as the other fifty-nine points of resemblance on the list. Scarcely anyone had bothered to study their earlier distribution. But I had noticed one or two things. For instance, they had formerly also been in use in Mexico, on Mediterranean islands, and on the Atlantic coast of Morocco below Gibraltar. The jump from Morocco to Mexico was not as startlingly absurd as the distance between the furthest points, Egypt and Peru.

I decided to build a reed boat.

43

CHAPTER 3

To the Indians in the Cactus Forest

THE COAST. A glimpse of the sea between giant cacti. A make-believe world. Feeling very small, I tilted my head back to look up at the tops of the green, spiky, giant cacti which towered above me like organ pipes and branched candlesticks in a world of swollen, overfed vegetation. Overfed and overgrown. And yet the ground I was walking on was nothing but a bone-dry crust of hard-baked, barren sand, without grass or flowers except for the red and yellow ones peeping out between the spiny tufts on the sinews of the cactus giants themselves. This was the cactus world. On the ground between the giants stood, lay and swarmed all manner of spiky plants, globular, sausage-shaped, articulated. In the evening sunlight some looked like silhouettes of dishes and cutlery combined in a juggling act, others like worn-out shoe soles bristling with nails, bent ends of barbed wire or long, waving cat's tails. This was a still and silent forest. Not even a rustle from the leaves of the gnarled iron trees which stood here and there, writhing as if to avoid the prickles on their ubiquitous neighbours in the cactus groves.

A desert hare leaped silently out among the cactus shadows in the evening sun, pricked up its long ears, and glanced about before it bounded off again and disappeared. Crossing the hare's path a tiny striped chipmunk came scurrying along at a tremendous rate, stopped dead with its tail in the air, and bowled on again like a little bristling ball through the fairy-tale wood. On the highest fork of a three-branched candelabra plant, towering over all the rest, an eagle sat motionless. It did not stir until I was close against the trunk. Then it spread silent wings and glided smoothly away over the enchanted wood. The eagle was not moving, it was I and the forest which were sliding backwards, as it hung against the vault of sky before disappearing from view. It was only when I moved my own feet that I could hear

44

the leather sole cracking the earth crust and breaking through into invisible cavities dug in the sand by rats, snakes and other desert vermin.

In the stillness I had just caught a very faint sound, faint but with the same effect as a lion's loud roar of menace. It sounded like a half-empty matchbox being gently shaken. It was a warning note of hypnotic terror, in a sort of natural Esperanto. One did not need to have seen a rattlesnake before in order to jump aside at this unobtrusive sound. Tongue darting, eyes glittering, tail-tip slightly raised and twitching, the beast lay rattling its tail, ready to strike. The dry rattle, like a set of plastic rings on the light tail-tip, was quivering with fury, and in the hope of leaving the field victorious I looked around desperately for a stick or branch. But just here there was nothing but cactus, with fleshy, thorny branches which simply snapped like cucumber when I struck out at the slithering, supple creature. Finally, a shrivelled, fibrous skeleton of a dead cactus proved hard enough to knock the rattlesnake senseless, and before it regained consciousness the victory was won, even if the tail end of the dead body went on quivering and rattling for a long time afterwards.

We were supposed to be hunting for boat-builders in this cactus country. There was not a single tree we could climb to spy out the way. My Mexican friend, Ramon Bravo, had disappeared into the cactus wood to the left in the hope of finding a rocky outcrop with a view, while his wife Angelica and German Carrasco sat in the jeep down in the valley where, for the twentieth time at least, we had lost the wheel tracks we were following. Where I was standing now, I had caught my first glimpse of the sea. The lookout point was marked by a living monument of a cactus, shaped like Neptune's own trident, with a trunk so thick that I could hide behind it. This was where the eagle had perched. From there it must have been able to see great stretches of coast and those savage red mountain peaks inland, through which we had been lurching before all the wheel tracks branched off and vanished into the cactus forest. I myself could see only a silver flash of sunlight on shining water, and blue-tinged mountains far away on the other side. That was enough to set our course. So the four of us jolted on through the enchanted wood, trying to make haste before the sun sank.

Suddenly the cactus forest opened up, giving way to low evergreen scrub, and there, just before us, lay the sea, with small, rippling waves and a wide, virgin beach. Five straining black whalebacks came bursting through the surface of the water, heading straight for us, and as they dived and disappeared a shower of glittering small fry shot up in front of them, cascading out of the water and close inshore, where they seethed and sparkled for a moment before they scattered and disappeared.

This was nature unadulterated. Before us lay the Gulf of California and on both sides behind us stretched the Sonora Desert. The bare blue mountains ranged on the other side were the Mexican desert peninsula of *Baja California*, Lower California, some 600 miles long. We would have to back out of the scrub and into the cactus wood again, for there was not a single hut and no trace of human life to be seen along the whole shore. We had to go further up the Gulf.

And there it was in front of us, the Indian village, just as the sun sank behind the line of mountains on the other side and the sea began to turn black. One could hardly say that this last surviving remnant of the once powerful Seris tribe had been converted to a romantic style of architecture by its encounter with the white man and his culture. Half a score of families, totalling some sixty adults and children, had settled here in the sand on barren Punta Chueca, where the head of each family had built a little shack of corrugated iron and tarred board. Inside there was scarcely room to lie full length on the sandy floor. The building materials and the scrap-heaps against the back walls, full of broken glass and tins, were the result of the sale of turtles, which the Indians caught alive and kept crawling round in a little pen at the water's edge.

The Indians did not react noticeably to our arrival. Most of them went on with what they were doing, sitting in small groups or walking calmly about between the huts in a medley of colourful headbands, home-made ornaments and long, gaudy raiment in gypsy style, bought up and put together Indian-fashion. The men had long, black pigtails hanging down to the small of the back. The women's faces were painted with lines and spots in symmetrical patterns, barbarically attractive and timeless, an age-old fashion that may crop up again as the very latest thing. A not unattractive woman in an ankle-length skirt sat surrounded by others, grinding natural colours with oil in small pots, while one of them had acquired an ordinary lipstick which lent itself admirably to drawing vertical lines on the chin. She beckoned authoritatively to Ramon's wife, who had been watching spellbound. Now she had to sit down on the sand and have her face painted in the same pattern. One or two aged gaffers and a flock of children had joined us, and Ramon was soon recognized. The children sped off like arrows to one of the huts to fetch Chuchu with all his family. He had been Ramon's interpreter and guide the last time he had been here, filming seal and other animals in the Gulf. Now at last there was universal recognition and rejoicing.

Ramon had brought a friend who wanted to see their reed boats? But there were no Seris Indians building *askam* nowadays. The one Ramon had seen two years ago? That was the last they had made. Not even the other Seris villages further north used *askam* today, since the government had helped every village to buy a wooden boat with an outboard motor. A little naked boy disappeared like a streak and came running delightedly back with a small toy boat. It was a torpedo boat made of yellow plastic.

Night fell about us. We were lent some cardboard cartons which we folded up under ourselves before lying down to sleep on the floor in a fishing-tackle shed. All night long the Indians kept up their monotonous, incomprehensible chatter. I was drowsily aware of them every time I turned over. They were sitting round small heaps of embers, debating, and most of them crept to their beds at last, an hour before the rest of us got up, as the stars were beginning to fade.

Before the sun had yet begun to redden the cactus crowns, the four of us were sitting, surrounded by a few Indians, looking out over the peaceful gulf. No one spoke. We just sat. Chuchu rose slowly and ambled down to the silent beach, where he threw out a little round net. After two casts he pulled in four fine fish under our very noses. Two tiny boys with three-edged throwing spears doubled the catch in an instant. That was food enough. Everyone sat. It looked as if nothing more was going to happen that day.

'Will you build an *askam* for me?' I asked circumspectly.

'*Mucho trabajo*,' they all responded in chorus. 'A lot of work.' This was about the sum of their vocabulary in Spanish. For anything else they needed an interpreter. Chuchu acted as intermediary.

'You will be paid,' I promised. 'In goods or pesos.'

'*Mucho trabajo*,' they repeated simply.

The offer increased. Silence. It increased again.

'It is a long way to the reeds,' said Chuchu, stalling.

'We will come with you,' I replied, and rose to my feet.

Four Indians stood up. They were willing to come. Chuchu, with

47

two brothers and a nephew. Only the eldest brother, Caitano, knew where the reeds were. They grew by a lake out on Isla Tiburón, Shark Island, whose rugged outlines we could just make out in the sunrise on the other side of the sound.

The government's outboard motor came into service. Soon we were bucking away over the ripples towards the distant horizon. I was surprised that there were no reeds nearer than this.

'They are fresh-water reeds,' Caitano explained. 'They cannot grow on the seashore by the desert here. It is a long way to the fresh-water lake.'

Shark Island, with its savage mountains, loomed out of the sea. It is not a small island. With a surface area of nearly 400 square miles, it is shown even in a world map. As we jumped ashore on a white sandy beach we found ourselves on the edge of a broad plain, thickly grown with low bushes and scattered cactus trees, between us and the dawn-flushed mountains inland. A single *berrendo* deer, with a great spread of antlers on its lifted head, stood motionless on the beach, staring at us. Out came the cameras, stealthily, to immortalize the beast before it took off. Still it did not move, and we crept nearer. Nearer. I went ahead and was included in the picture. Caution was indicated. The deer began to move. Slowly. It strode forward proudly and deliberately, bent its head and butted me in the stomach with friendly determination, an antler in each of my armpits. I tried in vain to push the deer away so that we could get a decent picture; but no, it intended to be immortalized like this, and all my pushing and shoving, all my efforts to withdraw from this humiliating position were useless. The friendly deer simply followed, now forward, now back, close enough to hold me between its horns without goring

14. *World expert* on ancient Egyptian boat illustrations, BjörnLandström of Sweden, drawing an Egyptian papyrus ship for boat-builders Omar, Mussa and Abdullah from Chad, while the author explains the principle of the straddled mast to them.

15. *Papyrus reed* from the source of the Nile is cut and examined by a papyrus boat builder from Chad.

16. *Behind the Giza pyramids* the Buduma Africans from Chad begin to build a papyrus boat, with Landström and the author looking on.

17. *The ancient Egyptian boat-builder's art* comes home again. The boat-builders from Chad train Egyptian helpers in an art which their forefathers forgot when the papyrus reed died out in Egypt.

and without wishing me any harm. It was a ridiculous situation. Not until the deer had been scratched on the neck and behind the ears was it sufficiently astonished to lift its head and stand staring, wide-eyed, while I backed slowly towards the two-legged company with whom I had come ashore.

We dragged the boat well up on the sand and began our walk across the level ground. I was expecting at any moment to see the reed-grown inland lake. But no, there was only dry sand here and we had to struggle through a labyrinth of low evergreens, thorn scrub and scattered cactus. No path. No trace of anything but deer, hare, lizards, snakes and rodents. Shark Island had been uninhabited by human beings since the last Seris Indians were compulsorily evacuated to the mainland, some time in Caitano's childhood. We plodded and trudged, right, left, straight ahead, wherever openings appeared in the rugged terrain, but always heading generally inland towards the mountains.

'Where is the lake?' we asked in turns.

'Over there,' Caitano replied, pointing with his nose without lifting a hand. We walked and we walked. Gradually a vast stretch of land lay between us and the sea. The mountains came closer. Soon we were standing at their foot. Half the day had passed, the sun was blazing straight down on our heads, and we were without water or provisions.

'Where is the lake? I'm thirsty,' muttered German.

'Over there,' repeated Caitano, pointing his nose upward. We began to clamber over the stony scree which ran down a cleft in the red mountainside. Up to now we had seen only lizards and hares, but here startled mountain sheep and deer ran off along the rocky shelves about us. They were anything but eager to give us the sort of welcome we had had from our lonely friend down on the beach. Once or twice we

18 and 19. *Mussa and Omar* boat-building with fingers and teeth.
20. *Abdullah* helped us to persuade his compatriots to give the boat a curved stern in the Egyptian style. This added section was to prove the boat's weak point.
21. *A thick rope cable* was fixed in the ancient Egyptian manner right round the gunwale of the finished papyrus boat, for fastening the mast stays.

came upon broken potsherds of Indian make. Indians must once have stumbled down here with their water supply from the lake. Higher and higher. Incredible that any lake could lie up here on the steep, arid mountain wall where only cactus grew now.

Then Caitano stopped. This time he pointed with his whole hand. We were standing on some huge, tumbled boulders, looking out over a rocky canyon. High up on the opposite mountainside the bare red rock split in a branch canyon running from a little bowl-shaped plateau, and up there the sun was shining on a lush green patch, more fertile and lush in its light spring-green colour than any cactus or desert plant. Reeds!

The lowland, with the plain and the sea in the distance, was already far behind us. Weary and parched, we hurried over the rocks, looking forward only to throwing ourselves into the mountain lake and gulping down great draughts of water. I noticed one or two rock shelters half-buttressed with crude stone masonry. Human beings had once been busy here. Reaching the green luxuriance at last, Caitano seized his knife and cut his way into it, until his brown back, with the black pigtail of hair, disappeared in the reeds, which reached high above our heads. I hurried after him.

'Where is the lake?' I asked when I caught up with him, standing in the greenery. We could not see further than an arm's length away. He stood gazing at the ground under his toes and pointed straight down with his nose. Black, moist earthmould. The rest of us pressed forward, wanting to push further in to the lake. Caitano crawled hesitantly into a dark tunnel made in the reeds by animals which had come there to drink. The tunnel ended in an overgrown cavern, so large that there was room for everyone if we huddled together. Here the ground was obviously swampy. Mossy stones felt like cold fungus, and in the midst of them was a shallow pool about as big as a wash-basin, but completely covered with green spirogyra. I was just about to lower my seat into it to cool myself when a suspicion struck me and I stopped without touching the water.

'Where is the lake?' I asked.

'There,' replied Caitano, pointing to the exact spot where I had been about to sit.

No one had anything to say. We gingerly fished up the floating greenery and filtered barely enough water through our closed fingers for everyone to wet their dry throats. Then we smeared the remaining dregs over our hot skins and squelched our feet in the mud to exploit the last drop of moisture.

In spite of everything, inside this shady cavern it was incredibly cool and comfortable and life was suddenly marvellous and attractive. It is the great contrasts which give the greatest pleasure; a little slush and shade after the gruelling walk made us feel better than a champagne lunch after a bus ride. The Indians squinted at the section of sun which could just be glimpsed through the thick roof of reeds above us. They were thinking of the long walk home, and two of them crawled out with their big knives and began to slice the longest stalks off at the root while the rest of us lay dozing idly.

There was something to be learned from this walk. I had assumed, like most of the experts, that it was natural for the Seris Indians to build reed boats. I had assumed that they did so because it was difficult to find wood in the Sonora Desert, while the coast was presumably thick with reeds. And now the reality had turned out to be quite different. The Seris Indians had not built reed boats because they had easy access to reeds. On the contrary, they had made their way right up here into the mountains to find a minute trickle of fresh water where they could plant reeds to provide the raw material for their boats. If building reed boats had not been a tradition brought by their ancestors from elsewhere or received from visiting sailors they would never have thought of trailing up to this pool to gather reeds for boat-building. They would certainly have made the framework of the boat from the branches of the sturdy iron tree and covered it with animal skins. Sealskin was ideal for kayak building, and the rocks on the south coast of Shark Island were covered with seals. The Seris Indians had learned to build reed boats from other men. From whom?

Soon we were on our way down the mountainside, the four Indians in front, each with his big bundle of bound reeds over his shoulder, the rest of us following with the camera tripods and equipment. As we scrambled down I noticed that the Indians had dropped a reed here and there. Down on the level ground the Indians began to move in scattered order, and soon we found ourselves in front, with them following. So that we should not go astray before the sun sank behind the mountains, I searched for the tracks we had made and followed them zig-zag fashion, while the Indians insisted on holding back. After all, they had the heaviest burdens to cope with, even if it did seem to me that they had shrunk a bit during the descent from the mountain.

The sun was just going down as we regained the boat. We knew we would see the light of the camp-fires on Punta Chueca after it had set, so we waited patiently for the four Indians. They appeared one after another, padding silently on to the beach. Chuchu came last, smiling bashfully, with three, literally three, reeds on his back. The others had none.

'*Mucho trabajo*,' one of them muttered, and was applauded by number two, who was drying his face with his pigtail while Chuchu carefully laid his three reed stalks in the boat. The fourth was already on board, waiting for the trip home.

My three Mexican friends were bitterly disappointed and expressed their lack of appreciation of the results in no uncertain terms. Three stalks, after a whole day's hard walking on an island without food or drink. We had expected to find reeds on the shore. My own disappointment was mingled with satisfaction. Three reeds did not make a boat. But they told me something more important. I had learned that this was not the original homeland of the reed boat.

In the village, Chuchu and his helpers were subjected to loud-voiced ridicule from the old people when he threw his three reed stalks down by the wall of the hut. One ancient crone was particularly irate and vociferous. In the end she stumped off, bent double, to her own hut and shouted through the opening. A moment later a wrinkled old Indian appeared and was dragged reluctantly out by his wife. He was almost blind and wore blue glasses. When he straightened up we could see that he had been an unusually fine figure of a man, with distinguished features, something of a giant. The Seris Indians were different from all the other Indian tribes in Mexico. The Spaniards who saw them first described the natives of Shark Island as giants. The old man hobbled round the hut with his wife, and there on the garbage heap lay a reed boat. The thin, bamboo-like reeds were grey and brittle with age and the ropes were rotten, but there was the boat in its complete form. We helped to drag it in front of the hut door, because the old man was intent on proving that a proper Seris Indian could build an *askam*.

The old giant turned out to have been the tribe's former chief. As dawn was breaking the next morning he took out a home-made coil of rope and a dagger-length wooden needle, polished smooth with use. Blind as he was, he groped his way out and with his huge needle he sewed his old craft together, trying to strain the collapsed prow up into an elegant curve again. Luck was with us after all. The rubbish heap had given us exactly what we came for.

Then the last reed boat of the Seris Indians, and perhaps of all Mexico, was carried into the water and Caitano and son jumped on board. They settled themselves comfortably with a pair of old paddles and a long wooden spear with a running line. Paddling was something they could do, and soon we saw the brown backs with the black pig-tails disappearing over the ripples on the long, slender reed boat. When they came back a huge turtle was waving its flippers on the reed floor between them. The old, dry reeds had absorbed a great deal of water and the ripples were slapping on board, but they were afloat.

This was Mexico. Where had the Seris Indians' tribal ancestors learned this distinctive art of boat-building? From one of the many neighbouring tribes? Once there had been neighbours on all sides using reed boats, from the Inca empire in the south to California in the north, and also on the inland lakes in Mexico itself. As late as the beginning of the last century, the French painter, L. Choris, painted three Indians paddling a reed boat along the wooded coast by San Francisco harbour. In Mexico itself reed boats similar to those of Peru had been observed on lakes in no less than eight different states, according to the noted Maya authority, Dr Eric Thompson.[1]

I watched regretfully as Caitano's struggling captive was carried over to the turtle-pen, while the lifeless hulk of the Seris people's last *askam* was thrown for ever on the rubbish heap behind the old man's hut. There it lay, like a full stop to the last chapter of an unwritten book on the reed boat's story, forgotten for all time in the central regions of America.

[1] *Journal of the Royal Anthropological Institute*, London 1951, Vol. 79.

CHAPTER 4

With Bedouin and Buduma in the Heart of Africa

AFRICA. No continent has a more evocative name. Hear the word and the country appears before your eyes. A wall of green jungle, the huge tropical leaves pushed aside as lines of Negro porters with loads on their heads walk straight-backed into the camera lens. Giraffes and baboons loping slowly across the screen. Tomtoms. The roar of lions. I had never been in the African interior, only glimpsed it as if through a window, in the darkness of a cinema or pressed between the pages of a book.

But there I was. In the African interior. In the heart of Central Africa itself. In a little hotel room in Fort Lamy, capital of the Chad Republic. I could not have been further from the sea. And that was a little para-doxical, because the visit was the first stage in a proposed voyage by reed boat across the Atlantic. The only water in the vicinity was a tranquil river. I could see it through the window: green landscape, red banks of clay, brown jungle water. Colours sparkled in the sun. A band of fishermen, their wet skins shining like liquorice, stood up to their knees in water on a clay bank, pulling in a net. They had fixed a dense thicket of bamboo poles in the river bottom as a fish barrier. Yesterday I had seen seven hippopotamuses loafing on another bank further up the river. They were protected here in the capital. Croco-diles had been virtually exterminated because the skin was an impor-tant part of the country's exports. The traffic at this season was limited to flat-bottomed canoes made of hollowed-out tree-trunks; there had been no rainfall since the rainy season ended six months before, so the water was too shallow for motor-boats.

The Shari river flowed smoothly and steadily northward, but the water it carried from the jungle never reached the distant sea. From the vast jungle near the Congo border in the south it passed through

54

savannah and semi-desert on its way to the great inland Lake Chad on
the southern borders of the Sahara. Here the heat was so intense that the
water evaporated as quickly as it flowed in. Lake Chad had many tribu-
taries, but no outlets other than the blue sky which arched cloudlessly
over the vast surface of the desert lake and insatiably absorbed the
invisible vapour.

This was the lake I wanted to visit. But, easy as it might be to find
on the map, it was extremely difficult to reach. On all the maps it
stands out as the blue heart of Africa, but no two maps give the lake
the same shape. Now it is drawn as round as a plate, now curved like a
fish-hook, and then again scalloped like an oak-leaf. The fairest maps
show the great inland sea with dotted outlines, for no one knows the
shape of Lake Chad. It is variable. Thousands of floating islands drift
about on the surface, now sailing in one direction, now setting course
for another part of the lake. They collide and amalgamate, they
drift ashore and are transformed into peninsulas. They are torn apart
and sail off in different directions to new, unknown destinations.
The lake, which sometimes covers an area of 10,000 square miles
(the Lake of Geneva is about 225), often dries up to half that size, because the depth varies from three to fifteen feet. About twenty feet is
the greatest depth. In the north much of it is so shallow that papyrus
reeds cover large areas, and papyrus also grows on most of the islands
which sail around in an everlasting regatta.

The Republic of Chad has no railways. Nor has it any roads open
all the year round. It is a paradise for sportsmen and for those who
want to see one spot in the world which does not simply reflect our
own ubiquitous existence. The capital has first-class hotels, chemists,
bars and many ultra-modern administrative offices full of black
officials, most with parallel scars on chin or cheek signifying their
tribal origin. The wide asphalt roads, running between the small gar-
dens of French bungalows from the colonial period, which ended in
1960, become more rugged and exotic as they run out into the sand
between rows of Arab houses in the suburbs, to disappear across the
landscape as interminable caravan routes running between isolated
groups of round, native kraals. When the rains begin one must ride or
fly to make a journey overland outside the capital. But then the river
is navigable for small boats, right down to the trading stores in the
marshes where it runs into Lake Chad.

Three days earlier I had flown across the Mediterranean and the

55

whole of the Sahara in a French plane which stops once a week at Fort
Lamy on its way to more southerly parts of Africa. Anything destined
for the Republic which is unsuitable for weeks of camel transport
must be brought in by air: cars, steam-shovels, refrigerators, petrol.
Yes, even lobsters and tender beef for the master chef at 'La Tchadienne'.
They all come by air.

We left the aircraft, three men laden with film equipment and goods
for trade with potential African boat-builders. My party consisted of
two film photographers, the Frenchman Michel and the Italian Gianfranco. We were going to study and film local boat construction. I
had stumbled on a photograph in a travel article on Central Africa.
It showed some Negroes standing by the water with a distinctive craft
of the same type as the reed boats I knew so well from South America
and Easter Island. The picture had been taken on Lake Chad and the
author himself was very emphatic about the striking similarity between
this craft in the African interior and the type of boat which had been
built since time immemorial by the Indians on Lake Titicaca in the
Peruvian uplands. In Egypt this ancient African type of vessel had
died out long before, but here in the heart of the continent it still survived. An old caravan route ran from the Upper Nile area through the
mountains to Chad. In more recent times it was known as the trans-
African slave route. I knew that the anthropologists had reason to
believe that part of the population in the Chad area had its ancient
roots in the Nile valley. Chad was an African melting-pot. Here the
tropical sun sent its burning rays down on a welter of human types and
one would have to be a specialist to distinguish between the different
tribes and languages. But one thing was clear to everyone. Just as Chad
provides a passage from the Sahara Desert, whose sand dunes roll in

22. *Reluctant inland Africans* add more papyrus to the stern they did
not want, while the author holds the fateful bow-string which was
later removed.
23. *The 'paper boat'* in the desert sand was guarded night and day. One
cigarette end could have sent the papyrus up in flames.
24 and 25. *Five hundred Egyptians* from the Cairo Institute of Gymnastics
drag the papyrus boat from the building site. The building camp, inset.
Standing, from left to right, Muhamed, Mussa, the author, Abdullah,
Omar, Corio; seated, second from left, Yuri; lying, Carlo.

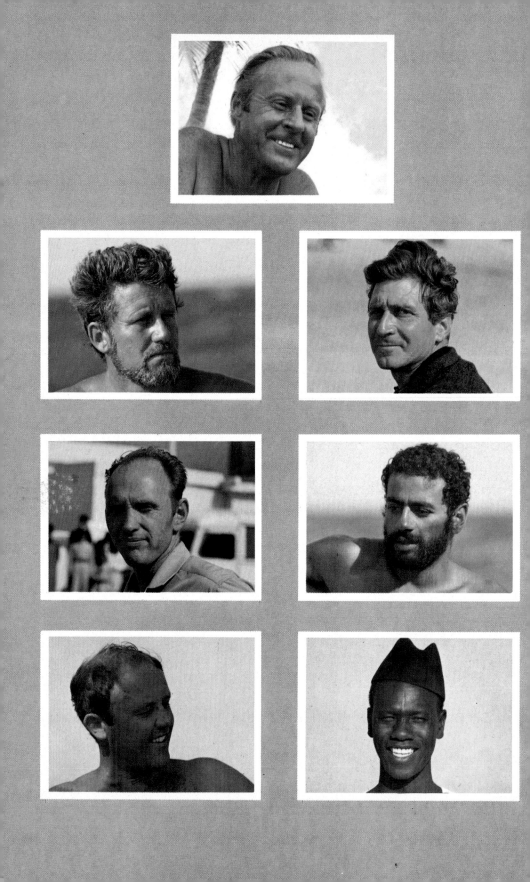

over the national frontiers in the north, across to the boundless jungles of the tropical belt rolling in from the south, so the northern part of the country is full of Bedouin and other Arabs, while the southern part is exclusively inhabited by Negroes. They meet on the central plains and in the capital, Fort Lamy, where they join in a common effort to forge a nation from what chance once demarcated as a temporary French colony.

After a cold shower in our air-conditioned hotel rooms we crawled into a scorching-hot taxi and drove to the official National Tourist Bureau. The wide main road was seething with cars, bicycles and pedestrians. Here and there we saw a few white faces among all the Africans. These were French officials and colonists who had chosen to stay on in the capital after the liberation. The tourist chief was one of them.

We explained that we had come to ask the best way of reaching Lake Chad, as we could find neither railway nor road marked on the map. The tourist chief spread out a colourful map and some illustrated literature on lions and all kinds of jungle game. We could go and shoot them all for a reasonable fee, but we would have to travel south, in the opposite direction from Lake Chad. We explained that it was the lake we wanted to visit, as it was the only place where we could see papyrus boats. The tourist chief folded the map and said that if we did not want to go where he, the expert, recommended he could not help us. He calmly aimed his paunch in the direction of his inner office and betook himself there. I had to fish out of my passport a heavily stamped letter of recommendation from the Norwegian Foreign Minister and send it in by a clerk. The tourist chief's paunch reappeared in the doorway and this time he explained kindly that it was impossible to get to Lake Chad before the river reached high water level. In any case, to find papyrus one had to go right round to the village of Bol on the north-eastern shore and one could only reach that by air. Did I wish to charter a plane?

26–32. *Seven men from seven nations.* Thor Heyerdahl, Norway, leader of the expedition. Carlo Mauri, Italy, film photographer. Santiago Genoves, Mexico, quartermaster. Norman Baker, USA, navigator. Georges Sourial, Egypt, underwater expert. Yuri Senkevitch, Russia, ship's doctor. Abdullah Djibrine, Chad, papyrus expert.

57

I did, if that was the only way.

The tourist chief picked up the telephone. There were only two single-engine aircraft in the country, and both were in hangars, under repair. A third taxi-plane had two engines, and therefore needed about half a mile to land in. The landing-strip at Bol was only 650 yards long. The tourist chief added that filming was forbidden in the country except with a government permit.

Moreover, there was unrest in the Republic at the time. The Arab population in the area behind Bol was Mohammedan and had begun to rise against the Christian Negro population, which held power in the government. So it was unsafe to venture into the northern part of the country just now. To prove his good intentions the chief placed the Tourist Office car and driver at our disposal. We could drive round and see anyone we liked in Fort Lamy and question people who knew conditions at the lake.

He gave us the address of a smiling, sturdy Frenchman with tattooed arms who was there to study the possibilities of improving the stocks of fish and developing modern fishery in Lake Chad. He explained that the only way of reaching the papyrus swamps round Bol was to drive by jeep across the desert east of the lake. This was confirmed by a French doctor who was an animal trainer and the most enthusiastic huntsman and local expert in the country. Both called attention to the point the tourist chief had made, that there was unrest in that quarter of the country at present. There was in fact a large river-boat on the lake, which made periodic round trips, buying up a sort of native corn, but it would be impossible to find it now.

Not many countries have felt the need to keep an embassy in the Chad Republic, but France had one in its former colony. Michel presented us there, but the Ambassador had only been there a month and none of his staff had ever been to the lake.

This was our third day in Fort Lamy and all we had done was to go from office to office, from bungalow to bungalow, calling on friendly people who offered us coffee, cold beer or whisky and gave us the address of someone else who might be able to offer a solution. And we had come full circle, to the addresses the tourist chief had given us and all the people we had questioned on the first day. We decided to try to reach Bol on our own, by jeep. We had the formal permission of the authorities. They had installed in Bol the only radio telephone in the whole lake area, and as a safety measure the Minister for Home Affairs would inform the sheriff in Bol of our arrival. I had only to go to the Minister of Information and get a document which would autho- rize us to take films. Here, as usual, there were Negroes, not Arabs, in almost all the public posts. The Minister ran his fingers through his crinkly hair and roared with laughter as he proof-read the document his own secretary had filled in at his own dictation.

'The man is an archaeologist, ar-chae-o-log-ist,' he told her, handing the paper back as he nodded towards me. 'Change that to ar-chae-o- log-ist, otherwise the Mohammedans will chop off his head in the area he's got to cross.'

I peeped cautiously over the frizzy-haired beauty's shoulder. French was the official language of the Republic, the only one which the many different ethnic groups had in common. On the paper I had been entered as '*archevêque*' instead of '*archéologue*', so I had turned into an archbishop instead of an archaeologist.

The mistake was rectified and the Minister reassured that there was no question of becoming involved in religious controversy on the government's side.

With appropriate documents and two Negro drivers, of whom one, Baba, said he had been in Bol before, we set out on the road from Fort Lamy long before sunrise next morning. We thought it safest to divide up into two jeeps in case of accident in the desert, and this proved a very wise decision. In the lead car we had a yellow map without contours, on which the names Fort Lamy, Massakory, Alifari, Kairom, Ngouri, Isseirom and Bol were underlined in red. We had no difficulty in finding the first villages. They were efficiently signposted and the sand roads were firm enough for us to drive across the flat country at over sixty miles an hour, with no escape from the dust clouds which we ourselves sent whirling up towards the starry sky. Along the first stretch to the north, steam-shovels and many road gangs were busy raising the road up above surrounding ground level so that it would still be usable in the rainy season. The first hundred miles were behind us when the sun rose over the plain. But then we branched off on smaller and smaller side roads and soon the twentieth century had vanished over the horizon. Even just outside the capital, the buildings had given way to scattered groups of round, straw-roofed native kraals, mostly deserted, but gradually we found ourselves crossing large uninhabited tracts of desert, with occasional wheel-tracks following the caravan route between villages where rows of low houses made of sun-baked clay harboured a medley of Arabs, goats, donkeys and camels. Then we were heading for sheer wilderness.

This was the desert. This was the southern border of the Sahara. The last thermometer we had seen registered nearly 50°C (122°F) in the shade. But where we were now there was neither thermometer nor shade for miles around. Behind us lay the savannah with fan-palms and arid-looking trees, here and there enclosing stretches of genuine parkland, where gazelles, wild pig and troops of monkeys leaped clear of the track in company with gaudy tropical birds, while fat guinea-hens scarcely bothered to hitch themselves out of the wheel-tracks. Where we were now the sand lay like snow on bare mountainsides, in drifts and dunes, over low, rolling crests and hollows in the landscape, where only sparse desert scrub broke the sun-drenched infinity of sand. Sun. It was now directly above our heads, glittering on all the jeep's metal, which was so hot that we could not touch it. The brooding heat pinched our nostrils whenever we tried to take in air – hot desert air, saturated with the dust which surged in from every side.

We were constantly getting stuck in deep sand dunes, and one jeep had to tow the other out on a steel cable while long, scorching metal plates were thrust under the wheels to provide a solid surface. At intervals, first one jeep and then the other would break down in the heat, its motor stone dead, but Baba and his friend were brilliant mechanics and, armed with spanner and screw-driver, they always managed. Where the sand was firm enough we travelled at dizzying speed. Time and again we lost sight of all wheel-tracks and drove on a looping course until Baba thought we were on course again. And so we arrived at a lonely village which was unknown to Baba and unmarked on our map. On a bend beside the first mud huts both jeeps became firmly embedded in deep sand and we had to get out and dig again.

For the first time we felt slightly ill at ease. Arabs swathed in grey rags and white burnouses, with expressionless faces and eyes fixed on us, came slowly – remarkably slowly – drifting towards us from all sides, never turning their gaze from our own, and showing no desire to greet us or to help dig out the jeeps. Soon they were standing shoulder to shoulder, fixing us with eagle eyes, unresponsive to all our attempts at a smile or a greeting. No women. They were as dark-skinned as our two raven-black Negroes, but the sharp features, hooked noses and narrow lips proclaimed them as Arabs. The harsh life of the desert had set brutal scars on skins and minds alike. There was no charity here. No pity. No telephone. The world beyond the sand dunes was represented only by our two jeeps, which were stuck fast in the sand.

The metal plates were now in position on the sand and Baba and his friend sat helplessly behind their driving wheels, accelerating until the sand flew. The Arabs stood quite still, as if waiting for something, holding something back. There was tension in the air; the look in their eyes made one think of a wary pack of wolves, all ready to leap or run at the first move of one male. It seemed imperative to act first. I tramped over to an apparent leader among them and politely handed him our two spades, indicating that he should get two of the other men to dig. He hesitated in some surprise, then took the spades and began passing the orders on, barking like an irascible sergeant. As we now beckoned to the rest of the pack to come and help push, the powerful shoulder of the newly designated boss was suddenly at my side, while we were nearly trampled underfoot by the helpful mob who fought for elbow room to join in and shove. We shook hands and thanked them, then drove off with our swirling dust cloud, through the village and along a well-worn camel track, as fast as our wheels could turn.

In mid-afternoon we passed through another village, completely buried away in the wilderness, where we felt equally unwelcome. Here we had to force our way through dense masses of people and closely-packed flocks of resting camels, donkeys and goats in a market-square in the midst of the adobe houses. Angry, glaring Arabs pressed forward silently, without returning our greetings, as if by reading our thoughts they might find out if we were government representatives, come to impose Christianity, or collect taxes. What else could strangers be doing out here in their desert realm? It was obvious that we were not welcome guests and again we bowled off at top speed into the desert.

It was nearly evening, but the heat still kept its choking stranglehold. Baba had a headache and the two in the second jeep, completely surfeited with dust, dropped further behind. The water we had in a large can was sickeningly warm, with no power to refresh because it burned on our lips. In the villages we passed we saw not a single fruit, only clay jars and dried calabashes filled with earth-coloured oasis water and dirty goat's milk. We had driven all day without seeing an empty bottle, a tin-can or a scrap of paper anywhere near our wheel-tracks. Only on the road just outside the capital had we once noticed fragments of glass from a broken bottle. Everything here was home-made: houses, clothes, harness. The traffic consisted of long caravans of small, heavily laden donkeys, Arabs swaying high up on their tall camels, and barefoot women trotting behind with pots and baskets on their heads. What you did not need for yourself was taken to market in the next village. It was a world set apart from ours, self-sufficient, unaltered, independent. The whole of our civilization could founder and they would get on just as well, as simply, as modestly, as steadfastly, bound to tradition and to the earth.

Then the lake came into view. Blue and shining like cold steel it lay, reflecting the desert sky, behind a belt of sappy spring-green reeds – papyrus reeds. From the top of a sand dune we could see it, like an unreal mirage, tempting us to leave the jeeps and rush off, make our way through all that fresh green stuff and cast ourselves into the blue, blue water, drink, dive, cool off, get the dry yellow crust of sand out of our ears, nostrils and eye-sockets, clean all the pores of our body, wash, drink again, drink, drink. We had been sitting in the jeeps for thirteen hours and were just about to stagger, stiff and dazed, to the ground, when Baba stopped us. It was not safe to leave the jeep here. Better to wait till we reached Bol. The village was on an open beach and if we kept going at full speed we would be there before nightfall. The desert was not safe at night.

We managed to control ourselves with difficulty. Water, so near, so divinely blue and beguilingly beautiful in its cool nakedness behind the curtain of reeds. But we took our seats again with dust in our mouths, and roasted and frizzled in the hot metal jeep, while Baba turned the wheels in the opposite direction and tore down off the sand dune and into more sand, sand and desert.

We would be grateful to Baba later. When, just before sundown, the two jeeps met the firm surface of the caravan route which runs to Bol from the desert villages in the east, we rushed straight through the deserted market-place and down to the beach below the houses, where we were about to dive in with all our clothes on, when we heard a warning shout. There stood an apathetic and bearded young Frenchman who had been put ashore by the research team working in a boat on other parts of the lake. 'Go out there and you'll be perforated with bilharzia in minutes,' he said dryly. 'The whole lake is full of them.'

We looked at Baba. He shrugged his shoulders and sat down again, all dusty, in the jeep.

That celestially beautiful lake was full of bilharzia, one of Africa's most insidious creatures. The little beast is an almost invisible worm, a millimetre long, so thin that it can bore its way at high speed right through a man's skin and lay eggs in his body, which is soon riddled with worms crawling about and eating him up from inside.

We thanked the Frenchman for his warning and asked him if there was a place where we could wash. He shook his head sadly. All the water here came from the lake and must be either boiled or left to stand for a day or two before it could be used.

The villagers kept their distance until a giant of a Negro came striding out of a whitewashed house with a small cortège, all making straight for us. This huge man was the real chieftain type. He was acting sheriff in Bol, deputizing for another man who was on tour up-country. No one in Bol had received the promised advice of our arrival. Who were we, and where were our papers? Sheriff Adoum Ramadan had toothache and was not in the best of spirits. Moreover, he had Bol's total population of 2,000 Arabs and Negroes to look after, of whom 200 were village headmen, so he had not much time to spare. Michel gave him a dose of aspirin and explained that we were looking for lodging for the night, as we had driven continuously since leaving Fort Lamy the night before. 'Then you have driven fast,' said the Sheriff tersely, affecting to miss the point. He inquired again why Fort Lamy had not advised him of our coming. The radio telephone was in order. What's more, we could thank the fates that we had got through, on the route we had taken. And now we learned that five separate jeeps had been burned by Arabs along the caravan route between Fort Lamy and Bol that month. The month before, sixty rebels had been shot in the area we had passed through. Two severed Negro heads had been found on the roadside and had recently been displayed by the authorities for identification. We were explicitly ordered to stay in Bol until there was a chance of leaving it other than across the desert.

The toothache-sufferer sent one of his escort to show us the way to a cement hut which lay by itself down by the beach, while he himself disappeared in the darkness towards the village with the rest of his silent staff. The hut consisted of a passageway with small rooms in the form of open cubicles, where we had to step over men and women already lying asleep. This was Bol's public guesthouse, where any traveller could simply go in and lie down to sleep, and the faces lifted to peer at us as we stepped over them were hardly angelic. In one corner there was a shower, but there was no water other than a dirty, soapy puddle eight inches deep in a hollow on the earth floor. We tried to pump, but gave up when we saw that the pipe led straight from the lake and was therefore full of bilharzia. We had no choice but to sleep in our desert dust.

Baba had just swept the floor where we were to unroll our sleeping-bags when the sheriff dashed in, his big, kindly face now lit by a huge smile. The toothache had gone. If he could have the rest of Michel's medicine three beds would be brought down for us from the sheriff's house. We slept with mosquito nets over our heads and pistols under our pillows. All night long invisible strangers prowled about in the pitch darkness, and several times I heard breathing close to my ear.

As the sun rose over the sea we were awakened by the muttering of a row of Arabs kneeling along the wall, prostrated in prayer towards Mecca. Others sat silently brewing tea on tiny open fires of dry, broken reeds. We ourselves were taken in to eat with the sheriff, who was in radiant mood and refused to let us touch our own provisions. We were to take all our meals as his guests as long as we were in the Bol district. His cuisine was in fact quite excellent in its own way, only one had to be careful not to close one's teeth completely because they would then inevitably crunch on desert sand.

That day I saw my first papyrus boat. It came drifting silently past

33. *Expedition members.* Different languages, political background and religion. From the left: Abdullah, Yuri, Norman, Santiago, Thor, Georges and Carlo. In the background the expedition's Belgian adviser, Captain De Bock.
34. *United Nations' flags* flank the row of participants' flags, arranged in alphabetical order by Captain Hartmark from Norway.
35. '*I name you Ra* in honour of the sun-god,' said the papyrus ship's Berber godmother, Aicha Amara, wife of the Pasha of Safi, who received a model reed boat as a christening present from the author and his wife, Yvonne.
36. *Baptized in goat's milk. Ra* being launched in the old port of Safi on the west coast of Morocco. *Ra* was the name of the sun in Egypt and in all the Polynesian islands.

me over the glassy water on that enchanted lake, which had completely changed its appearance from the day before. When we arrived, one large, low island had been lying straight in front of our hut, but now it had disappeared without trace and three other islands had loomed up in quite different places in its stead. The smallest of them changed position slowly as I watched it, drifting off to the right, leaving a faint hint of a wake behind it on the left. It looked like a big, well-arranged flower basket, a thick bouquet of golden papyrus flowers, delicate unruly crowns, the tallest in the middle and the shortest leaning gracefully out at the sides, reflecting their yellow crowns and green stems in the sky-blue water. Small climbing plants and other flowers and leaves were dotted about to make the composition aesthetically complete. The whole island, with its turf floor of interwoven roots and plant fibres, floated majestically away without benefit of oars or engine. The papyrus boat was travelling smoothly and surely past the floating flower basket. On board stood two tall Africans, dressed in white and erect as toy soldiers, punting the boat along with long poles. The yellow boat and the straight black bodies were also mirrored in the lake and the reflection, sailing upside down, reminded me of those other reed boats which actually were sailing upside down in relation to us, because they were on the other side of the globe, on Lake Titicaca in South America. The boats on Lake Titicaca were so strikingly like the boat we were looking at now that they could easily have replaced the mirror image.

I was longing to try out one of these boats on the lake after learning how they were built. The uninitiated could not hope to produce a boat in this particular shape simply by lashing papyrus reeds together on impulse.

The sheriff took us in solemn audience before Sultan M'Bodou

37. *Yuri, the ship's doctor*, checking the provisions, which consisted of dried meat, fish, Egyptian biscuits and durable natural products.
38. *Fifteen wooden boxes* to provide floor and bunks for seven men in the basket cabin. They contained personal possessions, books, film equipment and radio.
39. *Egyptian hardtack*, baked according to a recipe from Cairo Museum, was both tasty and easy to preserve.
40. *160 ceramic jars* of ancient Egyptian design containing water, oil, honey, curdled butter and all kinds of dried fruit and nuts.

M'Bami, the religious leader of the district and the most powerful man in the whole area. The sheriff himself and his deputy were Africans from the south, sent up from Fort Lamy to foster the political interests of the Christian government, while the sultan belonged to the local Buduma tribe and had the whole Mohammedan population of the area on his side.

The sheriff was broad and big-boned, like a good-natured gorilla, while the sultan was a beanpole of a man, a head taller than the average, with his head and the lower part of his face swathed in a length of cloth over an ankle-length cloak, so that only the hooked nose and piercing eyes were visible. All the village headmen slipped off their sandals before stepping on the earth forecourt of the sultan's simple adobe house where the audience was being held. Afterwards we were installed round the wide sandy area in the middle of the town, the parade square where the sultan would appear on his rearing white thoroughbred in honour of his guests. While two men held the reins and constantly urged the stallion up on to its hind legs, the sultan sat immovably, surrounded by a flock of colourfully dressed brothel girls, who ran round and round him, brushing him with their airy veils.

When the parade had completed its round, accompanied by drums and wooden trumpets, a dense line of horsemen appeared at the end of the square and thundered past us at a furious pace, swords drawn, yelling hoarsely. One of the riders was particularly aggressive. Time after time he raced past, his horse's hooves close to our boot-tips, while he leaned towards us, howling and grimacing savagely, his sword whirling appallingly close to our scalps. I tentatively asked the sheriff what this meant and was told that the rider was simply showing off. But Baba added that he was showing his contempt for us, who were not Mussulman. The sultan, on the other hand, showed no contempt. On the contrary, he evinced the greatest interest when he heard that we wanted to learn how to build papyrus boats. He sent us to his own kinsman, the splendid Buduma Omar M'Bulu, who lived in a large beehive-shaped straw hut like all the other huts in the Buduma quarter of the district capital of Bol. Only the sheriff and deputy sheriff had their own white-painted bungalows with red bougainvillaea growing on the walls. The rest of the houses, apart from the round straw huts of the Buduma and Kanembu tribes, were the low adobe huts of sun-dried, hand-formed clay belonging to the dominant Arab population.

Omar was a dignified man, tall, straight-backed, black as a stove pipe, with smooth-shaven skull and big, smiling eyes and teeth. He spoke both Buduma and Arabic in a low, friendly voice and ended every sentence with a hint of a smile. Omar was a fisherman. He did not hesitate for a moment when Baba asked him in Arabic to show us how to build a papyrus boat, but took down a long machete knife from the straw wall and walked ahead of us to the lake with his long blue cloak slung over one shoulder. The black sinews rippled as he bent and began to swing the knife at the root of the tall papyrus reeds and long soft stems were thrown one after another in a heap at the edge of the marsh. His half-brother, Mussa Bulumi, volunteered as a helper. He was older and smaller, equally shaven-headed, but without Omar's regal bearing. Mussa understood nothing unless it was said in Buduma, but made up for that by laughing at everything, whether Baba spoke to him in Arabic, Michel in French, Gianfranco in Italian, or I in Norwegian. But Mussa was quicker than Omar at handling the reeds.

Large heaps of green papyrus were dragged up and dropped beyond the swampy ground. We were going to learn how to build a boat. Two big reed boats which could carry a dozen men each lay moored at the water's edge. We explained, by drawing in the sand, that we wanted a little one, about twelve feet long, which we could transport on top of the jeep. Two other Buduma tribesmen were summoned. They sat down in the sand under a solitary tree and began scraping the pulp away from the leathery leaves of the Doum palm until the tough white fibres emerged, split as thin as sewing thread. These the Africans rolled between palm and thigh until they had spun them into a sort of twine, and this in turn was plaited into solid rope. Now Omar and Mussa could begin on the boat while the others worked against time to keep them supplied with rope.

The papyrus reed was at least six feet long and about two inches thick at the root, with a tricorn-shaped cross-section. It was not jointed and hollow like bamboo but compact and spongy throughout its length, like a sort of stiff white foam-rubber covered with a thin, smooth sheath. Omar began by taking a single reed and splitting it part way lengthwise into four strips, still joined at the thicker end. In the forks he stuck four whole stems, root first, and tied them with a loop so tight that the spongy ends were solidly compressed. Between them again he inserted a steadily increasing number of reeds, which he

67

lashed fast all the time with loops of rope so that the bundle gradually increased in thickness like the head of a projectile. Mussa joined him and the two boat-builders each took an end of cord in their mouths and tightened the knots with all their combined strength, using fingers and teeth, until black arm and throat muscles swelled. The point was apparently to squeeze the cut end of the spongy reeds together until the pores closed. When the bundle increased to a thickness of about eighteen inches, it was continued lengthwise, keeping the same diameter, like a giant pencil. Finally the pointed end was lifted on to a sturdy tree stump and the boat-builders began to jump and trample on the reed bundle until it curved like a huge elephant tusk. The shape of the upswept prow was now ready and two shorter reed bundles were added outside the first, one on each side in a chain of loops; by inserting one reed at a time the bundles fitted tightly together.

When the length of the boat reached the mark we had made on the ground the whole vessel was ready, in symmetrical detail, except for the stern, where the papyrus reeds still stuck out like the bristles on a broom. From here the boat-builders could, if they wished, increase the boat's length indefinitely. The problem of shaping the stern was solved by Omar and Mussa in the simplest way. They took the longest machete knife and cut all the superfluous reed straight across as if slicing the end off a sausage. Then the papyrus boat was ready for launching, with pointed upswept prow and thick, flat, sawn-off stern. The work was completed in a day.

'*Kaday*,' said Mussa, patting his finished product with a grin. That was the Buduma word for the reed boat on which the whole of their lakeside existence had depended since the morning of time, no one knows when. No one knows who were their teachers. Perhaps they themselves. Perhaps they had distant ancestors who had travelled the caravan route from the Nile valley. This ancient type of boat had survived here, in any case, wherever reeds grew beside the lake, even on the distant shores which belonged to the Republics of Niger and Nigeria. Everywhere in this vast area the ingenious papyrus boats were built in the same traditional way and looked precisely the same, except for variations in length and breadth. However, four large wooden canoes, the hollowed trunks of mighty jungle trees which must have come down when the Shari river was in flood, also lay moored in a gap between the reeds where we carried out the grass-green *kaday*, and we used the canoes as a bridge to go aboard dry-shod.

Omar pointed scornfully at these cranky boats, which looked like elongated bath-tubs half full of water. Those were the boats of the Kanembu. They did not know how to build *kadays* like the Buduma.

I was just about to jump aboard our brand-new *kaday*, which was floating on the water like a curved cucumber, when I saw Abdullah. That was my first meeting with Abdullah. He was just standing there when we needed him most, like a genie from Aladdin's lamp.

'*Bonjour, monsieur,*' he said simply. 'My name is Abdullah and I speak French and Arabic. Do you need an interpreter?'

That was just what I did need. How else was I to learn anything from Omar and Mussa when the three of us were out on the lake in the little vegetable boat?

Abdullah behaved like a well-bred gentleman, swathed in an ankle-length white robe and with a bearing like a Caesar. His face was blacker than night, his head smooth-shaven like Omar's and Mussa's, with a long scar running centrally down his forehead and over the bridge of his nose. Strangely enough, this tribal mark was more piquant than disturbing, and, with his unusually intelligent eyes, lips which were always curling into a smile and teeth quick to part in joyous laughter, Abdullah Djibrine was a true, full-blooded child of nature, an alert assistant, a really merry companion. He had already conjured up two roughly hewn paddles and he handed one to me.

As the four of us jumped aboard our narrow papyrus boat one after the other and the camera whirred to preserve the event for posterity, we witnessed a singular drama. It was market day in Bol and a colourful crowd of several thousand men and women had come in from the desert and from the islands on the lake. The market-place was literally seething with life; not an inch of the sandy ground could be seen for the men, women and children elbowing their way about, with jars, baskets and large trays on their heads, covered with fragrant vegetables, straw, skins, nuts, dried roots and African corn. Scarred faces, bare breasts, yelling children. Bright eyes, angry looks, laughing glances. The fragrance of spices mingled with the smell of donkey dung, dried fish, billy-goat, sweat, and sour milk. The sun blazed down on them all; the buzzing of flies was completely drowned by babbling, screaming, muttering human voices crying their wares and haggling in three different desert languages. Hundreds of horned cattle bellowed and some thousands of donkeys, goats and camels brayed, bleated and trumpeted in vain against the rhythmic hammer blows of the weapon-smiths on dagger blades and spearheads of ringing metal. Now a picturesque group of black figures was making its way out of the chaos towards the lake. With shouts and blows they drove all their domestic animals before them – mostly African cattle with huge, curving horns. Down on the shore they took off their clothes and tied all their possessions in a bundle. Then they drove the cattle into the lake and, with bundles poised on their heads, set about swimming after them. In contrast to Europeans, many of them seemed to be immune to bilharzia, though the disease does play havoc with the lake-dwellers and has reduced many of them to complete wrecks.

The people swimming out there with their cattle had propped themselves on tusk-shaped floats, some of a balsa-like wood, others of papyrus, exactly like the one-man floats I had seen in Peru and on Easter Island. Soon all we could see were the black heads with high loads balanced on the crown, the curved tusk-tips projecting from the water, and in front a welter of large-horned animal heads making for a long island on the other side of the sound. Abdullah explained that this was a Buduma family who had been to market to buy cattle which they were now taking home to their own island. A white, sandy shore and scattered Doum palms proclaimed that the island was anchored to the bottom. Two other islands covered with waving papyrus flowers, but sandless, were just bearing into the sound.

As we ourselves paddled out, we learned from Omar, with Abdullah interpreting, that many Buduma families were living on the floating islands, too. Omar and Mussa had been born on such an island and Mussa still lived on one. He had only come into Bol with some fish. There were masses of fish in the lake, the largest bigger than a man. There were crocodile and hippopotamus as well, but not many were left now. Cattle and other domestic animals sailed around with their owners on many of the floating islands and it was often a problem for the customs posts in Nigeria when a Buduma family drifted into their Republic with herds and other worldly goods from the Republic of Chad without having left the threshold of their own hut. When families moved their pasturage from one island to another they would usually swim, but if they wanted to go fishing or cross the great lake itself for distant shores, they always used papyrus boats. In Bol we had heard that a few papyrus boats were built so large that they could carry forty tons or more, and Mussa claimed that he had once helped to build a *kaday* big enough to transport eighty close-packed cattle across the open lake. Another had navigated with two hundred men on board.

Accounts of the *kaday*'s loading capacity sounded incredible, but when Mussa, Omar, Abdullah and I had all jumped on board our little rush-job of a boat, I began to believe in them. The boat was so narrow that I could only sit astride it, yet there we were, all standing on it together and swaying, and the papyrus gave no hint of a bend or a wobble. The water, so blue at a distance, was far from limpid and I was not anxious to capsize into the worm-soup. Here in the sedge it was especially perilous, for the little worms come swimming out of a snail which lives on the reed itself. The two boat-builders began to change places, swaying to and fro, squeezing past the rest of us, but hanging on to us at the same time, so that we would not topple overboard. Whatever they did, the little craft floated quite imperturbably, as high in the water as an inflated rubber dinghy. Out among the reeds on the biggest island we found an old, half-rotten papyrus boat drifting about, level with the water line. Many of its ropes had rotted, but the wreck still bore me when I ventured cautiously aboard. How old was it? A year, suggested Omar, but of course he could not be sure. In any case the boat was not newly built. And there it was, still floating on the lake.

We paddled about all day among the marvellously beautiful papyrus islands. The other men followed in one of the larger *kadays* which had been moored beyond the wooden canoes. Soon we were four papyrus boats out there together, playing out the lines of a fishnet while big *capitaine* fish splashed in the water about us. Evening came. Our first day on board a papyrus boat was over.

We three Europeans stood together outside the guesthouse, looking at the twinkling stars. The other, more local wayfarers were already asleep on the floor, but we had just arrived home from a little hut where a solitary young man, Bill Hallisey of the American Peace Corps, had treated us to a shower from a home-made spray nozzle on a suspended petrol can. Bill was one of those extremely rare men who drove about in the desert alone, and his contribution had obvious results in the religious war. He sank wells and created water where conditions were most appalling, and in the villages where the water bubbled up, there were no Mohammedans who felt the urge to slaughter Christians. Now he was boring for water here, in Negro and Arab quarters alike.

We felt new-born after our washing ceremony with Bill and stood for a while enjoying the last breaths of fresh air before creeping into the stifling communal hut. We would have preferred to sleep outside in the sand, but it was not safe because of poisonous snakes on their nightly raids in the desert.

It was a hot, dark, moonless, tropical night and the stars blazed with adventure and romance. Only the cicadas and countless numbers of frogs whirred, hummed and croaked from near and far in the papyrus reeds. The desert was dead; both it and the village were dark, silent, lost in the night. We took a last look at the stars and were just crouching to enter the doorway to the guesthouse and sleep, when I heard something and gripped the other two by the arms. We all listened. Suddenly from the desert came the distant, almost inaudible roll of drums and the sound of a tremulous wind instrument. The whole of the Orient was in this sound, which seemed to be made of the desert sand itself, played by the mild night air and carried by it through the darkness. There was not a light to be seen. I could not go to bed without seeing the strange sights which must be associated with this mysterious, barely audible, nocturnal concert. I wanted the other two to come with me in search of the sound. They were not tempted. They wanted to sleep. I took the smallest torch and put it in my pocket. It was no good using this torch except in emergency; the thing was to be inconspicuous if one wanted to look on undisturbed and if one hoped to remain undisturbed oneself. I did not feel entirely safe after all I had heard. The torch might be quite useful in a tight spot.

It was damnably dark. I took a bearing on the stars so that I could find my way back across the featureless ground to the guest-hut, which completely disappeared in the darkness as soon as I had taken the first groping steps. I had to lift my feet high and warily to avoid stumbling, but then footsteps were almost inaudible in the powdery sand. I had been walking for some minutes, but the sound of the drums seemed just as far away when I bumped into an adobe wall. The village. An Arab house. It was easy to feel my way along the wall to a corner and then turn again in the direction of the sound. All went well until my groping fingers came upon a reed barrier. Not a single hut betrayed even a glimmer of light. Here a wide sand road led between two reed barriers, directly towards the music, which sounded clearer now. I could even perceive the outlines of conical grass roofs against the stars, but below that everything was quite black. I began to walk faster. Then I stumbled over something large, shaggy and mobile, which uttered a strangled shriek and pitched me headlong on the sand. A recumbent camel had been startled awake. Its dry joints creaked as it walked off, still invisible.

I stood still. Not a light, Not a sound from the houses. Only the music, which was now clearly audible. Drums and wooden pipes, or perhaps some sort of trumpet. I groped my way on, right through the village, and now the music was quite close. Now I could also see the glimmer of an oil lamp. I had come out on the far side of the houses and I saw shadowy figures passing the lamplight in an unbroken stream, always in the same direction. There was an open space here, probably the beginning of the desert plain itself. I groped my way round the corner of the last barrier, which was of clay and useful to lean against without making a noise. Now I began to see still more figures, standing, and seated onlookers. I stepped over a couple of children squatting by the same wall and staring hypnotized at what was going on in the pool of light. No one reacted to my presence in the darkness. There were crowds of people here. Best to keep still and unnoticed, by the wall. There were swathed figures everywhere and all were staring at the endless procession passing the light.

But this was not a procession. It was a ring of people dancing round the light, masses of men, shuffling their feet, bending forward and back, reaching down to the earth and up to the sky, round and round in a big circle, while the imperative drums and the wind instrument sent their seductive oriental sounds out into the darkness. I caught the barest glimpse of the musicians inside the circle. Something strange was happening in there too, which I could not really see. Two female figures came into view now and then, inside the circle of dancers. Sometimes they seemed to be teetering on some sort of chair, sometimes someone seemed to be dragging them around backwards by the hair. There was no way of getting a good view, but I was peering and concentrating in an effort to see better when I saw something which captured my whole attention. A dancer had left the circle and was dancing straight towards me in the same rhythm, holding in his hand a short sword which he swung in time to the dance.

It was a coincidence of course; of course he had not seen me in the darkness. Or rather, yes, he was heading for me alone; there was no longer any doubt about it. In the end the sword was whirling and flashing right in front of my nose. I forced a smile at the dancing man to show that I could enjoy a good joke, but no white teeth gleamed back at me from the black face. Sombre and impervious, the dark Arab continued his rhythmic dance and his defiant mock fencing. In the background I caught a glimpse of the whole ring of dancers carrying on unperturbed, all but this infernal fellow. After a few more attempts at a conciliatory smile it suddenly struck me that there really was nothing to smile about; the man was brazen and offensive, the situation was extremely humiliating, the skirmishing was now so aggressive that the sword was just shaving my nose and soon it was being thrust terrifyingly past me into the wall on either side of my head.

I thought desperately. If I seized the sword blade it would sever my fingers. I could not reach the man behind the sword. As he danced he seemed a little unsteady on his legs, almost as if he were in a trance. Was he drunk? I had seen no alcohol. Was he under the influence of drugs? I did not know the answer. I did not know the answer to anything, but now I must act, or I would get the sword in my face.

So I began quite intuitively to do something which made me wonder if I had lost my reason. I was actually thinking that if the people at home were to see me now they would be certain I had gone raving mad. I began to dance myself. I began to dance in time with the sword-swinging bandit, marking time at first, in order not to run my nose on to the sword tip. The Arab must have been taken by surprise if he reacted at all. I felt him lose the beat for a split second, but then he danced on, and the two of us danced, he backwards, I forwards in the same rhythm, out into the circle of light and into the ring round the light. They automatically made room for us and no one showed the slightest sign of surprise or change of rhythm. I was so blindly absorbed in following and doing exactly as the others did that I took no further notice either of the man with the sword who had summoned me to the dance, or of the figures we were dancing round inside the wide circle. When I had fully regained my powers of observation I saw only the four musicians stamping round close to the lantern. I myself was part of a great ring of dancing, coal-black men: Arab, Buduma and Kanembu, as black by day as by night. The dance was relatively simple; it came naturally if one followed the rhythm with a shuffle, hop and bend, just like the others in the ring.

It was a long time before I noticed that the ring was growing smaller. People were stealing away almost imperceptibly. Soon we were a tight circle of a dozen men revolving round the lamp and the musicians. The trumpeter might have been blowing from his earliest babyhood, because his cheeks were puffed out like a cherub's. When he blew on the wooden trumpet it looked as if black rubber cheeks were stretching until they turned brown. Perhaps the lamplight produced the effect. But one thing was certain. The sweat was trickling down his forehead, and when I looked closer I could see that it was streaming down the faces of all the others as well, especially the dancers. Then I saw something else, which I had not noticed before. The others in the ring were holding a small coin in their fingers, which they raised and lowered and slipped to the trumpeter when they fell out and stole away into the night. I must at all costs be equally generous if this were to end well, so I danced with a Chad banknote between my finger-tips. The trumpeter immediately came tripping out with the drummers at his heels and enthusiastically stuck his strident instrument in my face, the beat quickened, the ring grew smaller.

Now there were only four of us left and the musicians were obviously concentrating all their efforts on the one who had the most money. The sweat dripped off the others and to my amazement they seemed exhausted, as if they were taking part in an endurance test, although it seemed no worse than a long 'twist' or 'shake' at home. Perhaps the desert horsemen were less used to personal exercise and endurance than skiers in the north, because this was no more than fun. But perhaps the others had been keeping it up for hours; after all I had only just arrived. One could go on like this for ever, just dancing, shuffle-shuffle-hop-bend-and-stretch; but now it was going faster, faster and faster; the musicians wanted to put a stop to it. Another man fell out, and yet another. It was frankly a contest, faster and faster; yes, now one really had to breathe hard. I was dancing alone. The trumpeter fell on my neck and secured his bank-note; people pressed in from all sides, with staring white eyes and a medley of indefinable expressions; everyone wanted to have a good look.

I gulped in the night air, pleasantly tired and relieved to have escaped the man with the sword. Him I could not see, but now a heavily built man came up to me, pulling two hefty female figures out of the darkness. They were not particularly young and not particularly beautiful by comparison with many of the well-proportioned women one could see on the shore by day. Moreover, the black skins were gleaming with sweat which was running from their foreheads as from those of the dancing men. Perhaps these were the women who had

75

been doing something or other in the mêlée within the ring. Now they were discreetly placed at my side like a sort of trophy. Hundreds of Arab and Negro faces thrust towards us in the dim lamplight. What now? How to slip away from this increasingly involved situation, away from the mob, back into the night from which I had come?

It was then that I felt a powerful hand slap me on the shoulder and there was Omar, his face shining like a sun in the lamplight.

'*Monsieur, brave tamtam,*' said he, flashing his teeth in approval. That exhausted his stock of French. Omar was my salvation. One familiar face. This was obviously a celebration for the masses, because neither sultan nor sheriff was present. Omar was respected, and when the onlookers saw that I was on friendly terms with the sultan's kinsman the ranks parted and we went off together through the empty village to the music of the cicadas.

Next day my standing in Bol had risen. Lively rumours were circulating about my prowess as a tom-tom dancer, and the large sum I had paid to the musicians. The sheriff, on the other hand, had received new reports of terrorist activities and Arab uprisings in the interior and insisted on our being his guests until we could leave safely by plane. It was hopeless trying to contact Fort Lamy by radio telephone, but the African telegraphist could wire to say we wanted a taxi-plane.

We had a number of good friends in Bol by now and were enjoying the days spent in papyrus boats on the lake. A week passed. Then the sound of engines was heard over the floating islands and a little aircraft flew in low over the papyrus, skimmed the roofs of the village huts and landed on the levelled strip of sand, where we met the French pilot a moment later. He was ready to set off with the three of us at once, but the little plane could not carry the heavy film equipment, only the most essential clothing. The newly-made papyrus boat was hoisted to the roof of one jeep and all the equipment stowed inside with Baba, because both sheriff and sultan thought that no one would attack the two Negro drivers if they drove alone through the desert, with no strange white faces on board.

The last people to whom we said good-bye were the two boat-builders, Omar and Mussa, and the interpreter, Abdullah. Both sheriff and sultan assented with obvious pleasure when I asked if the two Buduma brothers could join me later, in Egypt, if I needed expert reed boat builders. When Abdullah had translated my question from

French into Arabic for Omar, and Omar had retranslated from Arabic to Buduma for Mussa, the two brothers were so delighted that they shook with laughter and nodded repeatedly, gripping my fist in both hands to confirm their enthusiasm.

'They say Yes,' Abdullah explained solemnly, 'and I am coming along to interpret!'

We were already sitting in the aircraft, which would not start, so I did not pay much attention to my own reply, but Abdullah obviously did. Cables were coupled to the plane from Baba's jeep and with their help we trundled forward and into the air over the Buduma huts, *kadays* and papyrus swamps. We had a perfect view of limitless golden sands behind us, which we had jolted over on our way to Bol, and below us lay the world's most extraordinary island kingdom, Lake Chad. Beyond Bol it looked like a green-speckled jig-saw puzzle on a blue ground to which someone had given a casual shove. The floating islands were all the green pieces, with their infinite variety of sinuous outlines, and an endless chaos of narrow blue channels wriggled round them like gaps in the disintegrated puzzle. On some of the pieces there were tiny round native huts and flocks of toy cattle moving about and grazing, and here and there in the blue cracks the little yellow mustard-seed of a *kaday* appeared. Then we saw only blue and more blue until we reached the mouth of the Shari river. It took only an hour to fly straight across the lake, up to Fort Lamy. And there we waited for the jeeps, one day, two days. Three days. The radio telephone to Bol was in operation and the sheriff was able to confirm that the jeeps had left there long ago.

With the help of the garage owner in Fort Lamy we sent out a jeep which drove half-way to Bol and came back again without finding anything but our own outgoing wheel-tracks. Then we sent out the little aircraft to get a better view. It criss-crossed the route for three hours without finding any jeeps stuck in the sand. The scientists who had boats on the lake sent a jeep searching from Bol to Fort Lamy and back again. When it returned the driver had nothing to report.

We informed the authorities. They could do nothing. The chief of police explained that this was not robbery, it was civil war. We missed the scheduled flight we were to have taken, which stopped at Fort Lamy only once a week. The two cinematographers should have been on another job in Ethiopia, but they missed out on that because they could not go without their expensive equipment.

Then we had an idea. With Michel as spokesman, we went to the headquarters of the French military forces. Chad had become an independent republic. The French had withdrawn discreetly from the government offices, where there was not a white face to be seen, but it was not difficult to find them when they were needed and it was no trouble for the French military chief to spot the two stolen jeeps. Owing to the risings among the Arab tribes in the north and east, the French had military patrols stationed at strategic points in the desert; they had mobile radio stations and were prepared to summon French parachute troops if terrorist action took the form of organized rebellion. This happened some weeks later. But it did not take the military chief many hours to report that the two stolen jeeps had been found hidden in the shade of a big tree in a remote desert village. Our two drivers had taken off on their own with their valuable booty and tried to sell it to the Arabs. The newly-made papyrus boat, so important to us, meant nothing to them so they had simply discarded it in the desert. To their disappointment they had found no one in the desert prepared to buy the film equipment, so all they had been able to sell was the petrol, of which they had managed to tap the last drop from both tanks. The patrol which caught the two fugitives reported on the air that if the jeeps were wanted back in Fort Lamy we would have to send out another jeep with petrol.

What happened to the faithless Baba and his fellow conspirator we never knew. They were not in the jeep which swerved in at the aircraft steps and delivered the stolen equipment as the big airliner stood ready and waiting to leave for Europe a week later. On the other hand, our loyal interpreter Abdullah was later arrested and imprisoned by the local authorities, suspected of being my agent in Bol for the black slave trade to Egypt. But no one yet knew about that.

So the fascinating melting-pot of Central Africa slipped away under our wings, with jungle and desert, Negroes and Arabs, blinding sun and our own giant aircraft casting the racing shadow of the twentieth century over the limitless Sahara as it passed, leaving no furrow on the sand.

Au revoir Africa.

CHAPTER 5

Among Black Monks
at the Source of the Nile

To BUILD a reed boat you must have reeds. I needed papyrus reeds. Where would I find them? In Chad, the desert lake? But no arteries lead out from the heart of Africa to the surrounding world, no rivers, roads or railways. I needed more reeds than I could transport with a caravan of camels. Boat-builders could be brought out by plane, of course, but not enough papyrus to build a ship. It was useless merely to think of transport from the reed swamps at Bol to the airfield near the capital.

In Egypt? Surely. Pharaoh lies in his tomb with reed boats painted on the stone walls. Stone and reeds. Stone in the desert and reeds on the shores of the Nile. Stone and papyrus reed were nature's gift to the ancient peoples of the Nile. And mud, which spilled over the river banks in its flight from the Ethiopian mountains. The peasant based his livelihood on the mud, the fisherman made his boat of the reeds, and Pharaoh assaulted the rock itself for the sake of the next life. On paper made from papyrus reeds, Egyptian scholars wrote chapters of mankind's earliest history. Stone was transported on papyrus and the papyrus boat was immortalized in stone. The papyrus flower appears again and again in the art of ancient Egypt. It was the national symbol of Upper Egypt, and in mythology it was united with the lotus flower of Lower Egypt by the bird-man Horus, son of the sun-god *Ra*, when all Egypt became united in one kingdom.

To build a balsa raft one must do as the Incas did, penetrate the rain forests of Ecuador in search of fresh jungle trees full of sap. To build papyrus boats one must do as Pharaoh's men did, wade out into the great papyrus swamps along the shores of the Nile and cut fresh reeds. When a pharaoh wanted a boat built he had no special problem. His skilled boat-builders knew everything about papyrus

79

and papyrus boats, after generations of experience. His labour force was unlimited and the building materials grew in boundless numbers just outside the palace gates. The papyrus swamps, on both banks of the Nile, stretched from the Mediterranean coast for many miles into the Egyptian desert.

But that was long ago.

'No papyrus grows in Egypt now,' Georges Sourial assured me. Georges was an Egyptian frogman and knew the Nile like a motorway. 'There is plenty of stone, if you want to build a pyramid, but not enough papyrus for a toy pram,' he added and steered the motor-boat we were sitting in closer to the bank to give me a better view.

On the Nile was an endless train of sails and masts, gliding up and down between palm trees, sandbanks and cultivated fields, but not a single golden-haired papyrus reed bowed its bushy head over the bank to mirror itself in the brown water. Papyrus had died out in Egypt at some time in the previous century. No one knew why. The gods had taken back one of their oldest gifts, as if they had simply pulled it up by the roots. There was plenty of stone left, in mountains and in pyramids, but even the mud had almost gone, checked in its course by the country's new rulers, behind the huge concrete walls of the Aswan Dam. When the papyrus disappeared from the banks of the Nile the last Egyptian master of the art of building papyrus boats also faded away for ever.

On camel and horseback, by car, train and boat, we travelled up and down the picturesque course of the Nile. We were guests on old weather-beaten fishing boats and freighters. We sat on grey, sunbaked decks, eating Arab bread and swallowing sour milk cheese scraped with our fingers from a lump on the deck, all in the hope of extracting

41. *Goodbye* for heaven knows how long. The author's wife, Yvonne, waves as four rowing-boats tow the raft-ship *Ra* and its crew out of Safi harbour, escorted by Moroccan fishing vessels.
42. *All the boats in the harbour* wish us *bon voyage* by rocket and siren.
43. *The papyrus boat* was steered by three ordinary oars lashed forward and two long steering-oars of the ancient Egyptian pattern aft. Abdullah, who still had not realized that the sea was salt, stood the first watch with the author.

information from the ragged river boatmen who had never worn shoes on their feet and seldom, if ever, spent a day on land, because their wives, children, domestic animals and all their worldly goods were on board. They had been born on board. The patched wooden boat with a tent on top was the Nile fisherman's home, his village, his world. We learned quite a bit about how men could be packed together and perform all the activities of life on a deck area which scarcely afforded elbow room; how food could be cooked on an open fire in a clay oven on an inflammable deck; how dried food would keep under a burning sun on an open boat. But if anyone learned anything about papyrus it must have been the fishermen who learned it from us. They had never seen a papyrus flower, not even the little bouquet which is planted in honour of the tourists in the fountain before the steps of Cairo Museum. They had never seen the inside of a pharaonic tomb. Never heard from their forefathers that any type of boat had ever been used on the Nile other than plank-built vessels like their own.

But the Nile was long. It stretched right across Egypt, across the whole of the Sudan and on to its distant sources in Uganda and Ethiopia. There, in the lakes at the source of the Nile, the papyrus plant had survived and was said to thrive still, as it did on distant Lake Chad.

The ancient civilized peoples must have travelled far and wide, because several of the old pharaohs who ruled Egypt were born in distant Ethiopia, where the Blue Nile has its source. But in the Middle Ages the long course of the Nile had been completely forgotten and its legendary sources assigned to the mysterious and hidden 'Mountains of the Moon', until the Italians and Portuguese rediscovered the upper reaches of the river, when the Europeans in their turn were on the move again in Columbus' day. Then, for the first time, modern men learned that the Blue Nile flowed out of Lake Tana, which lay high above sea level in Ethiopia's central massif.

44. *The open Atlantic* was waiting outside Safi harbour as the Egyptian steering-oars had their first test in historical times.
45. *The sail is hoisted on the straddled mast* and the ancient Egyptian rigging is about to undergo its first trial.
46. *Under full sail*, with the solar symbol pointing our course westward and away from the threatening coastal cliffs of Africa.

By comparison with the Pharaohs we were handicapped by having
to travel right up to the source of the Nile for papyrus, for the Nile
is the world's second longest river. Papyrus grows in Morocco and
Sicily, too, but not in sufficient quantities for boat-building. The
Sudan was suffering from internal unrest and the authorities were
too suspicious of tourists to give a visa to someone who claimed he
had come simply to build a boat of papyrus. Ethiopia, on the other
hand, was throwing open its gates to tourism, and so we landed on a
scheduled flight in the capital, Addis Ababa, 8,000 feet above sea
level, on a green mountain plateau speckled with yellow wild flowers
in the heart of the proud old empire.

My companion on the trip, Tosi, was a newly trained Italian film
photographer, skinny, but head-and-shoulders taller than most people,
so we had difficulty in folding him up in the little taxi-plane which
was to carry us on to Lake Tana. His luggage consisted mainly of
numerous bottles of insecticide spray. Soon we were swooping like a
swing-boat in the gusts of wind over Ethiopia's grass-covered hills.
Below us lay the picturesque round grass huts of the country, scattered
in groups on ridges and hilltops. The landscape itself was like an undulating golf course in every shade of the greenest green. Then it changed
to mountain crags and savage, deep canyons with white torrents
raging down them. Soon afterwards we were swerving across the
upper reaches of the Nile, reddish brown flood water forced between
precipitous rock faces, describing wild loops in the depths of an angular
gorge. The loops below us were nature's mighty hieroglyphs, recording
that since the morning of time this ancient river had been gouging
its way down through the very mountain rocks, gnawing with the
inexorable teeth of time, and spewing millions of tons of Ethiopia's
mountain landscape, in the form of masticated mud and sludge,
down the mountains to the desert plains of the Sudan and Egypt.
Since pharaonic times the Nile had been feeding ceaselessly on Ethiopia's mountains and carrying their substance down to nourish the
cornfields of Egypt. The Nile's deep pot-hooks wrote history; from
them had come the fertile soil for one of the most vital first shoots of
world culture.

Our meditations came to an abrupt end. Suddenly the plane
plunged straight for the cliffs, while the pilot pulled hard on the stick
and with one wing-tip we brushed the treetops on a ridge filling one
loop of the gorge. The Nile disappeared; we could see only rocks and

treetops. At the same moment we heard a deafening roar, thundering at us from every side and completely drowning the sound of the little engine. My stomach glued itself to my backbone and I gripped the seat and held my breath while the Nile gorge suddenly opened before us in an infernal chaos. The whole huge river was torn straight across and hung foaming like a mighty vertical wall before our windscreen. Turbulent masses of water surged over the cliffs in front, to the sides, above, below, vertically, horizontally, seething white, thundering, booming and smoking. The sun had vanished behind the surrounding precipices. Then the pilot pulled on his stick again and once again we clutched our seats while the elevators, helped by a powerful current of air, thrust us upwards and we flew into a glorious rainbow painted against blue sky. Then we skimmed elegantly over the edge of the frothing witch's cauldron where smooth, rolling masses of water streamed towards us, collapsed and fell straight into the depths behind. As if at the touch of a wand the Nile was horizontally under our wings again, but one storey higher, and in a completely new version, sluggish, muddy and silent, high up on a green plateau without a sign of a canyon or enclosing walls. We had a vista of rolling hills, shining water and tropical evergreens.

'Would you like another look?' asked the pilot and without waiting for an answer he tipped the plane on its side and circled back again low over the same ridge, with the same exciting sensation as we dived into the steaming gorge behind it.

'Tissisat Falls,' observed the pilot briskly, when our ears were functioning again. 'The full breadth of the Nile drops off the high plateau here. Local tribes call the waterfalls Tis Abbay. Abbay is their name for the Nile and Tis Abbay means "The Smoking Nile".'

Turning our heads, we could see that where the whole broad river suddenly ceased to exist a fine spray rose from the nether regions, borne on an air current high into the cloudless sky like the smoke from a giant camp-fire.

Soon afterwards we landed at Bahar Dar, and minutes later we were filming the same roaring chasm from the ground. This was the dividing line between two worlds, or a world on two levels. We knew that somewhere just ahead of us people were still paddling about in papyrus boats as they had in the pharaohs' days. It was here that we hoped to find unlimited supplies of papyrus, because it was only a day's march from the Tissisat Falls to where the Nile flowed out of great Lake Tana. We were in the legendary Moon Mountains of the Middle Ages.

When we reached the source of the river, night was approaching. There was Lake Tana, serene in silver and black, reflecting a glimpse of late evening clouds and the silhouettes of mountains and treetops. There was a movement out in the bay; long shadows, as of swimming creatures with curly tails, glided silently to and fro over the strip of silver. In the shadow of the woods they were invisible, but they stood out sharply in silhouette when they slid into the silvery light. There were six of them – six papyrus boats gliding aimlessly about where Lake Tana ran between two jungly spurs and slowly began to move in the form of the Nile on its first noiseless passage towards Tissisat Falls. In each boat sat one, two or three figures, each holding his thin pole by the middle and dipping the ends alternately on either side of the narrow craft, as one paddles a slender kayak. Perhaps they were fishing in the river inlet, perhaps they were relaxing at the end of the day by playing in the peaceful eddies which marked the source of the Nile. A little further down, a single papyrus boat was racing down white rapids, perilously near to the great falls, but the black figure on board deftly manoeuvred his small craft out of the white ruffles of foam and returned towards the lake, hidden in the shadow of a calmer shore.

The Mountains of the Moon. Mountains towering towards the moon. This was how the landscape must have looked to the medieval explorers climbing up from the Red Sea far below, or from the plains of Egypt. Lake Tana itself lies about 6,000 feet above sea level and the mountains encircling it reach to a height of 12,000 to 14,000 feet. Yet the area of water was so great that you could not see the far shore. The lake itself was the home of the black monks. They lived on luxuriant jungle islands a long way out, and for centuries the papyrus boats had been their only link with the outside world. Even at a distance, at that late hour, one interesting observation could be made. While the papyrus boats on Lake Chad were sliced straight across behind and rose only in front into an elegantly curved prow, this type, which had survived at the Nile's own source, had kept the ancient Egyptian form. Both prow and stern curved up above the waterline and the stern was bent in the peculiar ancient Egyptian curl over the boat itself. This sight, in the still twilight at the source of the Nile, was like a vision down the river, down through the ages, into the peaceful dawn of history.

As the last of the tropical sun sank behind distant treetops the light dimmed slowly as in a cinema. With the passing of the light the dark mountains and the lake were left timeless. The mild night breeze carried pleasant whiffs of spice and a soft breath of ageless mystery, a breath from those islands where the calendar stood still and the Middle Ages still survived, protected and cherished by monks who for count-less generations had perpetuated the traditional way of life, the robes, the ritual and the faith which their pious predecessors had brought to the islands when the Middle Ages were common property. Although huge jungle trees grew on their islands, the monks had never taken to building canoes or plank boats. Their predecessors had paddled the papyrus boat from antiquity into the Middle Ages and now they were calmly continuing to paddle it into the nuclear age. We had come to learn from the monks, we wanted to profit by their experience of papyrus boats, and no one knew better how to find papyrus in sufficient quantities to meet our needs.

Who had been the monks' teachers? Not only were papyrus boats and pharaohs exchanged long ago by the countries at the two extre-mities of the Nile: the dawning Christianity of those days had also found its way from Egypt to Ethiopia a thousand years before the long hibernation of the Middle Ages interrupted man's memory of the former contact between the lowlands at the mouth of the Nile and the highlands at its source. As early as the year 330, while Christianity was still making its way through Europe, the Coptic Christian faith had spread from Egypt to Ethiopia. The early Christians settled then in the old kingdom of Axum, far up on the high mountains of Ethiopia north of Lake Tana. Later many of them fled southwards and out of the hidden islands on the great lakes Tana and Zwai to escape persecution for their faith. The black monks who hid on Lake Tana have now been there for 700 years and have recruited new genera-tions by paddling youths from the mainland out to the islands in their papyrus boats.

To meet the monks and investigate the papyrus supply at the lake we had hired a rugged old iron motor-boat with a papyrus boat in tow. Two such metal boats had been brought up to Lake Tana by an enterprising Italian, who used them to compete with all the papyrus boats which ferried corn from small wharves on the shore to the two big market-places north and south of the lake.

On the first island we came to, the huge jungle trees grew right down to the water's edge and their roots formed palisades and networks far out into the water. We wound our way through the stems on the light papyrus boat and jumped ashore under the foliage. Behind the first tree-trunks was a small path and there two monks waited for us, unmoving, as if we had come at their command. They were wrapped in ankle-length cloaks with open cowls; their feet were bare, their faces dark brown, with black beards. They fingered the diamond-shaped Coptic crosses which hung on their chests and bowed silently, indicating with an elegant gesture the way up the hill to the shrine at the top. Here small papyrus boats were propped against the sunny wall and loose papyrus reeds lay gathered in dry bundles. The church itself stood at the very highest point, looking like a larger edition of the monks' simple dwellings which were dotted about the lower slopes. All were circular, with walls of upright stakes and thick, conical straw roofs. Someone beat on a flat stone slab suspended as a gong, which emitted a deep, melodious sound. Several monks sauntered up. Many were proud and handsome, like most Ethiopians, with black skin, sharp features, hooked noses and black pointed beards, but quite a few looked undernourished and listless. There were really young boys, men in their prime, and bowed ancients with flowing white beards. All were poverty-stricken, shrouded in simple cloaks, with bare feet or open sandals. They ate what their small plots of earth produced, and fish from the lake. They prayed, sang and meditated.

We felt welcome. Here we would surely obtain valuable information. Two old men wearing turbans pulled out their barrel-shaped skin drums, beat on them with their palms and sang, in low, cracked voices, the completely alien, ancient church music which must have been passed down from the oldest Christian community of Ethiopia. So must their ecclesiastical forbears have sung when they came paddling over the lake on their first exodus from the kingdom of Axum.

The island was called Covran Gabriel and the angel Gabriel with drawn sword was the first to meet us when the monks took us into their straw-roofed church. He was painted giant-size, surrounded by a colourful array of biblical subjects which decorated every façade of a central shrine, a sort of altar which filled the centre of the church from floor to ceiling, leaving room only for a circular passage round it, with doors leading out in all directions. All the Coptic churches on Lake Tana were similar. Here one could see the whole history of the

Bible transformed into a colour cartoon, and the monks confirmed what the charming, naïve style suggested: that the paintings were two or three hundred years old, some perhaps older still. We saw Pharaoh in the process of drowning with his Egyptian army in the Red Sea, with only the commanders' bright helmets and the army's weapons protruding above the surface of the water.

We were courteously invited to enter in our stockinged feet, and came out again with several hundred fleas which had been fasting on the old church carpets. I got off lightly, but the photographer's violent antics showed that the vanguard had already advanced from his legs to his armpits and into his hair. He was in full retreat for the boat, where to the monks' horror he performed a not entirely discreet striptease with the insect spray. By then I had already extracted from the monks what little they had to say about the buoyancy of papyrus. Despite the fact that the papyrus boat was to these islanders what horses and camels were to the desert riders, none of them had tested its buoyancy-duration for longer than one day at a time. After use they had always pulled the boat ashore and raised it on end to dry; otherwise it would have gone on absorbing water. Waterlogged papyrus did not sink, said the monks, but it lost all its carrying capacity. The bigger the boat, the longer it would float, but it was not worth building big boats, because they were too difficult to haul up to dry. So we were not much the wiser. The next island we came to was called Narga. It was flat and papyrus grew in its shallow coves, but this encouraged the monks to renew their own boats regularly. 'Papyrus rots,' they said. 'We must build new boats at least once a year, even if we dry them after each trip.' In an old stone tower sat a solitary monk who said nothing at all. Nor did he move. The tower had been built by the Empress Mentuab 250 years ago and the monk had seated himself in the open top storey only a few years ago, and had vowed to his God that he would sit up there and never move for the rest of his life, until he died. His brother monks on the ground regarded him as a living saint as he sat silhouetted against the drifting clouds.

We hurried over to the neighbouring island, looming against the sky with its wooded hills. This is the holiest of all the islands on Lake Tana, Daga Stefano, the island so holy that no woman, not even an empress, may set foot on it. The last to try was Ethiopia's mighty Empress Mentuab, who was courteously turned away when she arrived with her court in a large papyrus boat and tried to land, two-and-a-half centuries ago.

The island was lushly beautiful from the lake. We glimpsed a grass roof with a cross on it between the treetops on the ridge. A ragged monk with severe elephantiasis of the scrotum stood guard at the island's one landing-place, and a line of small papyrus boats, set on end, leaned against the trees behind him. Full of curiosity and anticipation we jumped on to the rocks and stepped ashore on the holy island. The monk allowed us to study the boats and did not stop us when we started up the broad mud track to the ridge. Giant jungle trees, straw huts, monks. Silent bows, muttered prayers, fingering of small crosses. Papyrus? They all pointed in the same direction across the great inland sea. There. There it grew in unlimited quantities. That was where they gathered it themselves. Buoyancy duration? Eight days. A fortnight. If it did not sink under the load it would rot and break up in the waves in under two weeks. Papyrus must be kept dry. Hauled ashore. They too knew no more.

We did not get into the temple itself. It looked ramshackle, with oval walls of stone, bamboo and straw. But beside it stood a cave-like rock cabin, full of sacred relics. Two smiling monks invited us into the darkness, to a sort of chamber of horrors. Piles of white skulls, old crosses and the holy personal effects of dead prelates. The largest treasures were long coffins of glass covered with cloth. The cloth was folded to one side and the half-light revealed the shrunken, emaciated mummies of four old Ethiopian emperors who had been embalmed and lay with wrinkled arms and hands folded on their breasts, to spend eternity on the holy island. The funeral cortèges had once crossed stormy Lake Tana with these mummies on papyrus boats, just as the pharaohs' mummies had once been ferried in silent procession down the Nile for interment.

Back in the sunshine we startled all the monks by playing their

47. *Alone on the ocean.* Beyond the Moroccan coast, wind and current began to tug the papyrus boat away from the mainland of the Old World.
48. *Experimenting* with unknown rigging and steering gear. Before we learned the trick we had broken both steering-oars and the yard which supported the sail.

own voices back to them on a little tape-recorder. Now everyone wanted to speak. Everyone wanted to sing. Soon they were all arrayed on wide steps, peacefully singing ancient Coptic hymns in chorus. I squatted in front of them, recording. Behind me stood the tall photographer, doubled over his film equipment. Then came a roar and an oath so mighty that the needle on the tape-recorder flipped right over before it fell back and stopped at zero. The monks sat still, their mouths shut and eyes wide. Behind me I saw the photographer performing a wild war-dance. He had kicked over his tripod and was frantically hauling his shirt over his head. Off it went, then he grabbed for his trouser belt.

'Stop,' I hissed, appalled – and I was really furious – 'have you gone crazy?'

No use. The trousers fell to the ground in a frenzied striptease, while the gesticulating photographer clutched his rump with both hands.

'Wasp,' he yelled. 'Wasp in my trousers!'

It was not altogether easy to forgive the photographer for our disastrous retreat from Daga Stefano, even if he was suffering tortures and could not sit down when we were back in the boat. Nor were there many monks left to say good-bye to when I turned towards the steps, but those who had stayed thanked us kindly for a little contribution we offered, in gratitude for their helpfulness and in propitiation for the photographer.

The visits to the monks had given us the uneasy overall impression that the most important point about building a papyrus boat was to make it so small that it could very easily be pulled up to dry after a day's use. That was hardly an appropriate programme for an Atlantic crossing. To make them easier to pull ashore, all the larger reed boats on Lake Tana were actually built in two parts, which could be carried to dry land separately: a thin, boat-shaped shell with curved prow

49. *Streaming two sea anchors,* we drifted southward along the African coast without sail or steering-oar.
50. *The broken steering-oars* spliced with rope and hardwood by Abdullah the carpenter.

and stern, and inside this hull a sort of thick, flat, papyrus mattress, shaped to fill the hollow space. The boats of the Buduma Negroes on Lake Chad were far more robust. There was in fact one noteworthy difference: the monks on Lake Tana laid the greatest emphasis on making the reed boats light without altering their age-old external design, while the Buduma on Lake Chad concentrated mainly on carrying-capacity and strength.

On the way to the opposite shore of Lake Tana we passed some low, scrubby islets where half a dozen hippos waded out, ducked and reappeared all round us. The boat crew assured us that these animals hated papyrus boats and would overturn them if they had the chance, because it was from such boats that hippos had been harpooned since time immemorial. This was something we were constantly hearing, both in Chad and in Ethiopia. We pushed our papyrus boat out empty, but the hippos simply popped their heads up inquisitively all round it, snorted, blew, and stared curiously.

To the far south-west the shore-line of Lake Tana scarcely rose above the level of the water, and here we finally found the big papyrus swamps. The boat's crew told us that this area was unsafe because of bandits. 'Some call them freedom-fighters,' said Ali, the skipper of the motor-boat. 'Actually they are just common robbers,' he explained. 'They leave you in peace as long as you take care to pay.' One of the worst, who had held sway along the lake for twenty-three years and killed forty-nine men, had just been shot by the authorities, the men told us. They had no problems themselves, because Ali paid the tribute.

We reached a spot in the endless marshes where a muddy current oozed its way between the papyrus stems and moved out over the lake like a broad stroke of red-brown paint. This could only be the outlet of some stream. In fact it was a little tributary, its mouth well hidden by the thick reeds. Because it drains into Lake Tana, source of the Blue Nile, it has been called the Little Nile. Many varieties of big wading birds sat peacefully in or between the tall reeds. As a rule the Little Nile was so shallow that it was not navigable for more than a few hundred yards by motor-boat, but now the water level was quite abnormally high and we ran over five miles up the narrow red river, to a village of round straw-roofed huts. This was the home of the Abaydar tribe, and men and women stood close-packed along the bank to stare at the metal boat. Ali explained that only this and one other, still larger metal boat, were to be found on Lake Tana. Both belonged to his Italian boss and neither had made the trip up the river before.

Several small papyrus boats were lifted down from the hut walls and part paddled, part punted out to us. The smallest were simply floats, in the elephant tusk shape we had seen before, and we learned that they were called *koba*. They were made and used in exactly the same way as on Lake Chad in Central Africa, Lake Titicaca in Peru, and on Easter Island. A slightly larger version, on which a single person could sit, was called a *marotcha*, while the usual two-part boat, designed for two or more paddlers, was called a *tanqua*. The largest *tanqua* we saw had nine men on board, but we heard that there were many which carried two or three tons of corn across Lake Tana. Occasionally a *tanqua* had been blown adrift and left in the water for more than a week before the crew reached shore again with the corn, which had then begun to sprout. The Abaydar people believed, as the monks did, that after two weeks a *tanqua* would be completely waterlogged and sink beneath the waves. The hollow hull of the *tanqua* was so thin that the boat undulated like a worm on the swell.

My suspicion was confirmed: even if the design of the Lake Tana *tanqua* came closest aesthetically to the lines of the ancient Egyptian boats, it lacked the rigidity and strength which characterized the *kaday* on Lake Chad. The solution must therefore be to transport papyrus from Lake Tana, boat-builders from Chad, and use the wall paintings of old Egypt as a model for the reconstruction of the ancient boat.

The area beyond the village was quite unpeopled, and I was alone on the swampy shore when an exceptionally impressive Ethiopian suddenly rose up from a thicket of reeds. He wore a sleeveless cloak and carried a long spear like a fishing rod over one shoulder. With his haughty bearing, pointed black beard and sharp profile he was not unlike Emperor Haile Selassie, and when his little son, emerging from the reeds with a plaited fish-basket hanging over his back, proved to be equally picturesque, I enthusiastically seized the two of them and posed them as foreground for a series of papyrus shots by the photographer. I handed the man a modest coin in thanks and was about to climb aboard again when he smiled with subtle condescension and courteously indicated that he wished to accompany us. So the photographer's model and son became part of our little expedition down the river and out through the reed swamps to the lake. Once there, both thanked us politely and were about to go ashore when Ali, much agitated, made me produce the wallet from my back pocket. Then he brazenly extracted an Ethiopian note equivalent to a week's wages and handed it to the bearded man, who smiled and made a stylish bow before disappearing into the reeds with his son, as inconspicuously as they had appeared.

'That was the biggest brigand on this side of the lake,' explained Ali with relief. 'I always give him something to keep him sweet.'

That night a veritable cloud-burst descended on us. We tied the boat to a tree on the bank and pulled our little papyrus *tanqua* over our heads as a roof. The thunder crashed as it can only crash when the clouds lie low over open water, and the stunning noise, accompanied by dazzling flashes of lightning, showed that the storm was right over our heads. The lightning struck on both lake and forest. A flash and a crash together, we felt the blast, and a great jungle tree splintered on the shore close to our mooring. The rain spurted in like jets from distant garden hoses. All our possessions were floating around in the boat with the day's catch of fish. The photographer slept. In this weather there was no need for him to lie in wait with the insect spray.

In the deep south of Ethiopia the Rift Valley runs north and south between two mountain ranges in the direction of Kenya. The geologists have shown that this valley, parallel to the Red Sea, was produced by Africa's slow westward shift over many millions of years. A series of large lakes lies like a string of beads down this wide mountain valley. In one of them, Lake Zwai, papyrus boats are built. There is an excellent motor-road down the valley and the other lakes are popular resorts for weekend tourists from the capital, Addis Ababa, who come here to hunt, fish and bathe. But they do not come to Lake Zwai, the loveliest of them all. For here there is no road, and here grows the papyrus which is the home of the snail which harbours the bilharzia worm. No bather, therefore, can set foot in this beautiful lake.

There were two Swedes in Addis Ababa who were able to tell us about this lake and its inhabited islands. One had read about the islanders because he was an ethnologist; the other had been on its shores himself because he made his living in Ethiopia as a bird-catcher. With provisions and camping equipment in a hired jeep, we left our base in the capital and raced off on first-class, good, less good and ultimately appalling roads until we found a lodging for the night at a hospitable Swedish mission-station high up in the hills east of Rift Valley. With the resourceful Ethiopian teacher, Aseffa, as interpreter and a young Galla Negro who 'knew the way', we set off in the jeep next morning for Lake Zwai. A deep gully scoured by a foaming torrent barred all access to the vast plains between us and the lake, and to get there we had first to struggle fifteen miles south on a waterlogged earth road under construction. There we left the road, crossed an imposing stone bridge and continued thirty miles north-west, without road or wheel-track. We followed narrow rides, animal trails and open glades between the scattered trees, now this way, now that, and we constantly had to get out and walk in front of the jeep to find a passage. Our 'guide' sat stolidly without opening his mouth, and the few times when he did point, he led us astray. There were no wild animals but many old burial mounds, and often we saw Galla Negroes hunting in the woods, spear on shoulder and dog at heel. One boy was startled and lifted his spear defensively when we turned the jeep towards him to ask the way, then ran off as fast as he could and disappeared among the sparse acacia trees.

It was late afternoon when we reached a high rocky headland projecting into Lake Zwai which afforded a splendid view of the eastern shore and two of the distant islands. On the point were a tiny wooden hut and a large tent, the Swedish mission clinic. The nurse who ran the centre alone was on holiday in Sweden, but a watchman of the Galla tribe lived with his family in a grass hut near by, and allowed us to use the tent. On either side we could see the reed swamp stretching north and south from the foot of the escarpment, and far below us the evening sun shone on a yellow dot which seemed to be moving across the lake, a little papyrus boat slowly making its way home to the nearest island.

The light dimmed fast, as it must, only eight degrees from the equator. Then the play began. Monkeys chattered in the trees round about. Hippos lumbered ashore and went champing into the native maize fields. The howls and moans of more and more hyenas came nearer and nearer. Out on the lake, far, far away we could hear drums. From the tent we could see the light of camp-fires on the islands. Aseffa said the Copts were celebrating the prelude to their great Maskal feast. I was just stealing out to watch the panorama when I ran straight into two dark figures with spears, standing almost invisibly right in front of the tent door. It was the caretaker from the grass hut, with a

93

kinsman who asked if we would like to see the hyenas. They had found their mule dead, and now the hyenas were busy eating their fill. We crept into the grove. Ahead of us we could hear heart-rending screams, yelps, snarls and barks. Around us in the scrub on every side watchful hyena eyes shone like parking lights. When we switched on the torch everything disappeared, inaudibly and invisibly, as at the touch of a wand. Only the mule lay there, bloody and torn. We switched off again and waited. Then all the eyes lighted up again, pair by pair, on every side, and the beasts howled, moaned and gnawed. We heard crackling among the bushes and boughs. We switched the light on again. Only half the mule was left; it had been divided into two and the whole hindquarters had disappeared without trace. We hunted everywhere in the bushes, which were covered with trails of blood, but half the body and both back legs had vanished for ever in the night.

Next morning we clambered down to the papyrus lake. Part of the maize field at the foot of the cliff had been trampled down by a single hippo which had eaten hundreds of corncobs during the night. A neighbour was busy chasing away monkeys intent on taking over the lake giant's leavings. Far out on the surface of the water we could see small papyrus boats approaching from the islands. Where we were waiting, a passage had been cleared through the reeds to a small landing place on the quaking marshy bank, for here a narrow footpath led down to the lake. We waited with axe and rope and two branches which we had lopped in readiness, each as thick as a man's arm and twice his height, because we had made a plan and now we were only waiting for the papyrus boats to land.

Here they were. They were unlike those of the monks on Lake Tana, and more like the boats on Lake Chad, with shorn-off stern and only the prow curved up into a point. But they were small. There was room for only one man on each.

The first two to arrive had come from the islands to barter with the Galla Negroes on land. One had greyish-brown corn beer in a clay jar and in the dried shell of a bottle gourd. The other had freshly-caught fish. Soon the third came in too and began to drag his papyrus boat ashore. We stopped them. We offered to trade and soon we had hired the three small boats. We placed them side by side and lashed them together with our rope, reinforced by the two solid branches which we bound crosswise. This was our plan of campaign. We knew this was the only way of getting out to the islands. For out there lived the lake people, the only people who had boats of any type on Lake Zwai, and by ancient custom they made them so small that no interloping landlubbers could use them to force an entry to their age-old retreat on the islands.

The Laki people were not related to the Galla Negroes who lived all round the shores of the lake. The Galla tribesmen were typical Africans who lived exclusively by agriculture and cattle farming. Their feet were solidly planted in the soil of Africa and they never attempted to build boats or rafts to venture out on the water. But the Laki people relied quite heavily on the papyrus boats, because they not only cultivated the earth, but were also fishermen and traders. Despite their black skins, the Laki people were far from negroid. Like most Ethiopians, they had sharp, fine features, with profiles which conjured up the people of the Bible lands. Like the monks on Lake Tana in the north, they had migrated from the area near the source of the Nile, and like them they had brought with them the art of building papyrus boats when they fled into isolation on remote islands. As late as 1520–35 they had set out on their long journey to the Rift Valley, where they settled on the islands in Lake Zwai with all their religious treasures and ancient Coptic manuscripts. The manuscripts must still be out there, because, despite over four centuries of enmity between the Laki and the Galla people on the shore, none of those landlubbers had ever succeeded in invading the islands. In recent years the enmity had died out, barter had gained the upper hand, and a few Laki families had moved to the mainland; but true to tradition not a single boat was built on the lake even now which could carry more than one passenger in addition to the oarsman. And there was so little room for even one poor passenger on the slender bundle of reeds that it would overturn unless he sat as still as a mouse, balancing either with his legs straight out or up to his knees in water on both sides of the bundle.

So it was with triumph that we regarded our finished work, a stable raft of three boats lashed together. We collected the equipment and were about to board and set off for those alluring islands when we saw that one Laki tribesman was silently occupied in untying the knots and removing his own boat. He explained to Aseffa that he had come in from the island to collect wood for the Maskal fire, but now he had remembered that there was better wood somewhere else. A polite salutation and he hurried off with his vital third of our little raft.

It was late in the afternoon before we succeeded in hailing another

Laki who was paddling along the shore and casting his net. There was a sparkle of leaping silver almost every time he hauled in the net. We bought the catch, twenty-one delicate *tulumu* fish, grilled one each over live embers and made the fisherman a present of the rest. The trade included hire of the boat and this time we made haste to shove off as soon as the raft was ready. It floated admirably, with three men, and the film equipment perched on its stand; so Aseffa crept gingerly aboard to act as interpreter.

The banks around us were covered with short rushes, but we could see no papyrus. The water was choppy and we paddled as fast as we could until the mainland was far away and the green hills of the nearest island rose above us. We had come so close that we could clearly see picturesque round straw huts scattered among the foliage on the slopes. Then a tiny papyrus boat appeared from behind a headland and steered resolutely towards us. Astride the papyrus, paddling along with his legs deep in the water, we were amazed to see a grave, dignified man in a sort of khaki uniform. He flipped the boat round and parked neatly straight in front of us. Through Aseffa we were given to understand that the man claimed to be some kind of sheriff or chief of this island, which was called Tadecha, and that he demanded to see our papers before allowing us to land. With the brisk official perched on a papyrus bundle, his behind wet and his uniform trousers up to the knees in water, the effect of the ceremony was undeniably comic. Aseffa asked if I had any papers; anything at all would do. I pulled out of my shirt pocket a letter from the Norwegian Foreign Minister, in French, one intended for use in the Chad Republic. Aseffa did not know a word of French, but standing on our raft he read aloud and with feeling a lengthy tirade in Galla of which I understood only the

51. *Norman* announced that we were drifting towards the reefs of Cape Juby when he emerged from the basket cabin with his sextant after a bout of influenza.
52. *Safi the baby monkey*, a happy farewell gift from the Pasha of Safi, enjoying herself on the mast and swinging ropes.
53. *Salt meat* being sliced for soaking in sea water by Georges.
54. *A broken jar* of nuts solves the rationing problem for Safi.
55. *Fresh eggs* having preservative lime paste rinsed off by *chef de cuisine* Carlo.

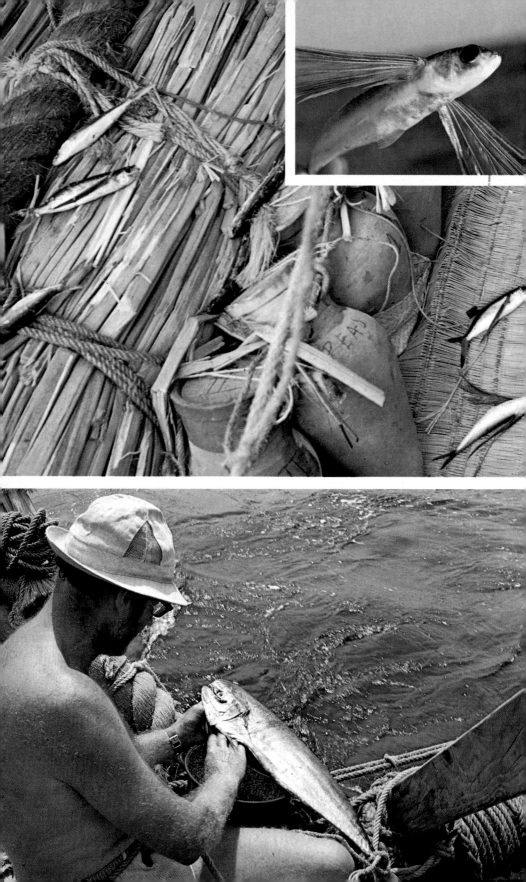

name of the Emperor Haile Selassie, which recurred constantly. What Aseffa had concocted only he and the sheriff knew, but the stern official raised his hand in a confused sort of salute, put his precarious craft into reverse and disappeared again towards the headland from which he had appeared, while we made for the nearest inlet in the grass-covered island.

It was a marvellously beautiful island, lush green, with rolling meadows and neat fields of maize. Naked boys were fishing in the inlet, women in home-woven garments made their way down to the landing-place with jars on their heads, a man was walking up the slope with his long and slender papyrus boat on his shoulder, while chickens and a medley of beautiful birds were fluttering everywhere. At the top of the ridge a cluster of sugar-loaf huts formed an open and orderly little village. They were covered with high conical straw roofs and the low walls were built in rings of stone and half-timber, daubed with clay and painted in simple patterns. Against most of the huts, at least one, and often two or three snub-nosed reed boats had been propped to dry in the sun. We were beckoned in by a handsome and polite married couple who offered us a bowl of freshly-brewed *aidar*, or maize beer. The man's name was Dagaga and the woman's, Helu. The hut had a trodden clay floor, neat and clean, with a weaving stool and enormous sealed ceramic jars, contents unknown. Bottle-gourd vessels and a few home-made tools hung from the crooked beams on the walls; the bed was of skins and the pillow the same little curved wooden neck-rest that they used in ancient Egypt. Dagaga and Helu were carefree; they had a minimum of possessions but a maximum of time in which to enjoy them. They had no refrigerator, but no electricity bills. They had no car, but no rush jobs either. What

56. *Galley* under the bottom step of the mast, presided over by Georges and Santiago while the cook takes photographs.
57. *Paymaster Santiago* found that the papyrus deck buckled so much that the jars had to be well padded in order not to chafe holes in each other.
58 and 59. *Flying fish* landed on board in large numbers and were either fried for breakfast or used as bait
60. *A dorado* caught by the author using flying fish as bait.

they lacked we would have missed, but they did not. What they had was what they needed. They had those things we struggle to obtain on those longed-for holidays from the office. When, some time in the near future, the modern world reaches them, they will learn much from us, and we, nothing from them; but that is a tragedy for both sides, for we assume that we who have most are wisest, noblest, happiest. Are we?

I sat philosophizing in the shade inside the doorway while beautiful Helu of the intelligent eyes graciously served her unknown guests. Dark-skinned, with sharp profile and narrow lips, there was something noble about her bearing. Dagaga, with a kid in his arms, was obviously delighted to be able to offer beer and hot roasted maize. It tasted extraordinarily good. The view from the door, looking towards the green hills, was unbelievably beautiful. I would have lain there on the skins enjoying the play of colours on the lake until the sun had gone down and the last reed boats had come home. Then I saw a flash on the horizon and heard a faint rumble. Black clouds were gathering. The film equipment! And all our things lying loose in the tent on the other side! If we were to reach the other shore before the storm broke we would have to hurry. The sun was low. Our wrist-watches frightened us. There were no clocks in the house we were leaving; time was not in short supply and needed no measurement there. We ran with long strides down the hill and shoved off in our three-part papyrus raft. Soon the island was slipping away behind us, its outlines blurred in the twilight. The last we glimpsed of it before the first raindrops obscured all vision were some subdued points of light high up on the ridge. Our Laki friends were sitting safe in their warm huts, calmly lighting the wicks in the bowls of their oil lamps.

The day after that was the Coptic Maskal feast, the most important day of the year, when all Christian Ethiopians celebrated what they called 'the discovery of the True Cross'. From our headland we could see great fires on all the islands. We had thought of going out again to ask the Laki people a few more questions about their experience of papyrus boats, but we were disappointed. Not a single Laki showed himself on the lake in a reed boat that day, and next day we saw only one or two fishing boats keeping their distance well out in the middle of the lake. Perhaps it was the sheriff who had hit on this method of avoiding a repeat visit.

We loaded the jeep and set off for home. The return journey was simple. Even though it had been pouring with rain, we could still see our own tracks. We had already left most of the plain behind us when we saw another jeep through the trees. It was following our old track, but coming towards us. It was full of dark Ethiopians, with one sturdily built giant who towered half a head over the others as we all climbed out and shook hands. His elegant embroidered tunic was hidden by a bushy white beard down to his chest, and a large Coptic cross dangled against his stomach. Aseffa kissed the cross and explained that this amiable giant was the highest prelate of the Ethiopian church, Bishop Luke. Now he was on his way to Lake Zwai to visit his fellow believers, the Laki people. He explained genially that he had a special mode of transport to the island. He would receive us on Devra Zion, the most important of the islands, if we returned the following week. We should approach the lake from the opposite side of the valley, where there was a little leper station which owned a small plastic boat.

Back to Addis Ababa. A few days later, the jeep loaded with new equipment, we were on the south-bound tourist road which runs along the west side of the Rift valley. From here it was an easy matter to reach the big lake, but this was the wrong side, where there was neither papyrus nor islands. The little leper station was closed, the windows shuttered. There was a Galla tribesman with elephantiasis in one leg sitting on the steps, who told us that the plastic boat was in Addis Ababa for repair. There were no other boats on Lake Zwai, apart from small papyrus *yevella*, which only the Laki people on the islands possessed.

We tried the jeep northward along the shore. Inaccessible. Southwards we got a little way, along a grass-grown path as far as a small convent school. Also closed and deserted. Further passage was blocked by a deep river, turning into fierce rapids. A sleepy monk sat swaddled on the grassy bank, gazing at a hippopotamus which was dozing with half its head above water in the shade of the hanging foliage of giant trees on the other side.

Boat? There was none. No one wanted to make boats on this bank, where so many hippos had been wounded by hunters in reed boats. A European and several Laki people had been drowned by hippos the year before. Jeep tracks? There were none. Not on this side of the lake.

Back to the main road. Further south along the tourist route. Lake Langana appeared in an open landscape, stone and gravel, no islands, no papyrus, no bilharzia – swimming-pools, tourist hotels, beer and pop. A sign boasted a plastic boat. We had come to hire it and take it

99

to Lake Zwai. So sorry. It, too, was in Addis Ababa for repair. Back along the main road. Night and tropical cloud-bursts. In the village of Adamitullu we found lodgings. A Galla woman had a boarded stall where she sold beer and Ethiopian pancakes filled with peppery spices and meat stuffing. In the back yard were two small bedrooms of planks and corrugated iron, a deep hole in the ground for common use, and a barrel of water and an empty tin for anyone who also wanted to wash.

The photographer opened his door a crack and inserted one arm and a large Flit spray. When he reopened the door he swept out a whole museum collection of lifeless insects. He slept on top of the bedclothes, Flit spray in hand. For myself I found a Galla Negro, whom I supplied with a torch, to guard the jeep. Then, after clearing the room of everything except the bare iron posts of the metal bed, I lit a fire on the floor with our hostess's incense wood, which smouldered all night and sent sweet-smelling clouds of smoke and all six-legged creatures out of the window-opening. Soon afterwards I heard an oath and uproar from the next room. The photographer rushed through the door and disappeared into the night. Next morning he was lying, curled up and completely consumed by bed bugs, on top of the load in the jeep. He had not slept a wink, he said, because a strange Negro had kept a torch shining in his face all night. My guard reported proudly that it was he – he had taken good care that the tall fellow who had left his bed in the middle of the night had no chance to steal from the jeep.

The guard was a find. His tribe happened to live near the southern end of the lake and he assured us that it was easy to get there, if he could come too. With guide and interpreter we lurched through groves of trees and crossed some sparsely grown wasteland, until we reached the southern continuation of the fierce stream which had stopped us the day before. Some crooked trunks, covered with stone and earth, had been laid as a cattle bridge over the torrent and here, inch by inch, we eased the jeep across. Then we followed bridle paths, creek beds, clearings in the woods and clayey maize fields from one idyllic Galla village to another. For miles at a time we were followed by racing village children, who beamingly tore a passageway for us through all sorts of man-made barriers and filled the deepest gullies with stones and branches. The scenery was varied and beautiful, the bird-life as exotic as in a zoo. The Galla tribes south of Zwai live their own lives in their own world, asking for nothing, getting nothing, and needing nothing. Their lives are completely undisturbed, untrammelled, unimproved and unspoilt. These were people who lived close to the earth and not one of them had been tempted to build a boat on the beach.

By the afternoon we had come so far that the largest Laki island was just opposite us. Its green hills were higher than any of the crests along the mainland coast. Soon only a broad sound separated us from Devra Zion, where Bishop Luke was supposed to be. We reached a Galla village on an open plateau. No one had a boat, but they all knew that Bishop Luke was out on the island now. He had been picked up in an extra large *obolu*, the Laki people's name for a papyrus boat which had been specially widened by lashing a shorter bundle of reeds on either side. What we had seen until now were simply common craft, so narrow that they overturned at the slightest careless move. In the Laki tongue they were called *shafat*, but the Galla people called them *yevella*.

We thanked them for the information and drove down steep, twisting paths to the shore, where we hooted until an inquisitive Laki came paddling across the sound in his little *shafat*. It was less than two miles from the spit of land to the island. We sent the man back to report that we had an invitation from Bishop Luke and must have an *obolu*. Not long afterwards the photographer and the interpreter were sitting with a Laki paddler on the Bishop's wide papyrus boat. I myself rode pillion on an ordinary *shafat*, back to back with a Laki who kept the reed boat balanced with his paddle and taught me to sit with my knees straight out and my back pressed to his, so we should not overturn. The camera equipment was carried by a third Laki on his own *shafat*.

The papyrus on our *shafat* was carelessly bundled together with strips of bark which proved to be old and half rotten. About midway, I tried to support myself on the papyrus with my hands in order to raise my seat a little, since it seemed to have sunk uncomfortably low in the bilharzia-ridden water; two of the bark lashings burst and at once the whole *shafat* was in the process of breaking up. The rowers on all three boats showed serious alarm, roaring incomprehensible orders to us and to each other in Laki and paddling in close formation in case we disintegrated altogether. We tried to keep our reeds together with arms and feet. It was quite evident that if we sank it would be futile to try to board the other boats, which would overturn at once.

The island which had been so near suddenly seemed infinitely far away and I sat stock-still, hanging on to both sides of the papyrus bundle to prevent more of the bark strips from splitting. I could feel the seat of my trousers sinking steadily deeper into the lukewarm ripples, the happy hunting-grounds of the insidious worms. Perhaps they were already on their way through the thin khaki trousers. Seldom have twenty minutes seemed so long.

The days of our *shafat* were over when we dragged the gaping papyrus wreck up on to the grass on the far bank, but we were now ashore on Devra Zion and it was well worth the discomfort. From the reed belt, grassland stretched towards the hills like an open park, with great, ancient trees. Further in, weathered rocks rose like the carved pillars and terraces of a ruined castle, overgrown with flowering evergreens, creepers, cacti and strange trees. We trotted and walked at a brisk pace along the almost imperceptible rock path, seeing no signs of life other than monkeys and gaudy birds. We had circled a good deal of the south side of the island without seeing cultivated fields, huts or men, when we found ourselves standing on the edge of a cliff, looking down into a deep horseshoe-shaped valley. The whole area down there was grass-green marshland, covered with papyrus and other reeds, and teeming with tall wading-birds and long-tailed apes.

On a dry sandbank by the lakeshore we saw Bishop Luke, leading a score of Lakis in the building of an extraordinary house. As we approached, it looked like a big two-storey bird-cage built of fresh-cut branches. The Bishop, who greeted us with a mixture of heartiness and astonishment, explained that when the timbers were covered with clay this would be a house where the Laki people could receive visitors from the mainland in the future. We stared at the marshland of this uninhabited and desolate valley. Steam rose from a hot spring which ran out into the lake a little further off.

The Bishop was obviously in a hurry to open his own food parcel, and to our embarrassment he insisted that we alone were to eat the best of the biscuits and fruit he had brought for himself. At the same time, he explained with ill-concealed anxiety that as soon as we had eaten we must start back again, because there was great danger from the hippos on the lake at night. We explained that we would have liked to sleep on the island. That was completely impossible, the Bishop assured us, and now he became earnestly though politely intent on getting rid of us.

The parchment books? Could we not see them?

The Bishop hastily consulted a tall, thin man with intelligent eyes, a beak of a nose and a pointed beard. They nodded. But we would have to follow the tall man at the double, up to the temple and straight down again to the boats. Hasty but still hearty good-byes were said. Our new long-legged guide was introduced as Bru Machinjo, chieftain of all the Laki people, who numbered some 2,500 individuals on the five islands in Lake Zwai. With chieftain Bru in front and a train of Laki men behind, we trotted as long as we had breath up the hillside among boulders and cactus-like trees and arrived completely exhausted, having staggered in single file for the last mile, at the island's highest peak. The landscape opened out into a magnificent view over the lake, the islands, the mainland shores and distant mountains. Below us, some 1,000 feet above the level of the lake, we saw the round straw roofs of a village built stepwise down the hillside. Above us lay a very small, square wooden hut, painted blue and green. Bru told us that this was the new monastery, where Bishop Luke lived during his visits. We were admitted by a monk, and on a rough wooden shelf in the empty room lay a great heap of ancient manuscripts and books made of parchment, yellow with age, with and without bindings, higgledy-piggledy, without order or system. Bru explained proudly that the Laki people's forefathers had carried them on their long migration from the north, many centuries before. I rummaged at random in the heap and pulled out the largest book. The pages were nearly two feet tall, of treated goatskin, magnificently illuminated with pictures of the ancient fathers of the church, painted with coloured cloaks and peculiar tiny feet. The text alone was a work of art: incomprehensible Ethiopian script, painted with delicate scrolls and decorations in black and red. Any library in the world would have locked such a work behind glass as an irreplaceable treasure.

The monk pulled out two big antique silver dishes with the Apostles engraved on the inside, which had also been carried on the migration. Here we were interrupted by exhortations to get down to the landing stage, for the sun was low on the horizon. We wanted to stay the night and delayed deliberately. We suggested sending a *shafat* over to the jeep for food and sleeping bags. Impossible. No Laki would venture out again in the darkness. We must sleep on the mainland with the Galla people and come out again the next day.

Now I was really curious. What was going on out here, if no stranger

103

except Bishop Luke was allowed to sleep on the island? It was twilight. I muttered something to the photographer, and in the confusion as everyone scattered and ran down the hill I hid behind a stone slab. There I sat while the whole company ran on down the terraces and disappeared. Silence fell. Only the wind murmured in the treetops. I sat alone, feeling as if I were sitting on the roof of Africa. Far below I caught a glimpse of our two reed boats paddling away from the island while the shadows spread over the lowlands. The huge lake swallowed the sun and the surface of the water glowed for a time like hot metal before it cooled, turning dark blue and then black, while darkness rolled on from the shore, up over the endless woods, over hill, over dale, in an unbroken wave to the world's end. Africa by night. I could no longer see the round straw roofs of the village below me. I could see nothing. I listened to an extraordinary warbling yodel mingled with the sounds of a religious choir somewhere down in the village. It was too dark to move. I had to sit and absorb impressions with ears and nose. Bats. Rustling in the grass. Suddenly I felt a hand on my shoulder. It was Chief Bru, who silently took me by the arm and made a signal for me to follow him. He held me in a friendly grip and led me like a blind man down an invisible path between boulders and rock terraces. We did not speak, for we had no common language. Since the interpreter had gone back across the sound there was no human being on the whole island with whom I could exchange a word. The chieftain knew every step of the way and saw to it that I came down unscathed. It was clear that, having remained among the Laki people, I was to be treated as a highly honoured guest.

We passed the first beehive huts and continued down a few more terraces to an assembly hut which was larger than the others. Light shone from the low doorway, and it was from there that the peculiar singing had come. Bru drew me in among the elders of the tribe, who sat on low, carved stools and wood blocks near the door. An oil wick was burning in a bowl, throwing huge flickering shadows of many men on the round, clay-daubed walls. Further in stood a row of young women in long white garments, bowing rhythmically and clapping their hands, while one yodelled and the others sang, monotonously and without accompaniment. In the half-light behind the white-clad nymphs I glimpsed some round jars, so large that each could easily have held two grown men. A clay oven was smouldering, but there was no smoke under the high roof supported by a pole with branches like the spokes of an umbrella. Together with the most aged of them all, a real Moses with a long white beard, Bru and I were placed inside the semicircle of men on elegantly carved stools, and a little table covered with a wicker lid was brought to us in the ancient Ethiopian manner. Under the cover lay enormous *wat* dampers as thick as foam rubber, in two layers, spread with morsels of fried fish. A cocoa-coloured powder, which made pepper as mild as candy, lay in a heap in the middle. In this you were supposed to dip the pieces you had torn off. All were invited to wash their hands before attacking the common meal with their fingers, and Bru spent his time tearing off the best pieces to place before his unknown guest. In a flash my hosts had turned a mute stowaway into a guest of honour. While the chorus of women swayed and kept up their strange incessant psalm-singing, a silent man went round filling all the mugs with sweet maize beer and finally with a very powerful sugar brandy. As the tongues of most of the men were loosened they engaged one another in an exchange of solemn monologues in Laki. I myself sat dumb as a post until I remembered the tape-recorder slung over my shoulder. At first there was sheer consternation, because the women's choir began to yodel full voice while the women themselves were enjoying a break, and the men choked because they heard themselves speaking while they were actually drinking. The evening was saved, the tape-recorder was my ventriloquist, conversing with everyone in Laki and bursting into shouts of laughter as if it understood all the jokes and everything that was being sung and said in the meeting hut.

In the end it was the eldest who rose and remained standing, when he felt the time had come to stop. All the women walked out first in line, yodelling in chorus with a warbling note like a night-owl's as they left us, and from the darkness the owl sounds came back to us individually until the women had all disappeared into their respective huts. The chief took me by the arm and led me to his own house, which was exactly like the round assembly hut, but smaller. By the faint light of the oil lamp I glimpsed the outline of someone packing up bundles of clothes and carrying them out so that I could make use of the hut's one bed. It was useless to refuse. Bru sat his guest down on the bed, which was of the same type as the ancient Egyptian pharaohs' beds in Cairo Museum: a wooden frame on legs, holding an open net of interwoven strips of leather. Bru and his family moved out their own mats and head-rests to lie on the floor in another hut, spreading clean skins and a home-woven cover on their own bed and signing to me to lie down. I pulled off my long jungle boots while the chieftain sat at the bedside and directed his son to bring a basin and wash my feet. When they were very thoroughly washed and dried, the boy bowed deeply and kissed my toes before he and the others were told to leave the hut. Here on Devra Zion the Bible story lived on in reality.

Fully clothed, but with clean, bare feet, I rolled up in the bed, where I lay wondering why Bru and his wife were still muttering together at its foot. They were consulting together irresolutely in hushed voices and kept looking at their guest in the bed, as though uncertain if I were all right or if there were anything else to be done. Then I saw that they were not alone. At the other side of the bed-end a vague figure was standing in the darkness. The oil wick was burning so low behind the roof pole that its outlines were barely visible. It was a young woman. She turned almost imperceptibly and as the soft light shone behind her profile I could see that she was beautiful. She must be one of Bru's own daughters. All three stood there for a long time, then the parents bowed and disappeared through the doorway. The lamp shed scarcely any light now and for a while I was uncertain whether the figure at the foot of the bed was still there or not. But then I saw her silhouette again. There she stood, almost without stirring. What now? Here I was in the chieftain's bed, his son had washed my feet, and now his daughter was standing like a guardian angel at the bedside. It was then that I heard the photographer's voice far away in the silence of the night. He was calling my name. I did not answer, in order not to break the spell. But the photographer would not give up and the shouts came steadily closer, until he was standing in the doorway with Bru and his wife. He had grown anxious about me, he said, and he and the interpreter had paddled back alone to the island in the bishop's *obolu*. They, too, were served now with maize beer and fish dampers, and skins were laid on the floor for the newcomers.

Next day we were still the chieftain's guests and with the interpreter to help we found out everything we wanted to know. The papyrus in Lake Zwai grew along such an inaccessible coast that it would not be feasible to transport it from this lake in large quantities. The swamps round Lake Tana were thus the only answer. But we learned something else from the Laki people. Their *shafat* and *obolu* were more reminiscent of the reed boats in Chad, Mexico and Peru than of the *tanquas* on Lake

Tana, which were built by their own Ethiopian kinsmen. It was not because there was no timber on the lake that the Laki people built reed boats. They did so despite the fact that wood was more readily available than reeds. The fact that nobody from the vast Galla area around the lake could transport us to the islands also proved that it was not given to everybody to build papyrus boats, even if they happened to live on the same lake. The art of building papyrus boats had been imported to Lake Zwai; it was not a local invention, but an inheritance from ancestors coming from the area near the source of the Nile, just as it had been with the monks of Lake Tana. Apparently, the papyrus boat had a tenacious way of accompanying migratory people as part of their tradition.

But the Laki people had the same unfortunate experience as the monks on Lake Tana. The papyrus must be dried after daily use. If an *obolu* or *shafat* were left lying in the water it would be unusable after eight, ten or, at most, fourteen days.

I travelled back to Egypt with mixed feelings. Was it worth attempting the Atlantic?

CHAPTER 6

In the World of the Pyramid-builders

'YOU WANT to rope off a bit of desert behind the Cheops Pyramid to build a papyrus boat?'

The thick-set Egyptian Minister adjusted his horn-rimmed glasses and looked at me with a questioning smile. He glanced half dubiously at the Norwegian Ambassador who smiled politely back, as he stood erect and white-haired beside his compatriot as a sort of pledge that this stranger from the north was in his right mind.

'Papyrus sinks after two weeks. Not my words – they come from the President of the Egyptian Papyrus Institute,' said the Minister. 'And the archaeologists say that papyrus boats can never have sailed beyond the mouth of the Nile because papyrus dissolves in sea-water and breaks up in the waves.'

'That is exactly what we want to test in practice,' I explained.

I had no better reasons to offer, faced with such a body of papyrus specialists. The Minister of Culture and the Minister for Tourism had done all they could, following a request from the Norwegian Ambassador. They had called in Egypt's foremost authorities as advisers and now we were seated round a large conference table with museum directors, archaeologists, historians and papyrus experts. The President of the Papyrus Institute had given his verdict in advance. He repeated it. But he admitted, laughing, that since I was the only one of those present who had seen a papyrus boat in real life he would gladly support the idea if I were absolutely determined to make the experiment.

To the head of the Cairo Museum the idea of a papyrus boat on the ocean waves was absurd. Egypt had exported papyrus to Byblos for bookmaking in ancient times, he said, but of course the Phoenicians collected it themselves, because only wooden boats could cross this open corner of the inner Mediterranean. For a papyrus boat to cross the Atlantic was completely inconceivable, now as then. Any specialist could testify that a papyrus boat would not be able to go beyond the mouth of the Nile.

A long technical discussion ranged from papyrus to pyramids and hieroglyphs on both sides of the Atlantic. Finally it was the Director-General for all Egyptian archaeological relics, Dr Gamal Mehrez, who had the last word. 'If anyone would reconstruct a papyrus boat from the wall paintings in our old burial chambers and try it out in practice, that would be a valuable experiment,' he stated. And that was that.

The Minister of Culture authorized the controller of the Giza Pyramid to let us rope off the area we needed for the tent camp and building yard, in return for our promise not to dig into the sand, because we would be right in the middle of the ancient graveyard of the pharaohs' families.

At the bottom of the steps of the Government building was the brick barricade familiar in Cairo, and sandbags were stacked in front of all the windows. Here we parted from the Deputy Minister for Tourism, Adel Taher, who shook my hand with a broad grin before disappearing up the steps again.

'You must build that boat,' he said. 'We are all in favour of your experiment. It is a good thing to remind the world that Egypt does not only make war."

I was left with the smiling Ambassador and thanked him sincerely for his invaluable support. Peter Anker had been a good friend from the start. Many years of work in the Middle East, both as a UN delegate and as Norwegian Ambassador, with ancient history as a personal hobby, had made him a walking encyclopedia on all questions of trade relations and cultural contacts in these parts, from the most ancient times.

'That was fine,' he declared. 'You got the building site, but no one shared your faith in the papyrus boat!'

'If there were no controversy there would be no need to try out the boat,' I remarked.

In the hotel room I sat irresolutely on the edge of the bed. Certainly, I had the building site. But I had not yet set all the wheels in motion. There was still time to withdraw. I had to decide now: full speed ahead on all fronts, or drop the whole plan, here and now. There was also the point that everything I owned was not nearly enough to carry out such a costly experiment. But my publishers would probably be willing to gamble on the account of the final outcome. What if there were no outcome? I sat fingering a small sheet of paper. The monks, the Laki people, the scientists and the papyrus experts all gave the papyrus boat a maximum of fourteen days in calm, fresh water and less in choppy salt water. I had personally sat for a few hours at a time on *kaday*, *tanqua* or *shafat*, and had already had the unpleasant experience of sitting in a papyrus boat while the reed bundle disintegrated. I knew that the *totora* reed in America was capable of long sea voyages and that it had a fibrous outer sheath and a spongy cellular centre which resembled papyrus in every way, but perhaps papyrus still did absorb water much faster than *totora*.

I unfolded the scrap of paper. The crabbed letters and childish handwriting on it read:

Dear Thor in Italy,
    Do you remember Abdullah in Chad? I am ready to come to you and build a big *kaday* with Omar and Mussa. We are waiting for orders and I am carpenter with Pastor Eyer in Fort Lamy.
                                    Greetings, Abdoulaye Djibrine.

The laughing, coal-black face of Abdullah, with the tribal scar over his brow and nose, appeared before me and I had to smile at the touching letter. At the same time it was a marvellous thing that this illiterate in the heart of Central Africa had had the initiative to take my address to a scribe in Fort Lamy and rouse me to action. Why did I hesitate? Abdullah was ready and Omar and Mussa were prepared to come with him. They built larger reed boats to freight their cattle on Lake Chad than those used by the Christians to escape alone and take refuge on Ethiopian islands, and they knew more about the floating capacity of papyrus than all the scholars in the world put together. They believed in their *kaday*. They were willing to build one big enough to float for months, and they were willing to come on board themselves and sail to distant lands which I could only describe to them in terms of the number of days and moons it took to reach them because they had not the faintest notion of geography.

It was Abdullah's letter which put an end to further hesitation. I would rely on the men from Chad.

That evening a telegram went back to Addis Ababa, to the Italian who owned the two big metal boats on Lake Tana. We had agreed that as soon as he received a telegram from me he was to send Ali with his people to the swamps along the western shores of Lake Tana to cut 150 cubic metres (or about 5,000 cubic feet) of papyrus reeds, to be dried and collected in bundles at the northern tip of the lake. Commendatore Mario Buschi was a middle-aged businessman, broad, red-cheeked and bursting with initiative. He had personally organized the transport of his two very heavy metal boats from the Red Sea up to Lake Tana, and it was he who had arranged for the 180-ton Axum monolith to be moved from the Ethiopian mountains to Rome in 1937. He was now hoping to be asked to move it back again, since the Emperor of Ethiopia was pressing the Italian Government for the return of the monument.

My first thought had been to float the papyrus down the Nile, but this would have been too tricky, with all the waterfalls and the restrictions of the Sudanese Republic in between. Buschi accepted as a sporting challenge the task of transporting 500 papyrus bundles 450 miles across the Ethiopian mountains from Lake Tana down to the Red Sea, because even if the stack of unpressed reeds bulked as big as a small house, they would weigh only about twelve tons.

There was not a day to be lost. It was nearly Christmas and if we were to cross the Atlantic before the hurricane season began on the other side, we must set sail from Africa in May. I was afraid of having the papyrus cut too soon, since old reed is not so strong, but unless it were cut now we could not be ready to start in May. Cutting two or three hundred thousand papyrus stems would take time, because it was high water in Lake Tana at present and if the reeds were to measure about ten feet long the stem must be cut far below the surface of the water. Afterwards the reeds must be properly sun-dried or they would rot in their bundles. Then would come the difficult journey over the mountains and finally up the Red Sea. There was war in the Suez area and all traffic was at a standstill. I would have to fight for special permission to unload cargo in this area. In fact, in Suez the inflammable reed must be landed and transported along blocked roads to rejoin the Nile near Cairo. Before the papyrus load reached the pyramids, a camp with all conveniences, including cook and provisions, must be ready in the desert for the necessary guards and labour force. The boat-building was to be headed by Buduma Negroes from Chad, who were still living their simple ancestral lives on floating islands in the most out-of-the-way desert corner of Central Africa. When all was set for the building to begin, it would be a lengthy process to lash the hundreds of thousands of thin papyrus stems into a compact sea-going vessel 50 feet long and 16 feet broad. Also, plans and preparations had to be made in advance for the transport of the finished boat to its launching place at some African port on the Atlantic coast. Sail and rigging, ancient Egyptian steering mechanism, wickerwork cabin, specially made water jars and ship's food in the old style – there were a thousand things to prepare.

So far I had only sent a telegram to Ethiopia. I sat down on the bed again, counting on my fingers: December to May. I felt my heart beating and began to pace the floor faster and faster. Paper and pencil: I must start all the wheels rolling right now. All at the same time. Most important of all, it would be necessary to find a crew who wanted to take part in the experiment.

Naturally I thought first of my companions of a hundred and one days on the balsa raft *Kon-Tiki*. We still met on every possible occasion to revive old memories. But Knut Haugland, already busy as head of the *Kon-Tiki* Museum in Oslo, had recently been appointed by the State to organize the immediate erection of a Norwegian Resistance Museum as well. Herman Watzinger, who had long been the FAO fisheries' expert in Peru, was just taking over responsibility for the Department's head office in Rome. Bengt Danielsson, the lone Swede among five Norwegians, who since the trip had been based on Tahiti as a free-lance ethnologist, had just accepted the post of Director of the Ethnographical Museum in Stockholm. Erik Hesselberg was still the same chronic Bohemian, travelling the world with his guitar and his palette. He would say 'yes' at once. But Torstein Raaby, who had once telegraphed 'COMING' in answer to the invitation to join the

61. *Lunch round the chicken coop.* When Norman and Thor took too long, Safi the monkey and Sinbad the duck came to book seats for the next sitting.
62. *The author's 'nasometer'*, notched with a knife, measured the angle of the Pole Star and thus showed *Ra*'s precise latitude.
63. *LI 2 B calling.* The author and Norman in the cabin: operating the little transceiver which kept in touch with radio hams, and keeping up-to-date with reports. Yuri sits outside the cabin door with the monkey.
64. *Change of watch* every two hours through the night. Georges struggles to wake up when Santiago and Yuri go off duty.

Kon-Tiki raft, had ended his adventurous life in the icy wastes north-west of Greenland as radio operator on an expedition which had set out across the North Pole on skis.

On the *Kon-Tiki* we had been five Norwegians and one Swede – six Scandinavians. But this time I felt tempted to assemble on the little reed boat as many nations as space would allow. If we crowded together we might manage seven men. Seven men from seven nations. Since I myself came from the northernmost country in Europe, the southernmost part of Europe should provide a contrast, so Italy would be the obvious answer. Since we Europeans were 'white' we ought to have a 'coloured' man with us, and the blackest Negroes I had ever seen were in Chad, so it would be logical to take one of the papyrus experts with us. Since the experiment was meant to demonstrate the possibility of contact between the ancient civilizations of Africa and America, it would be symbolic to take an Egyptian and a Mexican on the voyage. And, in order to have contrasting ideologies represented in this international group, it was an appealing idea to take one representative from the USA and one from Russia. All the other nations, excluded solely for want of space, could be symbolized by the flag of the United Nations, if we could get permission to fly it.

The times called for every sort of effort in the cause of bridge-building between the nations. Military jets thundered over Sphinx and pyramids, and cannons boomed along the closed Suez Canal. Soldiers from the five continents of the world were at war in one foreign land or another. Where there was no war, men sat poised behind atomic buttons, warheads primed, for fear of other nations. On a floating reed boat there was only room for people who could shake each other by the hand. The voyage itself was intended as an experiment, a study trip into the dawn of civilization. But there was room for an experiment within the experiment. A study trip into the crowded, over-populated

65. *Basket cabin interior.* Norman calculating the day's position which is logged by the author.
66. *The weeks pass* and hair and beards grow. Georges trims Santiago.
67. *The steering-oar* breaks again and the blade is salvaged by Yuri, Thor and Abdullah.
68. *The logs snapped* and the steering-oars were in constant need of repair, while the papyrus rolls bent like rubber.

world of tomorrow. With television, jets and astronauts, we are so busy shrinking the dimensions of our own globe that there is no elbow room left between the nations. The earth of our forefathers no longer exists. The once limitless world can be circled in an hour and forty minutes. The nations are no longer divided by impassable mountain ranges and infinite ocean gulfs. The races are no longer independent, isolated; they are connected and becoming crowded. While hundreds of thousands of technicians are working on atomic fission and laser rays, our little globe is whirling at supersonic speed into a future where we are all fellow-passengers in the same great technical experiment and where we must all work together if we are not to sink with our common burden.

A papyrus boat sailing along in the grip of the elements could be a micro-world, a practical attempt to prove that men can work together in peace regardless of country, religion, colour or political background, if they can only see as a matter of self-interest that it is necessary to fight for a common cause.

I took up my pen and wrote to Abdullah. I confirmed that I needed Omar and Mussa and that he himself must come as interpreter. Was it necessary for me to come and fetch them, or could Abdullah make his way alone to Bol and bring the others as far as Fort Lamy, where I would have air tickets to Cairo waiting for them? I would meet them when the plane landed at Cairo.

To my amazement a succinct reply arrived promptly from Abdullah via the scribe in Fort Lamy. Abdullah needed a certificate of employment to enable the three to leave the country; he needed three air tickets to Egypt; and he needed 150,000 Chad francs. If he had these he could arrange everything and I would be saved the journey to Chad.

It was a sizeable sum, even though the National Bank of Italy itself did not know the exact rate of exchange for Chad francs; and there would be endless problems before the funds were safely in Abdullah's hands. Safely? I had put my trust in an alert and reliable appearance, without knowing the first thing about Abdullah Djibrine, except that he was a man in a white tunic who had appeared in Bol from nowhere and disappeared again after acting as a voluntary interpreter. By his own account he was a carpenter. But if Abdullah was not deceiving me he would save me both time and money. If I did not have to pick up the Buduma Negroes in Bol, I would have time for an important last

114

visit to the Indians in Peru, since I had to go to Mexico and the USA in any case to find companions for the experiment itself.

Two important collaborators had now been set in motion. Buschi was to produce the reeds; Abdullah, the builders. Reeds and boat-builders should reach Egypt at the same time and by then the desert camp must be ready near Cairo. This was entrusted to the safe hands of a reliable friend, the Italian high school teacher, Angelo Corio, to whom the Department of Education in Rome had granted six months' leave for language studies with our international team in Egypt. Corio arrived at the pyramids tourist-fashion, with suitcase and camera, and foundered under a ring of struggling dragomans who wanted to show him the Sphinx and teach him to ride a camel. To survive in this peculiar oriental environment he obviously needed a local contact man who knew the laws and customs of the land and could find the right doors to knock on. Ex-Colonel Attia Ossama was just such a man. Because of the war, his real activities, which were connected with the Sinai Peninsula occupied by Israel, were shrouded in mystery. But being courteous and blessed with a winning manner he had an entrée everywhere and he undertook to act as middleman with the authorities and obtain permission to unload the papyrus in the Suez war zone.

The wheels were really turning now. Soon they were spinning in one country after another. Telegrams and telephone arrangements in foreign tongues, express letters with exotic stamps, and the whole project to be kept secret if the work were to be completed undisturbed before the deadline set by the hurricane season. Participants from seven countries. I had found an Italian, had a possible Egyptian candidate and intended to choose the man from Chad from among the three boat-builders, once they arrived. I was expecting a reply from Russia. I had to go to America. December had passed, January followed – three months were left. In New York I met my American contact man, Frank Taplin. In Cairo, Corio was waiting for the papyrus load which was now drying in the sun on the shores of Lake Tana, while Abdullah was out of reach, on his way to pick up the other two in Bol. Frank Taplin was a hyper-energetic American businessman, campaigner for peace and active cog in the World Association of World Federalists, an organization working for increased co-operation between countries, and expanded powers for the UN. The well-known New York editor Norman Cousins was president of the organization and a close personal friend of Secretary-General U Thant, who received all three of us on the top floor of the United Nations' imposing glass building.

Seven nationalities, black and white, from East and West, on a papyrus bundle, drifting across the Atlantic? We would be allowed to fly the United Nations' flag as long as we kept to the rules: all flags on board must be of the same size and hang at the same height. We could have seven national flags in a row, with a UN flag at each end. U Thant's good wishes came from the heart. Where would we start?

'I had thought of Morocco.'

'Then you must go and see my friend Ahmed Benhima, Moroccan Ambassador to the UN, who lives fifteen floors down, on the twenty-third floor.'

His Excellency on the twenty-third floor was a tall, distinguished man, the last scion of one of Morocco's oldest and most active families. He received us with routine amiability and we sank into deep arm-chairs. He listened with complete composure.

'So you are going to set sail from my homeland on a papyrus boat,' was all he said as he offered us cigarettes.

'Thank you, I don't smoke.'

'What port will you leave from?'

'Safi.'

'Safi! That's my own home town! Why Safi, in particular?'

Now his interest was suddenly aroused and he rose with an expression of great surprise and curiosity.

'Why Safi?' he repeated.

'Because Safi is one of the oldest African ports beyond Gibraltar. Casablanca is a modern port, but Safi has been known from ancient times. Safi lies just where a coastal sailor coming from the Mediterranean would be most likely to be swept out to sea by the elements. Just beyond Safi, the Canary current and the trade-wind seize anything that floats and send it to America.'

'My parents live in Safi. The Pasha of Safi is a good friend of mine. I will write to him and I will write to my brother, who is Foreign Minister in Morocco.'

This was an unbelievable bit of luck. We parted on the best of terms.

In New York I had a possible candidate for the trip and everything seemed to be going well until his better half was initiated into the secret plans. Then we all three hastily agreed that someone else must be found. There was barely time to have lunch with a possible new candidate before the plane took off for Lima in Peru.

A few days later I was sitting with a group of Uru Indians, frying fish on a floating island in Lake Titicaca. The whole island consisted of a network of floating reeds, reeds piled on top of one another in thick stacks. As the bottom layers rotted and sank deeper, fresh *totora* reeds were cut and stacked on top. All this part of the lake consisted of artificial reed islands lying side by side with narrow channels between them and living reed growing round them in all directions as far as the eye could see. Looking across this flat marshland where the Uru Indians passed their whole existence between fish and reed, one could see nothing but distant white peaks against the blue sky. House and bed were of reed. The boats were of reed, with a square-sail of reed stems woven together. Reed was the only fuel for their cooking fires. Rotten reeds mixed with earth from the mainland were laid out in small beds on the floating islands and there the Indians grew their traditional sweet potatoes. There was no fixed point in their existence; the ground rocked under the Uru Indians' feet whether they were walking on the floor inside the hut or round the little potato field outside. I had come to have a supposition confirmed. The Uru Indians, like the Quechua and Aymara Indians on the shores of the same lake, and like the Buduma Negroes in Chad, did not drag up their boats to dry every day after use. Yet the boats did not sink in a fortnight. The reeds certainly did submerge gradually. One could see that by observing these floating reed islands, on which the Indians had to keep on building up the surface. But the elegant boats lay beside the islands and floated without fresh additions, just as on Lake Chad in Central Africa. The explanation for this was obvious. The reed boats here in South America, like those in Chad, were lashed together with strong hand-made rope, knotted so tightly that as many as possible of the cellular channels inside were closed. The small boats in Ethiopia, on the other hand, were simply held loosely together with strips of bark or papyrus fibre and the porous reed was not sufficiently compressed to prevent the absorption of water.

There were still twelve days left before Abdullah and the boat-builders were due to arrive in Cairo. He had been sent air tickets for February 20th, calculated to coincide approximately with the arrival of the papyrus in Suez. Quite a lot could be done in the twelve days I had left. And with my friend Thorleif Schjelderup, a noted Norwegian

philosopher, author and film photographer, I left the bobbing islands
of the Uru Indians to visit the desert area on the north coast of Peru.
Here we were to see South America's most beautiful pyramid, an
enormous symmetrical construction of adobe bricks. The colossus lay
hidden and forgotten behind weathered sandstone mountains on the
desert plain in the Chicama Valley, unexplored by science but thoroughly plundered by grave-robbers, who had opened a crater right to the
bottom and transformed the stepped pyramid into a sort of square
volcano. This gigantic edifice towers so high above the desert that the
people of the valley simply call the ancient monument Cerro Colorado,
'Coloured Mountain'. But for the symmetrical stepped sides, and the
walled enclosure in front of the pyramid, one would, in fact, have to
look closely to see that this was not a mountain but a man-made
composition of millions of sun-baked bricks. For someone who had
been in Egypt the week before, there was an almost baffling similarity
in architectural form, astronomical orientation, dimensions and building materials to the oldest of the pyramids on the Nile. Cerro Colorado
had been erected by an unknown priest-king of antiquity when
mighty civilizations began to flourish in Peru, long before the Inca
culture succeeded the Chimu culture, itself a successor to those first
unknown preceptors whom science, for want of a name, has called the
'Mochica' people. It was they who built these very first and very
largest of pyramids on the coast. Who were the Mochica people?
Science has become more and more conscious that some form of contact
existed between the culture-bringers on the north coast of Peru and the
pyramid-builders in old Mexico. Beyond this little or nothing is known
of their origins. Among their realistic self-portraits in ceramic are
bearded men and individuals with strongly Mediterranean features;
some could have been portraits of typical Berber types in Morocco
today.

There was even time for a flying visit to Mexico, where my companion on the visit to the Seris Indians, Olympic swimmer, Ramon
Bravo, could think of nothing he would rather do than embark on a
reed boat. He had been having some stomach trouble, but was sure he
would be on top form before it was time to set out from Morocco
in two and a half months.

A small plane, a short drive, a few steps on foot, and we were
standing in the Mexican jungle, observing a pyramid in the rain. A
pyramid in the rain. Rain was just what we had been hoping for, and

down it came. Thorleif was soaked to the skin, standing in his shirt, wind-jacket tucked round camera and film, while the tropical rain poured down, dripping and streaming from block to block down the mighty Palenque pyramid. The clouds hung low over the treetops in the dense jungle which rolled over the ridge behind us, its gigantic trees thrusting forward on all sides to the very foot of the pyramid.

Tumbled and derelict in clearings round the pyramid lay moss-grown ruins of stately buildings, with something for every taste. Having come to the site for no other reason than to sense in one's own blood-stream a little of what had passed in America before Columbus, one had to overcome the first sentimental wave of enthusiasm and admiration, and then sit down and try to understand what lay behind this impressive complex of ruins. There was a curious aura of mystery here, something unwritten and unsaid which compelled attention, conjecture. This was not the time to be content with preconceived ideas. This was not the time to get absorbed by one fascinating detail, or fall into ecstasies over dimensions, beauty or ingenious technique. This was simply the time to absorb the fact that the enormous complex ruin, with its pyramids, temples and palaces, was the relic of human beings like ourselves, neither superior nor inferior. They had arrived here as pioneers a thousand years before Columbus and cleared a space for themselves in the jungle for house and home, farms and religious buildings. The spectacular pyramids and temples had been designed and calculated by skilled architects – remarkably skilled, if one thinks of most Indians who were living and still live in the same jungle, building huts of branches and leaves with no thought of making a single rectangular block out of what nature has given them in the form of boulders or solid rock. I had once tried to square off a round stone. I had not succeeded, although I had steel to carve with and the Indians had only stone tools. Only an expert would be able to cut smoothly polished blocks from the hard rock – not I, not one of my friends, be he town or country-dweller, and no Indian that I had ever met. It can be done, but not by just anyone. What was the truth about the jungle ruins of Palenque?

A mad idea occurred to me that archaeologists, in reconstructing the unknown, might benefit from consultants in the criminal police, someone who did not need to know archaeological terminology or excavation techniques, but who had the detective's all-round suspiciousness, practical insight and flair, and some experience in the calculation of probabilities. Here was a large pyramid in the deep forest. Had ordinary Indians decided to put it there? Or had people other than primitive hunters from Siberia mixed with the aboriginal population in Mexico's primeval forests?

It was natural, said those who believed that no civilized peoples before Columbus's day were able to travel, only barefooted savages: it was natural that human beings under similar environmental conditions should create things which looked alike. It was natural that people in both Egypt and Mexico should have laid stones on stones until they became a pyramid.

It began raining immoderately now, and we tried to find shelter under some outsize leaves.

Similar environmental conditions! Was there a greater contrast than Egyptian desert and Mexican jungle? Moist plant life made the hot air we were breathing as humid as a greenhouse. Nothing but dripping foliage, lianas, trunks, rich humus. Not a stone to be seen, except for the big chiselled blocks, once brought by man and now lying heaped in overgrown ruins. Was it natural to lay stone on stone in the Mexican jungle? Then why not in the African jungle, in the prairies, or in the meadows and pine forests of Europe?

Where had the architects of the Palenque pyramid found their materials? Perhaps they had dug deep into the mould beneath the roots of the jungle giants; perhaps they had gone to some handy ridge and hacked away at a solid mountain wall. Here in Palenque, in any case, the idea had come first and the right building materials had been found subsequently, after an expert search.

And in Peru? Was it natural to lay stone on stone until pyramids arose in Peru? Along the thousand miles of desert coast where Peru's pyramids lie scattered in the sands there is no usable stone; one must go far up into the Andes to find stone quarries. In the Mochica Valley, where we had just been, stone was of such poor quality that the

69. *At the masthead.* Norman was the expedition's only sailor.

70. '*No more beards,* after a year on the South Polar ice-cap,' said Yuri, rigging a shaving mirror on the broken steering-oar.

71 and 72. *Atlantic pollution. Ra* lay so low in the water that the expedition could see asphalt-like patches of oil in countless numbers all over the ocean. The photo was taken by Georges, swimming on a lifeline.

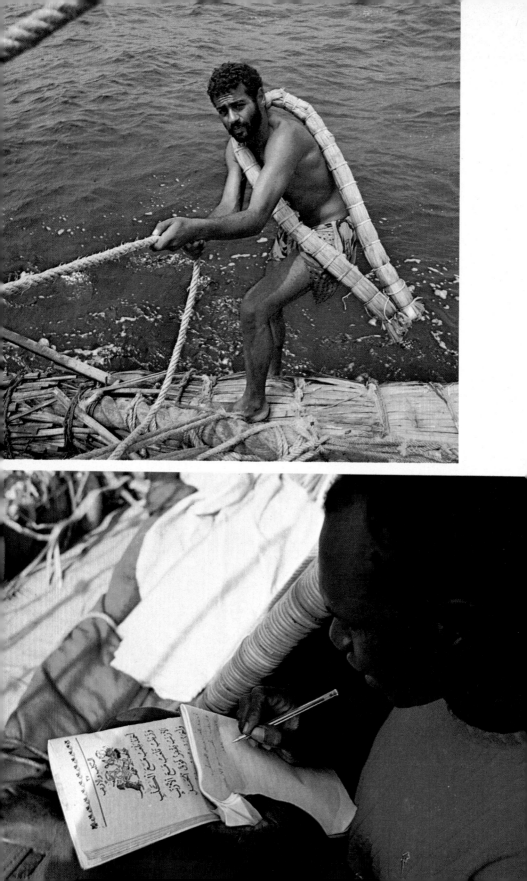

pyramid-builders had been obliged to manufacture some six million large, brick-shaped adobe blocks before they had sufficient materials to build their pyramid, which covered an area of some 4,000 square yards and was 100 feet high. There were other adobe pyramids in Peru which were even larger than Cerro Colorado.

It was thought-provoking to sit, cold and wet, under the big leaves and look at the streaming pyramid, with memories of Peru and Egypt fresh in one's mind. In Egypt it was natural to build with stone, to take tools to the rock itself, because naked cliffs rising from the desert sand were the only natural building material. But where in Mexico was stone natural? It was known that the Aztecs on Mexico's open plateaux and the Mayas in the dense jungles of Yucatan had learned pyramid-building from their predecessors. Archaeology had disclosed that the earliest civilization in Mexico, the one which had given the impulse to all the rest, had begun on the tropical coast of the Mexican Gulf, where the ocean current forges landward after its passage of the Atlantic. Was it more natural to build pyramids there? On the contrary. There the unknown originators of Mexico's earliest culture had made their way beyond the far horizon to find an accessible stone quarry. In some cases gigantic blocks of twenty and thirty tons had been transported from quarries as far as fifty miles from the building site. Today no one knows the identity of those dynamic masons and architects, who built in the jungle, but knew more about stone than wood. For convenience they have been given a name, Olmecs. If the many realistic sculptures on their abandoned stone monuments are self-portraits, then some of the Olmecs had round faces with flat, broad noses and thick lips, and looked completely negroid, while others had sharp features, hooked noses, moustaches and flowing beards and looked remarkably semitic. The Olmecs were the clue to the whole riddle. What was their real name, who were they, why did the Olmecs quarry stone and build pyramids? The Olmecs also manufactured

73. *Papyrus as a lifebelt.* Egyptian Georges reviving the art of his ancestors (see plate 12).
74. *Leisure pursuits.* Georges teaching Abdullah to write, in Arabic.

artificial building bricks in the jungle. Why? One of their 100 feet high pyramids was built of sun-baked adobe bricks like the biggest in Peru, like those of ancient Mesopotamia and like some of the pyramids in the Nile valley. Adobe is not a natural building material in the jungle.

The dripping edifice we were looking at confused the whole issue. A few years ago, in 1952, a discovery in this jungle pyramid had shaken the scientific world and immediately upset rigidly-held dogma. Quite unexpectedly, a secret entrance had been found to a narrow passage with a stone stairway winding down through the centre of the pyramid. It led to a heavy stone door which opened into a magnificent tomb with a colossal stone coffin where the body of a mighty priest-king lay buried, just as in ancient Egypt. There should not be burial chambers in Mexican pyramids. This was one of the two most cogent reasons for rejecting the idea of trans-oceanic contact. The similarity between the pyramids was superficial, they said. The pyramids on the two sides of the Atlantic not only had different functions but were also built in a different shape. In Mexico and Peru the pyramids had stepped sides; in Egypt the sides sloped smoothly.

However, this simple distinction had never been strictly accurate. Anyone who had travelled in the Nile Valley knew that there were stepped pyramids in Egypt too and that they were the oldest, the original form, not only in Egypt but also in Mesopotamia. Egypt's civilized neighbours in the Old World, the Babylonians, built their pyramids in step form and placed a temple on top, just as in ancient Mexico. And now, in addition, here was a priest-king, laid out in a coffin at the heart of a Mexican pyramid. His family also claimed descent from the sun and placed a sun-god of jade in the tomb, while his architect arranged the ground plan of the pyramid with astronomical accuracy according to the passage of the sun, as in Egypt. He had also been placed in a huge stone sarcophagus. He had also been given a splendid mummy mask over his face, as was customary in Peru and in Egypt. The mask was not of gold but of jade mosaic, with eyes of shell and pupils of obsidian. He had also believed in a life after death and was therefore equipped with jars and dishes for food and drink and adorned with crown, ear-plugs, neck-chain, bracelets and rings of mother-of-pearl and jade. The coffin was painted inside with red cinnabar, and remnants of red cloth still adhered to bones and jewels. In the Egyptian manner the sarcophagus was closed with a lid made from a single carved slab which weighed several tons, was as wide as the height of a man and more than twice as long. The lid and the walls of the tomb were decorated with reliefs of priests or priest-kings, all in profile, some wearing false beards as a badge of rank, just as in ancient Egypt. When everything was ready, half-a-score of young men were killed and laid outside the door of the tomb to serve as slaves in the next world. Then the door to the sun-king's burial chamber was sealed with a gigantic stone slab and a secret staircase was built up through the interior of the pyramid, which was finally filled in with stone and rubble and sealed. Inside and outside, the sun-king in Palenque had followed the ancient Egyptian formula for pyramid burial. The only innovation was the erection in the Mesopotamian manner of a little stone temple with local hieroglyphs on top of the pyramid, in the true Mexican style.

We had just been down and looked at the grave. It was built before the rest of the pyramid as part of the master architect's original plan, with gigantic smooth slabs in walls and roof, cut and fitted together, accurate to a hair's breadth, and the rest of the pyramid was constructed above it when the tomb was complete. White stalactites hung like rows of calcified icicles from cornices on the walls and gave the carved priests in their luxurious ceremonial garb an air of deep-frozen antiquity. The air was fresh and cool. Just as in Egypt, the architect of this pyramid had provided the necessary air-conditioning. A narrow air duct curved from the coffin all the way up the side of the stairway and two large ventilation channels ran right through the walls of the huge pyramid into the fresh air on either side, as in the Egyptian pyramids.

As we were climbing the long stone staircase between narrow walls I had another look at the construction. The staircase had a hexagonal cross-section, so that the flat ceiling was narrower than the width of the stair. Only in one place in the world had I groped my way up steps with precisely the same extraordinary design: in the pyramids in Egypt.

Was all this so completely natural? It was indeed hard to explain as the result of someone's merely stacking stones in a heap. We emerged between the big carved stone blocks and found ourselves engulfed once more in green jungle which would have overwhelmed the whole complex of ruins had the Mexican Institute of Archaeology not fought continuously to keep these national treasures out of the clutches of the rain forest, that strives continually to reconquer the fertile terrain once wrung from it by the energetic architects who settled among the trees.

Beside this royal burial pyramid was yet another, built above a natural cave, with stone stairs and a long shaft leading up through the interior of the structure, and containing a confusion of human bones. If this pyramid, like its neighbour, had been built for a single priest-king, it was certainly plundered before historic times, the bones of less prominent individuals being tossed down into the empty vault.

Here was food for more thought under the trees in the pouring rain. Either it was not true that people building pyramids as temples were different from those who built pyramids as tombs, or else two distinct peoples had begun to build pyramids side by side in the Mexican forests. So the problem would become more involved than ever.

Back in Mexico City we called upon Dr Ignacio Bernal, head of the national institute in charge of all Mexican pyramids and ruins as well as the National Museum of Archaeology, one of the largest and most modern in the world. Mexican archaeologists had gained a reputation for being in the forefront of the isolationists; the older generation in particular maintained rigidly that all the ideas underlying the Mexican ruins had been evolved inside the borders of the country by barbarians moving down from the north. Now we were about to challenge this opinion by sailing westward in an African reed boat. How would the Mexican specialists take that? I decided to ask their foremost representative, Dr Ignacio Bernal, who obligingly told the museum custodians to let us in with cameras and tape-recorders. He looked back over his shoulder a little sceptically as we took up our positions together in front of a large, stone stele bearing a realistic relief of an Olmec with a long beard, symbol of the enigma behind Mexico's earliest exponents of culture. Bearded Olmecs introduced pyramid-building to beardless Indians.

'Dr Bernal,' I said, 'do you think that the ancient cultures of Mexico developed without outside influence, or do you think that some ideas may have been brought across the sea in primitive vessels?'

'That's the most difficult question you could put to me,' replied the man we all regarded as the foremost authority in Mexico.

'Why is that?'

Surprised, I pushed the microphone closer to Dr Bernal.

'Because there are strong arguments which suggest that there may have been infiltration across the sea before Columbus, but equally strong ones to the opposite effect.'

'So what would be your answer?'

'To tell the truth, I don't know!'

'Then perhaps we can agree that the problem is still unsolved?'

He hesitated barely a second.

'Yes,' he said vehemently.

We recorded the same interview twice, to ensure against technical failure.

Just at that time the expedition's secret plans had leaked out in the daily press via Cairo. The news had reached Mexico too.

'You want to try out a reed boat at sea, do you?' asked Dr Santiago Genoves, smiling. He had come to see his colleague, Dr Bernal, just as we were about to leave the museum.

'Right,' I said. 'Would you like to come too?'

'Yes, and I mean that.'

I looked at Dr Bernal's Mexican colleague in astonishment. Dr Genoves was a well-known expert on the aboriginal population of America. I had met him at international anthropologists' congresses in Latin America, Russia and Spain. Small, but incredibly resilient and robust, he gazed calmly back at me.

'Sorry, but the place has already been taken by another Mexican. It will have to be next time,' I joked.

'Put me on the waiting list, then. If necessary I can come at a week's notice!'

'Agreed!'

Little did I suspect that these words were to prove prophetic, when the little scientist smilingly took my hand in a firm clasp and said good-bye.

New York next morning. A hotel room crowded with journalists. The expedition was no longer a secret here, either. The papyrus had reached Cairo. The building was about to begin. The three men from Chad would be sitting in the plane at that moment; Corio was waiting with camp and labour force ready; and tomorrow we would all assemble and begin. My own plane would leave that night, so I had the day free for the last hectic preparations in New York. Then a telegram arrived. I had to sit down as I read it:

ABDULLAH ARRESTED. BOAT BUILDERS STILL IN BOL. TELEPHONE IMMEDIATELY.

The telegram was signed by my wife.

A hasty call to our home in Italy confirmed that this was no joke. The post had brought an envelope from Chad with a little note from Abdullah. It said simply that he could not go and collect Omar and Mussa because he had been arrested. He would write again in a month. Greetings, Abdullah.

Abdullah was in prison. What had he done? Where was he? No one knew any more than Abdullah's note told us. Mussa and Omar were still living on their floating islands south of the Sahara, east of the sun and west of the moon. Without them, no boat. In eleven weeks we must put to sea from Morocco if we were to avoid the hurricane season. Behind the pyramids in Egypt a whole staff was waiting in a camp for the visitors from Chad, with beds made and table laid. Someone would have to go to Chad and bring the papyrus people to the building site. It would have to be me. There was a plane to Chad from France every Wednesday morning. So I would have to be in Paris on Tuesday, with a visa for the Chad Republic. Today was Friday, George Washington's birthday, and everything in the USA was closed. Tomorrow, Saturday, no public offices would be open. Then Sunday. I had one day, Monday, to arrange the visa and new travelling plans, as well as the financing of another trip to Central Africa which had not been included in the project.

I spent three days wandering among the New York skyscrapers, without taking one practical step. Everything was closed. On Monday morning the New Yorkers poured back to their offices. Telephones were answered. People from every nation in the world met in the UN building. But no one from the Republic of Chad. The Chad representative was in Washington for the day, a friendly voice explained, and I would have to go there to get my visa for Chad. My publisher was in Chicago. My wallet was flat. Tickets to Paris that evening were in order, but the long excursion to Chad called for both visa and money. The telephone at the Chad Embassy in Washington was silent. The Norwegian Embassy, on the other hand, promised to seek out the Ambassador for Chad if I would wait patiently at my hotel. From Chicago, however, came a request to rush immediately to a bank at the other end of New York. Abdullah's obscure fate in Chad complicated the situation further, as U Thant's office replied that the Secretary-General was prepared to write a helpful letter of introduction if I could come there at once. Before I was out of the door a man came rushing in – Mr Pipal, chief of a leading press agency, offering an advance against contract for news of the voyage. The telephone interrupted us. The visa was promised that day if I could get on the next shuttle plane to Washington. A press agency director helped to fling winter clothes into one suitcase and summer clothes into another, attended to the bill and would bring the baggage to the Paris plane that evening. Thorleif in the next room dropped his rolls of film and made for U Thant's office. Traffic jams in New York, in Washington, in the air, but brilliant co-operation between Norway and Chad in the capital. Two men welcomed me back at Kennedy Airport that evening as I came rushing out of one plane and into another with the Chad visa in my passport. One had an envelope from U Thant, the other, two packed suitcases.

'Thank you. Good-bye. Good-night America. Good-morning Paris.' A glimpse of my wife at a stopover in Nice on the way south in the next plane. Dictation pad, telegram forms: hold everything till we arrive with the boat-builders from Bol.

The Sahara was under our wings. The heat surged in when the door opened. We were in Chad. The low buildings of Fort Lamy seemed to stretch out endlessly now that I was searching for Abdullah. Abdullah's only address was a post office box. The key to the box belonged to a missionary. He had no idea where Abdullah was, because he had finished his stint as a carpenter. But kindly Pastor Eyer clambered into his car to drive round the Arab quarter and search.

The receptionist at my little hotel in the centre told me that the next outgoing plane left for the Sudan in a week, but my tickets for Egypt were invalid because no one in Chad could provide an Egyptian visa. Israel had an Embassy here, but not Egypt. Not Norway, Italy or England, either.

The room contained a bed, two pegs on the wall and a fan which sounded like a prop-plane starting up. I sat on the edge of the bed for a long time, trying to solve the tangle with a pocket atlas. Someone knocked. There stood a tall black man in an ankle-length white tunic with a minute rainbow-coloured cap on his head. He flung out his arms and laughed aloud, teeth and eyes flashing in competition in his happy face.

'Oh boss, oh boss, Abdullah has had a hard time, but now everything is all right!'

Abdullah! He was literally dancing with joy at the reunion.

127

'Abdullah, what happened?'

'Abdullah went to Bol; four days I paddled about on the lake in *kaday* looking for Omar and Mussa, who were fishing a long way out. I found them. I paid their debts. I was going to take them to Fort Lamy. Then the sheriff came. He said I was a bad man, who would do anything for money. He said today I sold two men to Egypt. Tomorrow perhaps to France or Russia. I was arrested. I was sent under guard to prison in Fort Lamy. I was alone. I used the rest of the money to get out.'

What a story! Abdullah arrested in Bol on suspicion of slave-trading. The old slave route passed by Chad, and the memories obviously lived on. Now Abdullah could not return to Bol. In fact, Mussa and Omar could not leave Bol unless I collected them there myself with a formal labour contract stamped by the authorities in Fort Lamy.

For five days Abdullah and I toured all the imposing government buildings in the capital and tried to get a legal labour contract drawn up for the two men I was to fetch from Bol. Intelligent, alert faces everywhere. Friendliness ready to burst out from behind the official mask. Ultra-modern offices. Particularly elegant was the towering colossus of the Foreign Ministry ornamented by fourteen empty pools in a row in front of the steps. But when Sunday came I sat down hopelessly on the edge of my bed and turned off the deafening fan. Let flies and heat have their way. I was fed up. Five days and not one stamp, not one signature on one single document. We had succeeded in tracking down a missionary with a single-engined plane who could land on the lake with pontoons, but if I tried to carry off the two Buduma without stamped papers I would suffer the same fate as Abdullah.

We had begun by going to the Director-General for Home Affairs, who knew about Abdullah's problems, but he could only see a

75. *African Neptune* crossed our bows in mid-Atlantic while Sinbad the duck acted as *Ra*'s figurehead.
76. *A sack* fastened to a lifebelt was thrown overboard from the American ship and Georges swam after it while Santiago and Yuri held him on the lifeline.
77 and 78. *The catch* was some weekly magazines and a pile of fresh fruit.

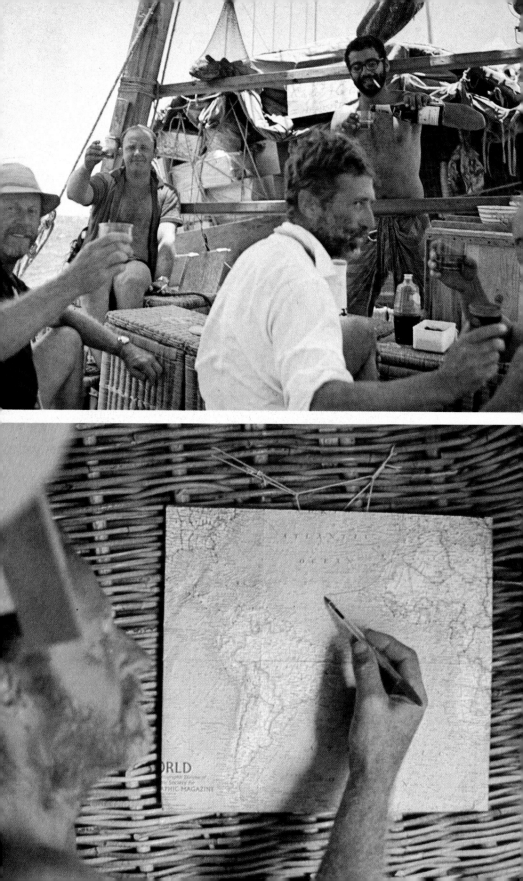

foreigner via the Foreign Minister, who could only be seen through the Chef de Cabinet who could only be reached through the Head of Protocol. Three days had passed before we got to the Foreign Minister, because everyone had to hear all the details and study U Thant's letter. The Foreign Minister, sitting behind padded doors, was a veritable giant, friendly and informal, with a wisp of black beard on his chin, bushy hair and parallel scars over forehead and cheeks. Before passing us on to the Home Office he took the matter up personally in two meetings with the President of the Republic, Tombalbaye. President Tombalbaye thought the whole case was so unusual that his Council of Ministers would first have to decide whether a citizen of Chad could be allowed to travel the high seas in a papyrus *kaday*.

To gain time I assured him that the only urgent problem was to get permission to take three Chad citizens to the calm shores of the Nile in order to build a *kaday* on land. We were then sent on to the Ministry for Home Affairs, which sent us to the Ministry of Labour, which sent us to the printers as they were short of forms. Twelve double-page contract forms were completed for the three men, then we had to go to the head of the Ministry of Works for stamps and signature. As fate would have it, he discovered two paragraphs in the printed contract forms which effectively stopped all further progress.

The contracts could not be stamped until they were signed by the two men waiting in Bol. Still worse, it was stated in print on the form itself that it was invalid without a medical certificate. How were we to get one? There was no doctor in Bol and the sheriff refused to let them leave there without a stamped labour contract. The head of the Ministry of Works summoned a representative of the Ministry of Labour, who stared gloomily at our fine contracts. The position was clear. Both were kindness personified, but they pointed at the words:

79 and 80. *Ra in mid-Atlantic* photographed from *African Neptune* en route from New York to Cape Town. The sail had faded but the hull was sound.

81. *Shipboard feast* at half-way point. From the left: the author, Yuri, Santiago, Georges and Norman. Special refreshments for the occasion.

82. *The author's chart* after a full month's voyage. We passed the fortieth meridian and were then in the American half of the Atlantic.

I could see for myself. Labour contract invalid without medical certificate, medical certificate impossible without departure, and departure illegal without labour contract. *Ergo*, impossible.

Dog-tired, I slammed the hotel door behind me and switched on the fan at full blast. Tomorrow was Sunday. I was seething with fury and sat on the edge of the bed, writing in my diary: 'Hopeless lunacy. But this parody of a system is not the fault of the people of Chad, who are basically friendly, intelligent and wonderfully uncomplicated men; it is a distorted image of *us*. African culture was not like this. It is *we* who have taught them this new way of life.'

One thought was buzzing round in my head: black shadows from white clouds. I turned off the fan and slept to the sound of distant military trumpets from President Tombalbaye's palace. Sunday. I went to see the flying missionary. He had petrol. Early on Monday morning he started the propeller on his plane and then he and I were skimming over the roofs of the government offices, over savannah, desert and floating islands. We landed outside Bol, sending up sheets of spray. We had twenty-four pages of printed contracts and an empty suitcase on the plane, so we would sink or swim on the fact that the documents bore no stamps or signatures but our own. The masses of printed words impressed both sheriff and sultan, who let Omar and Mussa step forward from the crowd.

That same evening two terrified Buduma Negroes were sitting behind us in the little plane when we took off again from the waves beyond their grass huts. The shore was black with friends and relations, the sultan and the sheriff at their head, gazing up at the two courageous adventurers, who sat gripping their seats and staring down like vultures at the little world they had grown up in. Their expressions gave nothing away, for was there not a row of burn marks on their arms to prove that they could voluntarily bear red-hot iron without complaint? The two long-distance travellers had come with what they stood up in, tattered tunics and home-made sandals. The case we had brought for them was as empty as before; they had nothing to put in it.

In Fort Lamy they embraced and rejoiced hugely at finding Abdullah a free man again. In the market-place Omar was fitted out in light blue from neck to sandals and Mussa entirely in yellow. In the fluttering new robes the blue and yellow figures strode ahead of us to the police station, wide-eyed with wonder at their new passport photographs.

'Names?' asked a helpful police sergeant.

'Omar M'Bulu.'

'Mussa Bulumi.'

'Age?' asked the minion of the law.

Silence.

'When was Omar born?'

'Four years before Mussa.'

'1927? 1928? 1929?'

'I think so,' said Omar diffidently.

'Born ca. 1929,' wrote the sergeant. 'And Mussa?'

'1929,' said Mussa quickly.

'Impossible,' declared the sergeant. 'You are four years older.'

'Right,' agreed Mussa. 'But we were both born in 1929.'

'Born ca. 1929,' the sergeant wrote for Mussa as well.

The passports had to be signed. Omar regretted that he could only sign in Arabic. He took the pen, sat down and made some elegant flourishes in the air over the paper, upon which the sergeant took the pen back and wrote his name for him. Mussa suggested that the sergeant should sign for him at the same time. But their passports could not be issued without labour contracts, so we went off to the Catholic Hospital for a medical certificate. There was a lively scene when a nun told Mussa to undress as far as the waist and he innocently pulled the long robe up to his navel. When Omar was to be X-rayed he was invisible on the screen until the baffled nun turned the light on again and found he had climbed up and was hanging over the top of the X-ray apparatus on his stomach. The Sudan required a smallpox certificate and the men were given the vaccine but no certificate, because the hospital had run out of forms. With Abdullah we rushed to the printers, who refused to print new forms until the hospital had paid off their old debt. At Sudan Airlines the clerk found three old smallpox forms in a drawer, but just as the hospital was about to fill them in, a French doctor appeared with Omar's X-ray photograph, which showed a large growth on the liver. Big Omar was seriously ill and strictly forbidden to travel. Mussa would not travel without his brother, who knew Arabic. The papyrus project was crumbling in ruins.

What could be done for Omar? We all trooped in to the French senior physician, a smiling colonel.

'*You*, here?'

The meeting was warm and we were both equally surprised. The last time I had met Colonel Lalouel he had been an army doctor in Tahiti. We worked out a solution together. If Omar were forced to return to Bol he would be without medical care. So I guaranteed that he would see a doctor in Cairo and took a prescription for injections and tablets, assuming responsibility for Omar's cure.

Then the Sudan flight left. At the last moment Mussa and Omar were pushed up the steps, finding it difficult to see because they had found yellow and blue glasses to match their clothes. Loud cries from Abdullah when he put his head inside and saw the aircraft fittings, while the other two were lost in admiration of the cabin which was larger than the sultan's house in Bol. Soon we were above the cloud ceiling and while Abdullah and Omar examined in detail the mechanism of the seat-belt and the adjustable seat, Mussa with stoical calm drew out a yellow handkerchief and sat polishing his naked skull and his sandals alternately. When the stewardess passed with the sweet tray, each took handfuls and sat holding his booty until he saw other people putting their sweet papers into the ash trays. They then pushed all the sweets in and spent the rest of the journey trying to coax them up again through the narrow opening. I was concerned for Omar's liver when I saw him start on his lunch tray with butter on his fruit salad. Then we crossed the desolate and arid frontiers of the Sudan and landed in the late afternoon at the capital, Khartoum.

Now there was no holding my companions. No one in Bol had seen a house with two floors, but here in Khartoum the houses lay on top of one another in layers, and even Abdullah went into transports when he saw a four-storey building. There would be trouble if my companions were let out of sight for one minute in this Arab city where we had to spend the night, and since my friends would not yet merge inconspicuously into their surroundings if they came with me to a big modern hotel, I decided to go with them to a fourth-class boarding house in the poorest Arab quarter. Reception and rooms were up on the third floor of an antiquated building, with kitchen and dining area out on the roof, and all three were overwhelmed at this fairy-tale house. The two brothers behaved very oddly on the stairs. Advancing with great circumspection they lifted their feet as deliberately and warily as if they were climbing a rugged mountainside. I realized that this was the first time they had been up a staircase. Both in Bol and on their floating islands all their huts were built on the ground, with only earthen floors. The hotel rooms faced inwards and were windowless, but had light bulbs hanging from the ceiling and several beds in a row. The two men from Bol had never seen a bed and when Abdullah explained that it was for sleeping, Mussa and Omar lay down on their stomachs and crawled underneath to try it. There they turned over and lay outstretched with their noses in the bedsprings, while Abdullah doubled up with silent laughter and beckoned them out again for the benefit of the astonished proprietress, who peeped beneath the mattress and wanted to know what they were looking for. On the roof we were given a little table with a fork and plate each, already laden with large pieces of meat, tomatoes, potatoes, leeks and beans. The function of the fork was quickly understood and appreciated. I was just about to stick mine into a tasty piece of meat on my plate when another fork forestalled me and quickly popped my morsel in Omar's mouth. I prepared to secure myself another, but – oops! – Abdullah's fork was there and I had to steer for a potato to avoid a collision. I surveyed the situation and saw the forks duelling to and fro across the table, each man eating from the plate where he had spotted something tempting at that moment. My table-fellows were used to eating with their fingers from a common dish in the middle and found the fork an excellent extension of their range at a meal where the food had not been placed in the middle, accessible to everyone.

I went to bed slightly hungry. The only water closet in the hotel resounded with amazed and admiring exclamations. Abdullah wanted Sudanese currency in case a lady should happen to visit his room. Next morning he woke me before dawn. He had heard that time was not the same all over the world and now he wanted to be certain that the pilot and I had agreed on a common time for the flight to Egypt to avoid his leaving the Sudan before us.

At the airfield there was a catastrophe. No one noticed that my companions from Chad lacked Egyptian visas, but the Health Department, checking all papers, discovered that their fresh vaccination against yellow fever would not be valid for another week. They had slipped into the Sudan through the Health Department's oversight; now at least they would not be allowed to slip out again until the vaccination was valid. My three companions were stopped and all bargaining was quite useless. In the meantime I had passed through to the airfield, where I discovered a wide gap in the fence. The watchful Abdullah saw my beckoning finger and withdrew from the queue with the two men who were not allowed to pass the barrier. The three

of them filed round the building in their white, blue and yellow robes
and the plane left with all four of us on board. The two men from
Bol sat down politely and fastened their seat-belts like experienced
globe-trotters, smiling at the pretty black stewardess and each taking
a single sweet from her tray.

Cairo. Reception committee at the foot of the aircraft steps, with
the smiling Norwegian Ambassador at its head. The Tourist Ministry's
representative waved us through without a word about visas or yellow
fever, and the Ambassador's chauffeur, in elegant uniform, bowed to
Mussa, Omar and Abdullah as they gathered their skirts about their
legs and manoeuvred themselves into the Ambassador's big car.
There were transports of joy and devout murmurs from each of the
men in the back seat at the sight of the first bridges, underpasses,
five-storey houses. A mosque, another one, the whole town was full
of mosques; it must be Paradise. But when the buildings in the centre
began to cover whole blocks and rose so high that the three of them
could not see the rooftops without rolling down the window, they
grew more and more silent. This could not be real. Mussa grew drowsy.
Omar sat stiffly and the whites of his eyes showed when he stole a
nervous glance to the side. Abdullah, on the other hand, sat with his
clean-shaven scalp thrust forward, drinking in with wide-open eyes
and mouth every last detail, from tram-lines and makes of car, to neon
signs and human types.

'What's that?' asked Abdullah.

We had left the modern city and were crossing the Giza plain.
I was prepared for the question, but wanted to watch Abdullah's
reaction. The others sat upright, dozing, but Abdullah had been
staring ahead for a long time, eyes and mouth growing larger and
larger in the dusk.

'That is a pyramid, Abdullah,' I explained.

'Is it a mountain or did men make it?'

'Men made it in the old days.'

'Those Egyptians! They are further advanced than us. How many
people live in there?'

'Just one man, and he is dead.'

Abdullah burst into admiring laughter.

'Those Egyptians, those Egyptians!'

Two more pyramids appeared. Now Abdullah too was quite silent.
The whites of his eyes gleamed. The three men from Chad were

guided by torchlight on a long walk from the car through sand-dunes to Corio's tent camp, which showed ghostly-white in the moonlight, down in the shallow depression behind the pyramids and the Sphinx. Little did the three men walking over the moonlit sand suspect that they were the first papyrus boat-builders to pass the Sphinx's paws for perhaps thousands of years and that the sand they were treading covered ancient tombs where the pharaohs' own boat-builders lay, lost and forgotten with their skill which was now return-ing to the foot of the pyramids again, by a long, a very long and roundabout route.

'Goodnight, Abdullah. You have a tent to yourself. Mussa and Omar will be in the next tent.'

Dazed with incredible impressions and new knowledge, all three stole a last glance at the pharaohs' broad, pointed, skyscraper mountains which towered over us like shadows thrown by our own tents against the unchanging multitude of stars. 'One man in each, and he is dead,' Abdullah muttered to Omar in Arabic. Omar did not bother to translate into Buduma, for his brother was already lying on his back and snoring, sated with experience, in his camp-bed.

The tips of the three pyramids glowed like hot lava on a row of volcanoes when the morning sun shot its first red arrows of light over the tent roofs from its cover behind the sand-dunes on the horizon. It was still dark and cold when the three men in their long garments crawled out and squatted to watch the red glow of the pyramid tops. They were waiting for the sun to reach down to ordinary human beings shivering on the cold sand, waiting for sunrise before prostrating themselves in prayer to Allah. When the sun rose the three black men knelt in a row and bowed their foreheads to the sand, their shaven skulls gleaming like polished shoes and pointing directly at the waking sun-god *Ra*, because Abdullah had worked out that Mecca must lie approximately in that direction. The sun rose and lit up the dunes. Then we all caught sight of something unusual, something from the living world amidst that dead sand and stone. The papyrus! There it lay waiting for us in huge stacks, some yellow-green and some golden as the sun itself. Abdullah took a long knife and we all gathered in tense expectation to hear the expert's verdict at this first critical encounter between boat-builders from Central Africa and raw materials from the source of the Nile. Abdullah sliced off a reed with a simple stroke and the other two squeezed the severed end and felt down the long stalk.

'*Kirta*,' murmured Mussa.

'*Ganagin*,' Omar translated to Abdullah in Chad Arabic and his teeth flashed delightedly.

'Papyrus, they say this is real papyrus,' explained Abdullah in French, and everyone felt relieved and happy. The papyrus was of the finest quality.

Together we chose a flat stretch of desert beside the tents and here we measured out a boat 50 feet long and 16 broad, outlining the contours with a stick in the sand.

'The *kaday* must be this big.'

'But where is the water?'

It was Mussa who asked, and Omar nodded.

'Water?' said the rest of us. 'Didn't you find a barrel of drinking water outside the cookhouse tent?'

'Where is the lake? We can't build a boat without leaving the papyrus to soak,' said Mussa, gazing suspiciously about him at the endless sand-dunes.

'But you told us that we must dry the papyrus in the sun for three weeks before it could be used,' I exclaimed.

'Yes, of course. Fresh papyrus breaks up; it has to be dried to strengthen it. Afterwards it has to be soaked before we bend it, otherwise it snaps like kindling,' said the three black men.

There we were. In the desert sand. The camels had water in their humps, we had some in a barrel with a tap. Far down in the valley ran the Nile. Far away. All the sewers emptied out there. Modern Nile water would certainly rot the papyrus twice as fast as the river water of the pharaohs' days. The two men from Bol had not warned us. In their world there was water everywhere, nothing but water and floating islands; their concept of our planet was a huge lake with a desert the length of one horizon.

'Where is the lake?'

Mussa looked distrustfully at us and Omar became uneasy. We had to find a solution on the spot.

'We will fetch it!'

There was no choice. It was too late to move the camp and the huge stack of papyrus. The Nile was filthy anyhow and we dared not soak the papyrus in the sea before it was really necessary, since the experts claimed that sea water dissolved the cell tissues in the reed. We had chosen this particular building site because of the environment, the pyramids as the symbol of ancient civilization and the tombs out here in the desert which gave us plenty of chance to check up on individual details in the old paintings, as work proceeded on our own craft. And in this desert climate we were certain of keeping the papyrus dry, as the boat-builders had said it must be, both in Chad and in Ethiopia.

'Abdullah, explain that we are going to fetch the water!'

In the jeep, Corio and I bounced over the sand ridge and down into the nearest Arab quarter. Here we bought bricks and cement, found a mason and a truck driver who undertook to drive twelve old petrol drums full of tap water out to us in the desert every other day. Our friends from Chad were taken shopping in Cairo; as far north as Egypt it was cold for them, with nothing under their robes. And Omar began his treatment. Next day the first bundles of papyrus reed were put to soak in a rectangular brick basin built in the sand in front of the tents. Now we could see in earnest how well papyrus floated. Three men had to jump and dance about to submerge a single bundle, and we had 500 bundles. If we thrust a single papyrus stem, thick end down, in a barrel of water it shot up into the air of itself like an arrow as soon as we let it go.

Two sharp-eyed scholars with laughter-lined faces and full, flowing beards, watched closely as we began on the papyrus boat. Both shook their heads, uncertain what to believe. One was Egypt's chief conservator, who made constant sorties from his near-by job on Pharaoh Cheops's big cedar-wood boat, which he was piecing together at the foot of the largest pyramid. The other was the Swedish historian, Björn Landström, the world's leading authority on ancient Egyptian boat design. He had come on one of his frequent visits to the country to catalogue and draw every single vessel depicted in the numerous tombs of the Nile valley. The week before, Landström had informed the press of his lack of faith in the seaworthiness of any kind of papyrus boat, but his first meeting with our stack of real papyrus reeds and our experienced boat-builders from Chad undermined his convictions and he offered to stay in Egypt and place all his theoretical knowledge at our disposal.

So the teamwork began. Landström knew nothing of papyrus reeds, nor of the technique involved in the chains of ropes which were to lash the bundles together into a boat, but he knew what the final shape of the ship was to be, besides all the minute details which were outside the Buduma Negroes' experience. He knew how the stern of a pharaonic vessel should curve gracefully into the sky as high as the bow, and also the shape and placement of biped mast with rigging, sail, cabin and steering mechanism. He sat down on a bundle of reeds and sketched a complete papyrus ship for us, and his drawing was to serve as our construction plan, showing the shape and all the proportions.

Mussa and Omar shook with laughter, because at Chad they had never seen a boat with a prow fore and aft, but they started building straight away. With four stalks bound together with twine at one end they began to build the boat we proposed to test at sea. They pushed in more papyrus reeds and the bundle and rope grew thicker and thicker, just as they had in Chad. When the cone-shaped bundle was about 2½ feet thick and the ropes as thick as a man's little finger, the bundle was lengthened into a cylinder, with rope rings of constant thickness placed two to three feet apart. Now there was room for Abdullah as well, and the work was in full swing. We had to go down to the Arab quarter and recruit more assistants. Abdullah interpreted to the best of his ability, in his Chad Arabic.

'*Bot*,' cried all the Egyptians. That was their word for reed. And then everything went like a conveyor belt. Two men hung on to the end of long wooden poles, pushing the rebellious papyrus bundles under the surface of the water in the brick basin. Two others sliced off all the rotten root ends and carried the fully soaked reed bundles up to assistants who were waiting to pass the stalks one by one to the three men from Chad, who forced them with all their strength into the bristling bundle of what was to become our boat, until the rope rings were stuffed as taut as barrel hoops. Abdullah was self-appointed foreman and worked and gave orders at breakneck speed. At first the Egyptian assistants looked down a little on the three raven-black men from Central Africa, for they had seen nothing blacker even in their own bakers' ovens, but Abdullah put them all authoritatively in their places with his sharp tongue and brilliant mind, and soon the other two had also won general admiration for their stoic calm, sense of humour and practical intelligence. Two rascally watchmen with turbans and old muskets, an excellent cook, and a laughing son-of-the-sun of a messboy, all helped to make up an agreeable camp, framed by a symbolic rope barrier which encircled tents, papyrus heap and building site. Already English, Arabic, Italian, Buduma, Norwegian, Swedish and French were in daily use round the same long table in the mess tent, and yet, even now, the whole international crew for the expedition was not present.

On the third day the clash between tradition and scholarship began. The reed roll was now so long that it was time to narrow it off into a point behind, but this the Buduma brothers flatly refused to do. They wanted to extend it without altering the diameter and then slice it off like a sausage, as they had always done on their own lake. No *kaday* could have a bow at both ends! With Abdullah as interpreter, Landström, Corio and I tried to explain that this was to be a papyrus boat of the special design which the ancient Egyptians used, but the generally cheerful Mussa turned and went off to bed. Omar tried to make us understand that although it was right to begin a papyrus roll with four reeds and make it thicker and thicker, it was not possible to make the thick end thinner and thinner and finish with only four reeds. With that he, too, trudged off across the sand and we were left disconsolate with all our Egyptian helpers.

Before the sun rose next morning the two brothers had slipped down to the building site and by the time the rest of us were up they had already done what they wanted to do. We ran down in the desperate hope of stopping them. Then we stood staring at the boat and at each other. Landström had made a construction drawing which showed seven separate rolls curved to a point front and back and then lashed side by side to give the boat width. But the two brothers had already begun the second roll by weaving it directly into and together with the first in a compact, firm whole. Not only were the ropes woven together in parallel chains across the boat, but a handful of papyrus reed from one roll was regularly woven diagonally into the rope rings of the neighbouring roll, so that they formed an inseparable whole. The technique was so superior to anything a non-initiate could have thought out that the scholars could only capitulate. A thousand years of practice swept away the theories of a single lifetime and the result was a compact amalgam of papyrus pontoons, of which only the very first had a full moon cross-section, while the rolls on either side had the graduated cross-sections of waxing and waning moons.

On the seventh day a sandstorm came ripping across the Sahara. The sand stabbed against the tents like petrified rain and the pyramids slowly disappeared from view. With stinging eyes and crunching teeth we had to hammer the long tent-pegs deeper into the sand and stretch a tarpaulin over the papyrus heaps because the dry, light reeds were beginning to fly through the air towards the pyramids. The reeds, bristling like hedgehog spines from the unfinished stern section of the two rolls, snapped like straw in the storm, while the finished section was as compact and robust as balks of timber. The storm grew more violent and the sand dashed itself against the camp like hot hail for three days. On the fourth day the storm died down and we went to work as drizzle began to fall over the desert. Jars of water were collected from the basin and poured over the pointed prow of the boat, which now consisted of three inter-woven cylinders, and when the bow was sufficiently malleable all the men were set to work bending it up into the high and elegant curve of the pharaohs' ships. But at the other end the bundles were still as straight and bristling as giant shaving brushes. Mussa and Omar would not yield. Then we took the three men from Chad on the adventure of their lives, to a big store in Cairo, where they travelled up and down the escalators and were allowed to choose a gift each. They gleefully chose wristwatches, and Abdullah promised to teach them to tell the time. That same afternoon an extravagantly happy Mussa discovered that it was possible to cut off enough papyrus to create a sharp point at the stern, bend it upwards and then patch on more reeds in a makeshift way so as to get the general Egyptian shape we wanted. We were all relieved. As the improvised stern curved into the air the construction assumed the form of a real ancient Egyptian vessel and, when the picturesque boat began to look like a crescent moon against the pyramids of the sun, it aroused enthusiasm among scholars and laymen alike. Little did we dream that this improvised afterthought of a stern was to prove the papyrus boat's Achilles heel.

Four rolls were gradually assembled on both sides of the longest central roll and then a second, similar layer of nine rolls was secured on top of the first. In addition an extra roll was placed along each side of the deck as a bulwark. The three central rolls were thicker, so that they projected eight inches below the rest, like a sort of broad keel.

In April the sun began to blaze down on the Sahara with an intensity which could be recorded in terms of work rate and water consumption. The boat-building in the sheltered valley behind the pyramids began to figure in the local press and television. The papyrus boat was constantly being confused with Pharaoh Cheops's cedar ship which Ahmed Joseph was reconstructing a few hundred yards away. Dragomans and tourist guides who were out of work, owing to the crisis in the Middle

East, hit on the idea of conducting such tourists as they could find to look at a genuine Egyptian papyrus ship. Tourists from every continent, and photographers and journalists who had poured into the country to report the war found their way by camel and on horseback, or trudging on foot, to the papyrus boat, which had now become the latest local attraction. While rope barriers were trampled down and disappeared, the guards struggled to hold back the mass of people from the fragile boat, over which the keenest onlookers scrambled in their eagerness to pose for photographs and without thought for the bone-dry reeds which snapped under their boot heels. The camels actually nibbled the boat. Papyrus scraps and whole reeds as souvenirs, with or without autographs, disappeared in all directions and Abdullah was so busy being nice to everyone who wanted his autograph that he forgot to oversee the work. Mussa and Omar stood with rolls of rope in their hands, flirting with beauties from Nigeria, Russia and Japan. We tried to work at night with lamps and flares, but the danger of fire from sparks and paraffin was so overwhelming that we had to stop. We really had built ourselves a paper boat. One match, and the whole thing would go up in a sea of flame and collapse, a few seconds later, in a little pile of ashes on the sand. We were panic-stricken over all the tourists who smoked and leaned with their cigarettes close to the wall of the vessel. We hung up large signs in English and Arabic, 'Smoking strictly forbidden', and told the day-watchman that he must point out the placard to everyone who came. Soon afterwards we found the old man himself sitting with his old rifle right under the papyrus prow, peacefully puffing at a home-rolled cigarette. I pointed furiously to the placard over his head, but he smiled back, unimpressed, and explained that he himself could not read.

The cabin was woven by an old basket-maker down in Cairo. It was bound together with flexible wickerwork, so that floor, walls and roof were connected in one large piece. This basket cabin where we were to live was 12 feet long and 8½ feet wide, with a curved roof under which we could stand with bent head at the highest point, and a door-opening three feet square in the middle of one long wall. Ceiling and long walls were continued three feet beyond one of the short walls, as an open storage alcove for the baskets of provisions.

During the work we had continually to make trips to the old tombs and study details of the fresco paintings. The pictures of long wooden ships always had a thick cable running lengthwise high above the deck.

It was kept up by two forked masts and ran all the way from prow to stern. By keeping the boat ends in tension this rigid cable should prevent the boat from breaking amidships if it collapsed fore and aft. The papyrus boats could evidently be allowed more flexibility lengthwise, because they lacked this tension cable. On the other hand, they had a short cable running diagonally from the in-curled tip of the stern to the after-deck, making the stern look like a harp with a single string. Little did we know how vital that string was. I spent hours pondering its function, convinced that it must have a practical purpose, though all the scholars and even the practical men from Chad said that its only function was to preserve the in-curved shape of the curl on the stern. Of course. But why, why this in-turned whorl? Just a matter of beauty, everyone said. None of us could work out a better reason, but that was reason enough for us to copy the old pictures on this point as well. The bow-string stayed there for many days, but one fine morning it had gone. Our friends from Chad had removed it; it hampered them in their work and was not needed any more because the curl on the stern now stayed immovably in place by itself. We asked them to tie the rope on again at once, but yielded to the logical argument that if the curl began to straighten out we could simply tie the bow-string on again ourselves whenever it was needed. It was not needed now.

Whereas the wooden boats had their giant cable strung between two forked masts, the paintings and reliefs of papyrus boats showed that they had a thick twisted cable made fast round the edge of the whole deck to hold the vessel together lengthwise, increase rigidity and provide a hold for the mast stays, which of course could not be lashed directly to the thin reeds.

As we wandered through subterranean chambers, corridors and colonnades, wall paintings three to four thousand years old helped us to relive the life of those days on the water, with the help of the artists' lifelike reproduction of every detail, often in low relief, covered with durable colours. We had to try to gain an insight into the forgotten life of former mariners through the ancient series of drawings, for no living man had experienced what we were now engaged on. Often it was difficult to distinguish between pictures of wooden boats and papyrus boats, because the wooden boats generally followed the papyrus boats in shape. But the tomb paintings sometimes showed workers actually collecting reeds in the papyrus swamps and carrying

This is how Björn Landström imagined Ra.
Right, detail of the mast foot.

the bundles on their backs to boat-builders, who tied the reeds into a water-craft with rolls of rope fed to them by small apprentices.

On board the various papyrus boats were depicted baskets filled with fruit, bread and other pastries, jars, sacks, cases, bird coops, monkeys, live calves, fishermen, hunters, traders, warriors, and cruising royalty. Here were whole funeral cortèges, with gods and bird-men. Here were naked fishermen working with nets, fish traps or hook and line. Here were flotillas of embattled papyrus boats. Here were warriors harpooning hippos from the papyrus deck and bird hunters catching feathered species among the reeds. Here were women sitting on the cargo, nursing their children. Here was Pharaoh himself, with his queen, on a ship's throne at a groaning table, with a servant ready to fill his cup. Some paintings depicted Pharaoh symbolically, as a giant straddling the length of the boat; others showed in detail twenty pairs of oarsmen in a papyrus or papyriform vessel with straddled mast, with rigging so big that half a dozen seamen were climbing yard-arms and stays and hauling on the halyards, and with a sail system so advanced that it testifies to a fully developed art of seamanship 5,000 years ago. The finest papyrus ships are represented with ornamental animal heads at the ends, and beautifully carved, painted and gilded cabin poles, sun roof, rudder-oars and other ship's fittings, all on a level with the ancient Egyptian skill and taste in architecture and everyday articles on dry land.

The pharaohs had enough stone to build pyramids as large as mountains. They had enough papyrus, too, so there was nothing to prevent them from building reed boats as large as floating islands. The papyrus boat we were to make was only a modest fifth of the Sphinx's length. We felt small when we came out of the underworld

83. *Opposite list* from ordinary sailing boats. Only bitter experience could teach us that a reed boat has to carry its ballast on the opposite side from other sailing boats because the reed bundles absorb more water on the windward side, where the waves splash higher.
84. *The problems were beginning aft*, but at first Santiago found it practical to be able to wash clothes on board.
85. *The afterdeck sagged* still further and it was difficult for Norman and Georges to work aft when the steering-oars broke in the darkness of the night.
86. *Abdullah praying* with a string of beads on nightwatch on the steering deck.

of mummies and stood between the paws of this stone monster. It made us realize what giant structures ancient men could have made out of reeds. The teeth of time devour papyrus, but not stone. If we had only had the wall paintings down in that subterranean world to go by, no one in our modern age would have believed that a sphinx and pyramids of such superhuman dimensions could have been made thousands of years before Columbus. However much we like to regard ourselves as the generation which has finally sloughed off the animal skin, the pyramids are there to remind us to tread warily. We must be careful not to underestimate the intelligence of others because they came into this same world of ours before we did. We are harvesting the fruits of their labours. They roamed about the world equipped with the same senses and inclinations. Their relics proclaim that in intelligence, imagination, inventiveness, taste, organization, curiosity, dynamism, aspiration, and all the other impulses behind men's actions, good and bad, we and ancient man have more features in common than we have setting us apart. It is only the calendar, and the technology we have built up together, which reveal the passage of 5,000 years.

When the last bulwark of papyrus began to take shape on each side of the deck, I had to fly off for a visit to Morocco. It was necessary to prepare for the arrival of our boat and our ultimate departure from the ancient port of Safi, which none of us had seen. Soon after my return to Egypt the last papyrus stems were put in place. Two hundred and eighty thousand reeds had been used. The building was finished. Six reeds were left lying on the ground.

On April 28th, the anniversary of the start of the *Kon-Tiki* expedition twenty-two years before, the papyrus boat was ready to be towed away. The area behind the pyramids was swarming with people. The Tourist Ministry had set up an open-air platform with chairs, and the

87. *There was no boat left* aft of the steering deck but Yuri held the course steadily as long as the rest of the vessel was riding high.
88. *Our only life-raft* was cut into strips by unanimous decision. The foam rubber was tied to the afterdeck to lift it but everything was washed away by heavy seas.
89. *In the grip of the sea.* Alpinist Carlo, knot and rope expert, helps sailor Norman to secure a sea anchor when both steering-oars break again.

K

Governor of Giza took his place with ministers and foreign ambassadors. Today others were doing the work and Abdullah, Mussa and Omar had put on their finest garb and taken their places among the audience. Broad-chested, with upstretched neck and curly tail, the papyrus boat looked like a big, golden hen brooding on round logs in the sand in front of the pyramids. We had built it lying free on top of a large wooden sledge, and our long cables were stretched out in the sand in front of this support. Busy men were laying out a slipway of telegraph poles on which the sledge could be towed over the sanddunes. For assistance in this task the President of the Papyrus Institute in Cairo had taken me to the Egyptian Institute of Gymnastics, where together we had convinced its head that we had set up a splendid training programme for rope-hauling out in the Giza sands. We would provide transport, how many men could the school bring?

The school could supply 500 physical training students, and here they were, arrayed in white shorts, with their gymnastics instructor organizing them in long rows along the ropes. Two men stood on the boat issuing directions, and one stood in front on the sledge, giving start and stop signals with a conductor's baton. There was something biblical about the scene. Perhaps it was because the old-fashioned boat, lying there, solid and home-made, with the basket cabin on its deck and the pyramids in the background, made one think of Noah's Ark lying abandoned in a desolate world after all the animals had left it. Or perhaps it was because Moses had come here to the pyramids, he who began his days drifting alone in a papyrus basket by the banks of the Nile. But what is certain is that when the man on the sledge raised his stick and 500 young Egyptians threw themselves into the traces until the desert resounded with rhythmic roars, when the wood began to creak and the big papyrus ship moved slowly forward against the still background of the pyramids, fixed in their ancient places, there were not a few of the onlookers who shivered, suddenly aware of ghosts walking under the broiling sun.

'*Ola ho-o-o-op!*' came the rhythmic shouts from 500 Egyptian throats, while timber squeaked and whimpered and stone grated, while the sun blazed down on the pyramids as it had always done, and played on the muscles of a thousand arms and a thousand legs conducted by the same baton, proving that men can move mountains without machines – if only they pull together.

The little desert valley seemed forlorn and strange when the tents were left alone with the pyramids, and the papyrus boat no longer provided a focal point, having moved out of the picture towards the asphalt road to Sahara City. There the wooden sledge with Noah's Ark was hoisted on to a large trailer, used in the building of the Aswan Dam. And while 500 cheering gymnasts were thanked for their hard work, the oldest and youngest means of transport in Egypt rolled together along the asphalt road, by the palm-covered shores of the Nile, to its mouth in the port of Alexandria.

Here we felt at once that the frail and fragile desert ship was beginning to absorb vitality and toughness from the moist sea air. The mummy-ship awoke to new life on its first meeting with the ocean.

CHAPTER 7

Out in the Atlantic

SAFI. The fresh scent of the salt Atlantic. The rollers broke against the steep coast, sending high white cascades up towards the old fortifications which Vasco da Gama's brother-in-law erected when the Portuguese took over the defence of the port in 1508 by agreement with the Berber chief Yahia ben Tafouft. Between medieval fortress walls and 450 year-old Portuguese castle, an energetic community of Arabs and Berbers now work peacefully together on the world's largest sardine fishery, and the port teems with colourful fishing boats, while large ocean-going vessels glide in and out to collect sulphate or exchange trade goods with Morocco's most important inland town, Marrakesh.

We were sitting up in the Pasha's palm garden at the top of the town, looking down on the endless open sea stretching from harbour to horizon. Safi's harbour had been used by the Berbers for a thousand years before the Portuguese came, and by the Phoenicians for at least a thousand years before that, for they used to trade along this open coast further down than the present Kingdom of Morocco. Just below Safi they had an important outpost on the little island off Mogador where the archaeologists are constantly excavating Phoenician relics. So long before Christian times there were already seafarers, traders, as well as colonists, trafficking between the innermost Mediterranean coasts and these old ports on the westernmost outpost of Africa's Atlantic coast, where the Canary current sweeps everything it can get hold of to the other side of the Atlantic.

All those who passed through the Straits of Gibraltar, the ancient Pillars of Hercules, had found shelter here if they, like the Phoenicians, ventured down along these low Moroccan cliffs and open sandy beaches. A reed boat could also have made its way down here to Safi, by progressing in short hops along the crooked coast of Africa, for no one doubted that such a vessel would float as long as it stayed close enough inshore to be dragged up at any time and dried when necessary. The question was, how long would it float if it left the coast and began to sail the open sea?

We know that the reed boat was used on the Atlantic coast beyond Gibraltar. It survived tenaciously on both sides of the Straits of Gibraltar. It is still in use among fishermen living in the shadow of the impressive and mysterious Nuraghi ruins on the west coast of Sardinia and our own version would not be the first the people of Morocco had seen. At the mouth of the Lucus River, on the Atlantic coast between Gibraltar and Safi, the reed boat survived as a fishing vessel and means of transport until it was finally replaced by Portuguese plank-boats at the beginning of this century. In 1913 members of a Spanish scientific expedition found that the ancient El Jolot tribe in this area was still building reed boats which could carry five or six fishermen and were navigated by both oars and sail. They expressly pointed out that it was the same type of vessel as the ancient Egyptians had used and they also emphasized that this design had not only survived in Morocco but was still in use on the Upper Nile, in Chad, and on Lake Titicaca in South America. They invited ethnologists to find out what connection could have existed between boat-builders in such widely separate places, and stressed that as far as these so-called *madia* on the Atlantic coast of Morocco were concerned, they seemed to be the most robust and perfect of all known reed boats.[1]

'You want to see a reed boat?' asked the head of the local coastal district, slightly offended, when I proposed to visit the Lucus River. 'Then you have come to Morocco a generation too late. Here we can show you boats of plastic!'

Colourful mobs of many racial types had gathered to watch as the reed boat built by our friends from Chad came rolling along the streets of Safi on wheels. Now it was ready for launching in the midst of the beached fishing boats in the harbour. Abdullah tried hard to explain our project to Berbers and Arabs in his own Chad Arabic dialect. Mussa and Omar had said goodbye. They had flown back from Cairo to Fort Lamy via Khartoum with heavy cases and the means to buy both wives and cattle at home in Bol. On parting, Mussa whispered that he had found a secret place in his fine new suit where he had

[1] A. Cabrera: "Balsa de juncos en el Bajo Lucus," *Revista del Istituto de Antropología de la Universidad Nacional de Tucumán.* Vol. 1, No. 2. Tucumán 1938.

hidden all his money so that no one could find it. Proudly he turned back the lapel of his jacket and showed me an ordinary inside pocket. Omar had finished his treatment and was envious of Abdullah, who with his knowledge of French and perfect health had been chosen to sail on the *kaday*.

Abdullah had no intention of returning to Chad until the guerilla war was over. He was coming to sea with us at all costs, even without the consent of President Tombalbaye and his Council of Ministers. With our Italian camp organizer Corio, he accompanied the papyrus boat as a passenger on a Swedish cargo boat supposed to sail from Egypt to Tangier in Morocco. No sooner had we waved good-bye to Abdullah in Alexandria than the captain received orders to change course and call at Port Said on the Suez Canal for a cargo of onions. Here Abdullah had a chance to observe how the white man lives up to his own teaching. He was awakened by cannons thundering along the Suez Canal, while missiles exploded at random on ramshackle Arab houses ashore. He stood on the ship's deck beside the inflammable papyrus boat and looked up, startled but unafraid, as something came sailing over the ship and exploded in the harbour area. The dock-workers disappeared and the ship was delayed for several days before it got away from Egypt. But now the papyrus boat had come safely through to the starting point in Morocco and Abdullah was busy tidying it up. It had shaken down a little on the journey overland from Cairo to Alexandria and from Tangier to Safi. It seemed slightly broader and flatter and the horntips, fore and aft, were a little battered and scorched after butting everything from bridges to high tension cables en route. But day by day the golden reeds grew steadily suppler and firmer as they absorbed the damp sea air.

Today the reed boat was to be launched. It happened to be May 17th and Norway's National Day. The Pasha had personally organized the launching from the same slipway which was used to launch the fishing smacks of Safi. As the King's representative he had almost unlimited authority, and he used it for the benefit of the expedition. From the day I arrived with the letter from his Moroccan friend, UN Ambassador Benhima, all doors in the Pasha's home were open and a spontaneous friendship arose between us. Pasha Taieb Amara and his wife Aicha were exceptional people. Both were equally active, equally alert and interested in social problems. He had used his power to establish modern schools, youth centres, workers' housing, seamen's homes and libraries and had brought activity in place of idleness to the old seaport. Madame Aicha was one of the twenty ladies chosen to make up King Hassan's women's council.

She arrived in her long Berber robe with a brightly coloured ceramic pitcher in her hand and we rose from our camel-skin pouffes to go down to the port.

'Since I, a Berber, am to baptize the boat, I think goat's milk would be most suitable,' she said, showing Yvonne the white contents of the pitcher. 'Goat's milk is Morocco's ancient symbol of hospitality and good wishes!'

The harbour was packed with colourful people. Our golden boat was decked out festively, with the flags of all the participant countries fluttering in the wind. Aicha smashed the fine pitcher into a thousand fragments against the wooden cradle, so that goat's milk and potsherds sprayed over papyrus and distinguished guests alike.

'I name you *Ra* in honour of the sun-god!'

Chains and cogwheels began to screech at once. The crowd pressed back. As the papyrus boat began to glide down the slipway towards the water I exchanged looks with the loyal patron of the expedition, Ambassador Anker, who stood straight and smiling, with milk-spots on the lapels of his dark suit. He and his wife had come from Cairo to see us off. We must have been thinking the same thing. 'Let's hope the worst obstacles are behind us now!' But others were thinking the opposite. Just as the bows touched the surface of the water a wide-eyed photographer leaned towards me and said:

'What will you say if it goes straight to the bottom now?'

There was no time to answer. *Ra* floated out. The wooden cradle sank slowly to the bottom with the iron truck to which it was secured, but *Ra* detached herself and lay on the water like a fat goose, while scraps of papyrus and wooden props from the sledge bobbed up round her and followed her out like a flock of goslings. A sigh of relief and admiration rose from the crowd on shore. Some had expected her to capsize. Most had thought that she was certain to list, because she had never been on trial and was a good deal short of symmetrical on either side of the centre line. This was handwork, and measured along the railing, Mussa's side proved to be some fifteen inches longer than Omar's. But the balance was perfect, no matter how many people jumped on board. The only part below water was the ten-inch depth of the three central rolls, which formed a kind of keel almost six feet wide. The rest of the wide boat lay right on the surface, like a lifebuoy.

A tugboat was ready to tow the reed boat over to a big lighter, where we made fast, so that the papyrus would not be shredded to ribbons against the stone mole in the tidal water. We lay here for a week, allowing the reed below the water line to absorb its fill, while we fitted our vessel out for sea. In this week the various members of the *Ra* expedition met one another for the first time. There would be time enough to catch up on each other's life stories in the tiny bamboo basket which was to be our common home at sea in the weeks ahead.

There was Norman Baker, from the United States. As the only real sailor on board he had been appointed the expedition's navigator and radio-operator. Thorough and reliable, he sat in the cabin entrance examining his equipment, allowing no detail to pass without an expert check. My own previous acquaintance with Norman was rather fleeting. He had come aboard my ship once, in his modest, calm way, when I was in Tahiti with a Greenland trawler I had chartered for an expedition to Easter Island. Norman had just reached Tahiti then, as navigator of a tiny ketch which he and an American biologist had sailed a good 2,000 sea miles from Hawaii. He could navigate. He was also a Commander in the American Navy and an instructor in oceanography at the Navy School in New York, though in civilian life he was a building contractor in the skyscraper world of that vast city.

'Have you really no experience of the sea?' asked Norman sceptically, turning to Yuri who sat, round and cheerful, beside him in the cabin-opening, fingering a breathing apparatus.

Yuri Alexandrovich Senkevich was Russian and the expedition's doctor. He grinned broadly.

'I have been in a Soviet ship to the Antarctic and back,' replied Yuri, and began to talk about luscious girls in Manila. But Norman was more eager to hear if Yuri had really spent a full year in the coldest place in the world. Yuri had. For a year he had been doctor to the Russian research station at Vostok, about 10,000 feet above sea level, right on the South Polar ice-cap, where the temperature can drop to –100° Fahrenheit. Yuri was the only one of the men I had never met before. We were both equally on tenter-hooks when his plane landed in Cairo. I had taken a chance on writing to the head of the Russian Academy of Sciences, President Keldysh, an intelligent and unassuming scholar who is in charge of all science in the Soviet Union, from sputniks to archaeology. I reminded him that he had once asked why I never took Russians on my expeditions. This was the opportunity. I needed a Russian and I needed a doctor; perhaps President Keldysh could recommend someone. My conditions were that the doctor must be able to speak another language besides Russian, and that he must have a sense of humour. The Russians had taken the last point very seriously. When Yuri emerged from the Aeroflot plane, laden with gifts and medical supplies, he had taken a vodka for fear of not being funny enough. And Yuri fitted straight into the picture at once. His knowledge of English was minimal, but enough to ensure that the point of a joke was never lost. Son of a doctor and born in Mongolia, Yuri was something of an Asiatic. He had been chosen from among the younger scientists at the Soviet Department of Health, and he specialized in the problems of astronauts under acceleration and weightlessness. After inspecting the bamboo cabin in which we were all going to accelerate out to sea, he had a number of humorous comments to make in the astronauts' favour.

The Italian, Carlo Mauri, was also quite a new acquaintance. He was to be the expedition's film photographer. A friend from Rome was to have come, a film producer who was one of Italy's best frogmen and had just been down filming *Andrea Doria* at the bottom of the Atlantic. But, when Abdullah landed in prison and I disappeared unexpectedly into the African interior just as we were about to build the boat, he lost faith in the whole project and proposed Carlo Mauri as a substitute, while he himself continued to organize the filming on land. Carlo Mauri, red-bearded and blue-eyed as a Viking, was another without the slightest experience as a sailor. He was a professional mountain guide and Italy's most noted alpinist. He had either led or at least participated in fourteen international mountain-climbing expeditions which had taken him to every continent. Many of the worst precipices in the Himalayas and the Andes were as familiar to him as some of the stiffest peaks in Africa, New Guinea or Greenland. One leg had been seriously fractured by a bad fall in the Alps which finished his ski-teaching, but as a mountaineer he was more active than ever. Carlo happened to be down on the South Polar ice-cap when he heard about the papyrus boat project; and as he had gone there after filming polar bears in the ice channels of the North Polar ice-cap, he liked the idea of a spot of hot, ice-free bath-water on the Equator.

At the eleventh hour we almost lost our Mexican member. My friend Ramon of the trip to the Seris Indians was rushed to hospital for an extremely serious operation on the very day when the papyrus boat was hoisted on board in Alexandria harbour. The tragic message arrived in the middle of a press conference and was withheld until a journalist asked for the names of the participants. Our otherwise smiling Ambassador sat seriously in the front row, fingering the paper.

'From Mexico – ' I was beginning, when nervous fingers passed me the telegram. It stung like a whiplash. If only Ramon pulled through everything else could go hang. It was difficult to finish the sentence. The press grew restless.

'From Mexico – Dr Santiago Genoves!'

The meeting broke up. Two telegrams went off to Mexico at once. One to Ramon in hospital and one to Dr Genoves, the Mexican anthropologist who had said half in jest that he would come if he had a week's notice. Now he had a week's notice. And he came. That energetic man even managed to stop over in Barcelona to receive Pope John XXIII's Peace Prize for 1969 as a reward for his campaign against war and aggression in the book *Pax?* which he was now in the process of filming. From Spain he reached Morocco just in time to supervise the transport of the reed boat overland from Tangier to Safi. Now he was already in action as the expedition's quartermaster, busy stacking pear-shaped Egyptian jars on the uneven reed deck, where they toppled over unless propped against one another, padded with reed fragments and made fast with rope. Coconuts in the shell served excellently as fillers. We had had 160 of these amphorae made, on the pattern of the ancient Egyptian jars in Cairo Museum, and Santiago handled them with the same solicitous care as he handled the ancient Indian skulls at Mexico University. He numbered and listed jars, baskets and goat-skin containers, writing it all down with a scientific thoroughness which reflected his long work as editor of the International Yearbook of Physical Anthropology. I had caught glimpses of Santiago at scientific congresses in many countries. He had escaped from Spain during the Civil War, but since then I had met him there, too, and now most recently in Mexico, where he was Research Professor at Mexico University, specializing in the problem of the apparently mixed origins of the American Indian tribes. He had absolutely no experience as a sailor. In one particular this muscular little scientist differed from all other scholars I knew. He had been a professional footballer.

If anyone could have had less knowledge of seamanship than Yuri,

Carlo and Santiago, it must have been Abdullah Djibrine, the desert dweller from Chad, who had grown up in the heart of Africa and did not even know that the sea was salt. Now he was to join the expedition as papyrus expert. Perhaps it was this exotic character whom I knew best, after two journeys to Chad and seven weeks spent together behind the pyramids. Resourceful and quick-witted, but wary as a gazelle with everyone and everything, perhaps Abdullah did not even know himself, when it came to the point. All I knew about him, after discarding his own tall tales about trips to Paris and Canada, was that he had been born in a little village near the papyrus swamps of Chad, where the men of the tribe had taken him from his mother by force in order to cut the distinguishing mark down his forehead and nose when he was so young that he could barely remember it. Apart from that, he had grown up to become a carpenter and a lady's man. As a good Mohammedan it was his right to have several wives, and my duty to provide for them. One Chadian wife with three children, and a second whom he had married at the last minute, created complicated monthly currency transactions with the Republic of Chad, and he had watched his chance to marry a third in Cairo during the one week when I was away on a quick trip to Morocco. A wedding feast in style had been postponed until I returned and could play host. It had taken place, with belly-dancing and Egyptian musicians, on the roof of his father-in-law's Arab house, and Mussa and Omar were so taken with the beautiful, shy bride that they stuffed most of their week's wages down her already well-filled brassière. So now I had monthly foreign exchange problems in Egypt, too, and vowed that, in Morocco, Abdullah would not be allowed out of our sight.

The youngest of the party was the Egyptian, Georges Sourial, a gifted chemical engineer, professional frogman, incorrigible playboy, six times judo champion of Egypt and once of Africa. Standing six feet five in his stockinged feet and, with a body like Tarzan's, Georges had not done a stroke of work since his college days, but frolicked in the clubs of Cairo and the waves of the Red Sea. He entertained horrified friends by breaking six bricks with one blow of his hand; he bore the scars of a shark-bite on his leg and was the only man I knew who dared to dive down to the lairs of the deadly moray eels and tempt them out with fish held in his own mouth, while he patted the big brutes as if they were peaceful domestic pets. Georges was no sailor: he knew the sea only from below, and when he asked to join us after reading the verdict of the papyrus experts he gave the charming reason that he came along because he was happier under water than above it. Like other old Coptic families in Egypt, the Sourial family also traced its origins back to the days before the Arabs arrived, bringing the teachings of Mohammed to the land of the Nile. From the day when he glimpsed the ghost of a chance of coming with us, Georges, who usually slept like a mummy for fourteen hours of the twenty-four, suddenly began to rise at dawn and make himself useful in the camp behind the pyramids. His odd acquaintances in the most obscure corners of Cairo brought us into contact with an old sail-maker who still sewed with needle and thread, a basket-maker who wove the cabin by hand, a baker who could bake Egyptian bread according to the recipe from Cairo Museum and a whole community of potters who lived on an isolated hillside in the suburbs, where they stood waist deep in clay slip, stirring it with bodies and limbs before they began to turn the potter's wheel with their bare feet, so that our 160 amphorae were made according to the 5,000 year-old example in Cairo Museum.

Day by day the papyrus bundles absorbed more and more sea water as they lay bobbing on the waves, while on board there was feverish activity. The weight of papyrus and rope had previously been about twelve tons, but ton after ton was absorbed below the water-line without sinking the boat. At the same time tons of weight were being loaded on deck without the vessel heeling visibly. She lay steady as an island. The heaviest burdens were the great straddled mast which was erected in front of the wickerwork cabin, and the bridge, built of lashed poles behind the same cabin so that we could see over its roof. If this weight was added to that of the cabin, the heavy steering-oars and the spare timber for repairs which lay on deck, then the papyrus rolls were carrying a good two tons of cargo in wood besides over a ton of water in heavy jars and at least two tons of food supplies, containers and equipment.

Activity during the last week was at fever pitch. Each day the papyrus spent in sea water represented a day of its life lost, according to the experts, and that was reason enough to hurry. A no less obvious reason was that, with every day that passed, the hurricane season on the other side of the Atlantic drew nearer. As if by a miracle our programme had held good, with a failure margin of only one week, despite the detour to Chad and all other obstacles; but now the bustle was reaching a real crescendo. We no longer had a day to lose. We packed and carried and rolled on the dock side. We climbed and hauled and knotted on masts and stays. We cut and whittled and lashed with ropes and leather on steering bridge and oars. The deck seethed with willing helpers. Captain De Bock, veteran of the Franco-Belgian expedition to Easter Island and an experienced sailor, had calculated the probable line of drift of the papyrus boat before taking leave from his post as Harbour Pilot guiding 50–100,000 tonners in and out of Antwerp harbour. Now he stood, stout and reliable, on the papyrus deck supervising stowing and lashing according to the best nautical traditions. His Norwegian colleague, Captain Hartmark, had previously captained my own expedition vessel to Easter Island. Here he was again, clinging to the masthead of *Ra*, securing the rigging in a seamanlike manner with mountaineer Mauri. Herman Watzinger from the *Kon-Tiki* expedition had come up from Peru, on his way to Rome, to give us a helping hand at the start, and Frank Taplin had come from New York with renewed good wishes from U Thant.

Our wives, with the Pasha's wife at their head, squatted round the jars in the warehouse on land, packing sheep's cheese in olive oil, fresh eggs in lime solution, dried fish, nuts and mutton sausages in baskets and sacks. Aicha Amara mixed ground almonds and honey, butter, flour and dates, into *sello*, a sort of powdered biscuit which represented Morocco's oldest and most easily-preserved travelling food. In the last days the Pasha of Safi had to provide us with a police barrier so that the work on the dock should not be brought to a complete standstill. Press, photographers and public had jostled shoulder to shoulder in a spirit of amiable curiosity so much that one man fell over the edge of the wharf, jars were smashed, and a paraffin lamp was trodden flat.

Then the great day dawned. *Ra* had now been lying in the harbour absorbing sea water for eight full days and had consequently lived out more than half its lifetime, according to the experts. The day dawned with a mild offshore breeze which increased in strength, and by eight o'clock on the morning of May 25th the flags on both *Ra* and the old Portuguese citadel up on land were straining straight out towards the open Atlantic. Rais Fatah, the sardine fishermen's spokesman and the expedition's local adviser, a black-skinned giant of an Arab, came rowing across the harbour with sixteen of his men, divided among four open rowing-boats which were to tow *Ra* out of the harbour.

There was hectic activity down on the long stone mole. The mass of people was jammed together in an impenetrable wall, and photographers were sitting in all the boats and on top of the cargo cranes. Aicha, the Pasha's wife, needed police help to get through to the dockside and present a parting gift: a lively little baby monkey which the Pasha's people had recently caught for us in the Atlas Mountains and named Safi. It clung desperately to the ship's godmother until it noticed that one or two of the men on board had fur on their faces. Then it jumped happily over to the boat and played a vigorous part in a mêlée of farewell embraces and good wishes in many languages, while the fishermen, unmoved by all the uproar, attached a rope from each of the four dinghies to the thick rope we had secured right round the reed boat at the water-line. Now they were waiting for orders to row us away from the seething mass of people. One after the other we tore ourselves away and jumped down from the high stone mole to the soft, vegetable deck of the papyrus boat. Abdullah, Georges and Santiago blew kisses, and handed autographs up to the dockside; Carlo gave his blonde Italian wife a last farewell kiss; Norman, who was struggling with a sore throat, escaped from the good wishes and admonitions of the American Ambassador; while the Russian Ambassador gave Yuri a touching hug on this, his first departure from Soviet guidance and organization. I myself found a microphone stuck into my hand and paid a last debt of gratitude to all the expedition's friends and collaborators who were now suddenly left behind on the dock, although we felt that their place was on board with us: Ambassador Anker from Cairo, Pasha Amara and his Moroccan helpers, Captains De Bock and Hartmark, Corio the camp master, Herman Watzinger, Frank Taplin, Bruno Vailati. Then I jumped on board with the rest. It was almost like walking on a mattress. I signalled to Rais Fatah, the men on land cast off, and the fishermen leaned to their oars and began to row. The time was 8.30. Slowly our broad reed bundle began to move away from the quay.

Then began a shrill chorus of wails, so unexpected that at first everyone jumped and then every man of us was left with a lump in his throat. All the fishing boats in the harbour had started up their rending sirens, accompanied by deep blasts from factory hooters, silos and warehouses on land. Ships' bells were rung, the crowd cheered, and a cargo-ship lying at anchor outside the harbour began to send up crackling signal rockets which burst in a shower of stars and slowly settled on the water ahead of us in a blood-red carpet of smoke. It was a royal farewell which almost scared us, as we stood on our strange boat, tugging experimentally at the curious rigging and fiddling about with two parallel, oar-like rudders, set aslant, of a type no man had tried since the last Egyptians recorded the system for posterity on their tomb walls, before the artists and their boats vanished from the surface of the earth. What if we could not make the mechanism work? What if we came swimming back to the mole from papyrus bundles scattered to the four winds by the waves outside the harbour wall? The whole harbour began moving behind us. An escort of fishing smacks, yachts and motor-boats followed us past the furthest mole, while all the sirens and bells continued to sound as if for the New Year celebrations. Above us circled an Embassy plane and a helicopter which had come down from the capital, Rabat. Outside the mole the uproar died away, the ocean seas began their leisurely swell, the smallest escort vessels turned about and put back to calm waters and we were alone with the Atlantic and the big fishing boats. Our four rowing-boats cast off, and with good wishes in Arabic the oarsmen headed back with the smaller motor-boats towards the high mole.

For the first time we hoisted *Ra*'s sail. Large and heavy, made of strong Egyptian sail-cloth, it was a good 26 feet high and 23 feet wide along the yardarm at the top, next to the yard, narrowing downwards in the ancient Egyptian manner to a mere 16 feet, the breadth of the papyrus boat itself, at the lower end, near the deck. A couple of light puffs of wind barely pushed the heavy yard clear of the straddled mast, showing that the good offshore wind was already dying away. Then the big, wine-coloured sail hung almost motionless, displaying its rust-red sun disk, the bright, freshly painted symbol of *Ra*. The whole row of flags arrayed in alphabetical order hung idly like a colourful clothes-line over the cabin roof: Chad, Egypt, Italy, Mexico, Morocco, Norway, USA and USSR, flanked at either end by the United Nations' optimistic flag, with its white globe on a light-blue ground.

Abdullah and I stood, each holding the tiller of a big rudder-oar, on the bridge behind the basket cabin, looking anxiously from the slack sail to the white breakers washing against the stone mole only a few hundred yards away. Were they coming closer? Yes. A sighting from the tip of the jetty up to a tower on the fortress wall showed that we were drifting slowly back towards land. Perhaps the long, mountainous point, which projected to the north and sheltered Safi, prevented the offshore wind from filling the sail. We tossed a rope end to the nearest fishing smack and soon we were moving at full speed in a straight line out to sea, with an escort of fishing smacks putt-putting all round us. At this speed we were not obeying the laws of nature. The first thing to happen was that a line with a net full of live lobsters which we were towing spun into our wake and wound itself round one rudder-oar, which bent in an ominous arc and threatened to break. A slash with a sharp knife, and the oar-blade was saved, but several days' banquets vanished in the waves behind us.

The next thing to happen was that one of the three thick rowing oars we had bound to the side of *Ra* as a leeboard was snapped across by the speed alone. It was to this very oar blade that Norman had nailed our future life-line to family and friends ashore: the copper plate which was to act as earth to our little portable radio. Metal obviously had no place on a springy papyrus boat, and the oar-blade broke at the exact spot where the copper plate ended and was barely saved by being trailed along on the earthing wire.

This was no good. Wind or no wind, we would have to manage on our own. We stopped the escort, hauled all our ropes on board, and hoisted our sail again. We noticed how violently the big fishing smacks round us were rolling by comparison with our own raft-like vessel which, like its predecessor, the balsa raft *Kon-Tiki*, simply rocked gently up and down on the long rollers. The wind blew first in light puffs, then with steadily increasing strength. But it was no longer an offshore wind. The north-easterly typical of the time of year had veered to the north-west and was blowing straight towards the low cliffs which stretched southward from the safe harbour of Safi. We were still so close inshore that we could make out all the houses and the treacherous surf creeping silently up and down the mustard-brown cliffs where the green lowlands of Morocco washed their sun-heated

90. *Central African Abdullah* did not fear the sea because he had three leather pouches of magic remedies tied to his back.
91. *Two Africans* bind reeds as a bulwark against the sea, Georges under the water and Abdullah above.
92. *'The sea is salt!'* exclaimed Abdullah, and asked for extra rations of fresh water to wash himself before saying his prayers to Allah.

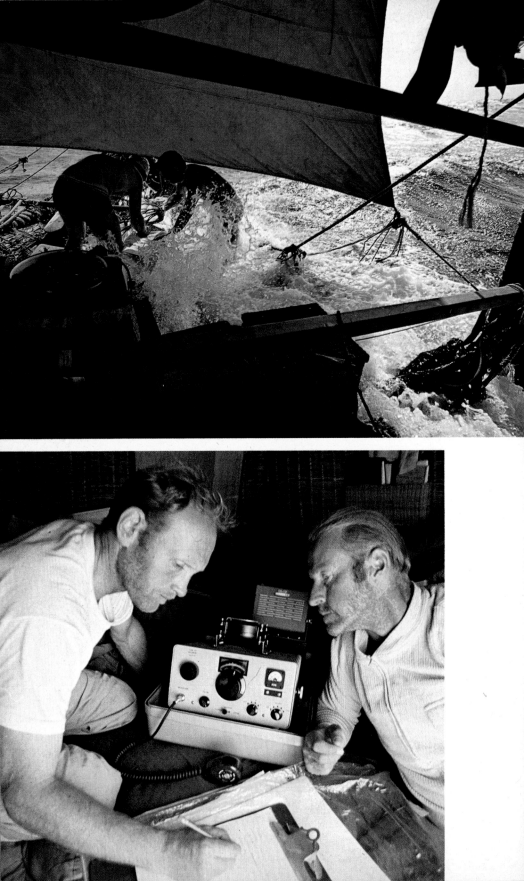

façade in their eternal confrontation with the sea. That was where the wind would send us, unless we succeeded in manoeuvring the papyrus bundle.

All seven of us on board were equally in suspense about one thing – how the steering mechanism would function. This was the greatest lurking factor of uncertainty, for we had no teacher. Our hope was that, beyond the Moroccan coast, wind and current would carry us directly away from land so that we would have a week or two for experiment without risk of being washed up against the cliffs. It was the coast we were afraid of, not the open sea. We had avoided the sea outside the estuary of the Nile for our experiment, for fear of being washed up on the coast before we had discovered how the Egyptian steering system worked. Out in the open Atlantic, off Morocco, we assumed there would be room for trial and error, because the elements there usually carried flotsam straight out to sea.

We had constructed *Ra*'s steering device according to the numerous models and wall paintings from the earliest Egyptian era. We had tried in vain to procure the cedar from Lebanon which the Egyptians had used for these huge rudder-oars, but the few cedars which survived in the ancient Phoenician kingdom were now protected in a national park. So we had to make do with a heavy Egyptian tree, the *cenebar*, for the biped mast, and we had carved two 25-foot steering-oars, with blades as large and wide as the average writing desk, from an African jungle tree which the Moroccans call *iroco*. These were now made fast slantwise aft on either side of *Ra*'s peaked stern. The lower part of the shaft, close to the blade, rested on a solid log which was lashed on across the boat aft. About twelve feet further up and forward, the oar rested on a thinner cross-log, which also served as

93. *New bunk sites* had to be found every time the sea smashed the boxes we were sleeping on in the basket cabin. Norman chose to sleep on the food baskets.
94. *Sharks* began to gather round the raft-ship as we approached the West Indies.
95. *The last storm* carried the galley overboard and smashed all the boxes, but the padded jars were still full of drinking water.
96. *Radio hams* on both sides of the Atlantic were following the *Ra* experiment through reports on the amateur wave-length. Norman and the author with the expedition's transceiver.

the stern guard-rail on the bridge. Where each of the two oar shafts met these crossbeams they lay in a rounded groove lined with leather and were rigidly lashed with thick ropes so that the oars could not jump out or swing sideways, but could only rotate round their own longitudinal axis. This made them useless as steering-oars in the ordinary sense of the word. They could not be used like the long, free-swinging oars in the stern of *Kon-Tiki*, because they were tightly strapped top and bottom. Instead, each of them had a tiller of hardwood lashed fast at right angles across the shaft near the top, and a long thin rod hung horizontally from the end of one tiller to the other, secured with freely-moving rope hinges, so that if a single person stood in the middle and pushed this rod from one side of the bridge to the other, both oars turned together round their own central axis, like two parallel, slanting rudders. The system was so ingenious and apparently different from the steering devices used by living peoples today that we all cheered with relief when for the first time I tentatively pushed the suspended cross-bar to port and *Ra* slowly, but co-operatively as an amiable horse, obeyed the signal by turning her bows to starboard. I promptly pushed the bar over to the starboard side and *Ra* swung slowly to port.

There was no doubt about it. We were using a steering mechanism which in historical perspective represented the forerunner of the rudder, the missing link between a primitive steering-oar and a modern tiller. At some point in antiquity the Egyptians had discovered that pushing a long steering-oar sideways to make a sailing boat turn was unnecessarily laborious. All you had to do was to twist the shaft so that the blade was not perpendicular in the water and the vessel would swing just as well. So they put a cross-bar on the shaft and had invented the steering device we were now testing. The thin rod suspended crosswise between the two tillers was simply an improvement to enable a single helmsman to control an oar on each side of the boat at the same time. All that was needed then was for the sailors of old gradually to discover that if they placed the oar-blade with the shaft vertical instead of slanting, and continued to twist the little crosswise handle, they had invented a modern rudder.

Abdullah, standing unafraid but with wide-open, glowing eyes, on the bridge at my side, now grasped the long, thin horizontal rod as well. Four hands made steering easier still, and down on the deck the others ran about, organized by Norman, hauling on ropes which set the mainsail in the position where it would always best catch the changing wind. Our first hesitant moves were now being followed by excited journalists and experienced old salts on board the puttering vessels which circled about us, and everyone seemed as relieved as ourselves when we found that the reed boat really could be navigated. The north-westerly was blowing us straight in to land, but we managed to beat almost 90° up into the wind so that we took it on the starboard beam and travelled south-west, parallel to the land. The combers were rolling steadily and strongly here beyond the open coast where Cape Badusa gave no lee and the fishing smacks, crowded for the occasion with more or less seaworthy passengers, began to turn back. One after another they blew their horns and waved good-bye. The last I saw was my wife Yvonne, trying, seasick as she was, to find her sea-legs long enough to wave both arms at once. The helicopter disappeared and the aeroplane made its last farewell pass just over our heads.

Then we were alone with the sea. Seven men, a monkey gambolling gleefully in the shrouds, and a wooden cage full of cackling fowl and a single duck. It was suddenly so strange and quiet, with only the sea swelling and frothing round our peaceful Noah's Ark.

As soon as Norman had managed to hoist the big sail and see to it that the sheets and tacks were secure, he came stumbling aft along the papyrus deck and confided to me that he was now feeling really ill. He was white-faced and red-eyed. Yuri wobbled over on unsteady sea-legs and to the general consternation confirmed that Norman's temperature was 102°. Influenza. The sea-wind was flinging itself at us in colder and colder gusts, and our Russian doctor ordered our American navigator to bed immediately in his sleeping bag inside the wickerwork cabin. With that, our only sailor was temporarily out of action.

The onshore wind strengthened and the sea began to pile up in foaming breakers. When the largest waves came surging towards us *Ra* simply lifted one side and amiably let them pass under the rolls of reed. But now and then they smashed so vigorously against the oar-blades that both shafts bent visibly and I had to roar to the powerful Abdullah to slacken his iron grip and yield a little to the pressure so that the oars would not snap.

Everything was going well and we were in high spirits – even the unfortunate patient, who lay bemoaning his uselessness. Carlo had quickly revealed himself as the vessel's supreme knot expert, quite used to both sleeping and eating suspended on a rope. Now he enthu-

siastically served hot coffee and the cold chicken legs we had brought
with us and informed me gleefully that life at sea was just like life on
the mountain-tops, the same fellowship with nature, the same challenging duel with the elements, the same *joie de vivre* and necessity for quick
solutions to unexpected problems.

We held our course steadily across the wind at a speed of about three
knots, and the coast did not seem to be coming any nearer. It was 3.15
in the afternoon and I felt that everything was going so well that Abdullah and I could be relieved by the two men on the next watch. Carlo and
judo-champion Georges took over, fresh and vigorous, and Abdullah
crawled into the cabin for a well-earned rest while I picked my way
forward along the papyrus rolls to take a look at the foredeck, which
was so stacked with jars, goatskins and baskets of vegetables that all
further passage forward was barred for the time being, unless one
balanced on the outermost round reed bulwark. Just forward of the
wind-filled sail Santiago sat with a broad smile on his face, leaning
against the chicken coop and enjoying the view of the distant coast.
Stiff after many hours at the steering-oar, I dropped down beside him
and relaxed for the first time in many hectic weeks. There we both sat
and revelled in the papyrus boat's superb ability to ride out all the waves
which lifted and flung themselves against us on the starboard beam without disturbing our trim, without even giving us a harmless drenching.
I stretched out and was enjoying the glow of happiness pervading my
whole weary body when I was suddenly jolted out of my blissful state
by an appeal from three panic-stricken voices:

'Thor! Thor!'

It was barely five minutes since I had been standing on the bridge
myself. I sprang up and grasped the edge of the suddenly flapping sail
in order not to lose my foothold on the reeds while I squeezed my way
past towards the stern with a thousand fearful misgivings buzzing
round my head. From behind the sail Yuri came wobbling towards
me like a drunken tight-rope walker, so overwrought that he could only
speak Russian and gesticulate towards the stern where the two men on
the bridge were leaning forward, shouting to me in helpless desperation. So everyone was still on board. As long as we could manage
to stay on board we would be all right. Georges waved his arms and
Carlo yelled in Italian that the steering-oars were broken. Both of
them! One look was enough to reveal the extent of the damage. Both
oar-shafts had snapped at the throat, just above the shoulders of the

blade, and both the big, yellow-brown blades had come to the surface and were being towed behind like two surf boards. *Iroco* could not possibly be the robust wood we had been told it was. Fortunately we had tied a rope to each blade in the Egyptian manner, so that the oar itself could not slip away aft, and we made haste to pull in the vital broad wooden blades before the ropes chafed away. Carlo and Georges were left with two empty shafts projecting into the water aft, with no flat surface to control our course, no matter how they twisted the handles.

It was like a punch in the solar plexus.

'Shall we have to give up?' Carlo asked in a low voice. The three men aft fixed me with looks of profoundly miserable enquiry.

Before there was time to answer, I realized that *Ra* was coming slowly about, until with sail filled again and bows pointing in exactly the right direction the reed boat continued serenely on the very course we had been trying to hold by force. In that second I understood what had happened and felt a surge of relief. The two perpendicular oars which were still made fast as a lee-board forward had truly come into their own now that there was no longer a rudder or anything at all projecting aft as a keel, so the stern was being pushed sideways to lee-ward of the onshore wind and the whole vessel thus obediently turned along a course which automatically pointed away from land.

'Wonderful!' I shouted in English, putting the most obvious joy into my voice in order to infect with my own new confidence these men who with good cause were about to abandon all hope of continuing the voyage across the Atlantic.

All the uproar brought the feverish Norman crawling out of the cabin just in time to receive his share of my jubilant shout. Startled, he asked what was going on.

'Wonderful!' I repeated enthusiastically. 'Both rudder-oars are broken, so for the rest of the voyage we can use the ancient *guara* method of the Incas!'

Norman stared blankly at me with bloodshot eyes, uncertain whether to laugh or cry. The others scrutinized me closely, all obviously wondering if I had gone out of my mind as a result of the accident or if I was conversant with some Indian witchcraft they knew nothing about. For, sure enough, *Ra* was holding her course more steadily than ever, as we could see both from the compass and from the line of the prow in relation to the coast. Carlo considered me for some time.

Then the unhappy expression disappeared from the blue eyes and he gradually began to roar with laughter, until the red beard shook. Then Abdullah in the basket cabin woke up too and soon we were all laughing uproariously with relief and delight at this vessel which steered herself, so that all we had to do was go and sit on the cargo. Up on the bridge the compass needle was left alone in its well-secured binnacle. The bearing was south-west; it was there we wanted to go, and that was the way *Ra* was obediently heading under full sail in briskly foaming seas, while we all enjoyed life as passengers.

'Now we really are castaways,' I admitted to my still slightly bewildered companions, but I hastened to add that for the experiment this was the best thing that could have happened. Something just like this might have befallen other vessels of this type which sailed past Gibraltar and tried to steer further along the Moroccan coast. Now we would really see where they would have landed.

Carlo was beaming like the rising sun. He just went on shaking his head and laughing. One only had to let nature have its way, he agreed, and the elements took care of the transport. We had one spare rudder-oar on deck but we did not put it out for fear of breaking that as well before we had seriously begun to cross the great Atlantic Ocean. In any case the *iroco* wood had proved so brittle and insubstantial that we would have to reinforce the reserve oar before risking it in the waves.

Towards evening Yuri came crawling out of the cabin with an anxious expression.

'Now we have two patients who absolutely must stay in bed,' he explained.

For the past two days Santiago had been tormented by a sort of eczema below the belt. The sea air seemed to have made the disease burst out in full flower. His skin had peeled away in several places and he himself feared that he might have caught the dangerous *tina* sickness which he had seen on the Canary Islands, for which we were now heading. Yuri was afraid Santiago might be right; *tina* was a dreaded disease, widespread in North Africa.

When night fell we saw the lights of several ships passing us in both directions, some at disturbingly close quarters, and Carlo clambered up and made a little paraffin lamp fast to the swaying masthead, since there was an obvious danger of our little haystack being rammed and sunk. The night watches on deck were divided between Italy,

Egypt and Norway. Russia had more than enough to do caring for USA and Mexico, and we preferred to let the carpenter from Chad have his sleep out so that he could attack the problem of repairing the steering-oars next day. The wind alarmed us by blowing in treacherous gusts from both north-west and west-north-west and I spent most of the night keeping my eye on a lighthouse blinking away on land, until that too disappeared. As long as it was pitch dark I dared not succumb to the temptation to take a nap. With the navigator struggling with waves of fever, our only hope of judging the distance from the land was to gaze into the darkness for a light. Each new ship which appeared ahead or to port made my heart thump with excitement. Was it a light from the coast, were we drifting towards buildings, or was it simply other seafarers? Not until we saw the red or green riding lights could we relax – and only then, when we had assured ourselves that they would pass out of range of a collision. As long as there was enough water round us we had no serious problems.

When day dawned in the east and there was no land in sight we turned a smiling Yuri out into the morning chill, equipped as if for the Antarctic, and he sat himself down, solid and trustworthy, in the cabin opening and filled his pipe while the rest of us crawled into our warm sleeping bags and let the papyrus bundles sail the sea for themselves. I was not the only one to be so dog-tired after twenty-four hours of hectic vigilance that sleep came before I had time to become really familiar with the strongly personal character of the basket cabin and its energetic efforts to outdo the papyrus bundles in peculiar creaks, snorts, cracks and whines.

Our first day on board *Ra* was over.

CHAPTER 8

Down the African Coast
to Cape Juby

A COCK crowed. There was a scent of fresh hay. I was on a farm. No, I was certainly not on a farm, because I was being carried helpless on a swaying stretcher. I woke up in a sleeping bag and heard water gurgling beneath me and waves foaming against my ear. Of course: I was on a boat. I half-opened my eyes and saw blue-grey waves through the chinks in the bamboo wall before my nose. I was on board *Ra*! The scent of hay came from the mattresses which were filled with freshly dried Moroccan grass.

The cock crowed again. I heard it again, now that I was awake, and shot on all fours to the opening in the bamboo wall to look ahead. We must be really close to the coast, about to run aground. Outside I could see nothing but breaking wave-tops as far as the eye could reach, but straight ahead the view was blocked by the burgundy-red sail, taut as a drawn bow, speeding us over the surface of the sea. Through the rushing of the waves on the other side of the sail I could hear a furious cackling and again a clear cock-crow. Of course, it was our own poultry in the big chicken coop forward. Relieved, I crawled out, clad only in my underpants. Outside the air was icy and Yuri was sitting on the deck of the bridge, wrapped up like an Eskimo, writing notes.

We must be far out at sea by now, because there was a biting north wind with chaotic wave crests leaping ten to twelve feet above the troughs, and even from the masthead the horizon showed only an undulating transition between sky and sea at all points of the compass.

'Where are we?' asked Yuri.

'Here,' I replied, falling into the cabin over the navigator, who lay sprawled as if unconscious, while pills and germs raced round inside him. Only he knew how to use a sextant. I only knew how to drift about on a log raft. Heaven knew where we were. What I needed was a sweater and a windcheater. An extraordinarily cheerful whistle cut through the orchestra of creaks and the roar of the waves, from the narrow passage between sail and cabin. Carlo's ruddy, bearded face appeared behind the bamboo wall.

'Grub's up! Hot *karkadé* tea à la Nefertiti, and mummy-bread-and-honey Tutankhamen!'

Abdullah woke up in the cabin and shook his African neighbour Georges awake. Ravenously we swarmed round Carlo, who had served breakfast on the lid of the chicken coop, and every man found himself a big jar, a potato sack or a water-filled goatskin container to sit on. We would get the deck tidy and make life comfortable gradually, as soon as we had mastered the steering gear.

'Where are we?' asked Georges.

'Here,' Yuri replied, on his way to the patients with two hot cups of *karkadé*.

'Africa is still there,' I added, waving a hand over to port. 'Is there anything else you want to know?'

'Yes,' said Georges. 'How did the old boys in the past find their position at sea without sextant or compass?'

'They could work out east and west by looking at the sun,' explained Carlo, 'and north and south from the Pole Star and the Southern Cross.'

'And they could get the latitude by measuring the angle from the horizon to the Pole Star,' I added. 'It's always at 90° to the North Pole and it's right down touching the horizon if you are looking from the equator. If you are at 60° north, the Pole Star is 60° above the horizon and if you are at 32°, it is 32°. If you can see the Pole Star you can read your latitude directly from it. The Phoenicians, Polynesians and Vikings could only make a rough guess at the longitude by calculating the distance according to their speed, and the invisible ocean current was always an uncertain factor once they had no land-sighting.'

In the Egyptian museum back home in Cairo Georges had seen his countrymen's instruments, many thousands of years old, for measuring the angles of the celestial bodies, and he knew how important both the sun and the Pole Star were in all their calculations, both astrological and architectural. I decided to concoct some sort of home-made instrument, so that without any special nautical skills we could at least check our own latitude. We could always see our direction from the sun and the moon and the best-known constellations.

The red Egyptian *karkadé* tasted like hot cherry juice and was both refreshing and stimulating. The Egyptian bread-biscuits looked like flattened buns. They were crisp and so tasty that, with or without honey, none of us had eaten better travelling rations. In good heart for a new day, we all went in and exchanged good wishes with the two brave patients in the cabin. Norman was really ill, but both his and Santiago's morale was first class. Santiago's problem was that the degree of damp on *Ra*, barely two hands' breadths above sea level, made all our clothes, sleeping bags and blankets sticky with salt sea air and his skin was being constantly chafed, so that the slightest movement hurt him. Yuri had his hands full with the two of them. Ill as they were, it must have been quite a strain to lie idle and listen to the heart-stopping, deafening bangs, squeals, creaks, and snorts which every single big wave forced out of the papyrus bundles, as they bent, buckled and stretched again in their many ropes. From time to time it sounded as if a hundred thousand Sunday editions of the *New York Times* were being torn to shreds under the heaving boxes on which Norman was sleeping. Sixteen wooden boxes were stacked on the wickerwork floor of the cabin, two under each man, with straw mattresses on top, and two spare boxes were reversed for Norman's radio and navigating equipment. As the papyrus undulated like a banana skin on the waves, the flexible cabin floor followed the movement, and with it, too, the boxes and straw mattresses, the vertebrae and back, if not the shoulder and hip, of the man on top, according to whether he chose to lie on his back or on his side. It was like sleeping on the back of a live sea-serpent.

Out on deck this sinuous action of *Ra* was no less obvious. If one stood aft looking along the deck one saw the yellow railing billowing companionably with the masses of water below, and if one stretched to catch a glimpse of the high, pointed bow forward of the sail, both it and the foredeck rose with rhythmic restraint, as if to take a look over the wave crests, and in the next breath plunged down so steeply that the tip of the bow was barely visible above the hen coop. The whole of *Ra* was like a great, puffing sea monster, swimming with long undulations and snarling, snorting and bellowing to scare any reefs or obstacles out of its way. The oddest thing was the straddled mast with the big sail. It was like a huge distended dorsal fin, moving to and fro in time with the movement of *Ra*'s big round muscle bundles. One moment there was a good three feet between it and the cabin wall where Carlo had stacked the cooking boxes; the next the distance had closed so much that one had to watch out in order not to get one's toes caught under the cabin floor or the foot of the mast. Mast, cabin and steering bridge were all simply lashed to the flexible deck with rope and were therefore allowed considerable mutual play. Had this not been so, we would not have survived the first day. Had we not followed all the ancient rules, had we hammered the bridge together with nails, made the cabin of rigid planks or secured the mast to the papyrus with steel cable instead of rope, we would have been splintered, sawn and ripped to shreds by the very first seas. It was the suppleness and flexibility of every part which ensured that the sea practically never had a chance to snap the yielding papyrus fibres. All the same, it was quite a shock on the first day when carpenter Abdullah took out his measure and showed us that the deck of the steering bridge sometimes gaped a full eight inches from the back wall of the cabin, while at others they were squeezed so tightly together that to have a finger caught between would have been disastrous. It was vital to keep really alert and have an eye on every finger until we were thoroughly at home on board. But we looked forward with some misgiving to the probable behaviour of our paper boat in a few weeks' time when it was already so elastic and loose-jointed on the second day at sea.

From experience of the *Kon-Tiki* I already knew before we set out that the most dangerous threat to raft voyagers was to have a man overboard. We could not go about and sail into the wind, at least not with our present lack of experience. A good swimmer could not catch up with us at the speed we were moving. We had a huge case containing a six-man life raft of foam rubber lashed fast between the legs of the steering platform, aft, but that was only for use in extreme emergency and could not be launched without cutting away the whole steering bridge. An axe hung ready for that purpose. But even the rectangular life-raft, if launched, would have no chance of overtaking *Ra* and we would drift separately. So rule number one was: stay on board. Never move from one place to another without your own rope's end ready for immediate attachment. Carlo Mauri had made each of us a six-foot life-line with a hook on it, and we always had this rope tied round our bodies, with the hook ready to be slipped over rope lashings, mast stays or the woodwork of the bridge, as soon as we moved outside the cabin.

I stuck to this rule to the point of absurdity, regardless of the weather, and told them about Herman Watzinger, who had only just been saved by Knut Haugland when he fell overboard from *Kon-Tiki*. Georges the diving champion and Abdullah the Central African had difficulty in understanding that it was not enough for them to be roped up only when alone on nightwatch, or hanging over the cross-bar aft, answering the call of nature. Georges finally took the order to heart when he realized it was important to me, but every other day I continued to find Abdullah singing happily on the very edge of the papyrus roll, with his lifeline hanging down like a monkey's tail. Finally I went for him.

'Abdullah,' I said. 'This water is bigger than the whole of Africa and a thousand times as deep as Lake Chad where Georges can dive to the bottom.'

'*Ah, oui*,' said Abdullah, impressed.

'And it is full of fish which eat men. They are bigger than crocodiles and swim twice as fast.'

'*Ah, oui*,' repeated the receptive Abdullah, always grateful for new knowledge.

'But don't you understand that if you fall overboard you will drown, you will be eaten, you will not see America?'

A broad and fatherly smile spread over Abdullah's face and he placed a huge hand kindly on my shoulder.

'You don't understand,' he said. 'Look here!'

He pulled up his thick pullover and revealed a well-filled black stomach. Round it was tied a thick piece of twine, and from the twine three small leather pouches hung against the small of his back.

'With these, nothing can happen to me,' he assured me. He had been given the pouches by his father and they had been filled by a medicine man at home in Chad. Judging by others I had seen on sale in the market place in Bol they contained leopard claws, dyed pebbles, seeds and dry scraps of plant. Abdullah pulled the jersey down again conspiratorially and nodded in triumph. Was my mind at rest now? Nothing *could* happen to Abdullah. But to please me he too agreed to rope himself up.

Abdullah's first shock came when early in the morning he rushed to tell me that salt had got into the water. Into all of it. How had it happened? I, too, was seriously alarmed and asked him which jars he had tried.

'Not a jar. There!' said Abdullah, shaken, and pointed out to sea. He had never realized that the ocean was salt. When I explained that it was salt all the way from Africa to America he asked wide-eyed where all that costly salt had come from. After the geological explanation he was in despair. Santiago had said we must be economical with our drinking water on board; we could only have one litre, or about a pint and three-quarters per man per day. Abdullah said he would need at least five times as much, because as a Moslem he had to wash arms and legs, head and face every single time he prayed. He prayed five times a day!

'You can use sea water for your prayers,' I assured him. But Abdullah could not. According to his religion, pure water must be used for the washing ceremony. There was salt in this water.

Before the problem of the salt was solved Abdullah had another fright. Georges had pulled the sleepy baby monkey, Safi, out of her bed in a perforated cardboard suitcase where she had spent the night, and in her excitement the little lady had made a tiny pool on Abdullah's mattress. Now Abdullah was really beside himself. Had the monkey done this? If a dog or monkey performed on a believer's clothes he could not pray to Allah for forty days! Abdullah began to roll his eyes in utter desperation. Forty days without Allah!

Georges settled Abdullah's moral scruples with a white lie. It was not the monkey, it was sea spray. Practical wishful thinking made Abdullah accept the explanation without poking his nose further into the slightly odorous problem. I decreed that in any case the monkey must begin to wear trousers and in addition must never again be allowed to sit on Abdullah's mattress.

'Abdullah,' I added, 'you who need pure water for your prayers, have you ever thought how many monkeys and dogs live round all the water sources in Chad? Out here there isn't a dog for miles around and the little that Safi produces we leave behind us. There is nowhere in the world where you can find purer water than at sea.'

Abdullah listened and thought. A moment later he was subjecting to lengthy scrutiny a canvas bucket of sea water. Then the ceremonial washing began, at breakneck speed and with the graceful dexterity of a conjuror. After that Abdullah went up to the compass, where Yuri helped him to find the approximate direction of Mecca. With the candour of a convinced monk he knelt on his own mattress in the cabin opening and bowed repeatedly towards the east with his forehead to the mattress cover. Then he took out his long string of beads and began to reel off prayers. The prayers ran along the string of beads like peas out of a sack, but Abdullah's spirit was so genuine that all of us, whether Copt or Catholic or Protestant, natural philosopher or atheist, had to respect his steadfast conviction.

The wind was increasing in strength. It became almost violent. Without steering-oars we had no control of the craft whatsoever, but *Ra* still chased along in a seemingly perfect direction. Abdullah, now feeling clean inside and out, joined me on the bridge with knife and drill. We had to find some way of lashing the broken oar-blades back to their shafts. Abdullah was in high spirits, humming Central African jungle tunes while struggling to keep on his feet with his long tunic catching the gusts of wind. Carlo joined us with his alpine knot-craft and we had almost repaired the first oar when the wind became really bad. A couple of powerful gusts from different directions suddenly took the sail aback and it twisted before we had a chance to readjust the sheets and tacks.

A head wind now flung itself with all its strength against the big sail. While the heavy yard, twenty-three feet long, from which the sail hung, crashed so violently against the top of the straddled mast that the wood at the top threatened to break, the whole of the big mainsail flapped in savage jerks, threatening to split itself against the mast. It overturned fruit baskets and caught on the chicken coop, making the poultry cackle and squawk to rival our shouted orders. A square provision basket was suddenly bobbing about on its own in our wake. No one knew what was in it, because quartermaster Santiago was lying in bed with his inventory. Yuri almost had to hold him and Norman down in their bunks by force while I clambered on to the bridge and tried to lead the battle against the giant sail. A man's voice was faint in the stormy gusts which flung it out over the foaming wave-tops, together with the flaps, bangs and screeches from sail and papyrus bundles.

It was no good trying to lower the sail now; it would fly out to sea like a kite. We must get the vessel back on course, partly by turning the sail and partly by turning the hull. Big Georges, with an ordinary oar braced against the papyrus where it rose aft like a tail, was set to row *Ra*'s stern section up into the wind. An umbrella-shaped canvas sea anchor was slung overboard on a long rope; nothing is more effective in reducing speed and keeping the stern to the wind. On the bridge I saw the compass needle turning slowly while I fought desperately to hang on without being pushed overboard by a sheet which jerked and lashed out like a whip as I tried to secure it to the side of the bridge, making sure at the same time that the meagre crew was also secured and assigned to hauling on the right ropes. In the gusts of wind I bawled orders in Italian to Carlo, in English to Yuri, in French to Abdullah and in English, French or Italian, just as it came, to Georges, but the truth was that I did not even know the names in my own mother tongue of the ropes I was asking them to haul on, so my admiration for the powers of comprehension of this international team of landlubbers reached a peak as the day passed.

When we had salvaged the precious sail, fastened the sheets, bound all our ordinary rowing oars like Indian *guara* to the side of the ship fore and aft and hauled the sea anchor in again, everything went peacefully, as before. We had a little breathing space in which I tried to invent some short words which everyone could understand when it was vital to save seconds, should anything of the sort happen again. Through the gaps in the bamboo trellis we could hear from time to time, between the powerful gusts of wind, weak-voiced fragments of good advice emanating from the feverish Norman. He had done his utmost in advance to teach all the rest of us the English expressions for pulling in, slacking off, or letting go the halyard which hoisted the sail, the tacks controlling each end of the long yard from which the sail hung, and the sheets attached to the sail's two loose bottom corners to port and starboard. But practice had now shown us that, since three of the active men understood either little English or none, the result was always a gamble if one shouted to Yuri or to Carlo: 'Pull in starboard tack!' or to Abdullah: 'Let go port side sheet!'

No sooner were the five of us sitting, panting but triumphant, on the bridge trying to work out a few short practical expressions, Esperanto style, than warning sounds started up again in the mainsail, and although this time everyone was at his post in a flash, sail and craft succeeded in turning round again. This happened time after time, time after time. We drifted farther on the same course, but sidelong, or sometimes even stern foremost, with sail and yard struggling at chaotic angles. We had to make sure the sail was always filled to save the yard from breaking, but sometimes we only succeeded by turning the sail to the wrong side. By turning it round outside the port leg instead of outside the starboard leg of the straddling mast, the sail would willingly fill, but then we automatically sailed almost at right angles to the course we needed in order to keep clear of land. For painfully long periods at a time we headed under full sail straight for the African coast while we rowed, hauled on ropes, wrestled with the sea anchor and tried to lash the rowing oars in different positions, *guara* style, in our efforts to return to the proper course. But without the big rudder-oars the boat absolutely refused to accept any compromise. The sail sent the boat either directly south-east or directly south-west; nothing in between. Every time an unruly gust turned us about, so that we were stuck with *Ra*'s nose pointing south-east, the invisible coast line of Africa came nearer and nearer. Carlo spent his time up at the wildly swinging masthead, but fortunately saw no sign of land. Nevertheless we knew that the coast, which swerved inward south of Safi, bulged out again towards us further down. No sooner had we got control of the sail one way than it twisted the other way and flapped about with such violence that every one of us had to use all his weight and strength in order not to be swept out to sea. One piece of headgear after another flew overboard; the most regretted was Abdullah's rainbow-coloured Moslem cap, which was practically part of Abdullah himself. But now each man was automatically making himself fast every time we changed places. The monkey had her own private little rope and performed rapturous gymnastics upside down on the mast stays, and the poultry were safe in their cage, which was now covered over and made fast out of range of the sail.

During the day the changing wind blew in such mighty gusts that there was constant danger of losing the whole rigging before we regained control of the steering. The sail would have to come down. We had no alternative but to try to lower it in the squalls.

No sooner had two men loosed the halyard, while the other three

97. *A little American yacht* came out from the West Indies to film the last stage of the expedition.
98. *It found Ra* devastated after the last storm, but with the crew of seven men, one monkey and one duck alive and the cargo safe. From the left, Norman, Georges, Yuri, Abdullah, Thor, Carlo and Santiago.
99. *The mast is cut away* by Santiago and Norman. With the ropes chafed through on the windward side, so much papyrus was lost that the heavy straddled mast could no longer support the sail.

stood ready with the sheets to guide the yard and sail down to the deck, than a mighty blast came and swept the heavy mainsail out like a flag over the sea, and Yuri and Abdullah fought desperately to re-capture the loose sheet which fluttered over the wave-tops to port. The other three of us hooked feet and knees round anything we could in order not to be lifted overboard with the starboard sheet – our last chance of preventing the sail from disappearing for ever beneath the waves. There was a frightful creaking from the mast and all the ropes which held it, and the papyrus bundles shrieked and heeled over so that for the first time we had an uneasy feeling that our miracle boat might actually be capable of capsizing. One thing was certain: no other fifty-foot sailing boat in the world could have withstood this gigantic pressure without immediately capsizing, unless the mast had broken first.

Inch by inch we managed to recapture the yard and most of the sail, but large sections of the sail still lay overboard on the combers in folds containing many bathtubfuls of water, and in our struggles to drag this heavy weight free of the sea's hold we knocked off yet another of our precious rowing oars, which disappeared under a wave and bobbed up tantalizingly in our wake.

'See you in America!' Carlo shouted at the oar. 'But we're going faster than you!'

Soaked with sea water and laden with the weight of a yard six feet wider than the whole deck, the sail had to be turned and stowed lengthwise along *Ra*'s port side. Triumphant, but as exhausted as if we had lasted twenty rounds in the ring, the five of us sat on top, trying to restrain this rebellious burgundy-red flying dragon, which was still jerking convulsively as the folds were inflated by the wild gusts. Finally the brute was securely bound.

It was suddenly extraordinarily quiet on board. Only a rhythmic, peaceful creaking made us feel that mother sea had adopted the reed boat *Ra* as a marine cradle full of unruly fellows who must now be rocked to sleep before they hurt themselves by overturning the whole cradle, or colliding with land. *Ra*, stripped to the bare mast, once again set her course as she wished, parallel to land, no longer threatening to run us ashore.

100. *Everything of value* is transferred to the yacht. Georges swims with the mast, the author passes equipment to Santiago in the yacht's rubber dinghy.

I looked at Carlo. He began to smile. He chuckled. Then he began to laugh without restraint. We all stared at him.

'Now we have neither sail nor steering oars. There is nothing left on this craft to obey human orders any more. Nature is in command now. As soon as we stop fighting her, we can just relax and enjoy ourselves.'

We began to look about us. Nothing but peace and order everywhere. No yard, no sail, no engine, no worries: here we were, rocking in a communal papyrus hammock, while the mighty ocean current took us where it liked, and that was just where we wanted to go. Abdullah crawled into the cabin and lay down with his tiny pocket radio against his ear. Georges wanted to fish. Yuri ate an orange and went off with the skin to make a glass of liqueur with surgical spirit, while Carlo began to poke about in sacks and baskets to find the raw material for a better meal. Santiago lay motionless in the cabin with his little inventory and called out the numbers on the jars which contained water, dates, eggs, olives or grain for the hens. I myself took the sheath knife to whittle an instrument which could give us our latitude. Then Norman could not restrain himself any longer.

'This is all very fine, fellows,' he groaned. 'But not for the people at home. We promised to go on the air yesterday. They have to know that everything is OK, otherwise they will think we have gone down.'

Yuri agreed and helped the feverish Norman to roll the mattress away so that they could open the locked case under his legs and pull out the little emergency transmitter with the built-in, hand-operated generator. A little later Safi radio replied clearly to Norman's call and was told that we had broken both rudders, but were continuing across the Atlantic Ocean with no problems. He also warned them that there would be no regular contact in the future, because the oar carrying the earthing plate was broken and lying on the deck. If we dropped it overboard in the seething waves the copper would cut through both rope and papyrus. Norman was so weak that he sank back in his sleeping bag while Yuri packed up the radio and Carlo crawled in with a hot drink.

Georges caught no fish but came into the cabin with an idea. Why not reef the sail? Even a tiny spread of sail in this wind would help us to travel faster. The sail was deliberately sewn in such a way that we could reef and lash either one or two-thirds of it, so that we need only use the top strip of sail if the wind was too strong. I thought this a good idea and Norman nodded feebly. The five of us crawled out on deck again, heartened by a mighty Stone Age lunch based on salt sausage and fresh vegetables. After a desperate struggle we managed to turn the yard with the water-filled sail from the port side so that it lay spread out across the vessel, projecting three feet into the waves on either side. It was difficult to reef the sail in a wind which varied in strength between stiff breeze and light storm, but with our combined efforts all went well, as we lay on top of it while sliding it out over the hencoop and the rest of the cargo, and then rolled it up until only a third of the surface was left unfurled. Great was our triumph when this narrow strip of sail filled with wind at the masthead. With the sea anchor hauled aboard and the small rowing oars bound in place, we skimmed south-westward over the wave-crests, rejoicing in this fresh victory over the elements.

Fifteen minutes passed. It was early afternoon on our second day at sea when a squall struck the sail again. We leaped to the tacks and sheets as one man when we heard the first thud of the heavy, wet roll of sail which now hung bunched together at the masthead and hammered the rigid yard against the mast. The next blow sounded like a scream for help from the masthead, and our hearts contracted as we heard the blow extend into a terrifying crash and a crack which jarred bone and marrow. We looked up and saw the whole, indispensable yard which held the sail outstretched slowly sagging on either side of the central point, while the sail shrank inward, like a bat folding its wings. Sharp splinters of broken wood stuck out of the yard like angry claws. We had to lower the whole conglomeration to prevent the canvas from being ripped to shreds. This was on our second day at sea. Our second day.

No sooner was the corpse of the broken yard and sail lying in a heap on deck than *Ra* became as docile as before and our magic reed rolls continued to undulate in the desired direction like a tame sea serpent with us on its back.

'There you are, you see,' said Carlo, and crawled into bed, gratified.

Abdullah scurried aft and washed himself up to the knees and elbows for his next prayer to Allah. Yuri sat down chuckling with his pipe and diary in the door opening and I sat down beside him with my whittling.

'Everything under control?' asked Santiago, cautiously sticking his nose out of his sleeping bag.

'Everything,' we chorused. 'Everything. Now we have broken everything that can be broken. Now there is only the papyrus left.'

The rest of the afternoon passed peacefully inside the cabin while the storm howled outside. We had not seen a ship, but shared the night watch between us, since we were lying right on the coastal route round Africa. We were constantly shinning up to the masthead on the lookout for a light from land. Collisions with ships and the perilous cliffs on shore were the only things we feared.

Half an hour after midnight I was shaken awake by Carlo, who was leaning over me, holding a paraffin lamp. With wide, anxious eyes he whispered that there were lights all along the horizon on the port bow. We were being driven sidelong by a strong north-wester, straight towards them. I had gone to bed fully dressed and had only to tie on my lifeline before rushing out on deck. A bitingly cold wind of moderate strength, and an overcast sky. Through the pitch-black night I saw all the lights spread out along the horizon. As Carlo said, they lay ahead of us in our line of drift. Four were very large and another faint. It must be the Moroccan coast. Carlo was up at the swaying masthead. We seemed to be approaching fast. The other three rested men were turned out. Now we would have to try to row our reed bundle to save ourselves from a tragic fate on the rocks. Then both Carlo and I thought we glimpsed a green light. Another, and a red one, too. It was not land! A scattered fleet of big fishing smacks was sailing straight towards us! Blue with cold, the crew crawled back to bed. Soon afterwards three big, rolling vessels puttered close past our bows. A fourth lay broadside on to us after stopping its engine so that *Ra* was heading straight for the pitching ship's side. I shone my flashlight on cabin wall and papyrus rolls and blinked '*Ra* OK, *Ra* OK'. The big sea-fishing boat started up again and glided away, so late that we barely avoided a collision. It sent some incomprehensible flashes from the masthead and gradually disappeared in the darkness. Georges stood watch, wrapped up like an Egyptian mummy in wind-jacket and blankets, and I crawled into bed. Even hoarse shrieks from a hundred thousand tethered papyrus reeds were not enough to drown the uninhibited, rapturous humming of the son of the Nile, which the stern wind blew in through the thin wickerwork wall, all that separated our cosy den from the ferocious universe outside.

It was still cloudy when day dawned, the third day on board. The wind was less fierce, but the seas were more agitated than ever. We observed with satisfaction that the waves leaping madly round us simply lifted us into the air. The sea carried us forward at arm's length like a ball and not even the most treacherous breakers managed to pour water on deck. The whole cargo was dry. With neither sail nor rudder, with neither sextant nor position, with no land in sight, the third day was a day of peace, when we managed to finish splicing one steering-oar and reinforced the middle section of a long reserve spar which was to replace the broken yard.

Abdullah was busy washing his smooth-shaven head for prayer when he stopped and uttered a hoarse cry of protest. The sea certainly was not pure! Someone had done his business out there and he had smeared it on his head. In the bottom of Abdullah's canvas bucket large and small black lumps were circulating. We looked overboard. Hundreds of similar clots were floating past us on both sides. Soft, asphalt-like lumps. An hour later they were still floating just as thickly round us. It must be the waste from a tanker. We looked for the miscreant from the masthead, but there was no ship in sight, and the sea continued to be covered with black lumps all day.

Towards afternoon we drifted past a big moonfish which lay idly on the surface and later we were visited by nearly a hundred dolphins which suddenly surged up round us, leaped vertically out of the waves in a cheerful reel, and gave Abdullah indescribable pleasure before disappearing as suddenly as they had arrived.

The fourth day was noticeably warmer and calmer and the sun appeared through rifts in the clouds. For a long time we could clearly see the distant blue silhouette of the mainland rising in a couple of hump-shaped mountains. Santiago was really sick but Norman was much better, with no fever, and Yuri allowed him to crawl out and take the sun's meridian. But since we had no chronometer on board and the emergency radio could no longer pick up Safi radio, we lacked a sufficiently accurate second time to fix a reliable position. This worried the two men in the cabin, because Norman thought that since we could still see the mainland we would not be able to pass outside the Canary Islands. We were drifting into the dangerous passage between Fuerte Ventura and Cape Juby on the African mainland. Santiago, who had lived in the Canary Islands as a boy, could confirm what Norman's reference books showed, that Cape Juby was the terror of all sailors because from the rocks a treacherously low sandbank slid out like a tongue into the most dangerous ocean current, just where the African coast turns south.

We were sitting forward on the heap of sail, eating, when we heard an eager yell from the ever-observant Abdullah, who had already finished his meal and was on his way to the cabin for prayers.

'Horses! Horses!' He corrected himself: 'Hippos!'

We looked where he was pointing and in a moment they came surging up again, two great whales which squinted at us with small indolent eyes and puffed through their blowholes, spouting up a mixture of air and spray. Abdullah had never seen such big hippos in Chad and it made his day. That a mammal could have a fish's tail sounded to him like something out of the 'Thousand and One Nights', but one of the whales raised its tail politely to wave good-bye and Abdullah was dumbfounded at the inventiveness of Allah.

On the fifth day we awoke to a bitingly cold north wind and a violently restless sea. We put on all the clothing we owned and Abdullah's teeth chattered. For five days, breaking seas had been flinging themselves constantly against *Ra's* starboard beam, just as we had calculated, because the whole of our journey would lie in the belt of the north-east trade-winds. For this reason we had built the cabin with the door opening on the opposite, that is the left or port side, which would be in the lee. We had also displaced the cabin and the heavier part of the cargo towards the starboard side so that the wind which filled the big sail from that side would not succeed in capsizing the whole boat. Both we and our advisers were well aware that sailing boats must be loaded with the main weight on the windward side in order not to capsize. By the fifth day bitter experience was beginning to show us that in this respect a papyrus boat runs counter to every other boat in the world. It is the only sailing boat which must be loaded more heavily on the lee side. The reason is that on the windward side the papyrus absorbs many tons of sea water above the water-line, because waves and spray are always washing up over the whole side of the boat, whereas everything above the water-line on the lee-side remains dry and light. The weight of water on the exposed windward side gradually becomes so enormous that the vessel heels over *against* the wind instead of *with* it in the normal way.

It was too late to move the cabin amidships. It was lashed fast with stout rope running crosswise right through the bottom of the papyrus

boat. We moved all loose cargo from starboard to port but that did
not seem to be enough. The rolls above the water-line on the starboard
side must have absorbed several tons of sea water, which now accompanied us on our voyage as an invisible cargo, weighing more than
the few hundred kilos of food and drinking water which we had
managed to transfer to the other side. We were actually sailing in a
vessel which listed chronically to windward.

Norman was now completely restored and while the rest of us
re-stowed the cargo he tried to secure the unruly copper-plate under the
water so that he could make radio contact and thus get an accurate
second time. He had good reason to suspect that we were nearer the
coast than he had estimated without chronometer time yesterday,
and that we were actually drifting straight towards land at Cape
Juby.

During the night a full storm blew up. The wind howled through
all the mast stays and *Ra* seemed to grow more and more dislocated
as the stormy seas flung themselves on us more savagely than before.
We kept double watch all night in order not to be caught unawares
by the sandbanks of Cape Juby, and we kept a close eye on all our ropes.
Not a line had snapped. Not a papyrus reed had worked loose. But the
timber of the bridge ground so violently against the bamboo corner
of the cabin that everything within that corner was covered with an
even powdering of fine sawdust. Santiago was suffering from sleepless-
ness, for at night it was almost impossible to get a wink of sleep unless
one was dead tired, as the boxes heaved about beneath us, while cabin,
bridge and masts swayed out of step, making a din like a thousand
cats stuck with their tails between the ropes. The whole cabin was
also leaning so severely to starboard that no one could lie on his side
without rolling over. The others lay four in a row, but we were three
because the radio and navigation corner was on our side. Abdullah
was always rolling down on Georges who rolled down on Santiago,
until Yuri, who was at the bottom of the slope, received the others
with knees and arms because the wall would not allow him to roll
further. I had bundled all my extra clothing under the starboard edge
of the mattress and Carlo had done the same, so that we did not roll
down on to Norman and the radio corner.

The storm continued to rage all night, with waves twelve to fifteen
feet high, which in the gusts sent a fine salt spray over the boat. During
the morning of the seventh day *Ra* seemed, oddly enough, to become

a little less disjointed; the ropes seemed to be tauter. The crest of an enormous, towering sea, which quite inexplicably broke over us aft and buried Norman to the waist, had difficulty in running out through the papyrus. The sea spray on the deck and the moisture from below had apparently made the papyrus reeds swell to bursting point until they filled all the ropes and all the interstices. So the vessel seemed more rigid and robust than before; it was just unfortunate that she listed so badly to starboard.

We were all filled with admiration at the splendid way in which *Ra* rode out the storm, when Norman announced that we were heading for the rocks. We had a choice between trying to hoist the sail in the powerful north wind or drifting straight towards land. We agreed unanimously to try to hoist the sail, two-thirds spread, on the newly reinforced yard. Even Santiago came staggering out, and with the whole crew in action we got the sail up and the one spliced rudder-oar out into the water astern. We skimmed like a flying fish over the crests, away from land. Soon afterwards we heard another crack; the thick shaft of the spliced rudder-oar snapped like a matchstick and we could only haul the blade on board again. But the landlubbers had been gradually turning into a team of seamen. In one tiger-spring Abdullah was there, grasping the port-side corner of the flapping sail. Santiago crawled out and hooked himself fast beside him. Carlo and Yuri vanished without a word behind the cabin on the starboard side and slackened the sheets. Georges, clad only in his underpants, grasped one oar and rowed the stern up into the wind while Norman and I adjusted the small vertical oars, until *Ra*, with no helmsman, was pitching over the wave crests again like a weighty fish. So we held our course for the rest of the day, without a single reed being damaged by the

101. *The starboard side* had not enough papyrus left to keep the cabin above water and numbers of sharks put a stop to all further repairs. Norman and Georges salvage the mainsail.

102. *The port side* was undamaged and still afloat with the whole cargo. Norman and the author on board, Georges in the yacht's rubber dinghy.

103 and 104. *Farewell Ra, see you later.* Norman, Santiago and Georges hoist a small sail on two oars on the storm-racked vessel, which sails the last leg of the voyage west alone. The reed bundles had carried us 5,000 kilometres in 8 weeks. Inset, from left, Yuri, Santiago, Carlo, the author with monkey, Norman, Abdullah, and Georges with duck.

storm. It was the thick wooden parts outboard, not the thin reeds of the hull, which presented us with problems.

Next night the storm died down, but not the seas, which were running up to eighteen or twenty feet high. The cabin, no longer symmetrical, was leaning to windward like a tip-tilted hat. I crawled out on deck in the darkness before my own night watch to take a look over the whole vessel. When I crawled under the sail to get a clear view ahead, my heart almost stopped beating. On the starboard bow was a tall, broad lighthouse, illuminated with coloured lamps and surrounded with a multitude of other lights. We were steering to the left of the whole immobile complex and accordingly heading straight for land. This lighthouse, which lay so far out, could only be Cape Juby.

With feverish haste we began turning the sail to alter course as best we could without rudder-oars. This was not enough; we just began to lose leeway and continued to approach land to the left of all the lights. With pounding hearts we quickly realized that we could not pass outside, that we were racing blindly towards the invisible rocks. It struck us at the last minute that the lights were rocking slightly, as if tower and houses were built on a floating pier rather than on sandbanks. Then we rushed past on the inside: the complex was detached from land. It proved to be a huge oil-drilling platform anchored off the African coast, lighted to the top with coloured lamps to prevent collision with ships and aircraft. We just stood and stared. Then I yelled brusquely to Georges, who stood shivering, holding the little oar. Why the devil did he not put on some clothes or get back into his sleeping-bag before we had another man sick in bed!

On the seventh day we still had two-thirds of the reefed mainsail hoisted and seemed to be sailing in competition with high, surging swells travelling the same way as ourselves. Heavy banks of cloud were rolling up from both sides of *Ra*, but straight ahead there was a rift of blue sky between the two fronts. It all indicated that the Canary Islands and the African continent each lay hidden beneath one of the dense cloudbanks, and the blue strip of sky arched above the open

105. *Thanks for the ride,* Ra. You proved that even landlubbers can sail thousands of sea miles on papyrus bundles. You also proved that men from east and west and north and south can live and work together for the common good, even when they are short of space.

stretch of sea between them. *Ra* willingly allowed herself to be steered towards the blue. Yuri's medical skill had got both Norman and Santiago on their feet again, but Georges was temporarily sent to bed with severe back pains after straining himself with the oar, half-naked in the ice-cold night wind.

About noon, Carlo was busy hauling on ropes which might succeed in bending the basket cabin on to a more even keel. Standing on the bridge, I thought to my horror that I could see low green grassland through the telescope every time we were lifted particularly high on a wave-crest. A moment later Carlo was at the masthead with Norman at his heels. They called down that there was an uninhabited green slope running parallel to our own course, six sea miles away, at most, and perhaps even closer. We altered course as much as we possibly could. Soon the grassland disappeared from view. It must have been the low banks surrounding Cape Juby, where the coast swung southward. It must have been the last corner of Africa which we had put behind us, for there was no more land to be seen.

Carlo was going to propose our first big feast, so Abdullah slaughtered three fowls over the rudder bar. Yuri's liqueur was ready. There was a lot to celebrate. First we would drink a funeral draught to the *iroco* tree. It was much too brittle for steering oars. Then we would drain a beaker to the papyrus reed. What a phenomenal boat-building material! It was now May 31st and the papyrus had been in the water for a fortnight without rotting and without disintegrating. On the contrary, it was stronger and more pliant than ever. Not a single reed had been lost. We had been sailing for a week from Safi to Cape Juby, farther than from the Nile estuary to Byblos in the Phoenician kingdom. As far as from Egypt to Turkey. So we had already proved that the Egyptians could have delivered their own papyrus wherever they liked on the coast of Asia Minor without the help of foreign wooden ships.

Skål, Norman. *Skål*, Yuri. *Skål*, you fellows. *Skål* to Neptune and to all Abdullah's hippos. Safi sat between us on the hencoop, drinking from a freshly opened coconut.

Then I heard someone babbling about 'white houses' and leapt to my feet to look. Georges was lying on his stomach in the cabin opening, pointing inland to where we had seen the low banks disappearing. Now they had reappeared, this time carrying rows of small white houses. A typical North African Arab village. To the right of all the houses lay a picturesque old fort. Here it was, Cape Juby. We had been celebrating while in the greatest danger. We were gliding past the treacherous spit of land which had haunted our thoughts for a whole week and had claimed so many wrecks over the centuries. For a week we had been struggling to steer away from land, and here we were, passing within gunshot of Cape Juby on the current.

The white houses sank into the sea as quickly as they had appeared. We were drifting fast. Good-bye, Africa. Good-bye, Old World. We have no rudder. We don't need one on this voyage.

A big gull came out and landed on the upright papyrus bundle in the bows. It was chased off by the duck, which was taking an airing outside the hencoop. The gull took off. Soon afterwards we were surrounded by a whole flock of screaming seabirds, while the hens cackled in their cage which served as our dining-table.

'I know what that first gull flew off to tell the others,' said Carlo. 'It said it had found a floating bird's nest off Cape Juby.'

CHAPTER 9

The Sea Takes Over

THE CANARY ISLANDS were behind us. In eight days we had sailed the same distance as across the North Sea from Norway to England. A vessel which does not lose its battle with the seas on such a long voyage is usually regarded as a 'sea-going' craft. Despite broken rudder-oars and yard, despite the maltreatment of inexperienced, non-Egyptian landlubbers, and despite storm and waves, *Ra* was as buoyant as ever. The whole cargo still lay safely out of reach of the ocean. We sailed on in high seas which had little in common with the serene waters of the Nile.

We had passed the Canary Islands in a drizzle without catching sight of land. Now that the sky arched blue over our heads we could see the flat, low carpet of cloud, lying along the African Gold Coast, which marked the position of the continent to port. The position of the Canary Islands off the starboard quarter was clearly marked by the invisible volcanic cone of Teide on Tenerife, 12,000 feet high, which sent passing humidity up into cooler altitudes, where it condensed into a succession of little puffs of cloud which the wind carried out over the sea like the ribbon of smoke from a big steamer.

Abdullah, who knew no islands other than the flat ones floating on Lake Chad, was alarmed when he heard that there were islands out here in the fierce seas, with men living on them. He wanted to know if they were black like himself, or white like us. Santiago, who had lived on the Canary Islands and was also an anthropologist, told us about the mysterious *guanches* who were living on these distant islands when the Europeans 'discovered' them, some generations before they sailed further and 'discovered' America. Some of these original tribes on the Canary Islands were dark and rather short in stature, while others were tall and fair, with blue eyes, blond hair and aquiline noses. A pastel drawing from the Canary Islands of 1590 shows a group of such *guanches* with full golden beards, all fair, with long, yellow hair hanging in soft waves down their backs. Santiago could also tell us about a full-blooded, fair-haired *guanche* whom he had known personally when he was up at Oxford. This *guanche* was a mummy brought from the Canary Islands. The original population of the Canaries had practised both mummification and cranial trepanning, just as they had done in ancient Egypt. The fact that the fair *guanches* resembled Vikings rather than the races generally associated with Africa has led to endless speculation about prehistoric Scandinavian colonization, and even to theories that the Canary Islands are the remains of the lost Atlantis. But mummification and skull trepanning were never practised in ancient Europe. These and many other cultural features link the *guanches* with the ancient cultures of the North African coast. The indigenous population of Morocco, collectively referred to as the Berbers, whom the Arabs forced southward into the Atlas mountains over a thousand years ago, was just such a mixed race as the *guanches*, some short and dark-skinned, others tall, fair, and blond, with blue eyes. Fairly pure descendants of both these Berber types are common in isolated Moroccan villages to this very day.

We looked at the puffs of cloud from the sky-scraping but docile volcanic cone on the Canary Islands. In clear weather the peak itself could be seen from the Moroccan coast. There was no need to go to Scandinavia or dive to the Atlantic seabed to find the homeland of the *guanches*. They could quite simply have originated in the indigenous population of the nearest continent, who in ancient times had succeeded in crossing the same stretch of sea which we ourselves had now cut across in our reed boat.

The real mystery of the *guanches* on the Canary Islands was not so much who they were as how they got there. When the Europeans found them, some generations before Columbus, they owned no boats of any sort, not even log rafts or canoes. And there were large trees growing on the Canary Islands, so they were not short of timber. Both the dark and the fair *guanches* were typical farmers, who bred sheep. They had managed to bring live sheep with them from Africa to the islands. To leave the African coast with women and live sheep on board, you must also be either a sailor or a fisherman, at all events not just a herdsman. Why had the *guanches* then forgotten the boats of their seafaring forefathers? Could it be because their forefathers knew no boats other than the sail-carrying reed boats, *madia*, which have survived on the north coast of Morocco to the present day? A boat-builder who only knew how to build reed-ships and had never learned the principle of joining flat planks together to form a hollow, water-tight hull, would be left helpless and shipless on the beach when his own reed boat decayed with age if no papyrus or other floating reeds grew on the island where he had landed.

Ra suddenly began to pitch and complain so violently that we had to forget the *guanches* and rush to the sail, which was beginning to flap. The wind had not changed, but a series of waves had caught up with us which grew more and more tempestuous, with deeper and deeper troughs into which we sank, and higher and higher wave-crests which threw themselves after us from on high, but never broke over us because our golden paper swan simply raised her tall tail daintily and let the seas slip under us as quickly as they came. Abdullah had a headache and could not keep his food down. Yuri suspected sea-sickness, although Abdullah had shown no symptoms until now. He sent Abdullah to bed with dry Egyptian 'mummy' biscuits, while Santiago was allowed to come out on deck with the rest of us, for Yuri had now succeeded in making his skin grow. Norman was in tremendous form, and we were sitting round the hencoop, enjoying Carlo's hot risotto with almonds and dried fruit, when someone shouted, 'Look up!' Startled, we all looked up, and almost ran for our lives as a gigantic comber came reeling towards us, high above the cabin roof. Then it dwindled into a little drift of foam which trickled, sputtering, under our reed bundles while we stared down into a deep wave valley. More waves of the same type followed. When the sea behaves in this way for no apparent reason, it is usually off an estuary, where the waves are forced higher and higher by a strong current. We must have entered an area where the strong ocean current from Portugal had been intensified by compression as it passed the narrow straits between the largest of the Canary Islands. So we travelled still more briskly on our chosen course. This was the Canary current itself, running towards the Gulf of Mexico.

Up, up, up, and down into the depths. Abdullah was asleep and missed the five great cachalot whales which surged up right alongside the papyrus and sank before Carlo could reach for his camera. Up, and deep, deep, deep down. Then some piece of timber creaked and cracked again. Another of our small rowing oars had been reduced to matchwood, for only a stump of shaft was left hanging outside the papyrus rolls. Even the small oars were beginning to be in short supply.

Something had to be done. Should we try to steer in to the Cape Verde Islands and get some stronger wood? A unanimous 'No'. But we carried with us as cargo a strong square reserve mast of Egyptian *cenebar* wood. So far the masts had not broken; they had even weathered the storm. So we would probably never need the spare mast, and we bound it instead as reinforcement to the thick, round *iroco* shaft of the hitherto unbroken spare rudder-oar, which we had been keeping in reserve. The result was a rudder-oar so thick and heavy that all seven of us had to lend a hand in order to lift it when it was ready to be lowered into the waves late at night. There was a full moon and the stars were glittering. Running seas came chasing after us, shimmering, high, fierce and black, but they did not frighten us, for they never got the upper hand of the papyrus. It was only timber which the seas hated and destroyed as quickly as we pushed it over the side. Only as long as it lay unused on deck was the wood left in peace, together with 160 fragile ceramic jars and all the rest of the cargo. But now the giant oar must go out and do battle with the sea.

Santiago and I took our places on the steering bridge, where we held on to the end of the twenty-five foot oar-shaft which had to be made fast up at our level, while all the others stood down on the papyrus deck, hanging on to the big, heavy oar-blade. It had to be pushed out into the waves and then made fast with its neck section resting on the port-side end of the thick cross-beam which projected on either side of the afterdeck.

Sea and papyrus were tossing wildly when the order was given and the giant oar pushed out. A mighty wave rose at once and lifted the blade out of the hands of the five who were trying with every ounce of strength in their bodies to secure the thick ropes which were to hold it in place. On the bridge Santiago and I barely managed to cling to the upper, narrow part of the shaft which was to be bound to the solid guard-rail of the bridge. But as the wave hissed beneath us and passed amidships, a gap opened under *Ra*'s stern and the runaway rudder-oar slammed down with all its weight against the end of the cross-beam. It was like a colossal sledge-hammer whirling down on an anvil. The next wave lifted it again for a second blow; the five men below fought desperately to recapture the rogue hammer with lasso-loops and bare hands, while Santiago and I were tossed up and down like helpless, weightless puppets, unable to do anything but guide the thin end into position every time the oar floated, when its weight was not intolerable. When the wave-troughs allowed the full weight of the oar-blade to fall, the two of us on the bridge were flicked into the air, while the five men on deck slung all their ropes round the throat of the blade in unsuccessful attempts to fasten it to the cross-beam before the next wave tore it out of their hands and sent the oar up, and us, on the other end of the see-saw, rushing down again. We came down so hard and fast that our fingers and feet would have been crushed had they been in the way when the oar-shaft smashed into the guard-rail round which we were trying to hook our legs to prevent ourselves and the oar from disappearing overboard. So frenzied were the undisciplined antics of the leaden rudder-oar that we all soon realized we might have to let it go before it hammered the cross-bar aft to pieces, and with it all the ropes which held the papyrus together.

But the thought of being reduced to a haystack drifting helplessly sideways to America gave us the extra reserves of strength of wild animals, and before we knew what had happened the oar had fallen into a lucky position enabling all seven of us to catch it in the ropes at the same instant. We got the monster tethered to *Ra* top and bottom with rope cables so thick that the seas could not shift them. This meant that once again we had one of old Egypt's two rudder-oars in position astern. The shaft was shapelessly thick and awkward and rotated badly because it was spliced to a square mast, but it was so strong that when the waves tried to snap it off the whole papyrus boat would twist before the shaft broke.

Santiago said it had been the toughest job of his life. Yuri treated a couple of us for minor finger injuries, but that great hefty rudder-oar kept us on such a steady course that we were able to crawl exhausted to bed and share a comfortable night watch between us. The watch had only to look out for ships which might run us down. The moon, the constellations and for once the constant direction of the straight lines of frothing wave-tops showed the night watch that the course was steady. He sat enjoying himself in the warmth of the cabin-opening on the lee side and only when the watch changed did we crawl up to the bridge to take a look at the little man-made compass. But we soon learned that the starry sky above our heads served as a giant compass with its bright round disc turned downwards. We were heading due west. We did not bother our heads too much about where we were going. At all events it was now away from land.

For three days we sailed with no problems, while we repaired the other rudder-oar with patched-up bits of two different broken shafts. No spikes or nails were used. All the joints were made of rope, otherwise the wood would have splintered at once. The powerful running seas continued, drenching the windward side of *Ra* so that the papyrus rolls became still wetter, right up to the railing, and weighed the exposed beam deeper and deeper into the water. As long as the seas were running so high we were not going to risk putting out the other repaired rudder-oar, but we kept it ready in case the one strengthened with the spare mast should break, for now and then it bent ominously in its worst encounters with the sea. On the other hand, we did risk setting the full sail, and that went well. The wind was from the north and bitterly cold, although we could still glimpse the low sky ceiling along the coast of the Spanish Sahara. As far as possible we re-stowed the cargo on the port, or lee side, which was as high above the water as when we set out. Under full sail our heavy, broad reed bundle picked up speed again and moved westward at a steady rate of about 60 nautical miles in 24 hours, or 2.5 knots, and we could clearly see our own wake behind us. After eleven days' sailing we had covered 557 sea miles, or more than a thousand kilometres as the crow flies, and we had to put our watches back an hour.

For two days, ships had been constantly appearing round us. Once we could see three big ocean-travellers at the same time. We must be on the Great Circle route round Africa. The brightest of our paraffin lamps had to be hung at the masthead to avoid collisions at night. But soon the sea was empty of human voyagers and only schools of dolphins danced about us, some so near that we could have patted them. One or two lethargic moonfish drifted past, and the first flying-fish began to shoot up under our bows. The sky was empty of living things. Only the occasional lost insect blew aboard and a pair of small petrels flew in rapid darts between the wave-troughs. This little seabird sleeps on the water, because it floats over the highest seas as lightly as papyrus. In the last few days masses of small brown beetles had begun to creep out of holes in the papyrus and we only hoped that the sea water would kill off eggs and larvae so that we would not be eaten away from within. The sceptics who had seen the camels trying to eat the side of our boat had prophesied that the reed might well be fodder for hungry marine creatures. Up to now neither whale nor fish had tried to feed off our floating sheaf, but we were not at all happy about these emerging swarms of little beetles.

Sun and moon rolled westward in turn to show us the way. The lonely night watches gave us in full measure that timeless perception of eternity that I had experienced on *Kon-Tiki*. Stars and night-black water. The immutable constellations sparkled above us, and just as brightly beneath us the shining phosphorescence glittered: the living plankton glowed like sparks of neon on the soft dark carpet on which we were floating. With the sparkling plankton beneath us we often seemed to be riding under the night sky on a billowing mirror, or perhaps the sea was crystal-clear and bottomless, so that we could see right through it to myriads of stars on the other side of the universe. The only thing that was firm and near in these omnipresent stellar heavens was the supple bundle of golden reeds on which we rode, and the big, square sail which stood like a shadow against the stars, broader above, by the yard arm, than across the bottom, near the deck. This ancient Egyptian outline of the trapeze-shaped mainsail in the night was enough in itself to turn the calendar back thousands of years. Silhouettes of sails like these are not seen against the sky of today. Strange squeaks and snorts from papyrus, bamboo, wood and rope did the rest. We were not living in the age of the atom bomb and the rocket. We were living at a time when the earth was still large and flat and full of unknown seas and continents, when time was the common prerogative and no one was short of it.

Stiff, but fitter from the struggle which now lay behind us, we changed watches by the meagre light of paraffin lamps swaying above our undulating vegetable deck. It was unspeakably good to crawl to rest in a warm sleeping-bag. You woke up with such an infernally good appetite. You felt an extraordinary physical well-being. Small pleasures grew big; big problems felt small. The Stone Age life was certainly not to be despised. There was no reason to believe that people who lived before us, and had to make vigorous use of their bodies, merely had a hard time and did not receive their due share of life's joys.

Westward progress of over one hundred kilometres (or nearly sixty nautical miles) could be plotted on the chart every day, even though the horizon never changed. The border line between sea and sky was the same every day and at all times of day. The horizon moved with us and we were always its focal point. But the masses of water also moved invisibly with us. The Canary current was a fast-moving, salt-water river flowing towards the setting sun, keeping eternal company with the trade-wind, westward, westward, air and water and all that floats and blows. Westward with sun and moon.

Norman and I stood together on the bridge, he with a regular sextant, I with a 'nasometer'. 'Nasometer' was Yuri's approved designation for a home-made instrument I had carved from two flat pieces of wood, to measure the latitude. They were joined to a little wooden block which was cut in a curve so that it fitted against the nose, hence the name. With the block exactly at eye level, the idea was to look along the upper surface of one piece of wood with the left eye and hold it so that it pointed exactly towards the horizon. The other flat piece was attached to the same block with a leather hinge and was supposed to be tipped up under the right eye so that it pointed exactly to the Pole Star. The angle between the two pieces could be read directly off a disc placed on edge between them, and this angle represented our latitude without any further calculation. This extremely primitive 'nasometer' appealed to everyone's sense of humour because it was so incredibly simple and quick to use, and moreover seldom resulted in an error of more than one degree. This was close enough to enable us to make a chart of our daily position which was amazingly close to the correct version marked off on another chart by Norman.

We gradually began to learn interesting lessons from our testing of the papyrus boat. The slanted rudder-oars had been the first to disclose their secrets, showing themselves to be a missing link in the evolution of man's earliest steering mechanism from oar to rudder. Next the wash-through bundle-body of the raft-ship itself began to reveal its true qualities. In addition to an almost unbelievable loading capacity the papyrus reeds possessed both a toughness in rough seas and an enduring buoyancy which quite contradicted the preconceived verdict of modern man. Yet it was the rigging that revealed the most significant secrets about this ancient vessel's forgotten history, showing that it had been originally developed as something more than a mere river craft. In the design we followed, Landström had copied all the details of mast and rigging from the ancient Egyptian wall paintings. A strong rope ran from the masthead to the bow of the boat. But no corresponding rope ran from masthead to stern, although one rope forward and one aft would have been the logical requirement to hold the straddled mast erect on a river boat in calm waters. The ancient Egyptian ships' architects, however, carefully and strikingly avoided any rope running from the masthead all the way aft. Instead they secured five or six ropes at different heights on each of the two straddled masts and these ropes were stretched diagonally down in parallel lines to either side of the vessel a little aft of midships. In this way the whole sternmost part of the boat was free of mast stays and could rise and fall on the waves with no attachment to the mast. No sooner had *Ra* begun to pitch on high seas than we realized how extraordinarily important this special system was. The stern hung behind the rest of the boat like a trailer which must be allowed to ride up and down freely over all the bumps. Had it also been secured by a stay to the masthead the mast would have broken as the first big ocean rollers surged beneath us. In our dance over the high wave-crests the middle section of *Ra* was rhythmically thrust upwards while the full weight of bow and stern sagged simultaneously in the wave-troughs on either side. Had both ends of the hull been attached to the mast, it would have broken under the pressure. As things were, the mast was well able to support the curved prow while holding the central part of the soft deck suspended in a straight line. Everything which lay farther aft was allowed to follow the motion of the sea.

We all daily praised this ingenious arrangement and special function of the rigging. Norman the naval expert, in particular, saw at once what it meant. There was no mistake about it. The creators of the old Egyptian rigging had prepared their flexible reed boats for the meeting with ocean swells. After the third day at sea I was already writing in my diary: 'This rigging is the result of long experience in navigation on the open sea; it was not born on the calm Nile.'

But there was another detail of the special Egyptian ship design which we took longer to understand; and for that, we were to pay dearly. Every day we looked admiringly at the broad, in-turned curl on the high-peaked stern. What purpose did it serve? We placed no reliance on the general conviction that this curl was simply intended to beautify the shape of a river boat. Yet as the days passed we ourselves were as unable as the egyptologists to detect any practical function for it whatever. We did constantly make sure, however, that the curl was not beginning to straighten out. It remained in perfect shape, so our friends from Chad seemed to have been right in thinking that they had done their work so thoroughly that it would keep its curve without having to be fastened to the deck by rope. The only mistake we could see we had made so far was in stowing the cargo as for an ordinary sailing boat in those first days. No living man, only our own costly experience after long sailing in the trade-wind belt, could have taught us that a papyrus boat should have its heaviest cargo concentrated on the lee side. Now we were already so waterlogged on the windward side that the starboard gunwale was inexorably approaching the water level. This was most conspicuous far back on the starboard quarter, where as time passed we were able to wash over the side without hanging head downwards with our legs in the air as we had to do on the rest of the boat. After a time all the washing was done there and in fact everyone found it extremely handy.

On June 4th the rough seas about us began to calm down, and next morning we awoke to a new world. It had turned nice and hot, and the sea was a procession of long, shining rollers. We received another quick visit from five big whales: a majestic assembly. Perhaps they were the same ones which had called on us before. They were beautiful and friendly in their own element and we thought with horror of the day when mankind would have succeeded in launching its harpoons into the last of the sea's warm-blooded giants, so that in the end only the cold steel hulls of submarines would be frolicking in the ocean depths where the Almighty – and most men – would rather have seen the whale suckling its young.

It was so nice and hot that Georges tore off his clothes and dived overboard with his lifeline on. He disappeared under the *Ra* in his diving mask and came up again with a shout of delight which made Yuri and Santiago dive after him, each on his lifeline, while the rest of us watched and waited our turn. Only Abdullah still sat in the cabin-opening watching the calm seas, sulking. Unless the wind came back we would be becalmed here and never get to America. Norman consoled him with an explanation of the invisible ocean current. Perhaps we would not cover over a hundred kilometres a day as we had before, but we would certainly manage fifty.

Soon everybody had been under *Ra*'s belly except Abdullah. He washed himself in the canvas bucket on board and knelt facing Mecca for lengthy prayers. Perhaps he was praying for a wind.

The exhilarating salt-water bath made everyone feel new-born again. And to see *Ra* from below was among the greatest of all thrills. We felt like little pilot fish swimming under the curving belly of a gigantic yellow whale. The sunbeams were reflected like search-lights from the depths and played up against the papyrus bundles over our heads. Sea and cloudless sky together created the bluest blue round the big, shining yellow whale which glowed above us. It was swimming so fast that we were dragged along behind it on our ropes unless we ourselves swam as fast as we could in the same direction. For the first time we were able to see that we had zebra-striped pilot fish faithfully swimming in wedge formation in front of the reed prow, just as I had seen them swimming in front of the logs of the *Kon-Tiki*. We sailed past the trunk of a big African tree stump with roots which lay wallowing heavily in the rollers. A fat little *pampano* fish peeped out from under the trunk and waggled its tail as hard as it could to get across to *Ra*, where it found one or two smaller relatives already darting to and fro round the big oar-blade. Now and then they flirted off and took a playful nip at Yuri's white skin.

Here and there on the underside of the papyrus hull, small long-necked barnacles were beginning to grow, waving from their blue-black shells with orange gills like soft ostrich feathers. But there was no sign of verdancy or seaweed to be seen anywhere. The papyrus reeds, which in the Sahara sand had been greyish-yellow, shrunken and dry, had swollen under the water into smooth, shining stalks of gold and when we pressed them they were no longer brittle and fragile as before, but hard and resilient as motor tyres. Not a single reed had worked loose or broken. The papyrus had now been in the water for three weeks. Instead of dissolving by decomposition after two weeks it had become stronger than ever, and there was no sign of the reeds losing buoyancy. The list to windward was due to water absorption above the ship's water-line, amounting, in effect, to added cargo.

Overjoyed at what we had seen, we scrambled back to the papyrus deck and soon afterwards chicken feathers were floating in our wake again as Carlo cooked us a banquet.

Emboldened by our observations we now decided to lower the other repaired rudder-oar into the sea as well. We would never know more peaceful seas than these. But the giant oar with its spliced double shaft was so long and heavy that darkness had fallen before we managed to manoeuvre it clear of all the stays and over the cabin roof to windward, where it was to be pushed out. The rollers were peaceful, but still high enough for problems to be inevitable when the oar-blade began to jump before we could get it down in the right groove and make it fast. Having learned by experience, we decided to postpone the launching until daylight, so we left the mighty rudder-oar safely lashed with the long shaft in the air and the blade on deck, furthest aft on the windward side.

Next morning the weather was still wonderful and I clambered over the jars aft for a morning bath. There sat the morning watch, Yuri, happily enjoying himself washing his underclothes, but on board, without the canvas bucket. Every roller sent a little ripple over the papyrus gunwale at our lowest point, where the steering-oar weighed us down, and the rhythmic trickle was just enough to keep a little pool at the deepest point aft.

'This yacht is getting more and more practical,' observed Yuri happily. 'Now we have a washstand with running water.'

We hastened to launch the heavy rudder-oar so that the waves would support most of its weight, but our lowest corner continued to let in the ripples and as long as it simply provided us with a wash basin this was generally popular. We checked the curl on the stern. It was just as before and showed no signs of straightening out. For safety's sake Georges swam underneath *Ra* and discovered for the first time that the bottom was beginning to sag just aft of the basket cabin. But the papyrus bundles were just as whole and strong and when he squeezed the reeds air bubbled out. The reed was just as buoyant as before. We must simply have been carrying too much weight aft.

Now we moved all the cargo from the afterdeck so that the only weight left behind the cabin was the heavy cross-beam on which the two steering oars rested and the steering bridge itself, which stood on poles and sheltered the crate containing the life-raft.

The ripples continued to wash in over the starboard quarter. We made another thorough inspection both above and below water. It was obvious that *Ra* had preserved her original shape perfectly, from the bows back to the exact point where the backmost pair of stays ran down from the masthead and were secured to either side of the boat. Aft of this point there was a visible kink where the whole after part of *Ra* began to tilt gently downwards.

We began to ponder again. It was the freely trailing section of the boat which had taken a downward turn, while everything which was attached to the stays held up by the mast was still as it should be. The prow was as high as ever. Our proud golden swan still stretched her neck; only her tail was beginning to droop. If the mast could only have supported the strain of a stay to hold up the stern as well, this would not have happened. But if we tried to hoist the stern up with such a rope, the mast would break when the first roller passed under us. The stern must be allowed to undulate. But it must not be allowed to sag at a permanent angle in this way. We tried to pull it up with ropes stretched diagonally to either side of the cabin. We tried to fasten thick stretchers from the stern, over the guard-rail on the bridge and on across the cabin roof to poles erected on the foredeck. This was the Egyptian method of lending rigidity to wooden ships, but there were no such horizontal hawsers shown on paintings of papyrus boats. And however much we strained and hauled on all these ropes we did not succeed in heaving the afterdeck up again. Carlo tied all sorts of ingenious knots and hauled harder than anyone on wet ropes, until the palms of his hands began to swell up like white macaroni.

The days passed. More water washed in over the stern every day. While its lower section slowly gave way beneath it, the fine curl at the upper end of the stern arched as elegantly inwards as ever, showing no sign of losing its decorative shape. But it served no purpose, and as it became sodden it began to overload the weak afterdeck which supported it. All the storm waves which had washed over the peaked stern had caused it to absorb quantities of sea water over the water line. Since the stern was broad and thick and stood taller than the cabin roof, it must now, in its waterlogged state, weigh at least a ton. Should we lop it off? Then perhaps the bottom would float up again. But it was like cutting the tail off a swan. We had not the heart to cripple our proud craft.

But how, how, how the devil had the creators of this extraordinarily ingenious vessel succeeded in keeping the flaunting tail in the air without a rope to pull it up? On the contrary, it had had a rope which pulled it down towards the deck. The boat-builders from Chad had fortunately dispensed with that. We had not missed it up to now. Or? Or! I threw down the coconut which I was scraping out and began to draw frantically. Well, blow me down! I shouted for Norman, Santiago, Yuri, Carlo, the whole crew. I had found the mistake. We had not known how to put the curly tail to its intended use. Only bitter experience could have shown us that, too, because all those who had learned the purpose of the curly tail from its inventors had been in their graves for thousands of years. The peculiar arch over the afterdeck was not built for beauty. The rope, which everyone thought would serve only to hold the cocked tail in tension, had a completely different function. The cocked tail stood by itself. The rope was not intended to pull the tail-tip down, but the afterdeck up. The high, harp-shaped stern was meant to act as a powerful spring, supporting the free-swinging afterdeck as the stays to the masthead supported the rest of the papyrus boat. To enable the papyrus ship to sail the open sea without breaking, its brilliant architects had divided it into two linked components. The forward part was kept up by the straddled mast with its parallel stays, the after part was allowed to move independently, but always returned to its place, thanks to the bowstring attached to the big spring arching above it.

We tied the bowstring in position, but it was too late now. After three weeks the afterdeck had developed a kink and without a fixed point in the air over the tail-tip no rope could repair the damage. We were the sufferers because we, like all the others, had assumed the peculiar arch of the tail to be the ancient boat designers' end, whereas it had been their ingenious means.

Yuri and Norman stood in the puddle of water astern, staring at the slowly sinking golden tail. Suddenly they began to sing with one voice:

'We don't want a yellow submarine, a yellow submarine, a yellow submarine. . .'

They did not want a yellow submarine and neither did we, so soon all seven of us were standing in the stern, singing Yuri's refrain in chorus. No one took it more seriously than that. Indeed, the rest of the boat was bobbing like a champagne cork, so Yuri and Norman set about washing socks and trying to find a rhyme for 'submarine'.

To my own mind our main problem was not so much how the papyrus reed would ultimately survive its interplay with the sea, but how we seven passengers on board would ultimately survive our interaction with each other. In the basket cabin, which measured nine feet by twelve, there was not even elbow room between us when we lay down, and the papyrus deck was so full of jars and baskets that there was no room to put a foot down. This meant that, outside our sleeping bags, we lived either on the narrow papyrus roll in the shelter of the port cabin wall, or up on the little steering bridge which could be spanned with both arms, lengthwise and crosswise. Everyone was within speaking and touching distance of everyone else, day and night. We were stuck together like seven-headed Siamese twins, with seven mouths speaking seven languages. We were not only black and white, from communist and capitalist countries; we also represented the extremes of educational levels and living standards. When I visited one of our two Africans in his home in Fort Lamy, he was sitting on a fibre mat on the earth floor with no other chattels than a paraffin lamp which stood in the middle of the mat, while his passport and travel tickets lay on the floor in one corner. With the other African, in Cairo, I was ushered in by bowing oriental servants between the pillars of a rich man's home, with massive French furniture, tapestries and antique heirlooms. One crew member could not read or write; another was a university professor. One was an active pacifist; another an officer. Abdullah's favourite occupation was listening to his little pocket radio and dispensing news about the war on the Suez Canal, of which he himself had caught a glimpse. His own African government in Fort Lamy supported Israel against the Arabs and now they had asked France to drop parachutists to suppress the Arab rising in the desert beyond Bol, where we had met. Abdullah was a fanatical Mohammedan and therefore supported the Arabs. Norman was a Jew. Georges was Egyptian. Their distant relatives were shooting at each other from opposite sides of the Suez Canal, while they themselves lay side by side in a wickerwork cabin, afloat on the Atlantic. Abdullah dispensed news with equal enthusiasm about the war in Vietnam. He was completely bewildered because Yuri and Norman, who were both white, represented two countries which were hostile but wanted peace and therefore helped the yellow-skinned men in Vietnam to kill one another. He wanted Norman and Yuri to agree on the same explanation of this anomaly. There was ample fuel on board for a serious conflagration. Our paper boat was loaded with psychological petrol and the heat generated by friction in the little basket capsule could only be extinguished by the ubiquitous waves.

The most insidious danger on any expedition where men have to rub shoulders for weeks is a mental sickness which might be called 'expedition fever' – a psychological condition which makes even the most peaceful person irritable, angry, furious, absolutely desperate, because his perceptive capacity gradually shrinks until he sees only his companions' faults while their good qualities are no longer recorded by his grey matter. The first duty of an expedition leader at any time is to be on guard against this lurking menace. In the days before departure this had been thoroughly impressed on the whole crew.

I was therefore not a little alarmed when on our third day out I had already heard the peaceable Carlo roaring in Italian at Georges that he might be a judo champion, but he was so disorderly and untidy that he was in need of a nanny. Georges hit back, but after a quick and heated verbal duel both of them shut up and only the papyrus could be heard creaking and whining as usual. The next day there was another explosion between the same two men. Carlo was tightening a mast stay when Georges angrily threw down his fishing rod and ostentatiously went to bed. On the bridge Carlo confided to me that playboy Georges was beginning to get on his nerves. Carlo himself had gone to work, carrying heavy rice sacks, when he was twelve years old. He had made his own way with his own bare hands without benefit of schooling. This lazy rich man's son from Cairo was a spoiled rascal who simply dropped everything and expected the rest of us to tidy up for him. I promised to speak to Georges, and agreed with Carlo that Georges did not yet quite understand the spirit of expedition teamwork. To him this was all a new sort of game, a contest of endurance and muscle power. But Carlo must also try to understand that up to now Georges had only lived in a home where he *did* simply throw everything down without a thought and still always found it in its right place, because the house servants or his wife or his mother picked it up and kept everything tidy. Carlo had learned in the school of life, Georges had not. We would have to teach him.

Soon afterwards I found a moment alone on the bridge with Georges. He was unhappy because he had answered Carlo rudely, but he had done so because Carlo was always interfering in Georges' own affairs. It was easy to explain to the attentive Georges that there was no room for one's 'own affairs' on board, except inside each man's private box. No one was obliged to clear up after anyone else and no one was entitled to strew the deck, inside or out, with hand-harpoons, flippers, reading matter, wet towels, soap or toothbrushes. Everyone on board was equal and no one had to clear up after anyone but himself.

A moment later Georges' fishing tackle, tape-recorder and dirty clothes had been picked off the deck and cabin roof and Carlo and Georges were suddenly hauling together on the same rope.

The next serious threat to peace did not come until we had everything so well organized on board that we introduced galley duty. Carlo had voluntarily offered himself as permanent cook, a generous gesture which assured him great prestige and popularity. Now the rest of us were to take turns in being orderlies and cleaning up the galley boxes, pots and pans for one day at a time. The orderly list was chalked on a black-board on the bridge and no one had remembered that Abdullah could not read. He did not realize that two of the others had taken this turn before him, and when Santiago showed him the dirty pots and the scrubber, Abdullah got a headache and flung himself on his bed growling:

'I know what it is. You are white, Santiago, and I am black. That's why you want me to be a servant to the rest of you.'

Santiago was an apostle of peace, but this hurt him worse than a dagger wound. He flared up.

'And you say that to me, Abdullah!' he snarled in pure rage, 'when I have spent six years fighting for Negro equality. The most important thing about this whole voyage for me is the very fact that—'

Abdullah heard no more. He pulled his sleeping bag over his ears. When he looked out next time he happened to catch a glimpse of me staggering aft with the dirty stack of pots. His eyes widened.

'You and I have simply changed days,' I explained.

Next day Abdullah was standing happily in the stern humming and singing his rhythmic African songs while he scoured the pans.

The next day brought a shock for the lot of us. Georges came and asked me quietly if he alone could be responsible for order in the kitchen for the remainder of the voyage. It was such a tedious business rotating the job and there were others who had more important duties to perform.

So it was Georges – yes, Georges – who became permanent orderly, and after that the kitchen on *Ra* was spick and span and no one else had to think about washing the pots.

Then there was a time when Norman and Carlo began to react ominously against Yuri and Georges, who did nothing without express orders, while they themselves were always on the lookout for work from morning till night, quite apart from their own duties. They could accept the fact that Abdullah took no personal initiative, but the other two, who both had university backgrounds, should not simply wait for orders. At just the same time, Yuri, Georges and Abdullah were beginning to be irritated by Norman and Carlo. They were too military, they gave orders instead of speaking pleasantly, as one does among friends, and they did not know how to relax and enjoy the mere fact of being alive. Moreover Santiago was an artful dodger. If there was something heavy to be moved he would stoop down himself and take hold, then call the others to help, and the next moment he would be standing smiling and pointing while the musclemen, Georges, Yuri and Abdullah, did the lifting and carrying. And then there were those who felt inwardly aggrieved because I as leader would not chase a sleepy man out of his sleeping bag if he was taking a nap while others worked on their own initiative – and the other group which thought I ought to have more control over those who chose to bark military orders instead of calling in a friendly way. This was neither a naval vessel nor a company of Alpine troops: we were seven companions on an equal footing.

But the miracle happened. Instead of all these small frictions growing into expedition fever, each man tried to understand why the others behaved as they did, and here Santiago's philosophy and research on peace versus aggression benefited all of us. Yuri and Georges began to admire Norman and Carlo because their initiative and energetic efforts improved conditions for all of us, and Norman and Carlo changed their view of Yuri and Georges, for no one on board tackled stiffer tasks or was more willing to help as soon as he was asked, or realized that help was needed. Santiago was the diplomat and psychologist who helped Dr Yuri to bandage invisible wounds. Yuri was hard-working, responsible and tireless as our doctor. Abdullah was admired by everyone for his lightning intelligence and eagerness to learn, and for his ability to adapt to cultural modes completely different from his own. Abdullah himself liked everyone, because he could see that he was one of the family although the rest of us were white. He would coax Yuri to produce a medicine which would give him, too, a beard like all the rest of us, and simply could not understand why the well-groomed Yuri would sit in the pool aft shaving every morning, when all the rest of us were beginning to grow red or black moustaches and beards. Unable to grow hair on his face, Abdullah completely stopped shaving his own head, which until now had shone like patent leather, and soon he at least had crinkly hair growing on top, so thick that he carried his big carpenter's pencil stuck in it like a red hairpin.

Georges had one or two peculiarities. During the day he slept easily. But at night he could not sleep unless he had a pillow on his chest and music by his ear. For this purpose he had brought a tape-recorder with a limited number of his favourite pop tunes. The noise from the papyrus and ropes drowned the music for those of us who lay furthest away, but that same noise meant that Yuri had to give sleeping pills both to Georges himself and to Santiago. Georges' tape-recorder played Georges' tunes day and night. One day the tape-recorder disappeared. I had seen it half a minute before. At that time it was lying on the bridge and playing alone at Abdullah's feet as I passed, while Abdullah stood with his back to it, steering. Norman was hanging half overboard, making an oar fast. Carlo, Santiago and I were passing to and fro in the stern, moving the cargo, while Yuri and Georges worked on the other side of the cabin. Suddenly the music stopped. A minute or two passed before Georges clambered back over the cargo to start it up again. The tape-recorder had gone. Georges searched everywhere. In the stern, in the bows, under the mattress, on the cabin roof. Gone. Gone for ever. Who was the miscreant? The African judo champion swelled like an angry gorilla. Who, who had thrown his tape-recorder into the sea? Now the voyage was finished for him, done for: without his tunes he could not fall asleep. Who – who – who had done it? The air vibrated. No more sleep! Little Safi clambered as far up the mast as the rope reached; she did not intend to take the blame.

Abdullah could have kicked the tape-recorder overboard, but he was much too fond of music to do that. Norman could not reach it, and Georges had Yuri in sight the whole time. It could only have been one of us three who had been passing to and fro in the stern. Carlo was the only one who went on moving jars imperturbably, as if nothing had happened. Carlo! There was no doubt in my mind. He must still be fed up with Georges, so he had done it. Crazy. Unlike Carlo. Now we were all sitting on a powder-keg while the fuse burned.

'Georges,' I said. 'You really have turned into an orderly man, but how could you have managed to leave your tape-recorder so far out that it fell into the sea?'

'It may have been near the edge,' said Georges, 'but at worst it would have fallen on deck, not overboard.'

Inwardly I agreed, but I must save Carlo.

'It was right out on the starboard corner,' I said firmly. 'If anyone brushed against it while we were heeling sharply to starboard it would have fallen into the sea.'

Georges continued to search in the most absurd places, then slipped off into his sleeping bag. He instantly slept like a log and we did not waken him until Carlo whistled his special mealtime signal and served fried eggs with salt ham next morning. Who could be angry with Carlo? The tape-recorder was never referred to again on the voyage. Not until we had landed on the other side did Santiago lay his hand on Georges' broad shoulder one day and say calmly:

'Georges, how much do I owe you for the tape-recorder?'

We were all equally astounded. Georges turned slowly, terribly slowly, until he was broadside on to the smiling little Mexican. Then he himself beamed from ear to ear and said:

'What tape-recorder?'

That was the end of the discussion.

'How could you take such a risk?' we asked Santiago later. He admitted that he had been very doubtful whether he was doing right or wrong when he flipped the recorder into the sea, but he was quite convinced that if it had been allowed to go on playing the same tunes much longer one of us would have gone insane and hit the owner over the head with it.

While the weeks passed with the seven of us in the cramped cabin crowded together as if we were at a non-stop party, *Ra* rolled on in the centre of an unchanging horizon which accompanied us like a magic circle. From June 4th to 9th the sea ran in gentle combers, the wind was fitful, and some of the men felt the urge to sleep at all hours of the day. The papyrus had stopped whining and growling and had begun to purr like a cat enjoying the sunshine. Norman disclosed that he was worried. We were drifting slowly south-westward and unless the wind returned there was a risk of our being caught in the eddying currents off the coast of Mauritania and Senegal. We had come into one of the trans-Atlantic shipping lanes, constantly sighting passenger steamers and cargo vessels far and near, and on the night of June 6th a big, lighted ocean liner headed straight for us. It was steering so directly towards us that the officers on the bridge could not possibly have spotted the glow from our little paraffin lamp at the masthead, so we gesticulated violently with our torches. The reluctant wind gave us very little chance of escaping with the help of the rudder-oars. The monster racketed along, lights blazing, and was beginning to loom threateningly over us when it suddenly turned towards our starboard beam and silenced its mechanical thunder. Some angry reprimand was flashed at us from the bridge, so fast that we could only catch the word 'please' before the giant glided silently past under its own impetus, a few hundred feet from the papyrus bundles. Then the propellers were churning the water again and the steel giant rumbled on its brightly lit way to Europe.

Next day we were sailing in slack winds through an ocean where the clear water on the surface was full of drifting black lumps of asphalt, seemingly never-ending. Three days later we awoke to find the sea about us so filthy that we could not put our toothbrushes in it and Abdullah had to have an extra ration of fresh water for his ritual washing. The Atlantic was no longer blue but grey-green and opaque, covered with clots of oil ranging from pin-head size to the dimensions of the average sandwich. Plastic bottles floated among the waste. We might have been in a squalid city port. I had seen nothing like this when I spent 101 days with my nose at water level on board the *Kon-Tiki*. It became clear to all of us that mankind really was in the process of polluting its most vital well-spring, our planet's indispensable filtration plant, the ocean. The danger to ourselves and to future generations was revealed to us in all its horror. Shipowners, industrialists, authorities, they would all have seen the sea gliding past at a fair speed from an ordinary ship's deck and would never have literally dipped their toothbrushes and noses in it week after week, as we had. We must make an outcry about this to everyone who would listen. What was the good of East and West fighting over social reforms on land, as long as every nation allowed our common artery, the ocean, to become a common sewer for oil slush and chemical waste? Did we still cling to the medieval idea that the sea was infinite?

The strange thing is that when you are bobbing over the wave-crests on a few papyrus bundles, aware at the same time that whole continents are gliding past, you realize that the sea is not so limitless after all; the water which rounds the African coast in May passes along the American coast some weeks later with all the floating muck which will neither sink nor be eaten by the inhabitants of the sea.

On June 10th the wind strengthened. On the same day Abdullah slaughtered our last chicken and then there was only a duck left in the poultry coop. When the coop was thrown into the sea, where it would gradually absorb water and sink, no one had the heart to slaughter the duck. It was spared and christened Sinbad, and after that it waddled about the deck, to the intense indignation of Safi. With a line tied to its foot and a basket as its one-room residence, it became master of the foredeck, while Safi kept to the cabin area, and if one of the two wandered by an oversight into the other's territory it ended either with Safi screaming with fury because she had been nipped on her tailless behind by Sinbad, or with Safi leaping triumphantly home with a duck's feather in her paw.

During the night the seas piled up and became really fierce. Often it was quite uncanny to stand on the creaking, swaying steering bridge and see nothing in the world but a lighted patch of sail and the lamp at the masthead, which swung like an unruly moon among the stars when one glimpsed their light between the racing storm clouds. Now and then a venomous snake seemed to be hissing right at one's back and a foaming wave crest would come rushing along at the height of one's head, invisible in its blackness apart from the white foam on top which seemed to be sailing alone through the air, whispering to itself. The body below reached us and lifted us in the air with its huge watery muscles, only to let us go again and drop us so deep that the next white phantom following behind hovered over us at a still greater height. We were worn out, dead tired, after two hours' intensive night watch at the two steering-oars, even if we were generally using only one of them and allowing the other to work in a fixed position.

Daylight found *Ra* more loose-jointed than ever before. At roof height the mast was swaying to and fro as much as two feet and the thirty-foot high masthead was swinging about so violently that Carlo only just managed to hang on through the wild antics up at the top. In the Egyptian style, each of the two straddled masts was simply planted in a shallow groove in a flat plank lying like a broad foot on top of the papyrus base. A short, naturally knee-shaped stump was fixed with its horizontal part tied to the wooden foot and its vertical end to the lower part of the mast. These rope lashings round the foot-pieces were now so slack that the swinging masts threatened to jump out of their slots. All the stays which ran like parallel harp-strings from each side of *Ra* to the masthead were also so slack that at one moment they hung in loops, giving the masts no support, while at the next they all tautened together with a jerk so violent that we were afraid the mast would break, or the papyrus bundles would be torn to shreds, for all the stays were fastened to a single thick rope cable tied right round the edge of *Ra*. We hammered thick wooden wedges round the mast-foot and tautened the boisterous shrouds one by one, at the risk of the first taut stays being jerked away while the rest were still slack. At last we had the dancing mast captive again.

The sea was full of life that day. Flying fish rained about us. Another moonfish drifted by, large and round and inert. Something invisible engulfed the hook on Georges' fixed fishing rod and made off with the whole line. Before he could pull it in, a hulking great fish swallowed the first, so Georges' catch was a severed fishhead. Meanwhile *Ra* was skimming over the wave-ridges at record speed and we were all disappointed when Norman announced a moderate day's run after taking our noon position. We were being pulled south by a lateral current. In the last twenty-four hours the starboard corner of *Ra*'s stern had sunk so far that the lower cross-beam of the steering gear was always dipping into the waves and acting as a brake. The water was permanently ankle-deep aft, and wave-tops were constantly washing right up to the crate containing the life-raft under the bridge. The crate shifted every time and chafed at the ropes.

The sea was equally agitated and unpredictable next day and an increasingly strong north wind brought the cold back with it. While Yuri was trying to adjust the ropes on the steering spar as it splashed in the waves, he caught sight of a blue bubble which he grasped and tried to pull off the end of the spar. Yuri had never seen a Portuguese man-o'-war and had no idea what had happened when the next moment he was entangled in the long, stinging tentacles of one of the Atlantic's smallest but most lethal monsters. That wily bubble is not a single animal but a whole colony of minute creatures which live in an extremely complicated symbiosis in which each and every one has its special properties and tasks. The largest creature, which constitutes the bubble itself, has no purpose other than to keep the extraordinary community afloat. It tows a bundle of filaments several yards long, made up of all the bubble's little fellow-citizens. Some are hunters which provide food for the rest of the colony, others are responsible for reproduction, while yet others are soldiers which literally shoot caustic acid into victims and enemies of the bubble colony. Very large Portuguese men-o'war have even paralysed and killed human beings.

The violent burning pain spread through Yuri's skin into his nervous system, paralysed the muscles of his right hand and began to affect his heart. It took our unfortunate ship's doctor a good four hours draining the medicine chest of everything from ointments to nerve and heart pills before he allayed his own pain and got the movement back into his right hand.

On June 13th an icy north-north-east wind was howling through the stays and whining in the wickerwork cabin walls, while the seas rose higher and boiled more savagely than anything we had seen up to now. There were howls, creaks and groans from every section of the heaving vessel and breakers running across each other and over one another's backs crashed aboard aft. A few wave peaks sent tons of water surging over us at a time and we could actually see the stern section sinking gradually deeper under the pressure of the heaviest cascades. There was nothing we could do but wait until the masses of water had rushed out again on both sides of *Ra*, leaving us with our once popular bathing pool now knee-deep in water. Abdullah was in high spirits and assured us that this misfortune aft was unimportant. We would not sink as long as the ropes held. Blue with cold, but humming, he ambled about in oilskins with his transistor to his ear. He had tuned in to a French-speaking Arab station which was reporting on the revolution in Chad, where the Mohammedans currently had the upper hand.

A splendid blue-green dorado was playing round the papyrus bundles most of the day, but after breaking the line it would not allow itself to be either hooked or speared. Carlo was going to prepare dried fish for lunch when a wet fish crashed in full flight on to the back of his neck while others hailed against the cabin wall around him. Eleven flying fish lay floundering on the deck ready for the pan.

From June 14th to 17th the sea was constantly seething round us and inexplicably high waves crossed one another from two or three directions at once, an interplay of currents and counter-currents from unseen coasts. Georges had pains in the back and had to be helped to bed. Abdullah was sick, but cured himself with a concoction of twelve boiled garlic cloves. The bridge began to creak and sway and had to be hastily reinforced with fresh ropes and stays. Yuri had the bright idea of moving Sinbad the duck aft, where she swam about happily in the inboard pool. Safi was so cross that she got diarrhoea, but kept to the outer edge of the papyrus rolls as always on such occasions. She had become incredibly clean. Suddenly a school of tunny fish, about six feet long, shot out of the water, frightening Safi into hysterics so that she hid in a basket and no one could persuade her out of it until Georges put her in her special sleeping box inside the cabin, after dusk.

Once again the masts were jumping in their flat wooden shoes, while *Ra* writhed about in the wildest gymnastics to follow the chaotic dance of the waves. She was making a new, hoarse sound we had not heard before. It sounded like a mighty wind roaring to and fro as our ten thousand bundled reeds bent in the water. The floor, walls and ceiling of the basket hut were also twisting and heaving with a new sound. The boxes beneath us jammed askew, so that the lids stuck, and we could lie, sit or stand on nothing which did not twist us with it. The stays were holding the masts in ominous tension, but we dared not slacken or tauten them in these powerful seas. It was bitterly cold, but Georges, Yuri and Norman all took a swim under the reed bundles for safety's sake. They came up and assured us with chattering teeth that the papyrus below us was in perfect condition, but now the sagging stern section was exerting a real braking action. Something must be done.

Then the starboard rudder-oar tore itself loose from the steering bar and danced madly in its efforts to wrench itself free of the steering bridge as well. There was a fierce battle in the deluges of water before we captured it and bound it in place with our thickest rope. There were fish everywhere and Georges managed to spear a dorado in the chaos. Something must be done to check the water which was at last breaking in with insane fury aft. How long would the stern section support this mighty strain? A wooden boat would have broken in two.

We must try to stem the flood of water. We collected all the spare papyrus we had and Abdullah, assisted by Santiago and Carlo, stood up to the thighs in water aft, tying on papyrus rolls as a bulwark against the seas. The water rose to their chests when the worst seas sent their crests surging on board. Abdullah was washed overboard several times, but clung to his life-line and only laughed as he scrambled on board again. After all, he was wearing his magic belt. When the work was finished he gave thanks to Allah.

What I had feared happened. The higher we built the dam, the more water found room on board the papyrus tail, because the papyrus bottom had swollen tight and held the water in. Since there was no free outlet, the stern section was being pressed still lower by the enormous weight of water. So we tried to remove Abdullah's bulwark again. But as the original railing had now been pushed further under water than before, so many tons of sea water surged in that the box containing the life-raft began to float between the poles of the bridge. We could only tie the reed bulwark hastily on again. We even took a knife and cut away the ropes of two small papyrus boats we had on board for an emergency and used all this liberated papyrus to raise Abdullah's reed gunwales. Finally we undid our own Egyptian life-belts, made according to the paintings in the ancient tombs. When at last we had not a single papyrus reed left to fall back on, the sides were higher, and the pool aft therefore even deeper than before. It now filled the whole afterdeck, but there was much less force in the water cascading in over the papyrus barrier. Midships and foredeck were as dry as before.

On June 17th the storm reached its height, the wind turned westward and the high seas grew calmer. We found flying fish everywhere; there was even a little creature floating in the coffee pot. We must have returned to the main current, for, thanks to a momentary gap in the heavy cloud ceiling, Norman was able to report that we had sailed 80 nautical miles, or 148 kilometres in the last twenty-four hours, even with a broad, sagging stern slowing us down like a lobster's tail. That counted for something, even on the map of the world.

During the worst of the storm we moved about 500 nautical miles off the West African coast, heading straight for the Cape Verde Islands west of Dakar. Both the north wind and the current were carrying us straight towards this large group of islands which might loom up around us at any moment, and this gave us an uncomfortable feeling of insecurity as we drifted and struggled in the storm with an intractable stern section behaving like a yellow submarine. One late evening, when the thought of the islands out in the darkness was haunting us badly, Norman took out the US sailing directions for the area we were in and read aloud to us by the light of the paraffin lamp. It swung from the heaving ceiling, making our shadows dance about us, distorted and elastic, in time to *Ra*'s deafening spectral orchestra.

We learned that cloudbanks and haze could lie so thickly round the mountainous Cape Verde Islands that the surf against the rocky coast often appeared before land itself had been sighted, although the highest peaks reached 9,000 feet. In addition there were powerful currents round the islands, so treacherous that they had caused innumerable shipwrecks. The heavy rollers round the island group were most active when the moon was changing. 'Great caution is therefore necessary when navigating in the vicinity of these islands,' Norman concluded his reading.

'Listen to that; be cautious, chaps,' remarked Yuri, pulling his sleeping-bag up and his leather cap down until they met at his nose.

It so happened that the moon was changing just then. The night was as pitch black as the day was misty. For the last four days the islands had lain straight ahead in our line of drift and now they must be lying somewhere just in front of us. They might appear that night or next morning, if we were caught by a strong southerly cross-current. Rain was falling from low clouds and neither sextant nor 'nasometer' could tell us where we were.

June 18th was a dramatic day. The Cape Verde Islands must lie somewhere ahead or across the port bow, swathed and hidden in fog and rain-clouds. Just two weeks ago we had passed the Canary Islands at close range without seeing them through the cloudbanks. But today more serious problems were brewing up than the ones which lurked beyond our decks. We had been together in tolerance on the papyrus bundles for twenty-five days and the reed had been floating in sea water for at least a month. Despite all our adversities *Ra* had sailed over 2,000 kilometres round the whole north-west coast of Africa and now the voyage across the Atlantic from continent to continent was to begin in earnest. If the Egyptians had sailed as far from the mouth of the Nile as we had now sailed from Safi harbour they would have been far up the Don, in Russia, or beyond Gibraltar. The Mediterranean was obviously not big enough to exhaust the range of a papyrus boat.

But damn that stern section! If only the ancient scribes had left directions, we would have understood the principles of the papyrus boat in advance; then we could have looked forward to crossing the ocean without problems. Now the waves were not slipping under us and lifting us up any more. They were creeping over our stern and pushing us down. The night before, a big sea had crept right over the cabin wall and I was awakened by getting a bucket of cold water on my head. Salt water was running down inside my sleeping-bag.

'We are starting with a handicap,' I admitted to the others.

It was then that Santiago threw a match into the powder-keg.

'Let's cut up the life-raft,' he said suddenly.

'Of course,' I said. 'Now we have broken up the two little papyrus boats, so just let's cut up the rubber raft as well.'

'I mean it,' said Santiago. 'We must try to raise the stern. We have no papyrus left, but the life-raft is made of foam rubber. We can cut it in strips and use it in the same way as the Egyptians would have used spare papyrus.'

'He's mad,' came mutters in several languages.

But Santiago was obdurate and refused to give in.

'You brought a life-raft which only takes six men and there are seven of us,' he challenged me. 'You explicitly said you would never get into it yourself.'

'The next size up was a twelve-man raft,' I explained. 'That was too big. But it's true that I shall stay on our nice big reed smack if you six decide to move to that tiny little rubber thing there.'

'Me too,' said Abdullah. 'Let's cut it up. The wooden case is just gnawing away our ropes.'

'No,' I said. 'The rubber raft is meant to give everyone a feeling of security. This is nothing but a scientific experiment. Without the rubber raft no one on board would be able to leave the papyrus boat.'

'Come on, where's the saw, what's the good of something we will never use?' insisted Santiago provocatively.

The rest of the crew were indignant, but everyone went aft to have a look, at least, at the heavy packing case which Abdullah wanted to get rid of.

There was no ship behind the back wall of the cabin any more. The only thing which projected out of the water there was the curved tailpiece which rose in lonely majesty, separated from the rest of *Ra* by the rippling waves which swept across from one side of the boat to the other. The case with the life-raft in it was sloshing about in green water between the legs of the bridge.

Abdullah seized the axe which hung ready, but Yuri protested furiously. It was absolutely crazy! We must think of the people at home. Norman agreed with Yuri: our families would despair if we had no lifeboat. Georges took the axe from Abdullah. Carlo began to waver. He wanted me to take the decision. For the first time on the voyage a serious breach was opening. On a vital decision, opinions were sharply opposed and both parties grew steadily more bitter in their uncompromising claims.

We sat all together on the foredeck, on our goatskin containers, sacks and jars, while Carlo served salt meat, onion omelette and Moroccan *sello*. But this was the calm before the storm. The dry reeds in the papyrus deck at our feet bent and straightened like strips of paper, keeping time with the seas which were still high and choppy. The reed was stronger under water where it was wet. With our two spliced rudder-oars lashed fast and her lobster tail hanging down and acting as a brake, *Ra* steered herself before the wind. Yuri, Norman and Georges resembled the murky thunder-clouds hanging over us on all sides, as they grimly cracked almonds in their fists, prepared to defend their position. It was essential to lance the boil.

'Lots of odd things could happen,' I said, trying to keep my voice cheerful. 'Let's think about all the situations where the life-raft might be useful. I'm most scared of someone falling overboard.'

'I'm most scared of being rammed by a ship,' interjected Norman, 'and then of fire on board.'

'The bows are floating splendidly, but not the stern,' said Yuri. 'No one knows if we will still be afloat in another month's time.'

'True enough,' I admitted. 'And it's still theoretically possible that the sceptics are right and the papyrus will gradually rot and disintegrate in the sea water.'

'What I'm scared of,' came quietly from Georges, who was never afraid of anything, 'is a hurricane.'

No one could think of more than these six good reasons for keeping the life-raft in reserve. But six reasons were enough. We therefore agreed to find out what each man would do in each of these six eventualities. We counted on our fingers.

First possibility: man overboard. Everyone felt safe because we were all roped up like mountaineers. We also had a lifebelt trailing on a long rope astern. If a lonely night wanderer stumbled over the jars and fell overboard, launching the life-raft would not help him. First of all, the life-raft was intended for extreme emergency and could not be launched without cutting down the entire bridge. Furthermore, it was deep and rectangular, with two inflatable tents which opened both below and above deck, no matter which side came uppermost. It was thus not intended for fast sailing and would be left far behind *Ra* even if we lowered the sail. The life-raft would be of little avail if a man fell overboard. No argument about that one.

Second possibility: collision. Everyone agreed that if *Ra* were split in two we would not have time to launch the raft, and if it was already afloat we would still all prefer to clamber back on the much larger remaining portion of *Ra*.

Third possibility: fire. In the Sahara, *Ra* would have burned like tissue paper, but here it would be difficult to set fire to her. In any case we had a fire extinguisher. Smoking was only allowed on the lee side, where sparks blew overboard, and the windward side was so soaked with water that it would float, fire or no fire elsewhere on board. No one would prefer the little life-raft to the large, wet, unburned portion of *Ra*.

Fourth possibility: the papyrus might sink under us. One month's experience showed that even if the papyrus absorbed water, it sank so slowly that there would be plenty of time to send out an sos. But we would also have to send out an sos if we transferred to the crowded lifeboat. We would all rather be able to stretch out in our comparatively spacious basket cabin than sit squashed together in that little lifeboat tent, waiting for rescue.

Fifth possibility: the papyrus might rot and disintegrate. We already knew from sight and touch that the papyrus experts had miscalculated on this point. Their laboratory experiments had certainly been made in standing water. Everyone agreed wholeheartedly that both the papyrus reeds and the lashings were stronger than ever, so we were absolutely unanimous in ruling out that emergency.

Sixth possibility: hurricane. More than likely, as we neared the West Indies. A hurricane might carry away masts and oars and steering bridge, might even rip off the sunken stern. But we had lived through more than one storm on *Ra* now and were certain that the tough wicker cabin would continue to cling to *Ra*'s central reed bundles, leaving us a raft with more room, water and food on board than the little foam rubber raft could possibly provide. Nobody would move to the rubber raft in a hurricane.

Before we had finished we were all in high spirits. No one had preferred the life-raft to *Ra*'s reed bundles in any conceivable situation. Yuri was visibly relieved. He grinned and shook his head, marvelling. Carlo laughed. Norman drew a deep breath and was the first on his feet.

'OK. Let's find the saw!'

Everyone wanted to make for the stern, but such heavy seas were breaking over the submerged deck that three men made quite enough extra load there. Norman, Abdullah and I waded out. With axe, knife and saw we attacked the heavy packing case and threw the nailed planks and plastic container overboard. That sort of thing was out of place on *Ra*. The green foam rubber raft came into view. Under it Abdullah was appalled to see that several of the ropes holding *Ra* together had been chafed through by the movement of the case under the pressure of water. Rope-ends bristled from the papyrus like ghastly skeletal claws. Only the swelling of the reed had prevented the ropes from slithering through and allowing the whole stern to break apart. Abdullah fell on the loose ends and tied them together with extra rope. We stood knee-deep in foaming water and Abdullah showed us how the skin on his legs was peeling in wet white flakes, after all the work in sea water over the last few days. Then I felt one of the mightiest of the towering waves crashing against *Ra*, lifting us up and twisting us abruptly sideways. I was staggering in an attempt to regain balance when I heard the deafening roar of tons of falling water and breaking timber. The sea surged in up to my waist from behind, while wood and rope yielded to the power of the ocean and slowly collapsed. I was swept to port by the torrent of water and stooped to grab a papyrus rope before I could be washed overboard, when I felt a great weight of broken timber thumping over my back. I heard Norman's voice bellowing: 'Look out, Thor!' and had not a moment's doubt that this deafening sound of breakage came from the entire bridge subsiding in its lashings and collapsing over our heads. As our foundations rocked and broken wood held me down in the flurry of water, I expected at any moment to find ourselves being towed along behind *Ra* on our lifelines while bridge and stern were left floating in our wake. Then the floods subsided and we were left knee-deep as before, I with broken timber pressing me down.

'It was the double rudder-oar that went,' shouted Norman, helping to free me.

Above us bobbed the splintered ends of two big logs lashed together. The thick, round original oar-shaft and the rectangular balk of the spar mast, bound to it as reinforcement, had broken off side by side. The big oar-blade was left hanging on the ropes, lashing like the tail of an angry whale, but in a flash Norman was there with Carlo and Santiago to haul it in, while Abdullah wrestled alone with the rubber raft, now floating freely, and I myself struggled with a 200-pound keg of salt meat which had suddenly broken loose among the bridge poles and threatened to cause disaster unless it was prevented from crashing about in the cascades of water.

That night Abdullah assured me, when I came out for the change of watch, that we were now surrounded by nice big waves with no nasty little waves on their backs. *Ra* rode smoothly and rhythmically, with two small rowing-oars temporarily attached where the big port rudder-oar was missing. When we switched our torches on we could see squid swimming as though behind glass as the water rose again on the lee side under us. The Egyptian sail occasionally stood out clearly against bright gaps in the cloud ceiling, but the horizon was invisible in the darkness. What sometimes seemed to be twinkling stars low on the horizon often proved to be plankton twinkling brightly at our own eye-level, carried up on an invisible wave-crest.

It certainly felt very odd next day to begin attacking our undamaged life-raft with a saw. Norman and I looked at each other and I paused uncertainly for an instant before sending the saw rasping through the canvas cover and into the foam rubber. Then we all set about dis-membering our only means of getting away from the boat we were standing on, knee-deep in water.

'People would think we were crazy. No one would understand,' said Yuri, grinning.

But the decision was unanimous and well-weighed. The life-raft was reduced to narrow strips, the shape of papyrus bundles, then pushed under water and lashed fast to the surface of the sunken deck. The miracle happened. The stern began to rise. It lifted enough to give us better steering control over the boat, and once again the waves slid under us without filling our swimming pool with such floods of water. The event was appropriately celebrated. Little did we dream then that the sea would gradually steal on board and pluck the sawn-up foam rubber away bit by bit, until only the natural papyrus stems were left. Neptune might have been telling us: 'No cheating. Pharaoh's men had no foam rubber.' So our delight was short-lived, but with the disappearance of the heavy cradle holding the life-raft we had removed a dangerous load from the afterdeck.

On June 19th we found ourselves dancing in heavy rollers augmented by counter-waves from cliffs on shore which stirred the sea into indes-cribable turmoil. The deck of *Ra* billowed like a carpet and in some places dry papyrus crinkled itself into little curls on top of the bundles. Between mast and cabin, where two men could usually walk side by side, one man had to watch out before slipping through alone, and the little gap between bridge and cabin wall opened and closed like a nutcracker. If we sat on the narrow crack between two of our sixteen boxes in the cabin, we were nipped in the bottom. For the first time a clay jar was crushed to pieces and the nuts ran out, to Safi's delight. We discovered that another was empty of water because friction with the neighbouring jar had ground a round hole in its side. The starboard rudder-oar was repaired and launched, while water gushed round our bodies, but soon afterwards there was another crack and the blade was floating astern again, while the sail swung round and imprisoned Carlo and Santiago, who were busy tapping water from a goatskin. They were bowled over towards the open railing and would have finished up in the sea had they not been roped up. A big flying fish sailed on board and swam happily round for a long time in the pool aft while Abdullah floundered about vainly trying to catch it.

In the struggle with rope and sail and broken rudder-oars I got my hand pinched and it was hurting even more that night when I came on deck to relieve Santiago. He pointed silently to a light to port. We clung to the guard rail, legs braced, so as not to tumble over while we stared. Cape Verde? No, a boat. It was heading straight for us. It was signalling. The flashes were too fast for us to read, but it was asking about something.

'*Ra* OK, *Ra* OK,' we flashed back in morse. The boat was close to us now and we guessed that it was a patrol boat from Cape Verde. It was rolling violently, while we were calmly undulating with the waves.

'*Ra, bon voyage*,' it finally flashed slowly. Have a good trip. Then it turned away and the comforting lights vanished in the darkness.

'Have a good trip,' I said to Santiago as he went to bed.

Two hours later I had already begun to whistle guardedly through the bamboo wall to waken Yuri in all the noise. He was to relieve me, but the others must be left to sleep. Then I felt as if Neptune himself had taken hold of the oar-blade out there in the blackness of the sea. Vast forces wrenched the oar from me and the whole vessel heeled, while white furies thundered out of the darkness and buried everything under my legs. The bridge vibrated and the crack of breaking wood was loud in my ears again. Was it the bridge collapsing this time? No. It was the other rudder-oar. Now we had nothing to steer with. I had to yell through the wickerwork and rouse everyone. The sail thrashed. The water seethed. Ropes and timber screamed louder than shouted orders. It began to rain. We threw out both our sea anchors. Then all was well.

'They wished us a good trip,' said Santiago, staring out into the night. We felt alone as never before. There was no light to be seen now from land or ship. At last the whole Atlantic lay open ahead of us.

'Good watch, Yuri. You have no problems – nothing to steer with.'

CHAPTER 10

Into American Waters

We were having a party on board *Ra*. Sky and sea smiled. The tropical sun burned down on the dry foredeck and the Atlantic washed quietly to and fro over the afterdeck. Inside the bamboo cabin it was cool and shady. A blue Atlantic chart was tied with twine to the yellow bamboo wall. On it was drawn a string of small pencilled circles. The last was quite new and showed that today we had crossed longitude 40° W and were therefore in the American half of the Atlantic. For several days Brazil had been our nearest fixed point, because we were now much closer to the South American mainland than to Africa, but as we were sailing almost directly westward we would be crossing the widest part of the ocean, and then the West Indies would be the nearest landing place ahead.

This was an occasion for celebration. Our Italian chef, Carlo, had extra help in the galley from gourmet Georges, who produced the choicest dishes out of the contents of our ceramic jars. After an *hors d'oeuvre* of Moroccan olives, sliced salt sausage and sun-dried Egyptian fish roe, we were each served an enormous omelette of fresh eggs filled with artichoke hearts, onions, whole tomatoes, scraps of smoked mutton and peppered sheep's cheese, and with a choice seasoning of all sorts of special spices, from Egyptian *kamon* to Moroccan desert herbs and red pepper. For dessert we had raisins, prunes, almonds and best of all, treble rations of Madame Aicha's honey-sweet Moroccan *sello* crumbs.

Who missed refrigerators and tin-openers? None of the representatives of seven countries who sat stuffing themselves with this variation of a pharaonic feast, while our papyrus boat marked the occasion by heading under full sail in the right direction, with no watch on the steering bridge.

We had a floating grocer's store on board. Santiago, our Mexican quartermaster, kept order in the store and Carlo was the only legal customer. Only Safi was caught pinching the stores. Unable to read Santiago's numbers, she had a peculiar talent for removing the cork from precisely those jars which contained nuts. From Santiago's little book the rest of us knew that jars 1 to 6, for instance, contained fresh eggs in lime solution, 15 to 17 were full of whole cooked tomatoes immersed in olive oil, 33 and 34 contained peppered sheep's cheese cut in cubes and also immersed in olive oil. Into jars 51–52 Aicha had pressed Moroccan butter, boiled and kneaded with salt, in the Berber manner. Jars 70–160 contained only clear spring water from a rural well outside Safi, but as they do in the desert, we had slipped small lumps of pitch into the water with which the goatskin bags were filled, or it would have gone bad. In the other jars and in baskets and sacks we had honey, salt, peas, beans, rice, various types of grain and flour, dried vegetables, *karkadé*, coconuts, *karubu*-beans, nuts, dates, almonds, figs, prunes and raisins. Our baskets of fresh root crops, green vegetables and fruit had come to an end after two or three weeks. From the roof of the bamboo alcove projecting rearwards beyond the cabin roof we had hung salt and smoked meat and sausages, bunches of onions, dried fish and nets of pressed Egyptian fish roe. Under this hanging grocer's store stood wickerwork baskets containing dried bread of various types, made from ancient Egyptian, Russian and Norwegian recipes. We wanted to find out if a papyrus boat could really be used at sea, not if we could survive solely on proper Egyptian dishes. On the other hand, we also wanted to find out if jars and baskets could last the journey, and if raft voyagers could live without tins and frozen food if their fisherman's luck gave out. Obviously there were no problems in filling a papyrus boat with any food that could be stored on any ocean-going vessel.

Crossing the fortieth longitude inspired Georges to break the rules by opening one of *Ra*'s two champagne bottles, while Yuri served out hand-painted wooden Russian beakers, filled with his own hair-raising home-brew. Abdullah refused. He patted the visibly taut skin of his stomach and disappeared beyond the cargo of jars to wash in our inland sea before giving thanks to Allah.

When he returned to his earthly friends he wanted an explanation of the pencil line on the chart to which he owed such a splendid meal. That we were constantly adjusting the clock, because the earth was round and the sun did not shine at the same time on all sides of a sphere, he could understand. And that Carlo had a watch with an automatic winder which went just as well after lying unworn in a box on board for five weeks because *Ra*'s wickerwork cabin was more mobile than any walking person he could also understand. But what he did not understand was why every day we marked our route on a chart on which the sea was divided by straight lines running down and across. Today we had passed the fortieth longitude and up to now he had not set eyes on a single one of them. Norman explained. Land and sea were divided into imaginary squares with numbers on them, so that people could tell by the numbers where they were.

'Aha,' said Abdullah. 'On land the squares keep still, but at sea they move west with the current even if there is no wind.'

'We have to imagine the lines on the ocean bed,' interrupted Norman. And then he explained that we had begun our journey in Safi, which lay on longitude 9° W, and today we were passing longitude 40° W. At the same time we had also been travelling south, all the way from latitude 32° N down to 15° N, so now we were just as far south as Abdullah was when he was at home in Chad.

Then Abdullah himself pointed out that the westernmost point of Africa, Dakar, lay 18° W and the easternmost point of Brazil, Recife, lay 36° W, so now that we ourselves were on 40° W we had passed the nearest corner of Brazil and had good reason to celebrate the fact that we were in the American half of the Atlantic.

Out on deck the feast went on. Yuri had climbed on the lid of the galley chest and stamped and leaped in the Russian manner as vigorously as the pitching boat would allow, while he sang Russian folk songs. When he came to 'The Song of the Volga Boatmen' we all joined in. Then Norman jumped on to the box with his harmonica and led the whole chorus in 'Down in the Valley' and other cowboy songs. Italy followed with heroic Alpine marches, Mexico with catchy revolutionary tunes, Norway with gay sea shanties and Egypt with exotic whimperings, to accompany belly-dancing. But Chad went off with the honours, partly because Abdullah was so genuine in his performance and partly because there was such an absurd contrast between the ubiquitous backdrop of sea and the Central African standing on a box drumming on the bottom of a pot while he sang his pulsating jungle tunes.

The watch disappeared aft at intervals to look at the compass. We were sailing due west with the wind at our backs, still at an average speed of 50–60 nautical miles, or approximately 100 kilometres a day. For six days after passing the Cape Verde Islands off the west coast of

Africa we had had the devil of a time keeping control of our sagging stern section, with the help of our clumsy stumps of botched-up rudder-oars. But out here in the middle of the ocean the waves had become much more co-operative and we had achieved a sort of *status quo* with the sea about us. As long as we let the waves tag along free of charge as far up the boat as the cabin wall, the ocean let its current send both waves and men speeding westward at a good pace. Carlo was one of those who suffered in silence at the sight of *Ra*'s tall tail emerging in solitary splendour from the sea astern. It was humiliating to see our once proud golden bird swimming swan-necked and toad-tailed. But on a day of celebration like this we just had to keep to the swan's big torso and forget that aft of the cabin we were a frog.

By sundown we had created an orchestra from Carlo's kitchen tools. *Ra* was creaking so softly that we drowned the mewing of the papyrus with our chosen instruments. Carlo could not get into the galley box, so he simply served Russian dried bread and honey. The bread tasted better to us than the finest cake, but it was handed out in big black lumps as hard as coal. I had eaten a good many when there was a snap and my only crowned tooth flew off across the papyrus and I sat there feeling foolish and exploring the revolting little hole with the tip of my tongue.

'Bad communist bread!' remarked Norman with a side-long glance specially aimed at our Russian ship's doctor.

Yuri bent and picked up the little chip, which he examined closely.

'Bad capitalist dentist!' he parried.

With shouts of laughter, song and music the party went on until the sun-god Ra sank into the sea, right in front of the nose of his marine namesake. The shining celestial sphere seemed to be enticing our own swan-necked *Ra* westward, ever westward. This eternal movement westward must have offered an immense enticement for genuine sun-worshippers. Resplendent lancets which no royal crown could match radiated like a diadem from the sea's edge into the sky. A tropical sea's attempt to emulate the northern lights: first in dazzling gold, then red as blood, orange, green and violet, turning gradually to black, while the twinkling stars emerged equally slowly from their invisibility as the sun-king disappeared. His majesty had gone. His little people of the sky flocked out to join the procession to the west.

We lay on our backs on full or empty goatskins, philosophizing. Outside the cabin there was no limit to our view, nothing to hinder or confuse our thoughts. We had had a fine day, we were full, we had

224

feasted and laughed, now we simply wanted to look at the stars and let our thoughts linger or wander where they would.

'You're a good chap, Yuri,' said Norman. 'Are there any more like you over there in Russia?'

'Two more,' said Yuri. 'The rest are better on the whole. But are there any passable capitalists left in your country, now that you have come with us?'

'Thanks for the compliment,' said Norman. 'If you think I'm passable, you'll have something to look forward to on the other side!'

There was a peaceful discussion on communism and capitalism, on anti-communism and anti-capitalism, on autocracy and dictatorship of the masses, on whether to prefer food or freedom, on why the peoples' representatives hate each other while common citizens everywhere get along so well as soon as they are able to meet. Whether the hippy movement in East and West was created by youth or by its parents, whether it would die out or increase with the advance of civilization, whether it could be thought of as a sort of warning barometer, showing that the civilization which we and our fathers had believed in and feverishly built up night and day was not going to be accepted by future generations. Egyptians and Sumerians, Mayans and Incas built pyramids, embalmed mummies and thought they were on the right track. They defended their ideas with slings and bows and arrows. We think they were wrong about the purpose of life. So we build nuclear missiles and go to the moon. We defend our policies with atom bombs and anti-missile missiles. Now our children are beginning to sit down in protest. They hang Indian ornaments round their necks, let their hair grow and play guitars on the floor. They retreat by artificial means into themselves, a longer journey than to sun or moon.

One grows philosophical when stars and plankton are twinkling in a world which is as it was before human beings saw it, before they got going on it with their thousand million busy fingers. It is easier to be tolerant of each other's views when you are sitting together in the starlight and know that you will sink or swim together, than when you sit on opposite sides of national frontiers with your nose in a newspaper or the TV screen, drinking in carefully chosen words. There was never any heated verbal duel of a political or religious nature on board *Ra*. To each his own opinion. We were supposed to represent the most extreme contrasts, and so we did, but we found that the highest common factor was not so small after all. It was easy to find. Perhaps it was because we seven on board saw ourselves as a unit in relation to our only common neighbours, who happened to breathe through gills and had quite different interests and ambitions from our own. In spite of everything, human beings were confoundedly similar, even if some had beaky noses and others flat.

There was a splash in the darkness; a heavy fish flailed against papyrus deck and bamboo wall. A jubilant shout from Georges announced that he had speared a two-foot long dorado. By the light of the fishing lamp we saw squid keeping pace with us by swimming backwards in jerks with all their arms stretched over their heads. They filled themselves with water and forced it out in powerful squirts which shot them backwards through the water. The jet system. They had acquired it as a means of escape from their pursuers. They acquired it before we did. The cachalot whale which had visited us could dive to a depth of three thousand feet, where the tremendous pressure was a hundred times that of the atmosphere, and yet it would not bang its head against the bottom in the absolute darkness, because it had a built-in radar. It had acquired it before we had.

'Yuri, as an atheist, do you think there may be an intelligent system in all those constellations twinkling up there, when no human beings have been up yet to put things in order?'

'I'm not a real atheist, it's just that I don't believe in all that nonsense that goes on in church.'

'In any case, Darwin and the Church agree that sun and moon, fish, birds and monkeys were created first. When man got his chance at last, everything was ready and waiting. In fact, now we are simply trying to find out how our own brains and intestines as well as the entire universe are composed and made to function.'

It was pleasant to lie completely relaxed in friendly comradeship with a peaceful sea and to gaze up at exactly the same view that seafarers and desert wanderers had gazed up at for thousands of years before us. Modern city dwellers, dazzled by street lights, have lost the starry sky. The astronauts are trying to find it again. I dozed. We decided we would all go to bed except for the watch. We had hard days behind us and did not know what was to come. Another storm would be no joke. The afterdeck was not there to protect us and we had spread canvas over the short back wall and long starboard side of the cabin after torrents of water from the stern had poured down the necks of those of us sleeping with our heads against the back wall. I thought with mixed feelings of my chief impressions of the last few days, before we had come out into calmer seas.

The first night, after being robbed of both our rudder-oars off the Cape Verde Islands, Yuri and Georges had worked out a temporary method by which two men at a time could steer tolerably well by simply hauling on the sheets of the sail. After all, the important thing was to keep the stern into the wind, so that the sail was filled and did not flap and slat against the mast. All we had to do was to ride with the weather. The first night after the Cape Verde Islands, we had been beset by huge waves which thundered against the back wall of the cabin, high up the canvas cover, before pouring overboard on both sides of the boat. These incessant crashes against our bedhead had made it difficult enough to fall asleep, and if we did sleep we were very soon roused to crawl out into the night and do battle with the vast canvas sail, increasingly indistinct as it rose into the darkness, as if we were being beaten by a fly-swatter from the heavens, slashing and twisting about. Waves and canvas. We were tossed around like dolls, thrown headlong across the cargo of jars and tumbled about from cabin wall and ropes to the outermost edge of the boat like punch-drunk boxers. Salt water ran off our backs and faces. Back into our sleeping-bags. Out again. Fourteen flying fish on deck for breakfast. Seven dorados caught in a row. Crazy Georges. Abdullah cannot eat them all. Let them swim with us, then we will have them fresh when we need them. Two disappeared in the pool aft, one swam about under the bridge and one hid under the steering spar. There was an underwater battle between fish and man before they were caught with bare hands. The fish was one powerful slippery bundle of muscle. One hand round the narrow tail root and one through the gills prevented the floundering fish from following the water as it poured overboard from the rolling vessel. The crossbeam on which the bridge poles were supported slid away. A crack, and the whole bridge gave way. Rope, rope! Water over our heads. Splendid job. Now it's holding. Enjoying yourself, Carlo? It's just like the Alps. Don't go to sleep here, Georges. We'll carry you to bed. Damn, how my arms ache! Was I asleep? Not quite. Are we still on *Ra*? Yes, the papyrus is creaking. There are stars outside; we are far away from the misty coast.

It was difficult to keep the first days after Cape Verde distinct in one's mind. Time flowed together. But in the logbook is a note that

June 20th was the hardest day up to then. On June 21st the entry
reads that the night was the worst we had seen, and the day no better.
But without sail or rudder-oars, and with sea anchors trailing to
slow us down, we were still able to log a day's progress of 31 nautical
miles or 57 kilometres towards America, the lowest recorded on the
voyage. On June 22nd the submerged end of the steering spar had
such an unsteadying effect on our course that Georges had to dive
down in goggles and saw off the thick spar under water. While three
of us hung completely or partly overboard in the twilight a dozen
black-and-white spotted dolphins came up and played along the
papyrus roll we were hanging on, so close that we could touch them.
The small whales gambolled up to the reed bundles and rolled about
without a splash in graceful play, more like soap bubbles than hundreds
of pounds of solid muscle. With Georges overboard and the waves
rhythmically rising to Abdullah's chest and mine, we were meeting
the whale in the whale's own habitat. It did not disturb us and we let
it play in peace in our common bath water. That day we discovered
for the first time that the waves which struck the cabin wall were
forcing their way further in, over the wickerwork cabin floor, between
the wooden boxes we slept on. The bottom of the case where Norman
kept his radio was soaking wet. The cabin was beginning to tilt so
sharply to starboard that several of the men tried to turn their mattresses
crosswise.

On June 25th there was a strange atmosphere. It vacillated between
cold and tropical heat. Once or twice there was a wave of heat carrying
a distinct scent of dry sand, just as I had known it in the Sahara. Had
I not had confidence in our approximate position, I would have thought
that we were navigating just off a desert coast. Only later did I learn
that sand from the Sahara regularly rains down on Central America.
That night the seas were worse than ever. We had to move everything
we could still farther towards the foredeck. All the boxes we had been
sleeping on in the cabin were awash, although the pliant *Ra* was
hurling herself over the chaos of waves as never before. She rode like a
magic carpet.

So it was that we eventually emerged into quiet weather, with a
fresh breeze, rolling seas and sunshine. The trade-wind blew steadily
from the north-east and the elements behaved more or less as one is
entitled to expect in these latitudes. As the weather changed, the first
shark came patrolling towards us and suddenly skimmed so close by

Georges' legs that he had to draw them in, but it simply glided on and disappeared in our wake.

June 28th was one of the most splendid days we spent on *Ra* and everyone busied himself peacefully with his own affairs. Georges sat in the door-opening with Abdullah, teaching him to read and write in Arabic. Others sat with laundry, fishing rods or diaries. Then we heard a heart-rending wail – from the equable Norman! For a while he had been overside on the foredeck, securing the broken oar-blade holding his beloved earthing plate, but now he was hanging as if paralysed, his face contorted, unable to pull the rest of his body on board. Everyone thought the worst: shark. We ran to pull him on board. There were no limbs missing, but the culprit was hanging on. The lower part of Norman's body was entwined in the glistening pink filaments of a big Portuguese man-o'-war. Norman was in a coma when he was dragged into the cabin and given cardiac stimulants.

'Ammonia,' said Yuri tensely. 'We have no ammonia. It's the only thing that helps to neutralize the caustic acid which is permeating his body. Urine is full of ammonia, all of you, and this is serious.'

For two hours Yuri sat massaging Norman with a rag dipped in a coconut shell full of urine while the patient writhed in pain and convulsions until he became inert and slept. His legs and the lower part of his body were covered with red sting marks like weals. When Norman awoke and looked from his own leg to all the innocent bubbles of foam which were floating as usual on the shining waves he shouted like a drunken man, 'Look, now the whole sea is full of baby men-o'-war!' He subsided with a bowl of hot dried-fruit soup. Next day he was still out of sorts and raged at Georges, who had suddenly got under his skin. But by evening the two of them had shaken hands and were sitting together singing cowboy songs.

On June 30th we drifted once again into a part of the ocean which was covered with oil clots. We were travelling the same way, but with the big sail we were moving much faster. Still we seemed unable to get away from them; we were passing untold numbers of the black floating lumps from morning till night. Then a splendid full moon rose far behind us in our wake. An unforgettable night, with moonlight on yellow papyrus and burgundy-coloured sail. The stars were beginning to fade on the eastern horizon. It was no longer May, nor even June; it was the beginning of July and we were still afloat with tons of useful cargo left.

On July 1st a ship bristling with masts and derricks appeared on the horizon to the north-west and passed us at close range, heading south-east. We were just crossing the shipping route between the USA and South Africa. We all stood on the bridge, the cabin roof and the steps of the mast to watch this homely fragment of our own twentieth century with something like nostalgia until the last masthead disappeared over the horizon. Then we were alone again with the sea. More alone than before. Georges stayed up on the bridge, humming in a rather melancholy manner. Then he gave a roar.

'They're coming back!'

It was true. Over the horizon where it had just disappeared the same ship hove into view again and now it was heading straight for us. The crew must have been discussing the extraordinary contraption they had passed and now the skipper had decided to come back and take a closer look. The ship came steaming straight towards *Ra*. *African Neptune*, New York, was the name on the bow as it swung in alongside *Ra*, with all the decks filled with waving people.

'Can we do anything for you?' Norman yelled to his countrymen, bubbling with exhilaration.

'No thanks, but perhaps there's something we can do for you,' came the shout from the bridge.

'Fruit!' the crew of *Ra* called back in many languages.

But *Ra* herself continued to forge ahead and was in a fair way to run her papyrus nose straight into the iron hull when our frantic shouts and gestures startled the skipper into starting up the propeller and hastily getting out of the way. Having something delivered to such an uncontrollable wanton was not easy. The sea-god's namesake made a wide detour round the sun-god's little namesake and as she crossed our line of drift a bag attached to an orange lifebelt was thrown into the sea. It whirled away far out of reach in the boil of the big ship's propeller. Georges had already put on his rubber suit for protection against Portuguese men-o'-war and dived out with a long line tied round his body. When we pulled him in he brought an unforgettable catch: 39 oranges, 37 apples, 3 lemons, 4 grapefruit and a wet roll of American weeklies. We waved and yelled our thanks. The foredeck had suddenly turned into a rainbow of Christmas presents. Fresh fruit and fruit salad in a world of salt. Cores for Safi and seed for Sinbad.

These were some of our best days on board *Ra.* Abdullah's papyrus bulwark and Carlo's jungle of guy-ropes on all sides of the cabin and stern seemed to be holding us up a little by the hair. Seen from the rolling ocean vessel we must have looked quite presentable. We on board the reed boat were all equally impressed by the incredible strength and loading capacity of the papyrus. Paper boat? Perhaps. But it was only the wooden parts which broke. Papyrus had proved to be a first-class building material. Its strength in sea water had been completely misjudged by the theorists, whether anthropologists or papyrus experts. It was equally wrong to believe, as we ourselves had believed, that the ancient papyrus boats, as painted on the walls in Egypt, were primitive vessels. The only thing an Egyptian papyrus boat had in common with a raft was that both floated equally well even if their bottoms were holed. Both the *Ra* and the *Kon-Tiki* were raft ships, because they had no hull. But otherwise, to compare the reed boat *Ra* with the log raft *Kon-Tiki* was like comparing a motor-car with a cart. Even a horse can make a cart go, but to drive a car you need an instructor and a licence. We had neither. We had set off on a sophisticated Egyptian vessel, never dreaming that it was so special-ized and unlike a simple raft in that one had to know the ingenious principles which made it work. It was made of first-class materials, but, like a car, if one was not instructed in the purpose and use of all the parts one could easily ruin something important before discovering by experiment how to make it all function. We were learning constantly, both from our failures and from our successes.

On July 4th Georges shook me awake with an anxious expression. He thought he could see water spouts in several places on the horizon. Black ribbons between sea and sky looked menacing as the sun rose, but they were simply scattered showers. Soon rain was pouring down on reed deck and bamboo roof. The unaccustomed rumble of thunder woke the crew and everyone came out into the dawn to wash the salt off their hair and bodies. We had so much water in the jars that we did not need to collect it. Scattered showers continued all that day, and the next, and the next. The waves flattened out as the rain subdued them, but the reed boat became completely drenched. After three days of showers it was heavy and sodden. The trade-wind turned fitful and shifted here and there, playing idly with draperies of rain-showers. *Ra* seemed to be stealing along on tiptoe, with barely a creak. Was it the calm before the storm?

There was plenty of opportunity to bathe and enjoy a fish's-eye view of the swollen strength and toughness of the papyrus bundles. One fly in the ointment was that once again, for two days running, we sailed through hundreds of thousands of small black clots travelling, as we were, to America. Out in the middle of Columbus' ocean we floated among them, and our hands turned black when we fingered them. Some were covered with small shells. Hundreds of long-necked barnacles and a terrified little crab had made themselves at home on *Ra*'s belly. Now and then we saw big shoals of flying fish swimming ahead of us like herring. They were timid, but our little pilot fish and pampano, the first striped, the second spotted, became so bold that they took nips at us and bit holes in the sacks of dried fish when Carlo hung them overboard to soak.

On July 5th, Egyptian Georges saw a rainbow for the first time in his life. The sunset on the same day was at least equally vivid. Enough paint for a hundred rainbows was smeared by invisible paint-brushes across the arch of sky towards which we were sailing. Norman sat doubled up in the cabin, working with chart and ruler on a board hung on the wickerwork wall. The rest of us lay on dry straw mattresses, waiting for the sum to be done. Through the chinks in the front wall we could see the riot of colour fading while Carlo lighted the paraffin lamp, which then disappeared with him up the steps of the mast.

'We have now sailed 2,150 nautical miles, or 4,009 kilometres,' said Norman at last. 'That means we are now much more than half-way. The distance from here to the West Indies is 1,300 miles or 2,425 kilometres, that is much less than the distance back to Safi.'

'The tail is holding us back, otherwise we would have sailed even faster,' said Yuri. 'Yesterday we were down to about forty miles.'

'The tail slows us down, but the worst thing is that it makes us yaw, too. Today we oscillated between 30° north and south of the main course the whole time, although we all took turns at the rudder-oars. Sixty degrees of error, that's a good many extra miles. I am simply calculating on the shortest distance between each midday position,' said Norman. 'If the tail had not sent us on such a zigzag course we would have been there by now.'

'The people who knew all the tricks of the papyrus boat could have been across long ago without problems,' said Georges.

The papyrus creaked peacefully and there was a gentle splashing behind our bedhead, as if someone were using a bathtub behind a screen.

'I thought the sea got worse the farther out one came but it's the other way round,' murmured Santiago. 'Among anthropologists we often speak about how primitive sailors might have reached this or that place, as long as they could keep close inshore, but that's the worst place of all!'

'Along coasts and round islands the seas and currents are squeezed into all sorts of extraordinary eddies and backwashes,' I confirmed. 'Close to land the sea runs amok much more easily than in the open, where the waves can stretch their full length. Even a storm is more dangerous on the coast.'

'The mistake is that anthropologists and other scientists are always arguing about whether reed boats and rafts can cross an ocean or not, and they never reach any agreement. But if anyone tries to find out in practice he provokes wrathful indignation, because the answer is presented in an unscientific way.'

This was a problem with which both Santiago and I were intimately acquainted. I was independent and could laugh it off, but Santiago had had a hard time getting permission from his university to join in anything as unscientific as a voyage by reed boat. Papyrus could be tested in a bathtub. Scientists work in libraries, museum offices, laboratories – not on the Atlantic, playing savages.

The only thing was that here we were, at sea, with our beards and sunburnt noses, getting an answer quite different from the answers in the textbooks. A result quite different from that of the specialist who had put his papyrus stalk in a water container. If you test a bit of balsa wood in the laboratory it sinks in a week or two. But if you do as the Indians did, fell standing timber and leave it in the sea with the sap in, the unexpected happens and you can keep afloat on balsa wood for 101 days, and land in Polynesia. Now, the papyrus experts had put bits of papyrus stalks in a tank of still water, and besides quickly losing buoyancy, the plant tissue began to develop bubbles and decay. Two weeks, at most, the textbooks said. Seven weeks had now passed. We and tons of cargo were being carried by exactly the same type of reed that sank in the laboratory. Why? Because the specialist experimented with loose reeds in a bathtub, while we sailed a completed reed boat on the salt sea. Experience had shown reed boat-builders from Egypt to Peru that reed absorbs water through the shorn-off, porous end, not through the tight fibrous sheath which covers the stalk. So they used special techniques to build their reed boats, compressing the ends of the reeds so that they let in almost no water. *Papyrus* and papyrus *boats* proved to be two quite different things.

'As long as the ropes hold,' Abdullah said daily, 'we shall float. If the ropes get slack the papyrus will absorb water. If the ropes break, we shall fall through.'

Before two months had passed we had long been so familiar with our environment that we often felt as if we were contemporary with the men who had created the papyrus boat and loaded it as we had with jars and baskets, skin containers and coils of rope, salted and dried food, nuts and honey. Ancient and medieval seamen must have experienced our many moods before us. Nothing was new, nothing seemed strange. Common problems, common joys, the yellow reed craft floating between sky and sea was the same. On our reed bundles we were outside time; none of us was a scientist now, we were all statistics in a scientific experiment which had been started up and ran by itself. Gradually time had begun to lose its dimensions. As our ancestors seemed to crowd in on us, past centuries became foreshortened, the image of time distorted. The Vikings were just over the horizon up there in the North Atlantic, Columbus was bobbing along in our wake. Soon the pyramid-builders had become Georges' grandparents, or at least he was beginning to feel prouder and prouder of his Egyptian forebears, whom he had previously regarded as something unreal in an old-fashioned school curriculum.

'If the stern holds I would gladly go on through the Panama Canal and across the Pacific,' Georges would daydream. 'If it's no good this time I shall build a new one and sail across again. It's obvious that my ancestors were the first to cross the Atlantic, at least in one direction.'

'It's not so obvious,' Santiago and I would argue, to Georges' bewilderment. 'What is obvious is that if they had tried they would have made it. The reed boat is much more suitable for sea travel than anyone thought. But it was not only the Egyptians who had reed boats; they were used from one end of the ancient civilized world to the other, from Mesopotamia to the Atlantic coast of Morocco.'

'Why did we copy Egyptian tomb paintings if we did not want to copy the Egyptian sailors?'

'Because only Egypt has contemporary illustrations which show all the construction details. It is thanks to the pharaohs' religion and the preservative desert climate that we know so much about everyday life in Egypt four or five thousand years ago.'

One of the sixteen wooden boxes we used to lie on in the cabin was full of books about the world's earliest civilizations. In a work on ancient Mesopotamia there was a picture of a stone slab from Nineveh, showing a splendid relief of reed boats at sea in war and peace. The ruins of Nineveh lie far inland, over 800 kilometres from the mouth of the Tigris and 600 kilometres from the Phoenician port of Byblos on the Mediterranean. Mesopotamian stone-masons, soldiers and merchants had contacts with both the Mediterranean and the Persian Gulf. The stone slab from Nineveh shows that their sailors used two types of reed boat. Three of the boats on the slab are depicted as reed bundles lashed together in the Egyptian manner, with both prow and stern curving upwards. They are full of men, and the waves round them represent the ocean itself, since a most realistic giant crab dominates the centre of the picture, surrounded by swimming fish. Double ranks of armed warriors have boarded the vessels and are busy chasing the crews of the two largest reed boats into the sea. Some are diving overboard, others are swimming, and a third reed boat is fleeing from the naval battle, with its bearded sailors humbly praying to the sun. A straight coast and two small islands covered with tall reeds encircle the seascape, and three more reed boats are hidden among the reeds. On board the one by the farthest island, archers kneel side by side, ready for battle, but by the mainland and the nearest island the scene is peacefully idyllic: groups and rows of men and women sit in reed boats, chatting and gesturing amicably.

This relief told us a great deal. For instance, we noticed the difference between the boats on the open sea and those among the reeds by the shore. In the former, both prow and stern were peaked and curved up as in the ancient ships of Egypt and Peru, while the sterns of the boats in the reed swamps were sheered off broad and straight. They offered no protection from the waves but were ideally suited to being beached and up-ended for their daily drying, as small reed boats always were in both the Old and New Worlds.[1]

While in Mesopotamia small reed boats have survived until the present day, hardly anyone would have thought that reed boats had

---

[1] The complete relief, now preserved in the Nineveh Gallery of the British Museum, shows a total of ten reed boats, seven of which are sea-going types with up-turned bow and stern.

ever existed in Egypt, too, had they not been preserved for posterity in the old tomb paintings, for the reed boat has vanished from Egypt with the papyrus reed itself. But both the types shown on the stone slab from Nineveh have survived in Peru to the present day. The Spaniards found both types side by side right along the coast of the Inca kingdom; scattered specimens are still in use, and numerous pictures on mummy cloths, ceramic jars and reliefs from the earliest pre-Inca period show that both types have remained unchanged from the days when the first pyramid-builders settled on the coast and portrayed reed boats engaged in sea fishing.

Thanks to the realistic art from the ruins of Nineveh, the burial chambers of the Nile Valley and the mummy tombs on the east coast of Peru, we know that fully-manned reed boats of the same design were once an important cultural factor common to the earliest civilizations in Asia Minor, North Africa and South America. Since the mighty civilizations of old collapsed, small reed boats of both types have survived in a circle round Egypt: in Mesopotamia, Ethiopia, Central Africa, Sardinia and Morocco on one side of the Atlantic, and also throughout the early American cultural area, with Easter Island as an off-shoot, on the other side. Now we ourselves, with a monkey and a duck, were far over on the American side of the Atlantic, on board a specimen which originated in Africa, and we were beginning to ask ourselves if the dividing line between the Old and the New World reed boats was as real as it might appear from the chart. Was the Atlantic divided down the middle, which we had passed some time ago, or along one of its continental borders? As far as floating vessels are concerned, should we draw the dividing line between them on the map, that is on the sea-bed, which is still, or on the surface, which is continuously moving from one continent to the other? Were we the first for thousands of years to have had the steering mechanism on our primitive vessel broken on its encounter with the Atlantic ocean currents south of Gibraltar?

The Egyptian Georges, who had previously been interested only in judo and frogman techniques, had suddenly developed a passionate interest in the fantastic world of antiquity. Was there no written evidence to show that the ancient Egyptians had voyaged beyond Gibraltar?

No, there was not. But the Phoenicians, who for thousands of years were their nearest neighbours in the eastern Mediterranean, had plied regularly beyond Gibraltar and down the whole open coast of Morocco, far beyond Safi and Cape Juby. Potsherds with Phoenician inscriptions and other relics from organized Phoenician colonization, including purple production, are now constantly appearing along the west coast of Africa, further south than we ourselves had followed it. Only a few years ago science had no idea that these earliest known seafarers from the easternmost corner of the Mediterranean had had an important trading colony on the flat island off Mogador, south of Safi. Phoenician relics are now being dug up both there and right down on the Rio de Oro coast, south of Morocco. Modern archaeologists have discovered that the Phoenicians had a solid foothold among the *guanches* out on the Canary Islands and that they used these oceanic islands as a staging post in order to pass Cape Juby and Cape Bajador in safety. Because of their advanced trading posts they had to sail beyond these dangerous points, which we ourselves had now barely managed to clear in our reed boat.

There is a written record by the historian Herodotus, after his visit to Egypt, stating that in the time of Pharaoh Necho, who ruled about 600 BC, the Egyptians had dispatched a Phoenician fleet to sail round Africa. It is likely that some of the Egyptians, being responsible for the expedition, did participate, although it is expressly recorded that ships and sailors were Phoenician. They sailed down the Red Sea and returned through Gibraltar three years later, having twice encamped to grow crops. They could report that the sun had moved to the north as they sailed round Africa. More than a century later one of the greatest Phoenician voyages on record was led by Hanno, with the aim of establishing colonies for trade outside Gibraltar. Sixty galleys, each equipped with sails as well as fifty oars and packed with a total of 30,000 prospective settlers of all trades, navigated into the unsheltered Atlantic. The vast fleet passed the ancient colony of the Eternal City of the Sun, and anchored six times along the Moroccan coast to disembark colonists. They followed the dangerous shores further than us, rounded Cape Juby and passed the Cape Verde Islands off Senegal, to reach as far down as the jungle rivers of tropical West Africa.

It is known that the Phoenicians even had overland trade relations with jungle tribes of West Africa. They made use of Numidian caravans which crossed the continent to bring back ivory and gold as well as lions and other wild animals wanted for the many ancient circuses entertaining spectators in all important cities westwards from Syria and Egypt to the Mediterranean islands and the Atlantic coast of Morocco. Centuries before Christ, all of North Africa was thus entangled in a cobweb of explorations and trade routes in which the intrepid Phoenicians were deeply involved. Again, who were these Phoenicians about whom we know so very little; from whom did they descend and who taught them to sail? Thanks to the Romans we have simply inherited the word 'Phoenician' as a convenient sack into which we put anything sailing from the inner Mediterranean before Roman times.

On a desolate beach just south of our starting place, an angled mole made of tens of thousands of megalithic stone blocks still projects towards the reefs and provides a magnificent harbour. Fantastic quantities of gigantic quarried stones have been dragged out into the sea by experienced marine architects, who built such a lasting bulwark that the Atlantic waves have not succeeded in washing it away after thousands of years. Who needed such a big harbour on that desolate sandy point before the Arabs and Portuguese had begun to sail down the Atlantic coast of Africa?

On a height where the broad Lucus River flows into the Atlantic on the north-west coast of Morocco stand the gigantic ruins of one of the mightiest towns of antiquity, with a past disappearing into the darkness of pre-history. Huge megalithic blocks weighing many tons were transported up the cliffs and lifted on top of one another in giant walls several metres high which can be seen from the sea. The blocks are cut and polished, the joints accurate to a millimetre, with the specialized technique characteristic of megalithic walls in Egypt, Sardinia, Mexico and Peru, the very areas where reed boats were in use. And it is also here, on the Lucus River which curves down to the sea at the foot of the ancient ruins, and only here, that Moroccan reed boats, *madia*, have survived to our own times. The oldest known name of the megalithic town is *Maqom Semes*, 'City of the Sun'. When the Romans found it they wrote that fantastic legends were associated with its earliest history. They called the town *Lixus*, the Eternal City, and built their own temples on top of the ancient ruins. Their buildings and colonnades seem pitifully small compared with the colossal blocks in the walls on which they rest. Roman historians placed the grave of the hero Hercules himself on an island in the river at the foot of these massive ruins, and with the open Atlantic for background, Roman artists made a giant mosaic portrait of the ocean-god Neptune, with crab's claws bristling from his hair and beard. Then the Romans disappeared, and the Arabs who followed, and have now merged with the original population on the surrounding plain, call the ruined town *Shimish*, 'Sun', and in their stories the last queen who ruled there was called *Shimisa*, 'Little Sun'.

The very few archaeologists who have embarked on small test digs have found that the Phoenicians used 'Sun City' long before the Romans. But who founded it? Perhaps the Phoenicians. If so, Phoenician stone-masonry was equal to the best on both sides of the Atlantic. The Phoenicians' home was in the distant eastern Mediterranean, the present Lebanon. 'Sun City' was no Mediterranean port, but a true Atlantic harbour established at the very edge of the powerful current which swings westward through the Canary Islands and ends in Mexico. How old are the walls? No one knows. They are covered to a depth of fifteen feet by the detritus of Phoenicians, Romans, Berbers and Arabs. The Romans believed in Hercules and Neptune, but not in the sun-god, and the Roman ruins lying uppermost are therefore not solar-oriented. But recent test digs down to the very bottom have shown that the lowest and largest of the giant blocks, those which were already covered with detritus when the Romans came, and which the Romans therefore failed to demolish or rebuild into their temples, provide the foundations for extensive buildings which were carefully oriented according to the sun. The Phoenicians, like their Egyptian neighbours and most of the earliest Mediterranean civilizations, were sun-worshippers.

The Sun City, the Eternal City, Hercules' last resting-place, older, according to the Romans, than Carthage – why all this tribute to a remote megalithic Atlantic port; why should it lie beyond Gibraltar? The founders of this Eternal City apparently lived as many sea miles from the Phoenicians in Asia Minor as from the Indians in America. To keep in touch with Asia Minor they must have been real masters of navigation, manoeuvring off the dangerous coast of North Africa, where no regular current and wind could help them there or back. It would have been infinitely easier for the residents of this Eternal City to cross the ocean and teach their stone-masonry techniques to the Indians. They would only have had to pull in their oars and let themselves drift like us. If it was the Phoenicians who founded this eternal Sun City their sailors must have taken priests, architects and other representatives of the nation's élite with them on their voyage of colonization outside the Mediterranean. In fact, the maritime Phoenicians are known first and foremost as the intermediaries of civilization in the ancient world. If it was the Phoenicians who lived in this Atlantic city, they knew all about the ancient pyramid types of the Old World, both the stepped and the smooth-sided ones. We know Phoenician exploration expeditions sailed at the request of Egypt: there was Phoenician timber in the ships buried round the Egyptian pyramids, Egyptian papyrus in the books of Phoenicia, and Pharaoh Rameses II had his own portrait, with inscriptions, carved in three places on the Phoenician coastal cliffs. In peace and war there were intimate contacts between the two countries. In fact, since modern scholars did not believe in the seaworthiness of Egyptian papyrus ships, it has been assumed that the Egyptians used Phoenician ships even to collect their own tribute from the Mediterranean islands and the Syrian coast. Still better did the Phoenicians know the terraced adobe pyramids of Asia Minor, which differed from the Egyptian in having a narrow staircase or ramp leading up the middle of one or more of the pyramid's terraced sides to a little stone temple on top, just as in the earliest pyramids built on the American side of the Atlantic.

'But we Egyptians sailed on the sea, too,' Georges would argue, and as a good Christian Copt he quoted the Bible, where Isaiah (18. ii) reports that his homeland was visited by Egyptian messengers who came across the sea in boats made of reeds. In the new edition of King James' Bible it was even specified that these reed boats were of papyrus. Georges also reminded us that Moses himself (Exodus 2. iii) was set adrift on the Nile by his mother in a papyrus ark daubed with pitch and bitumen. In Egypt, Georges had shown me the walls of Queen Hatshepsut's temple at Luxor in the Nile valley, covered with paintings showing that she had sent an expedition of several large wooden ships right down the Red Sea to Punt in Somaliland, to return with all sorts of merchandise, including complete exotic trees for replanting in the queen's garden.

What Georges did not know was that modest merchants with ordinary papyrus boats had sailed even further than the queen's famous fleet of wooden luxury ships. Eratosthenes, chief librarian of the huge Egyptian papyrus library in Alexandria on the Nile estuary, before the tens of thousands of irreplaceable papyrus manuscripts went up in flames, was able to report that 'papyrus ships, with the same sails and rigging as on the Nile' sailed as far as Ceylon and the mouth of the Ganges in India. The Roman historian Pliny (Book VI, XXIII, 82) later quoted that learned librarian in his geographical description of Ceylon, saying that while the papyrus boats took a full twenty days to sail from the Ganges to the island of Ceylon, the 'modern' Roman ships made the journey in seven days. This casual but most important written reference enables us to work out that the ancient papyrus boats made the same speed through the ocean as we did before we let our stern sink and become a brake. In fact, measuring the distance between the River Ganges and Ceylon, we can calculate from the information preserved through Eratosthenes that the papyrus boat, with Egyptian rigging like ours, must have averaged about 75 nautical miles, or nearly 140 kilometres, in twenty-four hours, that is slightly more than three knots.

But the Indian Ocean was not the Atlantic. Perhaps the Egyptians had also sailed beyond Gibraltar, but no evidence has been preserved to prove it. The Phoenicians, however, knew the rocks and beaches along the coast where we had begun our voyage. They had gradually learned the secrets of local currents.

The mystery surrounding the earliest traffic on the very ocean which washed up over our afterdeck, sent flying fish on board and drove us ceaselessly forward, became still more challenging when we lay with our beards stuck in learned books, feeling like ancient seafarers reading about ourselves and our own times. Looking up I saw the Mexican tapping water from a goatskin bag into an amphora; the Egyptian swayed past with a papyrus lifebelt over his shoulders, while the monkey poked its funny little face in and stole my 'nasometer' which I used to fix the angle of the Pole Star.

'Bearded men are floating westward across the Atlantic,' I wrote in a message to the head of the Archaeological Institute of Mexico, with a joking reference to the bearded Olmecs who founded the earliest Mexican civilization. It was only when Norman took our little radio set out of the case he was lying on that antiquity disappeared in a flash and for some minutes we were living in our own, modern world. Dick Ehrhorn, a ham radio operator in Florida, had built the little set, and soon after we lost contact with Morocco we suddenly heard a voice over the microphone saying, 'LI2B, LI2B, this is LA5KG Chris Bockelie in Oslo.' After that Chris travelled with us in the magic box right across the ocean, and beside him there was room for Just LA7RF in Ålesund, Frank I1KFB in Genoa, Herb WB2BEE in New York, Alex UA1KBW in Leningrad, as well as the builder of the set in person, Dick W4ETO in Florida, and many other voices which for the men of antiquity would have been genies from Aladdin's lamp, flying invisibly across the sea and landing in our little box among the goatskin bags and jars. Through the radio amateurs our families knew we were alive. Like us they had the chart of the Atlantic on the wall and marked our position at intervals. Half-way across we exchanged greetings with U Thant and the heads of state of our seven countries of origin. The presidents of the two super powers in East and West sent us friendly greetings which arrived on the same day. When Norman closed his 'Pandora's box' again we went straight back to antiquity, just as we had been wrenched into the present when he opened it and filled the cabin with a chorus of cackling metallic voices: radio hams in every conceivable country trying to help us with contacts. When they had gone the water gurgled and splashed and the ropes moaned desolately as before. In our world there were only sea and flying-fish, and now and then a green back gliding past, down in the bottomless depths.

Bearded men: that was one of our last humorous reports. Fate held us in the hollow of its hand. Our tail was under water, helping the waves to surge freely up to the back wall of the cabin, like breakers on a beach. Little fish were living on board, on the afterdeck. If we escaped a storm we would drift ashore in this way in a week or two, with cabin and foredeck chock full of food and other cargo. But if we met one more storm we would come out of it a wreck. Since leaving Morocco, only *African Neptune* had photographed *Ra* at sea under full sail. To see all of ourselves in perspective we had to swim out on a lifeline, and for us, who for weeks had seen only each other with some limited section of the vessel as background, it was a really thrilling sight to see *Ra* from the outside. Georges swam out with an underwater camera, craned up from the crest of a wave and snapped *Ra* struggling along, as others would have seen us.

On July 7th the papyrus boat was still looking beautiful, with its high golden prow and the burgundy-red sail tauter than ever, because we now had the east wind at our backs. But if a storm came *Ra* would never emerge looking as she looked now, and the film of the expedition would have no long shots of the papyrus boat sailing on the open sea. All the film Carlo had already taken might be damaged, too. So in the next radio contact with Italy I gave my wife, Yvonne, the job of finding a film photographer who could meet us with a small vessel at sea off the West Indies. Even if I did not hint at it by so much as a word to my own friends on board, I felt at the bottom of my heart that this might also be a safety measure. If lives were at stake the responsibility ultimately devolved on me.

What was the film photographer to bring with him? Everyone wanted a little fruit, Santiago a box of chocolates. Nothing else. We had more water and provisions than we could use. Salt meat, ham and sausages, jars and baskets full of honey, eggs, butter, dried fruit, nuts and Egyptian bread-biscuits. The deck forward and to port of the cabin was still so covered with food that it was hopeless trying to find room to put a foot down.

Bearded men. Only Yuri stood up to his knees in the bath water aft and shaved. Red beards and black beards. Abdullah now had hair on the top of his head. Black hands and white pulled on the same ropes. It had been so in ancient times as well. Nothing new. The wall paintings of ancient Egypt show men with yellow hair and men with black hair building the same papyrus boat. Under the sand where we had built *Ra*, at the foot of his own pyramid, the Pharaoh Chephren, son of Cheops, buried his queen and had her portrayed for all time with yellow hair and blue eyes. In a glass case in Cairo Museum, among the mummies of his kinsmen with their straight, black hair, lies Rameses II himself, with soft, yellow, silky hair topping his hook-nosed mummy skull. The north has no monopoly of blond, fair-skinned peoples. There were undoubtedly some living in Mediterranean countries, including Asia Minor and North Africa, long before the progenitors of the Vikings existed in Scandinavia. If there is any physical connection at all it must have been from south to north, because the Viking period began 3,000 years after the Pharaoh Chephren had buried his blue-eyed, blonde wife beside his father's mighty cedar ship in Egypt.

Blond men with beards. They were as common among the original population of the Atlas Mountains as among the Berbers on the plains round the City of the Sun on the Moroccan coast, where their descendants can still be seen; and they had sailed from the African coast with their women and beasts across the Atlantic to settle as *guanches* on the Canary Islands.

Blond men with beards, who were not Vikings, because they built pyramids and worshipped the sun, ran through all the legends associated with the ancient American cultures, from Mexico to Peru. Throughout tropical America, wherever pyramids and carved stone colossi lie – abandoned as ruins from bygone days – the Spaniards learned that they were not the first bearded white men to come sailing across the Atlantic. The legends told in detail of teachers, similar in appearance to the Spaniards, who had once mingled with the aboriginal Indians and taught them how to build adobe houses and live in towns, erect pyramids and write on paper and stone. In other words, white, bearded travellers were credited everywhere with having merged with the original local inhabitants and laid together with them the first foundations of local cultures. The Indians themselves had no beards. The Spaniards exploited the legends in order to conquer both Mexico and Peru, but the legends were not created by the Spaniards. A thousand years before the Spaniards came, American artists from Mexico to Peru were making ceramic figures and stone statues of bearded men. Before the Vikings began to sail the Atlantic the Mayans had painted white men with long golden hair in a legendary sea battle taking place somewhere on the Atlantic coast of Mexico. When American archaeologists opened a brightly painted pillared chamber inside one of the largest pyramids at Chichen Itza some decades ago, they found splendid mural paintings, which they copied in minute detail before the humid tropical air and countless tourists got in and removed everything. The paintings illustrated a dramatic attack on naked white men, navigating yellow boats with upturned prow and stern. As in the relief from ancient Nineveh, there is a large crab in the waves, with lots of marine fish and shells showing that the sailors are either coming from the ocean or trying to get away to sea. The white-skinned sailors are met on land by dark-skinned warriors with feathers in their hair, who tie their hands behind their backs, scalp their blond locks and lay one of them on the sacrificial slab, while others dive naked overboard from their capsized vessel, with long yellow locks floating on the waves among rays and other salt water fish. While some of the white-skinned men are being dragged helplessly away by their yellow hair, others have packed up all their possessions and are walking calmly off along the beach with large packs on their backs.

What legend or historical episode were the Mayans trying to perpetuate in this way, inside one of their most important pyramids, centuries before the Spaniards landed? No one knows. The three American archaeologists who copied the wall-paintings wrote soberly that the temple portraits of light-skinned men with yellow hair 'give rise to much interesting speculation as to their identity'.

We must have speculated more than most, on board *Ra*, where the elements were daily carrying us, as if on a mechanical escalator, towards the Gulf of Mexico, without our having to push or row. We did not delude ourselves that we could compete in seamanship with the professional navigators of old. Norman was our only seaman, but he had never seen a papyrus boat before. Abdullah had, but he had never seen the ocean. We would never have managed to navigate a papyrus boat with Egyptian rigging in the capricious water round Ceylon. Nor could we have sailed Phoenician vessels trading between Asia Minor and their colonies at Rio de Oro, a trip far longer than the distance from Rio de Oro to South America. But we could surely imitate men of old who had been caught by a storm off the African coast and lost their steering power.

Rain-clouds hung about us the length of the horizon and at regular intervals a shower came and washed us and the deck so that the papyrus became even more wet and soggy, and the water level on the afterdeck crept slowly but perceptibly farther forward up the narrow strip of deck on the windward side of the cabin, from which we had long since shifted the cargo. Sea water now stood in the depression pressed down in the papyrus floor by the starboard mast-foot, showing how low we were on the windward side, where all the papyrus was now soaking wet. On the lee side, on the other hand, we still had to hang over the edge on our stomachs to reach down to the passing wave-caps.

We were now so near to the mainland coast of South America that we were visited by the first sea-birds from the other side. Beautiful tropic birds, with long, trailing tail feathers, flew over the mast. A shark overtook us from the rear and made a savage attack on the lifebelt which we had in tow. Those of the men who had never seen a shark had an awful experience when Carlo shouted that something was fighting the lifebelt, and soon afterwards a dark monster, six feet long, came swimming majestically up with its dorsal fin above the surface. It rose and sank with the waves. When it was level with *Ra* it turned savage again, rolled its whitish belly upwards and thrashed its tail, attacking the underside of the papyrus rolls with gaping jaws.

Was it gobbling down some of the long, tasty barnacles? Whatever it was gobbling, the danger to the ropes was serious. With my experience of the low-lying *Kon-Tiki* raft I leaned over the railing and grabbed for the shark's rough tail which was like sandpaper to the touch. Then I saw that it had an open wound on its back and two big pilot fish were keeping station close above it. Twice I almost had it, but the lee side was still so high that I would have been dragged overboard unless I could get a better hold. Then big Georges drove his harpoon into the body of the shark. The brute fought for a moment with its steely muscles, until the water foamed about its tail. Then Georges was left standing with his tough harpoon line which the brute had snapped in two. It disappeared into the ocean depths with Georges' one remaining harpoon.

We sank back into peaceful daydreams about the unsolved mysteries of antiquity. Norman had been brought up on the doctrine that America was a world apart until his own ancestors came over from Europe, bringing knowledge and culture with them. The politicians believed that, and most of the ordinary textbooks were written by isolationists. Aztecs, Mayans and Incas had only primitive savages from Alaska and Siberia in their family tree. Europe had received its culture from Asia Minor and Africa via Crete and other islands in the narrow Mediterranean. But America had received nothing across the broad Atlantic, until Columbus. Primitive vessels could sail along coasts and reefs, they said, but not on the wide ocean. Now Norman wanted to hear the diffusionists' arguments. Were not the American Indian civilizations in Mexico and Peru completely different from the Afro-Asian cultures of the inner Mediterranean which had later laid the foundations of European civilization?

Basically not so terribly different, Santiago and I were able to explain. There are enough dissimilarities for those who are specialists and look for details. But if an unspecialized layman who does not delve into the thickness and grains of potsherds, or the motifs and designs on cotton textiles, tried to acquaint himself with the broader common features he would probably be quite amazed.

At a rate unknown to mankind elsewhere in the world, a series of jungle and desert tribes in the central parts of America managed to make up the Old World's cultural lead in the course of a few centuries before Christ, while all the rest of the native population of America, in the more favourable climatic zones north and south of the tropical belt, persisted with the primitive tribal communities of their ancestors until the Europeans arrived. The exact century when the tropical tribes in Mexico and Peru received their record-breaking urge and capacity to take this great leap forward from a primitive way of life to full civilization is known to no one living today: but what is certain is that the earliest American civilizations made their real breakthrough before the Christian era and yet after the civilizations of Asia Minor had reached their peak and were busy sailing out beyond Gibraltar, with everything carried on board that was needed in order to establish their important colonies along the Atlantic coast of Africa.

What was the essence of the sudden evolution which began just about simultaneously in the jungle thickets of the Atlantic coast of Mexico and among the sand-dunes on the opposite coast of Peru? The sun was suddenly worshipped as a god. It did not matter that, in one place, it was rainy and shady among the crowded trees of the primeval forest, while in another the sun burned down unhindered on dry sand; in both, the aboriginal Indians suddenly began to build step-pyramids to the sun. They built on the same principles and each under the command of an omnipotent priest-king claiming divinity and descent from the sun rather than from his own local tribe. Brother and sister marriage was practised in the priest-king's family in order to keep the divine blood as pure as possible. The priest-king put an end to the old tribal dance round the totem pole, to the sacrifices to invisible spirits and other traditional supernatural beings. Hereafter it was the solar disc which was to be studied and worshipped. Both on the Mexican Gulf and on the Peruvian coast the Indians stopped making family huts of branches and leaves. In both places they began to manufacture adobe bricks, of the same type and in precisely the same manner as men had been making for thousands of years in the Mediterranean area, from Mesopotamia to Morocco. A special type of earth was mixed with straw and water and compressed in small rectangular wooden forms. The contents were then turned out and baked in the sun into adobe bricks of uniform shape and size. While the neighbouring Indians continued to build the wigwams, leaf huts and plank houses of their forefathers, the sun-worshippers, from Mexico to Peru, moved into elegant adobe buildings constructed exactly as in the Old World, often on several floors and with gutters from the roof, and placed side by side to create organized urban communities with streets, sewers and aqueducts.

But although the invention or introduction of adobe bricks enabled these particular tribes from Mexico to Peru to build solar temples whose ruins still stand in jungle and desert like veritable mountains, they also began to attack the solid rock and hew and joint together gigantic blocks, with a skill and specialized technique in masonry to be found nowhere in the world except in that same restricted area from the inner Mediterranean and Egypt to the City of the Sun in Morocco. The Olmecs on the Gulf of Mexico, who had plenty of timber as well as adobe bricks, made long journeys across swamps and jungle to find solid rock suitable for quarrying. Almost a thousand years before Christ, they were transporting stone blocks of up to 25 tons each for a hundred kilometres through jungle and over swamp-land to a temple site near the Gulf, where they had already manufactured enough adobe bricks to build a sun-oriented step-pyramid 103 feet high. Who in Europe almost 3,000 years ago had the idea and urge to erect buildings as high as ten-storey houses? In Egypt the custom of building adobe step-pyramids to the sun was long dead when the Olmecs hit on the same idea. But in Asia Minor, the back-garden of Phoenicia, the sun was still worshipped from temples on top of stepped ziggurat pyramids, and it was, after all, they, and not the Giza-type pyramids in Egypt, which shared all the fundamental features of the Olmec and pre-Inca temple pyramids in America.

Before the Christian era the jungle Indians on the Gulf of Mexico had also learned, in record-breaking time, all the secrets of a perfect calendar system, and assembled a body of astronomical knowledge which had taken several millennia of study in the Old World. The ancient Egyptians, Babylonians and Assyrians, living in open plains and deserts, had the whole starry sky revolving openly above them. The Phoenicians harvested the fruit of this ancient cultural heritage, which enabled them to navigate out of sight of any land. How could the jungle Indians on the coast of Mexico have caught them up and won the race, living as they did under the foliage of the rain-forest where visibility was often reduced to the range of their own axe-shafts? Yet these early Indians had an astronomically more accurate calendar year than the Spaniards who came and 'discovered' them. Even our own Gregorian calendar is not as accurate as the one used by the Maya Indians on the Gulf of Mexico before Columbus. They arrived at an astronomical year of 365.2420 days, which is only one day short in every 5,000 years, while our modern calendar is based on a year of

365.2425 days, which is a day and a half too much in every 5,000 years. That sort of knowledge was not quickly or easily worked out. The Maya estimate of the length of the year was thus 8.64 seconds closer to the truth than our modern calendar. Their earlier neighbours, who entombed their sun-king in the dripping stone pyramid we had visited in Palenque, left an inscription stating that 81 months made 2,392 days, giving them a month of 29.53086 days, which deviates by only 24 seconds from the real length.

The Mayans had acquired the basis of all their astronomical knowledge from the still older Olmecs down on the coast, who even before the Christian era had been carving precise dates on their beautiful stone monuments. Europe had no chronology at that time. Zero in the Christian calendar is January 1st of the year allotted to the birth of Christ. Zero in the Mohammedan calendar is the year when Mohammed fled from Mecca to Medina, or AD 622 in our calendar. The Buddhist calendar begins with the birth of Buddha, that is about the year 563 BC. Zero in the ancient Maya calendar would have been August 12th, 3113 BC in our own. What decided this extraordinarily precise starting date? No one knows. Some believe that the Indians snatched this date out of the air, as somewhere to begin their calendar. Others think they may have worked back to some specific astronomical conjunction occurring long before civilization began to flourish in America. In Egypt the first dynasty of the pharaohs began between 3200 and 3100 BC, that is concurrently with the beginning of the Maya calendar, but as far as we know there was no civilization on the American side of the ocean as early as that. If the jungle Indians came to Mexico at least 15,000 years ago and waited until only a few centuries before our own era before suddenly producing the amazing Olmec civilization, why did they begin their own calendar at a date which coincided with the very time when the earliest civilizations elsewhere in the world were born? – precisely when they were beginning to flourish in Mesopotamia, Egypt and Crete?

How did the Mayans inherit a calendar which was accurate to a few seconds, if they began it at random at a time when their own ancestors were barbarians and when, as far as we know, the Olmecs themselves had not begun their astronomical observations in America? We have no answer. We only know that the Maya calendar began at 4 *Ahau* 2 *Cumhu*, that is August 12th, 3113 BC. We also know that both they and their Mexican kinsmen, the Aztecs in the highlands, had written and oral texts stating that civilization came to Mexico when a white, bearded man who claimed descent from the sun landed on the Gulf of Mexico with a large party of sages, astronomers, architects, priests and musicians. The Mayans called him *Kukulkan*, the Aztecs *Quetzalcoatl*; both names mean 'Plumed Serpent'. We do not know who invented this extraordinary name. A plumed serpent, often of enormous size, is painted on some of the pharaohs' tombs in Egypt as well, and on a great many of the Egyptian papyrus manuscripts. Perhaps a mixture of bird and snake as a divine symbol on both sides of the Atlantic is not so extraordinary, since birds of prey, snakes and felines were the three special symbols for the personification of the sun and the sun-king in Mesopotamia, Egypt, Mexico and Peru. These were the countries in which the sun-king's head-dress and other emblems were ornamented with the heads and often whole figures of these three particular animals. No less important in Mesopotamia and Egypt were the bird-men, who in symbolic art surround the sun-king and the sun-god. They occur again in Mexico, and in superabundance in Peru, where, just as in Egypt, they are shown as men with beaked bird heads, often helping the sun-king on his voyages aboard his sickle-shaped reed boat. From Peru the bird-men reached Easter Island, where they are also depicted with reed boats. But it is not these symbolic, imaginative figures who are credited with bringing civilization to tropical America. This honour is accorded by Mayans, Aztecs and Incas to perfectly normal men. They differ from most Indians only in that they had moustaches, beards and white skins. They did not come on wings but walking through the forest with cloak, staff and sandals, and they taught the natives to write, build, weave and worship the sun as the supreme deity. They instituted regular schools with the sacred history of the nation as a principal subject. The earliest American history-tellers follow them from their first landing on the Gulf of Mexico up to the Aztec highlands, down to the Mayan jungle peninsula, and on through the tropical forest, southward across Central America. The Indians throughout the vast Inca empire, from Ecuador to Peru and Bolivia, tell exactly the same story. Civilization was brought to them by white and bearded men who, under the leadership of the sun king, Con-Tici-Viracocha, first settled on the Island of the Sun in Lake Titicaca. Later they sailed away from there on a whole fleet of reed boats, to land and build the sun-pyramid, the megalithic walls and all the monoliths in human form which can still be seen among the remnants of the ruined city of Tiahuanaco. Hostilities with warlike tribes finally drove these first purveyors of culture north by way of Cuzco to the port of Manta which lies just where the equator crosses Ecuador. Here they altered course for the west and vanished across the Pacific, like 'foam on the water', hence the nickname *Viracocha*, which was later also given to the Spanish voyagers and all other white men.

We do not need to believe that there is any truth behind these traditions, even though they are as detailed as they are consistent, but in that case it is a still more remarkable cultural parallel that beardless Indians with raven-black hair decided to carve, paint and describe men with beards, fair skins and blond hair, such as we find on the tombs in Egypt and in historical illustrations from both Morocco and the Canary Islands. We believe in the complete mastery of masonry and astronomy among Mexican jungle Indians because the ruins cannot be explained away, but we reject their traditional memories, partly because they involve a religion alien to us, and partly because we only believe in the written word. We forget that the ancient Mexican civilizations had writing. They wrote on paper, wood, clay and stone. And we forget that they illustrated their hieroglyphic accounts with realistic images. The Olmecs, who were erecting monuments with engraved dates before Christ, also pushed themselves to quite inhuman extremes in order to leave for posterity huge stone representations of two widely disparate racial types.

Although their portraits are amazingly realistic in every slightest detail, they do not portray any surviving Indian type. One type is markedly negroid, with a round face, thick distended lips and a flat, broad, short nose. This type is popularly referred to as 'Baby-Face'. The other has a well-defined, sharp profile, with a strong aquiline nose, small, thin-lipped mouth and often a moustache and goatee or flowing full beard. The archaeologists have jokingly nicknamed this type 'Uncle Sam'. 'Uncle Sam' is generally portrayed with a majestic head-dress, full-length cloak, belt and sandals. This type, strongly semitic in appearance and often carrying a wanderer's staff, is illustrated from the Olmec area southward as far as the legends about the white men go. Modern religious sects have often cited this in support of their belief in the 'lost tribes of Israel' or the holy 'Book of Mormon'. A beautiful stone sculpture of the culture-bringer Con-Tici-Viracocha north of Lake Titicaca in Peru was confused by the arriving Spaniards with St Bartholomew, and a monastic order was established in his honour until the mistake was discovered and the old statue of the culture-bringer, with his ten-inch stone beard, was smashed to pieces.

The negroid Olmec type, on the other hand, appears warlike and primitive, often portrayed in grotesque dances, hunchbacked and crooked, or in the form of a spherical stone head lying loose on the ground, and yet so big that it may weigh up to twenty-five tons. Who were 'Uncle Sam' and his companion 'Baby-Face'? Which of them was the Olmec? Neither. 'Olmec' is a name we have coined because we have no idea who either of them was.

The Olmecs could write. Both Aztecs and Mayans learned writing from them, even if they chose to write a quite different type of hiero-glyph, so that one Mexican race could not understand another. It is easy to learn to write, but not to invent writing. The art is to discover that words and sounds can be converted into inaudible symbols which can be kept. Having learned that this is possible, it is a simple matter to think of new signs, letters, runes, cuneiform characters or hieroglyphs. In the Mediterranean area one culture acquired the invention of writing from another. Did the Olmecs discover the art of writing all alone on the jungle coast of the Gulf of Mexico? Why should we expect to find any Old World sign preserved unaltered in Mexico when, for instance, the Egyptians and Phoenicians, who had such an intimate cultural contact, chose to use mutually unintelligible scripts? The same could be said for Egypt and Sumer.

The invention of paper is hardly a natural consequence of inventing writing. Yet the original population of Mexico also manufactured genuine paper to write on. Not of wood pulp, as we do, but using the same recipe as the ancient Egyptians and Phoenicians used for papyrus manufacture. They used reeds, hibiscus bark, and other fibrous plants which they beat, soaked and rinsed of floating cellular tissue before hammering the wet shreds together with special clubs in several criss-cross layers. The art of producing real paper by this method is so complicated that the modern Papyrus Institute in Cairo experi-mented for several years before Hassan Ragab recently succeeded in reproducing ancient papyrus manufacture in practice. Mexican Indians, on the other hand, had learned this art to perfection before the Spaniards came, and, what is more, like the ancient Phoenicians they were busy producing books. Such books, for which the Spaniards used the term *codex*, did not have pages cut as in Europe, but folded together so that the whole book could be pulled out in one long, broad strip like the ancient papyrus rolls. The text was written in hieroglyphs and richly illustrated with coloured line-drawings, like the Egyptian papyrus rolls. Among other records these books contained the story of the bearded men, in text and illustrations.

While thousands of Indian tribes to north and south were living in the Stone Age until the Europeans came, their jungle and desert kinsmen along a consecutive belt from Mexico to Peru began, like Mediterranean voyagers, to look with the experienced eye of the metal-worker for mines where they could obtain gold, silver, copper and tin. They even alloyed copper and tin to forge themselves bronze tools, just as the ancient civilized people did on the other side of the Atlantic. Jewellers all the way from Mexico via the Isthmus of Panama to Peru made filigree brooches, pins, rings and bells of gold and silver, often set with precious stones, and with a stupendous workmanship such as only the very finest masters of the Old World could offer. This goldsmith's craft was, in fact, to cause their tragic fate, for the endless treasures of precious metal in Mexico, Central America and Peru were a far more powerful lure to the greedy Conquistadors who followed in Columbus' wake than were the crude stone and bone products of the Indian tribes elsewhere in America, which were first collected by peaceful modern ethnologists.

These same Indians who suddenly began to carve in stone, mould adobe, mine metal, manufacture paper, discover the inmost secrets of the calendar year and write down the traditions of their kin – these same Indians discovered in Mexico and Peru how to cross two useless types of cotton to produce an artificial strain with lint so long that it could be spun; the plant was thus worth cultivating in real planta-tions. When the cotton harvest was well established they began to card and spin just as in the Old World, and, when the skeins of yarn were long enough and had been dyed in all sorts of durable colours, they set up precisely the same two types of horizontal and upright loom as were used in the Mediterranean in ancient times. On them they wove tapestries which in many cases outstripped in fineness of mesh and exquisite quality the best the world has ever seen elsewhere.

Before pottery was discovered in the Old World the early civiliza-tions of North Africa had begun to cultivate bottle gourds, which they hollowed out, drying the rinds over a fire to make water containers. This plant was so important and popular that it is used for the same purpose to this very day by the reed boat builders from Ethiopia to Chad. By some means or other, this useful African plant fell into the hands of the cultured people of Mexico and Peru, where it was used in exactly the same way, and was one of the most important cultivated plants when the Spaniards came. It would seem more than probable that sharks and the corroding organisms of the sea would have finished a gourd off if it started to drift across the Atlantic alone, or that it would have rotted before the Indians found it on the opposite shore and realized how it could be used.

The creation of excellent containers from bottle gourds obtained from Africa was not enough for the cotton-growers in America; they also managed to duplicate the ceramic art of the ancient Mediterranean. With professional skill they located potter's clay, which they mixed with the correct amount of sand, moulded to shape, coloured, and fired. They made jars and jugs with all kinds of handles, dishes, vases with and without feet, pots with spouts, spinning-wheels, flutes, and ceramic figurines of the same general appearance and often with the same peculiar details as the ancient potters had used in Mesopotamia and Egypt. Even such unique products as thin-wall jars shaped like animals with a spout on the back, produced by the artist's first making a two-part negative mould, were made by potters on both sides. So were both flat and cylindrical ceramic seals, engraved for stamping and decorating articles respectively by pressing and by rolling. Perhaps the most extraordinary parallel is that small ceramic dogs, running on real wheels just like modern toys, are found in Olmec graves from pre-Christian times and also in ancient Mesopotamian graves. This is particularly noteworthy, not least because one of the main arguments of the isolationists until that discovery was made was that the Old World wheel was unknown in America before Columbus. It was indeed known, if not by others, at least by those who founded the earliest Mexican civilization. Why it was lost before being put to practical use is another matter; perhaps the muddy jungle soil and the lack of horse or donkey may provide the answer.

Where, besides, did the Mayans and Incas acquire their domestic dogs, as exemplified in the wheeled models of the Olmecs, the later local art, and the numerous carefully mummified creatures lying with their masters in graves from pre-Inca Peru? No one knows. The civilized peoples from Mexico to Peru had acquired at least two breeds of domestic dogs, both of unknown origin. Both breeds are quite different from the long-coated, curly-tailed, Eskimo breed which other Indians had brought from Siberia; they do not descend from known American canines, and are strikingly similar to the mummified dogs of ancient Egypt. The craft and custom of mummifying dogs and birds were also as characteristic of ancient Peru as of Egypt.

No mummies of men or beasts will last in a jungle climate, but we know that important persons were embalmed to attain eternal life by the sun-worshippers of ancient America, because hundreds of carefully embalmed mummies are preserved in desert tombs in Peru. Their grave-goods proclaim their high rank. While some Peruvian mummies have coarse, straight, black hair like modern Indians, others have reddish and even blond, wavy and soft hair, and their great body height is in striking contrast to the Indians living in Peru today, who are among the shortest races in the world. Relieved of their internal organs, filled with cotton, massaged with special preparations, sewn up and wrapped in mummy cloths, and finally provided with a mask over their faces, the pre-Inca mummies follow a traditional pattern which in all essential particulars is familiar from Egypt. The tall sun-priest, lying full-length among his ornaments under the five-ton lid of the stone sarcophagus inside the Palenque pyramid, also had a mask over his face, and his long body had once been wrapped in a red cloth, of which fragments remain on the bones. But no embalmer's art could save his mortal remains in the climate of the rain forests.

It was natural that a Mexican priest-king should be wrapped in red cloth and that his sarcophagus should also be painted red inside. Red was the sacred and favourite colour in Mexico and Peru, just as among the Phoenicians. In Peru special expeditions were sent north up the coast on large balsa rafts and reed boats simply to collect and bring home special red shells, just as the Phoenicians founded their colonies along the Atlantic coast of Africa mainly to satisfy their fanatical desire to make red dye from the 'purpura' mollusc.

In Mexico and Peru the Indians took up many customs which did not occur to the other Indians, and some of them were as strange as they were striking. They began to circumcise boy babies, as was the religious custom among the Jews and other people in their vicinity. They decided that sun-priests of high rank who lacked real beards must wear artificial ones, just as they did in Egypt. They waited until the particular constellation of the Pleiades appeared over the horizon before beginning their agricultural year, as the custom was among some of the inner Mediterranean peoples. And the surgeons in Mexico, and still more expressly in Peru, began to trepan the skulls of their patients, partly as a purely magical operation and partly to heal fractures. When the Spaniards reached America, the extremely difficult art of trepanning had a most restricted distribution elsewhere in the world. It existed exclusively along the narrow Mediterranean belt from Mesopotamia to Morocco, and, strangely enough, among the *guanches* on the Canary Islands.

The small details of daily life were not so staggeringly different, either, despite the distance from the Mediterranean to the Gulf of Mexico. Family life and community organization, from priest-king to slave and eunuch, followed roughly the same pattern in these hierarchic dictatorships; and domestic articles varied mostly in detail. Farmers in Mexico and Peru had begun terrace farming, with aqueducts, artificial irrigation and manuring with animal dung, just as they did in the Mediterranean area; and the isolationists themselves have pointed out remarkable coincidences of detail in types of pick, basket, sickle and axe. Fishermen in both places made the same sort of nets with sinkers and floats, the same sort of traps, and fish-hooks with bait and line on the same principles. Merchants sailed from Peru in search of red molluscs, using reed boats like *Ra*. The musicians in both areas had drums with skin stretched over the end, trombones, trumpets with mouthpieces, many sorts of flute, including pan-pipes, clarinets, and all sorts of bells. The isolationists themselves have pointed out similarities in the structure and organization of the armies, the use of military cloth tents in the field, the custom of giving the soldiers shields with painted designs to show their units, and the fact that the sling, unknown to the Indians who came across the Bering Strait, but characteristic of the warriors of the inner Mediterranean, reappeared as one of the most important weapons in the pre-Inca cultural area. Both diffusionists and isolationists have stressed that there are striking similarities in loincloths and men's cloaks, women's garments with belted waists and shoulder pins, and sandals of hide or coiled rope with very specific resemblances in design and manufacture. Personal ornaments, metal mirrors, tweezers, combs and tattooing, fans, parasols and litters with seats for important personages; wooden headrests; the use of the same sort of bismar or beam scales and the same sort of pan scales; board games and dice; stilts and whipping-tops and an unending series of parallels in patterns and designs. All in all, there is not such a fundamental difference between what the people of Asia Minor and Egypt had already created and spread to the islands of the Mediterranean when Europe was still living in barbarism, and what the Spaniards found when they arrived a couple of thousand years later in America. They came, under the sign of the Cross, to bring a new religion from Asia Minor to the Indians at the other end of the ocean current.

All this we contemplated and discussed as the perpetual Atlantic current drove our own reed boat steadily closer to tropical America. Perhaps, after all, the boat we were sitting in constituted one of the most remarkable parallels. The stern was sinking lower and lower. That was our Achilles' heel. Our boat-builders from Central Africa had at first been unwilling to give us any stern section at all. They were not used to making one; they had never learned how. The Indians in Peru were used to it, however. The art had been passed down unchanged from father to son since the country's earliest potters made models of the first crescent-shaped reed boats. Lake Titicaca in South America was now the only place in the world where reed boats still carried sails, and oddly enough, throughout that part of South America the sail is carried on just the same sort of strange, two-legged straddled mast as in ancient Egypt. Lake Titicaca is also the only place where really compact reed boats are still being built today, peaked and raised at both ends and with rope lashings running from the deck right round the bottom of the boat all in one piece, just as ancient artists have painted the lashings on tomb walls in Egypt. Our friends from Chad had bound many narrow bundles of reeds together in several layers, using numerous short ropes linked in the form of a chain; and although we had finally persuaded them to add an elevated stern, it was still only the outward shape which coincided completely with the Egyptian paintings. Except by the caravan routes, the great ancient civilizations had never penetrated across the continent to Chad in the same way as they had spread by boats bringing organized colonists along the Mediterranean coast to Morocco. Now, for the first time, I began to wonder if I might perhaps have allowed myself to be misled by the map. I had brought my reed boat builders from Chad because there were no better to be found in the Old World. But what if the cultures on both sides of the Atlantic had a common heritage? In that case the Indians who lived on Lake Titicaca, the most important and oldest pre-Inca cultural centre, had inherited their boat-building skill more directly than the remote Buduma tribesmen in the African interior. I remembered the isolationists' claim that there was an insuperable distance between the inner Mediterranean and Peru. Had I also allowed myself to be fooled by this dogmatic claim? Had we all forgotten that the Spaniard, Francisco Pizarro, who had neither aeroplanes, roads, nor railway lines to help him across ocean or jungle, had travelled straight from the Mediterranean to Peru with his perfectly ordinary men, just about as fast as Hernando Cortés made his way to the Mexican uplands? The Spaniards colonized the whole area from Mexico to Peru in one generation, the same generation which saw Columbus sail three times across the Atlantic and back. It is a sound isolationist lesson that history repeats itself. The Spaniards first discovered the islands lying in front of the Mexican Gulf, yet they delayed the establishment of their main settlements until they had pushed on to Mexico and Peru. We seven men from seven nations were here on board a reed boat to prove how alike human beings are, from north or south, east or west. And yet we found it so difficult to understand that the same likeness pursues us through time as well, from the days when the ancient Egyptians were writing their love-songs, the Assyrians were improving their fighting chariots, or the Phoenicians were laying the foundations of our own writing, and struggling with sails and rigging to explore the riches of West Africa.

When the first week of July was past I began in my heart of hearts to feel uneasy. I hoped the photographer's boat would be dispatched in time, before the constant showers which had kept us company for several days coalesced into a real gale. The hurricane season was beginning in the area we had now entered. The men took it all with devastating calm.

On July 8th the wind began to rise and the waves piled up as if a real storm had taken place beyond the horizon. Giant seas flung themselves on our wretched stern, and for the first time washed right over the steering bridge, which stood on long legs behind the cabin. We had a tough night of it. The wind howled in pitch-black darkness, the water rumbled, gurgled, splashed, roared and thundered everywhere. The chests we lay on began to racket about and float up and down in the cabin, with us on top. Those who lay furthest back on the starboard side had to empty the cases under them of all their possessions, as they were half full of water. They shifted all their things into the other sleeping chests, where the water was only trickling in, rising and falling a few inches where the gaps in the cases were leaking

most. At intervals of a few seconds a wave smashed against the back wall
of the cabin, which was now covered with sailcloth; the bamboo walls
shook and salt water trickled in on all sides – if we were lucky enough
not to get a whole deluge straight on our heads. Most of us got used
to the ceaseless rhythmic crashes over our heads, though Santiago
needed sleeping pills; but now and then there was a sharper, more
vicious thunder which had us all shooting out of our sleeping-bags – the
struggling sail had lashed back against the mast and once again we were
joined in battle with the giant which we could scarcely see above us
in the lamplight, while we stubbed our toes and stumbled over
Santiago's jars and Carlo's almost impenetrable network of backstays.
At about six o'clock next morning I was standing on the bridge, taking
the powerful wind on the starboard quarter with the help of a lashed
rudder-oar and another under constant handling, when the sea quite
unexpectedly rose about me and engulfed everything. A shining stretch
of water moved slowly up to my waist and without any appreciable
noise the cabin roof in front of my chest was submerged. Some seconds
later *Ra* began to quake violently, while the vessel lay hard over into
the wind, so hard that I had to hang on to the tiller of the rudder-oar
in order not to skid down the slope and overboard with the water.
At every moment I expected the heavy straddled mast to tear the
papyrus bundles under it to shreds and topple into the sea. But *Ra*,
shivering, simply rolled on to her beam ends to empty out the water,
then righted herself, though never again as fully as before. The starboard mast-foot had been pressed deep into the supporting bundle,
and the cabin also had become oblique towards the starboard side. In
the days to come the helmsman had to stand with his left knee bent to
keep upright on the slanting steering bridge.

With the stern shelving away like a bathing beach, we had to tie
ourselves on securely in order not to be washed out to sea when we
were bathing on board next morning. The waves soared forward
on both sides of the cabin, and on the lee side, aft of the cabin door,
we built a screen of empty baskets and ropes, covered with *Ra*'s spare
sail for which we had had no use until then. Dead flying fish lay everywhere. Although the stern section acted as a powerful brake, and
although we were constantly zigzagging along with no real steering
power, the strong wind drove us 63 sea miles, or 117 kilometres, closer
to America that day. This was only 20–30 kilometres less than the
average daily distance for the papyrus boats of old as given by Eratos-

thenes the librarian. Once again we were visited by white-tailed tropical birds from Brazil or Guiana, which now lay to the south and south-west. All the crew were in the best of spirits. Norman had made radio contact with Chris in Oslo, who confirmed that he was trying to help Yvonne secure a film photographer in New York. As soon as the cameraman was ready to leave home they hoped he would be able to come out on some boat or other from the West Indies.

On July 9th we had just discovered that the sea which had gone over the cabin roof had also forced its way through the lid of a cask containing almost two hundred pounds of salt meat, which later rotted. It was during this morning inspection that an agitated Georges came to report something much worse. All the main ropes which secured the outermost papyrus roll on the windward side to the rest of *Ra* had been chafed through as the floor of the cabin had shifted to and fro under the onslaught of the waves. Georges was pale and almost speechless. In one leap I was on the other side of the cabin with Abdullah. We were met by a sight I shall never forget. The boat was split in two lengthwise. The big starboard bundle, supporting one mast, was bulging slowly in and out from the rest of the boat down its entire length. The roll was attached to *Ra* only at prow and stern. Every time the waves lifted the big papyrus roll away from the rest of the boat we stared straight down into the clear blue depths. Never had I seen the Atlantic so clear and so deep as through that cleft in our own little papyrus world. Abdullah would have turned pale, had he been able. With stoic calm, and without a tremor in his voice, he said coolly that this was the end. The ropes had worn away. The chain was broken. The rope links would unravel themselves one by one and in an hour or two the papyrus reeds would be drifting away from each other in all directions.

Abdullah. Abdullah had given up. For a moment Georges and I too stood paralysed, our eyes turning from the rift of sea which opened and shut rhythmically at our feet, to the lashed top of the straddled mast. With a foot on each side it was really the straddled mast which had been holding the two halves of the boat together so that the ropes remaining fore and aft had not worn away long before. Then Norman was suddenly standing beside us, glaring like a tiger about to spring.

'Let's not give up, fellows,' he said in a strangled voice.

Next moment we were all bounding to and fro. Carlo and Santiago pulled out coils of rope and measured and chopped up lengths of our thickest cordage. Georges plunged into the waves and swam crosswise under *Ra* with a thick end of rope. Norman and I crawled all over the boat examining the chafed lashings to find out how long it would be before we fell apart. Papyrus stems were floating in our wake, singly and in sheaves. Abdullah stood with the sledge-hammer, driving in *Ra*'s huge sewing needle, a thin iron spike with an eye at the bottom, large enough to take a rope one quarter of an inch thick. With this needle we were going to try to sew the 'paper boat' together. Yuri stood the gruelling turn at the rudder-oar alone, hour after hour. First Georges swam under the boat four times crosswise with our thickest rope, which we cinched up on deck like four big barrel hoops, in the hope of holding the bundles together so that the straddled mast would not burst open at the top. Then he ducked under the papyrus bundles to the spot where Abdullah's big sewing needle had been pushed through. In the depths Georges had to pull the thin rope out of the needle's eye and re-thread it a moment later when Abdullah pushed the needle down again empty in another place. In this way we got the fatal gap 'sewn' up again to some extent, but we had lost a lot of papyrus and were consequently lying harder over to windward than ever. The straddled mast was askew, but *Ra* was still sailing so fast that Georges had to be held on a rope. We were delighted to be able to haul him on board for the last time without his having been spiked through the head by the sharp giant needle. Carlo apologized for the meal: spume was constantly washing into the galley chest and putting out the fire. A big basket from *Ra*, contents unknown, was observed at sundown bobbing up and down on the waves behind us. Before nightfall we inspected the cobbled-up papyrus roll, which represented almost the whole breadth of *Ra* on the starboard side of the cabin. It was wriggling ominously in the thin ropes we had used to sew it on, and was so depleted and waterlogged that we had to wade waist-deep to pass the cabin on that side. Then it was night again. The last things I saw were the whites of Abdullah's eyes in the corner just inside the door-opening, moving up and down above the mattress as he prayed, all amid the grinding and the whining and the gushing of water. Norman had a radio message that the boat Yvonne was trying to hire might be meeting us in four or five days.

On July 10th we awoke heavy-eyed at sunrise. The two cases on which each of us slept had been heaving and rolling wildly and irregularly all night. Norman could not keep his balance on his recalcitrant chests, so he had been lying across the legs of the rest of us. Our first thought was to tighten the four ropes we had secured round the whole boat yesterday, and yet another rope was swum round the place where the masts stood to prevent them from doing the splits. All day we went on sewing ourselves together with the long sewing thread which was pushed up and down through the papyrus, from deck to bottom.

That day Norman heard that two photographers were expected on the island of Martinique and that a little motor-yacht called *Shenandoah* was on her way there to pick them up. But Italian television had announced that we were disabled and had taken to the rubber boat. We thought with sardonic humour of the day when we had carved it up. No one missed it. No one would have boarded the lifeboat. We had more than enough papyrus left to float on. While the worst seas were breaking over us, and a yell from Carlo announced that his best saucepans had been carried overboard, Georges suddenly appeared with a dripping red object which he had fished up out of knee-deep water.

'Do we need this, or can I heave it overboard?'

It was a little fire-extinguisher from the days when smoking on the starboard side was forbidden. Volleys of laughter followed the apparatus out to sea. Even Safi hung from a mast stay and stared as the fire-spray vanished into the depths, baring her teeth and making throaty noises to show that she too appreciated the joke.

On July 11th the sea began to compose itself in gentler folds, but even peaceful waves washed a long way in from astern and over the starboard beam. As I stood my evening watch, several constellations, and also the Pole Star, appeared for the first time in many nights, and with my 'nasometer' I quickly fixed our position at 15° N.

In the middle of the night some big seas poured in over the starboard beam and drove right through the wickerwork of the cabin wall, so hard that the one case on which Norman had been sleeping until then was splintered to matchwood. The case had long been empty, and only broken bits of deal floated about in the seething water inside the cabin. *Ra* had begun to make some particularly disagreeable noises on the side where the papyrus roll was sewn on, and no one heard Safi's cries for help when her perforated sleeping suitcase was knocked off the wall by the next wave. She sailed about, imprisoned, among the splintered fragments of crate until, incredibly, she managed to open the lid and release herself. Santiago was awakened by her sitting, dripping wet, by his cheek, screeching to be admitted into his warm sleeping bag.

On July 12th birds flew out from the coast again to visit us. Over the radio we heard that the yacht which was to meet us would be delayed, as two of the crew had jumped ship when it reached Martinique to pick up the photographers. The surprise of the day was an absolute wreck of a ship which appeared on the horizon to the south and came yawing towards us. At first we thought it was some adventurers in a home-made boat, but then we saw that it was an old, patched-up fishing vessel covered with Chinese characters. Dried fish hung everywhere and the crew stood at the railing silently gazing as the *Noi Young You* staggered past us, some 200 yards away. There we stood, on our two boats, gazing at each other in commiseration and dismay, and taking photographs on both sides. The Chinese waved nonchalantly, with kindly condescension. No doubt they thought *Ra* was a native *jangada* or primitive balsa raft, come out to fish from the Brazilian coast, and they were visibly shaken to see that such a scrap-heap could still be in use today. The wash from the fishing boat rippled over *Ra*'s afterdeck as it lurched away, and then we were left alone with the sea. It began to rain again. The wind rose, and the seas with it. Soon everything was awash.

As night began to advance over a pallid, wet, overcast sky, we saw real storm-clouds rolling up like a herd of angry black cattle over the horizon to the east and stampeding thunderously after us. We made ready to weather the great storm which was tearing along, lightning flashing, in fiercer and fiercer squalls. There were limits to what the sail could take, but we let it stand. We had only a few days left, and we must make haste. *Ra* shuddered in the squalls. The seas rose. The Egyptian sail was drawing as never before and once again we seemed to be riding on a wild beast's back. The scene had a savage, barbaric beauty. Black seas grew whiter, boiling, streaked with foam; more rain fell from the sea than from the clouds. The wave-crests were flattened by the wind and *Ra* travelled so fast that the torrents of water overtaking us from astern had less force than usual. But those which did break over us did it so thoroughly that it was impossible to get more than a few seconds' nap between the shocks.

Dangers lurked everywhere if we were not properly secured to cabin wall or papyrus bundles. Heavy masses of water fell with a crash on the basket roof, which was subsiding, saddle-backed, further and further towards our noses. Santiago was washed overboard with the rope in his hands, but clutched at a corner of the sail. Now and then *Ra* heeled so violently that everyone gripped the stays and hung outboard as a counterweight. One of the galley chests was splintered and Carlo waded around to save the other, which was floating between the masts. The antenna blew off, so the radio was dead. The duck was washed overboard on its line time after time and in the worst of the chaos it broke a leg, which Yuri had to set. Safi was in great form inside the cabin. In the huge wave-troughs the biggest school of flying fish I had ever seen showered to and fro. Just before the watch changed I heard Abdullah trying to sing on the bridge in the darkness. A giant wave fell on the cabin roof from behind, and then it was my turn. Abdullah stood roped up, high on the bridge, his hair glistening with sea-water in the lamplight.

'How's the weather, Abdullah?' I joked.

'Not bad,' said Abdullah, undismayed.

The storm raged with varying strength for three long days. It was becoming more and more perilous to have the sail set, but we managed it for the first two days, while *Ra* raced over the stormy seas. The starboard mast danced alone through the semi-detached oscillations of the loosely cobbled roll, which had lost so much papyrus that what was left was pinned under the surface. Consequently the straddled mast was leaning steadily further into the wind, and this helped us to take the squalls better, even if the block in which the starboard mast-foot was set was sinking deeper and deeper into the poorly secured bunch of papyrus. Georges and Abdullah sewed as hard as they could under this mast-foot, which seemed to be making its way right through the bottom. The masts bounced up and down in the wooden shoes and only their own weight and all the stays pulled them back into their sockets after each leap. Because of all the ropes which had been worn away and worked loose on the starboard side, the papyrus reeds there were able to absorb unlimited water, and in addition the whole bundle became so limp and flabby that we never knew how much we could or should tighten the mast stays. When the straddled mast whipped backwards, all the parallel rows of shrouds on either side of the cabin bellied like a skipping rope, while the next moment they were jerked taut as bowstrings by a wrench of the mast so violent that only the giant hawser tied right round the boat as a bulwark in the ancient Egyptian style prevented the papyrus reeds from being torn apart.

The single reeds were as tough and strong as after one day in water, and floated when we lost them. But with every opportunity to absorb water freely, and with the leaning straddled mast throwing all its weight on to the wounded side, the loosely sewn remnants of the starboard bundles became more and more deeply submerged and the flexible wickerwork floor of the bamboo cabin bent elastically with them, without breaking.

We tried to fill up the empty space left by Norman's broken chest, but before we had finished a new wave broke in through the bamboo crevices and smashed the other. One chest after another was shattered to matchwood under us in the cabin. As each chest went, it became more difficult to control those that were left, for now they had room to sail around two by two like small boats in an overcrowded harbour, with a heaving straw mattress on top. Socks and underclothes disappeared in the undertow inside and popped up in quite different places. Norman and Carlo moved out and lay on provision baskets under the fringe of roof, forward of the cabin. Yuri's cases were smashed under him before he had emptied them of his medicines, which resulted in an inferno of broken glass bottles, squashed tubes, cartons, pills, ointment and test tubes, all of which emitted an incredible odour. It became dangerous to fall off the chests, and we packed mattresses, sleeping bags and anything we could spare into the empty spaces as padding against the waves bursting through the wall, so that we could lie safely on the boxes which were left. Yuri moved out. In the middle the roof was sinking lower and lower over our faces and the jigging paraffin lamp had to be moved up to a higher corner. Jokes and roars of laughter from the three who had chosen to move out to the other side of the thin bamboo wall confirmed that spirits were high, both inside and out.

Outside the gale raged, the lightning flashed, but we could hardly hear the thunder crashes for the awful sucking sound of water rushing in on the starboard side and gurgling round us until it disappeared in a backwash through the same starboard wickerwork wall again. The watch aft had a hard stint and we tried to change shifts as often as possible. The stilts under the starboard side of the bridge had sunk with the papyrus rolls and the platform on which the helmsman stood had become as steep as the roof of a house. We could no longer reach down to the tiller of the starboard rudder oar. We had to cling to the port corner, where the bridge was highest, and had therefore worked out a system which was as ingenious as it was laborious. With one rope tied to a foot and another held in the hand we swung to and fro on the starboard rudder-oar, but only when we could not hold the course with the port oar alone. For brief seconds at a time we made fast all the ropes we could in order not to be pounded to pieces. All that mattered was to keep the sail filled, and one tack from each corner of the sail was also secured to the railing of the bridge so that the helmsman could lean his weight on the hard-pressed yard if the rudder-oars alone could not cope with the situation. The whole bridge was covered with rope, while the sunken stern behind us acted as a completely unpredictable giant oar which made steering insanely complicated. If we thrashed helplessly about in the storm there was an overwhelming danger that the mast would jerk out or force its way down through the papyrus, since our waterlogged raft simply would not turn turtle.

On July 14th we made radio contact with *Shenandoah*, now heading east from Barbados. They reported that the storm had reached them, too, with waves breaking over the yacht's wheelhouse, twenty feet high. Their radio telegraphist had sent a signal that they were in danger and they had considered turning back, because the yacht was not built for major gales. Only the thought that we were lying still further out under the same conditions made them sail on eastward into the storm. The captain gave the maximum speed he could allow as eight knots. That was three or four times as much as *Ra* could manage, but in the teeth of the storm the yacht would travel much more slowly; at best it might reach us in a day or two, if we were heading straight towards each other on opposite courses. A radio ham had picked up a message that a merchant ship was said to be about thirty miles from our position, in case we needed help. But all of us on board wanted to sail on westward alone.

At one o'clock in the morning Yuri yelled that the yard had broken with a crash. Everybody out. But no one could see anything wrong; the sail was drawing as never before, on a straight yard. But just then steering suddenly became desperately difficult. As we relieved one another through the night we all agreed that steering watches had never been worse. It was not until sunrise that we realized what had happened. Carlo discovered that he was steering with a simple shaft and no blade. The thick, double-shafted rudder-oar had snapped off again as if struck by a giant sledge-hammer, and in the darkness the great oar-blade had disappeared for ever in the waves. That was the crack Yuri had heard, and we had all been working ourselves to death with two round poles while *Ra* held her course alone with her submerged stern as the only rudder.

On July 15th the storm reached a climax. The sail could no longer stand up to the strain, and in squalls which flung us so hard over that an ordinary boat would have capsized, we dropped the sail like a thunderclap. Lightning flashed, rain fell. When the sail had gone the masts stood with their gaping ladder bars swaying alone in the lightning flashes like a naked skeleton. There was a ghastly sense of emptiness and apathy without the sail. The waves seemed to pluck up more courage to attack us as our speed slackened. The rest of the galley disappeared into the sea. For a time egg-flip and powdered lime eddied round Carlo's legs, when one jar smashed. Still the foredeck and port side were covered with food in well-secured jars with tight lids. And sausages and hams hung from the roof and the steps of the mast. Worse than egg yolks was the sudden arrival of a number of Portuguese men-o'-war, sailing round the deck with their long, stinging filaments entangled in everything. I stepped on a bubble-body but was not stung. Georges and Abdullah got their legs entwined in stinging threads while they were working waist-deep in water to sew on new ropes where the old had been worn away. Each was thoroughly washed at once with Yuri's improvised natural medicine. Abdullah denied that it hurt. But he also bore the round burn-marks of cigarettes which he had stubbed out on his own arm to prove that a man from Chad is indifferent to pain.

Outside, the bench formed by jars along the wall with the door-opening on the port side of the cabin was the only place where we could be safe and more or less dry when the gale was at its height. All the film and all the valuable equipment were stowed here too, so that there was scarcely any room left for us. The duck and the monkey now lived in their own baskets one above the other on top of all our private possessions. Inside, the waves bursting through the walls continued to wreak their havoc. Box after box was smashed. By evening only Abdullah and I were left inside under the roof; all the others had moved out and were sleeping on the galley baskets, in the mast and on the cabin roof, which had become so sway-backed that it could scarcely support the weight of two or three men. There were only three whole boxes left of the sixteen which had once made up our beds. Two belonged to Abdullah and one to me. Because our sleeping places were furthest over to port, our cases had lasted longest, but now our turn had come. The box under my legs had already been smashed and clothes and books mixed like pulp with the porridge floating round us. I balanced a box-lid on edge with my heels to prop my feet up and clung to roof and wall so that the box under my back would not overturn when the watery mess surged over to our side. It was grotesque. Abdullah knelt praying in the door-opening for the last time. Then he slipped into his sleeping bag on top of two whole boxes and went to sleep. The gurgling sound about us was diabolical in the dark. My pillow skidded down into the maelstrom which revolved from wall to wall and let nothing escape. It was like being in the stomach of a whale, where the wicker wall was the whalebone filtering the food so that only the salt water ran out. I clutched at my pillow and fished up something soft. A hand. A rubber hand or some kind of bloated, water-filled glove from Yuri's surgical equipment. This was too grisly. I sat up and turned off the paraffin lamp, but then a pool of rain-water from the canvas on the roof poured down my neck and the lid of the case I was balancing under my feet slipped and vanished into the water. I crawled out to join the others. It was safer out in the rain; on the lee side. Abdullah was left sleeping alone in our once cosy home.

Long before sunrise on July 16th we regained radio contact with *Shenandoah*. We cranked and cranked and listened and listened until we heard the metallic voice of the radio ham. The captain asked us to send up signal rockets after dark. The wind had dropped. The storm had rushed further west and had now reached the islands. Apart from Sinbad the duck, with the broken leg, we were all unscathed. Norman looked out the signal rockets we had kept back when we cut up the life-raft. They were so sodden with water that we could not even light the fuse with a match. On a scrap of loose label we read: 'Keep in a dry place.' We asked *Shenandoah* to send up her own rockets. Shortly afterwards, the captain replied that they could not light theirs, either. Neither of us had a completely accurate position after the storm, but as far as we could judge we were travelling in precisely opposite directions on the same latitude.

The radio voice asked us to keep the hand generator going constantly, transmitting our call signal the whole time, so that they could try to home in on it. For although the wind had died down and the torrential rain had flattened the waves, neither of us had vessels large

enough to be visible over long distances. We learned that the motor-
yacht was an eighty-tonner, seventy-four feet in length. As we sat
cranking we noticed that the sea was once again covered with asphalt-
like lumps, and we had seen the same thing the day before. They were
left stranded on the papyrus while the water filtered through. I collected
a few samples to be sent with a brief report to the Norwegian delegation at the United Nations. We had now sailed through this filth on
both sides of the Atlantic, and in the middle as well.

While Norman worked with knobs and earphones, and the rest of
us took turns cranking, Carlo served the most delicious cold dishes.
He regretted that the galley was not operating as well as before,
partly because all the saucepans had floated off astern and partly because
he could not get the primus alight since it was lying at the bottom of
the Atlantic Ocean. But if we would like ham and Egyptian fish roe,
he still had a knife left. And there was no rationing of 'mummy
bread', which tasted better than ever, whether we spread it with
Berber butter and honey or ate it with peppered sheep's cheese in oil.
The storm had dealt kindly with the provision jars, packed down on
the soft papyrus reed. It was the wooden chests that had taken the
beating. Papyrus and rope, jars and skins, baskets and bamboo went
well together. Everywhere it was the rigid timber which had lost the
battle with the seas.

Late on the afternoon of July 16th the weather was fine again and
we kept a lookout in all directions from cabin roof and masthead.
Yuri was cranking and Norman was ceaselessly intoning our call
signal into the microphone, when suddenly something inexplicable
happened. Norman, who was sitting immovably in the cabin doorway,
turning knobs with both hands, suddenly stared strangely straight ahead
without looking at any of us and said in a voice full of emotion:

'I see you, I see you; can't you see us?'

A dramatic moment passed for the rest of us, sitting speechlessly
round him, before we realized that he was talking to the radio operator
on the *Shenandoah*. *Shenandoah!* We all turned sharply, Georges on
the cabin roof, keeping a lookout in the opposite direction and Carlo
swinging to and fro at the crazy masthead with his camera on his
stomach.

And there she was! She came into view at brief intervals, like a
white grain of sand on top of the distant crests. As she came closer
we saw that she was rolling wildly. What was left of *Ra* took the seas

with far more stoic calm. How we found each other is still a miracle to us, but here we were, leaping in turn, up and down, at sea off the West Indies. A big black bird circled above us. Shark fins appeared, cutting the water around *Ra*. The sharks must have followed the yacht out from the islands. Both sides filmed and photographed, but it was one day too late. *Ra*'s mainsail had been lowered for ever; the mast would support no more than a shred of sail without being driven straight through the flimsy foothold left to it on the starboard side.

A rubber dinghy was lowered from the yacht and Abdullah cheered delightedly when he saw a man with skin the colour of his own come rowing over to meet us. He shouted a greeting, first in Chad Arabic and then in French, and gaped speechlessly when the black man replied in English. Africa met Abdullah in America. An Africa which had become American through and through.

The first thing to be loaded on to the dancing dinghy was all the expedition film. We rowed over in several instalments to meet the men on board the yacht – cheerful, straightforward men. With its high superstructure and narrow keel, the pretty vessel rolled so badly that we who had spent eight weeks on *Ra* had difficulty in finding our sea-legs on the immaculately scoured deck. She rolled so violently that Carlo, and Jim from the yacht, each trying to film the other from his own boat, agreed that it was much easier to film the yacht from the reed boat than the other way round.

The captain and crew were all young men, most of them hired for the occasion, and all eager for us to come aboard so that they could start for home at once. This was not required by the hiring contract, and we continued to keep *Ra* manned. *Shenandoah* had brought us four oranges each and a box of chocolates for Santiago. But the improvised crew had set off without discovering that the provisions on board consisted mainly of beer and mineral water, so the captain was insistent on returning before we ran out of food. And before there was another gale. We borrowed *Shenandoah*'s dinghy and returned from *Ra* with several whole hams, cured mutton, sausages and enough jars of other food and water for all of us to eat and drink our fill for a long time to come.

Shenandoah waited. *Ra* floated with her port side intact, but the starboard side had lost so much papyrus that it was no longer capable of supporting our thirty-foot, extremely heavy, double mast. We decided to cut it down. As our proud mast toppled into the sea Norman erected a light straddled mast from two fifteen-foot rowing oars tied together at the top and provided with a little improvised mainsail. *Ra* sailed on. On July 17th and 18th we ferried all unnecessary cargo over to *Shenandoah* and worked at sewing the bundles together as securely as possible. While Carlo swam over with the straddled mast, Georges worked underneath *Ra*, Yuri danced alone in the dinghy on a perilous shuttle service between the two boats, and the rest of us waded about on the papyrus bundles with ropes and soaking-wet possessions. Visitors crowded in on us from down below. We began to see more and more shark fins slicing through the surface of the water all round us, like sails on toy yachts. If we put our faces under water we could see big fishy forms sailing slowly about, far down in the clear blue depths. The crew of *Shenandoah* began to fish for shark. A white-finned shark, six feet long, and another, slightly smaller, were pulled on board and we had *Ra*'s boiled rice served with tasty shark's liver. A blue shark, twelve feet long, was too crafty to be enticed on to the hook, and patrolled about restlessly.

Despite all orders to observe the utmost caution Georges suddenly terrified us all by flinging himself onto the submerged starboard edge of *Ra* with a hulking great shark in pursuit close to his legs. Georges had an old shark bite on one leg. I forbade him to swim any more as long as we were surrounded by these man-eaters and he said that in that case he would have to wait a long time, because he had counted between twenty-five and thirty sharks circling in the blue depths. It was pointless to risk human lives and we gave up any further sewing of the papyrus bundles. Better to let individual papyrus stalks and even entire sheaves of reed float away in our wake. We could afford to lose all the starboard side as long as the midships and port side were intact and showed no sign of breaking up.

The weather reports on *Shenandoah* were ominous and the captain had good reason to urge our return to harbour. The entire crew of *Ra* agreed that if another gale blew up we would be safer on board our own wreck. True, our papyrus boat was no longer navigable, with rudder-oars broken and a steering bridge on which we could scarcely keep our feet, but the remaining bundles were afloat and would continue to float westward like a giant lifebuoy until they were washed ashore. *Shenandoah* was navigable, even if both pumps and one of the two diesel engines had been put out of operation by the storm. But both captain and crew were fully aware that in a hurricane, however small, she could spring a leak or capsize, and then the whole metal craft would go straight to the bottom.

I summoned all the men of *Ra* to the first really serious 'pow-wow' since we had sawn up the rubber raft off the African coast. I explained that it seemed to me right to end the experiment now. We had lived on board the papyrus rolls for two months; they were still afloat, and, without taking our zigzag course into account, we had sailed almost exactly 5,000 kilometres – over 3,000 miles, the distance across the North Atlantic from Africa to Canada. This proved that a papyrus boat was seaworthy. We had the answer. There was no reason to risk human lives.

All the men, bearded and weather-beaten, with palms calloused from pulling cords and tillers, sat listening gravely. I asked each of them to say what he thought.

'I think we should go on in the *Ra*,' said Norman. 'We have enough food and water. We can make a platform of bamboo baskets and broken boxes to sleep on. It will be tough, but in a week's time we shall be at the islands, even with the little scrap of sail we have set now.'

'I agree with Norman,' said Santiago. 'If we give up now, no one will believe that papyrus boat sailors could have reached America. Even many anthropologists will say that it's not the long voyage behind us that counts, but the little bit left ahead. If there were only one day to go, that would be the one that counted. We must get all the way from coast to coast.'

'Santiago,' I said, 'the few anthropologists who do not realize that the people who used papyrus boats for generations would have handled them better than we have done, won't be convinced, even if we sail right up the Amazon.'

'We must go on,' said Georges. 'Even if the rest of you give up, Abdullah and I will go on. Right, Abdullah?'

Abdullah nodded dumbly.

'This is an Egyptian boat. I represent Egypt. I must go on as long as there is a papyrus bundle left to keep my head above water,' Georges concluded vehemently. Carlo gave me an enquiring look.

'If you think we should go on, I'll go on, too,' said Carlo, stroking his beard. 'It's for you to size up the situation.'

Yuri had been sitting, staring in front of him, for some time.

'We are seven friends who have shared everything,' he said at last.

'Either we should all go on, or we should all stop. I am dead against our splitting up.'

It was a painful decision for me to take. All the others were willing to go on. It might be all right, but a severe storm might wash one or other of us overboard. It was not worth it. I had set this experiment in motion because I was looking for an answer. We had the answer. A papyrus boat, with defective stern, wrongly loaded, and badly handled by a group of uninitiated landlubbers, in a time when no one living could give lessons or advice, had ridden out a major storm with men and animals surviving and all essential cargo intact, after zigzagging the open ocean for eight weeks. If we drew a circle centred on the ancient Phoenician port of Safi, where we had started, taking the distance we had sailed as its radius, the circle would encompass both Moscow and the northernmost tip of Norway. It would cut through the middle of Greenland, cross Newfoundland, Quebec and Nova Scotia in North America and touch the tip of Brazil in South America. If we had not set out from Safi but from Senegal, down on the west coast of Africa, the distance we had sailed would have been enough, as the crow flies, to take us right across the Atlantic and, further, up the Amazon almost to its source. For the Atlantic is barely 3,000 kilometres wide at its narrowest point, whereas we had covered 5,000. It was better to stop while the going was good. Here were two boats, each with its particular weaknesses, sailing west together in a sea area known as the birthplace of hurricanes. Little did we dream that the first hurricane of the year, Anna, had just been born in the sea behind us, where we had recently passed, and was travelling with rising momentum towards the northernmost of the West Indian islands ahead. Our own course was set for Barbados, in the far south of the same chain. Equally little did we dream that research planes from the American BOMEX project (Barbados Oceanographic and Meteorological Experiment), which discovered the hurricane at its birth, had found that the highest layer of air over Barbados was mixed with fine sand from the Sahara. Sand from the Sahara was raining over the jungles of Central America. And ahead and behind us, clots of oil were drifting from the coast of Africa towards the beaches of Central America. It was *Ra*'s fate to travel alone with the elements on their passage to the tropical land ahead of us. The decision was mine alone.

CHAPTER 11

Six Thousand Kilometres by Papyrus Boat

STRANGE APPREHENSION. Uncertainty. I awoke disturbed. Clutched at my support. Rolling. Rolling and pitching and the rush of water. Night. Was I dreaming? Was the voyage in *Ra* not over? Could it have been just a bad dream that the stern section sank and we cut down the mast? Or was it now that I was having nightmares and dreaming that we had not yet left the precarious wreck? For a moment I was confused, trying to separate dream from reality. The voyage in *Ra* was over. I had sworn to myself that I would never attempt such a thing again. And here I was. The same wickerwork cabin around me. The same low, wide opening out into the wind and the naked world, where savage waves, streaked black-and-white, reared up against the night sky. Ahead the same big Egyptian sail stood unchanged, set taut on the straddled mast, which we had cut down, and astern the slender tail of the papyrus boat soared above us in an elegant curve, though we had seen it sinking sluggishly into the foaming seas. I was dead tired, my arms were aching. I sat up when Norman came crawling in, large as life, and shone the torch first on me and then on a bushy head with a red beard, sticking out of the sleeping-bag close beside me.

'Thor and Carlo, change of watch, your shift.'

I picked up my own torch and shone it about me. There lay all the others, tightly packed as before, more tightly in fact, so that when Norman tried to dig himself out a modest sleeping space in the opposite corner, they all turned over in unison: Carlo, Santiago, Yuri, Georges. But squeezed between them was a strange head with Asiatic features and stiff raven-black hair. That was Kei. Kei Ohara from Japan. Now, how had he come on board *Ra*? Of course! I flopped down on my back and began to pull on my trousers. Much too low under the basket roof to stand; we could barely sit up. Lower than on *Ra I*. Of course. It was all clear now. This was *Ra II*. I had started everything off all over again. We were right back off Africa once more. We had not even passed Cape Juby. It was not Abdullah waiting to be relieved on the steering bridge out there in the darkness. It was another African whom I scarcely knew yet, a dark-skinned, full-blooded Berber called Madani Ait Ouhanni.

'Hurry up, Carlo, you've been lying on half my mattress and now you're sitting on my shirt sleeve.'

On the bridge it was damnably cold, but peaceful. Madani pulled down his Berber hood and showed me how far it was safe to turn the rudder-oar away from land without risk of the onshore wind's twisting the giant sail. Carlo took over the job of lookout for lights from both land and shipping. We felt threatened from all sides now, until we had once again cleared the perilous rocky coast of the Sahara and the constant traffic of the shipping lanes round Africa.

But we had done all that before. This was nothing but a risky repetition. We had already cleared Cape Juby alive, and here we were, sailing into the onshore wind again, in obvious danger of ruining everything we had achieved. Why had we not at least started below Cape Juby this time? Why a second *Ra*? Why was I beginning a thick expedition diary from page one again? Could I answer?

'We must make it this time,' muttered Carlo from the cabin roof. 'We must make those last few miles to Barbados.'

Was it he and the others who had persuaded me to set all the wheels in motion again? Because we were short of a few miles to satisfy the sceptics? Or was it continued curiosity? The desire to find out if we could cross the ocean in a better-built papyrus boat, now that we had practical experience of a single fumbling attempt to build and navigate a ship whose design we knew only from tomb paintings thousands of years old? Both, perhaps. Such an unbelievable amount had happened in barely ten months, between the landing of *Ra I* and the launching of *Ra II*. I had seen still more reed boats. They survived just where deep traces remained of ancient civilization on its way out from the inner Mediterranean into the Atlantic Ocean.

In the large lagoon of the Oristano marshes on the south-west coast of Sardinia, Carlo Mauri and I had embarked with the fishermen in their traditional reed boats, *fassoni*, and speared fish on tridents, while the impressive and ancient Nuraghi towers were silhouetted on the low hills about us. What an atmosphere of bygone ages! The archaeologists attributed the oldest of these magnificent stone ruins to inspiration from the inmost Mediterranean basin almost 3,000 years before Christ. But the same type of building was continued on Sardinia long after that. The fishermen had taken us into the best preserved of these giant cylindrical stone cairns, whose moss-grown megalithic walls were intact after the wars and earth-tremors of the millennia. No sooner had we fumbled our way through the little opening into the enormous boulder structure and switched on our torches than I seemed to recognize the place. I had seen once before this whole complex caracol system of narrow but lofty tunnels, one running in a ring inside the other, while the big boulder walls seemed to press in on us as they leaned over to meet in a pointed false arch high above our heads. And here, just as before, I followed a low passage which crossed these ring-shaped corridors and led to a narrow tunnel-opening further in, where it was possible to scramble up a spiral staircase which wound up through the compact boulder core to an observation point on the roof.

How strange! An extraordinary composition, but on the very same plan as the one used by the Mayans when they built their astronomical observatory, the famous 'caracol' of Chichen Itza on the Yucatan peninsula, before the Spaniards arrived. This was the pyramid that stood beside the Maya tower which contained the painting of blond mariners fighting black men on the beach. Was there a missing link? Had the unknown masters of the Mayan architects, the earlier Olmecs, also built ceremonial observation towers like the towers of Sardinia?

From the lookout roof of this ceremonial cairn I could see exactly what must have met the eyes of its Sardinian architects thousands of years ago: the distant surf sending white cascades into the lagoon where rows of golden tusk-shaped reed boats were set up on end to dry in the Mediterranean sun. The Mediterranean: the home of man's earliest ventures at sea, the home of deep-sea navigation, with the Straits of Hercules as an ever-open gateway to the world beyond. This water had helped culture to spread. We know that it had spread by sea from the corner where Asia Minor and Egypt meet to the island of Crete. From Crete to Greece. From Greece to Italy. From the original homes of Phoenician sailors to Lixus and other Moroccan colonies outside Gibraltar, centuries before the birth of Christ.

Reed boats were man's earliest kind of watercraft in this corner where Mediterranean culture was born. Reed boats built like those depicted from ancient Nineveh survived among Greek fishermen on the island of Corfu until the present generation. Their local name is still *papyrella*, although the plant and the term papyrus are unknown on modern Corfu. And we found them among Italian fishermen on Sardinia, still in use. We saw them from the roofs of towers built by unknown architects in whose memories they had travelled from somewhere in the inner corner of this historic ocean, this breeding-pond of culture criss-crossed since the morning of time by unknown navigators. Lost civilizations. Lost ships. No wonder the prophet Isaiah could speak of messengers visiting the Holy Land on boats of reeds that sailed across the sea.

Egypt, Mesopotamia, Corfu, Sardinia, Morocco. Yes, even Morocco. Having found the ancient Sardinian reed boats still in use, those that had once existed in Morocco again began to haunt my thoughts. They don't exist; all our boats are built from planks and plastic, was the categorical reply I received from a telephone call to the District Administrator of the Lucus region, where reed boats were reported shortly before the first World War. Returning to Morocco to build *Ra II*, I regretted that I had accepted his 'no' as a conclusive answer. Our good friend, the Pasha of Safi, now lent me his car and an interpreter-guide, and on good roads we reached the Atlantic port of Larache near the mouth of the Lucus River. In this modern town nobody had heard of reed boats other than a huge one that passed along the highway to Safi on a trailer the previous year! We wasted no time, but headed for the fishermen's wharf where some old seamen were sitting mending nets.

Reed boats? Did we mean *madia*? Sure!

With one old Berber as guide we were soon on the trail. For two days we tried to find wheel tracks through the sparse cork forest hiding a tiny Jolot village somewhere near the sea. We found our way at length on foot. Stone Age dwellings, hidden from the sight of nearby modern Africa by the lack of asphalt approaches and landing strips. Picturesque huts with walls of mud-covered branches thatched with the boat-builders' reeds. The bushy reed gables with big storks' nests were scarcely visible behind a labyrinth of impenetrable hedges of giant cactus. Goats, dogs, children, chicken and old people. Whole families were blond with blue eyes. Others were completely negroid. The Arab migration into Morocco had left no traces here. This was a striking sample of Morocco's mixed indigenous population. They should have been labelled 'unidentified'. Yet black and blond were for mere convenience mixed together and put in one bag marked 'Berber'. A black giant chased away the dogs and guided us through the cactus fences which barred the little sunbaked kingdom from view of sea, river or the sparse pastureland with its gnarled cork trees.

Madia? Of course. All the old people, bent greybeards and toothless crones alike, had known both *shafat* and *madia*, the two types of reed boat which had been in use in the Lucus River estuary until only a few decades ago. Two old men hastened to make a model each: a *shafat* with its flat, sliced-off stern, for floating cargoes across the river, and a *madia* with bow and stern curving upward as in ancient Egypt. A *madia* could be used out in the surf; it could be made as large as you liked, as *khab*, the thin flat reed they used, floated for many months. The old men built a bed-size sample with upturned bow and shorn end, and five persons jumped into it, paddling about to demonstrate its incredible load-bearing capacity.

As in Sardinia, here at the mouth of the Lucus River colossal ruins of megalithic structures overlook the waters where reed boats had survived: the mighty ruins of Lixus. In fact, but for my search for reed boats I would never have stumbled upon Lixus. The ruined city was as unfamiliar to my archaeologist colleagues as to the common citizen of Morocco. An expert on Egypt or Sumer, not to mention a specialist on ancient Mexico, knows little about the Atlantic coast of Africa and nothing about the sites on the Lucus River. Only a couple of archaeologists specializing in Morocco have had time and means to open a few small test trenches and disclose the colossal stones forming Lixus' oldest buried walls. I myself stumbled on these ruins merely because they towered above the modern road from Larache to the cork forest where I was to search for the village of the reed boat builders. It was only a few miles from the mighty ruin to the modest surviving village. The difference in magnitude, in proportions, and in cultural level, aroused much conjecture about the dimensional range of the watercraft once built in this area. It was on the outlet of the wide Lucus River, just where it wound past the hill where these colossal ruins stood, that reed boats had been in common use into the present century. Warehouses from Roman times emerge from the silt at the foot of the hill, testifying to a time when Lixus was the main Atlantic port for sailors from the Mediterranean world.

Reed boats had lured me to Lixus. Few sights have surprised me more. The Atlantic Ocean in front of us, the unbroken mainland of Africa

at our backs, stretching right to Egypt, with Phoenicia and Mesopotamia close behind. They had come there, from the innermost corner
of the Mediterranean, past Gibraltar and down the west coast of Africa,
with women and children, with astronomers and architects, with
potters and weavers, those travellers from distant Asia Minor who,
when the Romans later came out past Gibraltar, had been living here
since the morning of time. This was truly historic ground. Out here
on the Atlantic coast lay this ancient town, so old that the Romans
called it the Eternal City, connecting it with the giant Hercules, son of
the supreme deities, Hera (or Hra) and Zeus, and hero of the earliest
Greek and Roman mythology.

The oldest walls, now completely or partly covered by the compact
detritus of Phoenicians, Romans, Berbers and Arabs, were sufficiently
impressive to stir anyone's imagination. Gigantic blocks had been
quarried and transported to the top of this hill in enormous numbers,
carved in different shapes and sizes but always with vertical and horizontal sides and angles which fitted neatly together like pieces in a
gigantic jigsaw puzzle, even when right-angled indentations in some
blocks made their external surfaces not flat, but multi-faceted.
This special technique, unknown and almost inimitable, appeared as a
sort of signature carved in stone wherever reed boats had once been
in use, from Easter Island back to Peru and Mexico, and from there
back to the great civilizations of Africa and the inner Mediterranean.
Olmecs and pre-Incas had mastered this technique to perfection, just
as the ancient Egyptians and Phoenicians had, but Vikings or Chinese,
Negroes or prairie Indians would all be as perplexed as a bunch of
modern scholars if they were shown a mountainside and asked to carve
blocks and fit a wall together on these principles, even if they were
given steel tools and a pattern to copy.

As I wandered among the tumbled and half-buried blocks of the
Eternal Sun City and recognized that sophisticated special technique, I
felt as if America and the eastern Mediterranean were drawing closer
to each other. Lixus seemed to link them and divide the distance in
half. Thus far the eastern Mediterranean civilization had spread its
branches, many centuries before Christ. Here well-equipped and well-
prepared colonists and traders had been sailing to and fro at a safe
distance from the menacing cliffs of Africa, here and further down,
past the perilous Cape Juby, during just those centuries when bearded
Olmecs appeared on the opposite shores of the Atlantic and set about

clearing glades in the primeval forest. Just when Mediterranean stone-masons poured out through the Straits of Gibraltar, the unknown Olmecs began introducing stone-masonry and civilization to the Indian families that had roamed the wilderness for many thousands of years. Here at the river mouth, the classical reed boat had survived, although all sorts of timber were available on the shore. Here it survived, with the same ocean current surging off the coast, that very current which now had us in its grasp for the second time in a year.

I gave the heavy rudder-oar an extra shove outward, to give us the greatest possible chance of steering clear of the rocks round Cape Juby. How many vessels in the early days of Lixus had struggled, like us, to round the dangerous reefs where Africa swung southward to the furthest Phoenician colonies below Cape Bajador?

'This time the rudder-oars will survive, anyway,' I said laughingly to Carlo and patted the thick log I was steering with on the port side. The other, on the starboard side, was made fast with stout rope. Those thin shafts we had last time had broken on their first encounter with the ocean waves and reduced the whole voyage on *Ra I* to a process of drifting.

The papyrus hull itself was also infinitely stronger this time. The papyrus had once again been collected at the source of the Nile, because the sparse papyrus growing in Morocco, where we built *Ra II*, did not meet our requirements. Neither Abdullah nor I could reach Bol on Lake Chad to fetch Mussa and Omar; the rebels had struck again in the desert and French parachute troops had cordoned off the entire area. Nor had the Central African technique proved strong enough in the long run at sea. After two months we had lost the reed on one side because the makeshift tail tacked on behind had gradually subsided and allowed the waves to use the bamboo cabin as a saw, until the rope chains unravelled like knitting. I had decided to try out reed boat builders who were still regularly building robust vessels in the ancient Mediterranean style, with a pointed stern soaring as high into the air as the stem. That was how the South American Indians still built their reed boats in Bolivia and Peru. They also follow-ed the illustrations from ancient Nineveh and Egypt in another remark-able detail: their ropes ran continuously, from the deck right round the bottom of the reed boat, so that from the side the vessel consisted of a single compact bundle, while the boats on Lake Chad, apart from lacking a stern section, consisted of many small papyrus rolls, held together, on top of and beside one another, by short, linked loops of rope.

Strange that the Indians in South America should use a method which is far closer to the ancient Mediterranean building technique than the one which has survived in Central Africa. Perhaps the explanation was that the Buduma on Lake Chad had never had any close personal contact with the civilizations of antiquity. But the Quechua and Aymara Indians on Lake Titicaca had. It was the Aymaras' own forefathers who had helped to build the Akapana pyramid and the rest of the megalithic structures in Tiahuanaco, once South America's most important cultural centre, which stood in pre-Inca days on the shores of Lake Titicaca. It was they who had transported the colossal building blocks by reed boat across the lake. It was they who told the Spaniards that white men with beards had appeared among their forefathers to direct this stone work, and that when they came they had first appeared in reed boats of this type. The Aymara Indians themselves had never learned to work stone. But they had succeeded, to absolute perfection, in copying reed boats for fishing on the lake, right up to the present day.

All the crew of *Ra I* declared their willingness to join in a further experiment. Once again Santiago left his post at Mexico University, this time to look for reed boat builders on Lake Titicaca. In Addis Ababa my local contact, Mario Buschi, was discreetly asked to send his Ethiopian assistants out on Lake Tana to harvest another twelve tons of papyrus. Reed from Ethiopia and boat-builders from Bolivia were to be transported covertly to Morocco, where the building must proceed in all secrecy if I myself were to be left in peace to write the chapters on *Ra I* which were absolutely necessary if I were to bear the additional expenses of this continued experiment. Twelve tons of Ethiopian papyrus, shipped around Africa under the cover name of 'bamboo', were unloaded in Safi harbour, and vanished. Four full-blooded Aymara Indians and their Bolivian interpreter landed at the airfield in Casablanca with Santiago, and vanished. Sailcloth from Egypt, a wickerwork cabin woven in Italy, timber for masts and oars, quantities of rope, arrived unnoticed in Morocco from all sides, and vanished. Nobody but the Pasha and the closest circle of collaborators knew that a second *Ra* was being built in Morocco.

On May 6th, a section of the high wall around the city nursery garden in Safi collapsed, and out from the flowers and palm trees roared a mighty bulldozer, followed by a little frail ship of flower stems, which seemed to have grown naturally from the greenery.

Ra II was born.

She moved slowly through the crumbled masonry like a big paper bird emerging from its egg. With majestic dignity she rolled slowly on wheels down narrow alleyways, where Arabs and Berbers in hooded tunics and veils stood packed together to watch. Police paraded and barefoot children danced along in the procession. Excited gardeners and electricians hung from the trees and posts and on top of a red mobile ladder, to prevent branches and wires from tearing or setting fire to the dry papyrus tips rising fore and aft of the golden showboat. The authorities breathed a sigh of relief when the strange construction had jounced across the railway lines and stopped between rows of newly-painted fishing boats waiting to be launched for the first sardine fishing of the spring.

'I name you *Ra II*,' said Aicha, wife of Pasha Taieb Amara, as for the second time in a little under a year she splashed goat's milk over a bone-dry papyrus boat before it slid out on the water.

'Hurrah,' yelled the sea of people surging over the quay, applauding as the strange vessel lay bobbing around on the surface of the water exactly like a toy paper boat. The crew of the tug-boat just stood and stared without moving a muscle. We who were to use the little object felt a tremendous relief, for it was all made by hand and eye, and there were plenty of people who thought it would capsize or lie out of trim. Hurrah!

But what now? Stop! Help! Ay-ay-ay! A despairing shriek from the crowd. Panic on the tug-boat. A powerful squall came chasing unexpectedly over the mountain, twirled the paper boat round, and whisked it off alone, away from the tug-boat, at terrifying speed, straight towards a twelve-foot high jetty of solid stone. Howls and cries of distress, orders yelled in French and Arabic, faces buried in hands, photographers plunging into shallow water with their cameras, partly to snap and partly to push off. And there was the newly baptized infant, spinning round and high-tailing it at top speed, straight for the wall. Bang! The elegantly curved new papyrus tail took the whole shock and bent like a feather. It was heart-rending. The stern! The very part which must be invulnerable and perfect this time. The hull turned and danced recklessly on the wave-tops right up on to the stones.

No one could stop the boat in the gusts of wind. The experiment seemed to be over before it had begun. But no. The harp-shaped tail gave like a spring and the reed boat bounced off the wall like a rubber ball. Once. Twice. A wooden boat would have splintered and gone to the bottom. *Ra II* was unscathed. Just a scuffed grey patch on the outer sheath of some of the golden straws. Then the tug-boat captured the rope. Nothing to repair. *Ra II* followed cheerfully on her tow rope, over to the quay where the straddled mast was to be put on board, dancing to right and left in the gusts of wind. She behaved like a paper kite trying to get airborne.

I shivered at the rudder-oar as I thought back to the launching. But at the same time I thought that if we were now to be cast up on reefs and rocks in the mist over there, we would have a good chance of saving our lives before this ball of hay went to the bottom. It was so compact and solid that it did not bend an inch on the seas. *Ra I* had undulated like a sea-serpent. *Ra II* was as rigid as a baseball. Everyone on board was equally impressed with the Indians' brilliant design. Those perfect lines and the incredibly ingenious way in which the difficult construction problems had been solved were quite inconsistent with the style and quality of the Aymara Indians' other earthly possessions. This was inheritance. Even if the real secret of their ancient technique seemed to have gone unnoticed by laymen and scholars alike, our own research and experiments had proved that this Lake Titicaca method was the only one which could produce a vessel with shape and lashings coinciding with the details on ancient Mediterranean reliefs. All other methods of binding the papyrus together in the form of a crescent-shaped boat led inevitably to sagging and jerking, with catastrophic results to the ropes. It is easy to construct a makeshift raft of reeds, but not a sickle-shaped reed boat capable of resisting ocean waves. The system employed by our Indians was so simple and yet so ingenious that I know of no living tribe or individual who would be able to duplicate it without a teacher and much practice.

The four taciturn Indians, Demetrio, José, Juan and Paulino, and their equally calm Bolivian interpreter, Señor Zeballos, a museum curator from La Paz, organized the building of *Ra II* in masterl' fashion with a handful of Moroccan helpers. They were all so sile' that I was constantly having to put my manuscript aside and look ' of the tent, only to see that the building work among the palm ' really was progressing at full speed, with gestures and brief grunts in the Aymara tongue, Spanish and Arabic.

The Indians first stacked up two huge untidy rolls of loose papyrus stalks, elegantly packed into thin papyrus mats which were woven so that all the ends turned inward and were squashed flat. Before the ropes were drawn tight, these two thirty-foot cylinders were so thick that no one could get on top without the help of scaffolding. In the open passageway between these two big rolls a much thinner roll of the same length was now made, to which both the large ones were to be bound. This was done by first winding a rope, several hundred yards long, in a continuous spiral which at the same time encircled both the thin central roll and one of the thick outer rolls, and then a second rope which, without touching the first, ran in a complementary spiral round the thin roll and the other thick outer roll. So when these two independent spiral ropes were drawn tight by the united strength of the Indians, each of the big rolls was forced closer and closer to the little one in the middle, until it was jammed between them and finished up squeezed right into them, forming a completely invisible core. Thus only the two big rolls remained visible, pressed tightly together all along their centre line. This resulted in an unshakeably compact, double-cylinder hull, with no knots or criss-cross ropes; and all that remained was to extend the hull on the same principle, to produce the elegant upswept peaks at stem and stern. A sausage-shaped bundle was finally bound on either side of the deck to give it breadth and to break the waves. Then we ourselves lashed on ten cross-beams as a base for the light basket cabin, the steering bridge poles and the foot-plates for the heavy straddled mast. *Ra II* was finished: 39 feet long, 16 feet broad, 6 feet thick. The cabin was 13 feet long and 9 feet broad, tailor-made for 8 people, if we lay 4 by 4, feet together, stretched out like Egyptian mummies. Not only was *Ra II* about ten feet shorter than *Ra I*, but her cross-section was also rounder and thus much slimmer. I thought with regret of all the buoyant papyrus – almost a third of it – left lying unused on the building site this time. But neither rewards nor arguments could persuade our Aymara friends to add a single stalk or a single day's work to the boat. This was the absolute limit of their scope, and they wanted to be off post-haste, home to their abandoned wives on Lake Titicaca.

'A pleasant voyage and welcome to Suriqui Island,' said Demetrio

284

kindly, pulling off his stocking cap as the garden wall crashed and their masterpiece disappeared from the building site.

'To Suriqui Island?' we said bemusedly.

'Well, if not actually to our little island, welcome to our side of Lake Titicaca in any case.'

Geography was obviously not the Aymara Indians' strong point. They did not realize that they themselves had built *Ra II* on the other side of the Atlantic and had come down from a lake which lay 12,000 feet above sea level. But they knew how to build reed boats, with a perfection which no engineer, no model-builder, no archaeologist in our modern world could emulate.

'Rigid as a block of wood,' said Carlo. We both breathed a sigh of relief after a brightly lit cargo boat had thundered close by us without running us down. 'Rigid as a block of wood, but we're sinking,' he added.

'The sinking won't last. So far we have had too much load in relation to the small amount of papyrus under water.'

'Norman thinks we should have daubed all the papyrus with pitch, as it says in the Bible.'

'Not necessary,' I said. 'It's only the cut ends that absorb water. That was why we dipped the last inch of most of the reeds in pitch this time.'

But in fact I, too, was beginning to wonder whether we should have covered the whole vessel with a thick layer of pitch. Then we would not have sunk by as much as half an inch. Perhaps the ancient Egyptians had done this *inside* the visible reed mat. For otherwise the wall paintings would certainly have shown the reed boats as black, not green and yellow.

Several priests had written to me after the *Ra I* voyage, to say that according to the Bible, Noah's Ark was daubed with pitch, and Moses' mother had definitely used pitch on the papyrus basket in which she had launched her son on the Nile for Pharaoh's daughter to find drifting among the bulrushes. The idea had not just come out of thin air. There was surface pitch lying about for the asking in those days and it was in common use in ancient Egypt and Asia Minor. Nevertheless we had seen from *Ra I* that tightly bound papyrus floated without pitch, too, as long as the ropes held.

The ropes. On *Ra I* we had used much thicker ropes, and Mussa and Omar had knotted together hundreds of short, independent loops, which held even if others were chafed away. At first glance the Indians' rope lashing looked quite absurd. They had used only a single thin rope in a continuous spiral from stem to stern. Moreover they had blankly refused to use a rope more than half an inch thick. They said that in this way the rope would be subject to a more even strain, and even if it broke the lashings would not fall away, because wet papyrus would grip the rope. Could we rely on them? On whom else could we rely? Everyone on board was aware that this was a new experiment. We could have used the Chad method again, with the improvements we now knew to be necessary, and then we would not have been exposed to this fresh uncertainty. The fateful bow-string from the curly tail down to the deck behind the cabin was in position now, and wise from experience we had also concentrated the cargo on the lee side, but otherwise *Ra II* was full of unknown qualities. Not only were we afraid that the very thin, long rope, all that held us together, might snap in heavy seas, but while *Ra I* lay on the water as comfortably as a mattress, *Ra II* rolled so that we could neither sit nor stand without hanging on to something. On the very first day we tried in vain to rig hand ropes, because there was nothing to catch us at the edge if we fell. And we were sailing fast. While the papyrus was still lying high in the water we skimmed over the wave-tops with the sea frothing round our bows, and covered 95 nautical miles (or 177 kilometres) on the first day. It was all we could do to hold the big sail. Once both sheets blew out of our hands and another time the wind tore them to shreds, so that the mainsail, 26 feet high, 25 feet wide at the top by the yard, and 16 at the bottom, hung like a gigantic flag, battering, flapping and slapping until we expected the whole vessel to disintegrate. On the very first night we had rushed past the islet off Mogador, where one of the Phoenician purple factories had been, at such close quarters that we could see the lights of every single house on the mainland behind it. On the second day the squalls off the Sahara coast were so violent that we had to lower the whole sail at the risk of tearing the high slender papyrus prow to ribbons in the process. On the third day the wind died. It died so completely that sailing was out of the question and in the end we lay yawing helplessly. Now the coast had disappeared in a wall of fog and we twisted and tugged and hauled on heavy rudder-oars and on the ropes to heavy slack sails, in order to avoid shipwreck. We were aware, with every little gust of onshore wind, that we were only a few hours from the cliff walls.

Fortunately, equally feeble puffs of offshore wind, especially at night, carried us safely away from the shore again.

The wind did not return. On the fourth day there was a flat calm.

'We're sinking,' said one man after another. It was easy to see in calm water. The whole craft was on its way down, sinking by at least four inches a day. This was quite new to us. Nothing like this had happened on *Ra I*. Had the long spiral rope of the Indians not succeeded in compressing the papyrus sufficiently? Or was it a different kind of papyrus this time?

Santiago went round unobtrusively with pencil and paper, taking an anonymous opinion poll on whether we thought we would cross the Atlantic alive, or fail. Two thought we would get across, six thought we would fail. I don't know who the other optimist was. Perhaps it was Norman, who always said that if only we cleared Cape Juby safely we could let the craft steer itself; America barred the way ahead in all directions. Or perhaps it was Carlo, who suffered from an incurable devotion to *Ra I* because he thought *Ra II* had become too much the perfect sailing boat.

We were sinking frighteningly fast, and if the current had not maintained its hold on the sinking vessel we would scarcely have stirred from the spot. It was only the fourth day when Georges came to me with an unwontedly solemn expression to say that Santiago the quartermaster and Carlo the chef thought we had far too much food and water and should get rid of everything which was not absolutely indispensable at sea. He picked up a goatskin and began to finger the stopper preparatory to emptying the contents overboard.

'But that's the drinking water!'

'Better to ration the drinking water than sink before we have passed the Canary Islands. This time we *must* make it!'

'Let's start dumping things overboard, it's great fun,' Santiago tried to joke in an unusually hollow voice.

'We must chuck out all the food which needs long cooking,' came in almost cheerful tones from Carlo. 'The primus stoves are lousy this time. One is burnt to pieces and the other doesn't heat properly.'

Yuri stuck his head out of the cabin, looking extremely grave, and behind him I could see Madani, speechless, but with anxiously inquiring eyes. Kei stood like an inscrutable china figure on the steering bridge, betraying none of his feelings. Norman was busy fixing our position.

'We're sinking,' said Yuri slowly, 'and we know from the last time that what goes down never comes up again. We must throw out everything we can, at once.'

Norman was following the argument silently. The atmosphere was explosive. No wind, insufficient buoyancy. Why had this not happened last time? Could the home experts, wrong last time, be right now in giving us a fortnight to stay afloat? We had in fact voluntarily spent ten days floating in Safi harbour to allow the bundles to absorb water so that the light, top-heavy boat with its giant sail should not overturn. We had left port four days before, so that now a fortnight had passed. The papyrus rolls were already half under water.

'Let's pitch out those two reed boats on the foredeck,' Norman suggested. 'We don't need them as lifeboats and we've got a three-man inflatable raft for filming this time.'

We had barely time to attach a message in a bottle to the largest reed boat before eager hands pushed it into the sea. The other vanished overboard so fast that we had no time to tie anything to it. Farewell. They floated sidelong, like balloons, in a faint wind towards land. We had no idea then that the message would be found by a lonely guard on a barren Sahara beach a few days later. We ourselves lay deep, letting the current carry us parallel to land.

Then a big sack of potatoes went overboard. Potatoes need lengthy cooking. Then two whole jars of rice. Flour. Maize. Two sacks, contents unknown. A wicker basket. Better to starve than sink. Then most of the grain for the chickens went. A big beam, planks and hardwood boards for splicing and repairs. More full jars. Madani looked at me anxiously, big-eyed. Kei exposed his teeth in an enigmatic grin and stared up at the sail. A heavy coil of rope plunged overboard. A whetstone. A hammer. Georges' heavy iron spike for repairing the boat vanished for ever in the depths. Books and magazines floated about us in the calm water. Some only had their bindings torn off. Every ounce counted. I agreed. And yet I passionately disapproved at the same time. We had thousands of miles ahead of us. We had barely set out from land and at this rate we would need food for months, and spare materials. But they were right. We were sinking. Why? How long? I tried to convince first myself and then the others that the submersion would stop as soon as there was enough papyrus under water for its buoyancy to offset all the heavy cargo we had stacked hastily on board on the last day before departure on May 17th. Now it was May 20th. We were still sinking just as fast.

Yuri resolutely started to tear up a little plank deck we had lashed on top of the papyrus in front of the mast. It had been such a comfortable platform. Yesterday Santiago and Georges had used it as a stage in a lively display of clog dancing and sketches with which they had entertained the rest of us hugely as we lay drifting on an almost glassy sea. I got him to save a plank or two to walk on so that we would not stumble between the two thick papyrus rolls when we began to roll on high seas again.

But somebody was sitting in the shelter of the cabin, throwing all our almost weightless Egyptian *karkadé* tea into the sea. And the earthenware stove with all our charcoal. Lavatory paper. Spices. Everything counted.

There was a lump in my throat. Some of the crew were smiling joylessly. Others wore a look compounded of shame and misery. Better to let the havoc run its course within controllable limits than to let anyone be inwardly consumed by the dangerous feeling that we had not done everything that could be done, should we continue to sink. The greatest danger would be for anyone's own peace of mind to suffer. But then the chickens began to flutter overboard. Two of the men took hatchets and knives and were about to cut the whole chicken coop loose so that it could be heaved out to sea. Without a proper primus stove we could not eat poultry. Then it was time to halt the frenzy. The chickens' days were ended, but Georges pleaded for a single duck, which to Safi the monkey's indignation was allowed to strut freely about the deck and nip her tailless bottom just as the first Sinbad had done on *Ra I*. Safi had added a few inches to her stature, but was still the same carefree scamp as when we first had her as our mascot on the earlier voyage. The empty hencoop on the foredeck I myself broke up and turned into a light dining table, though there were some who wanted to get rid of both this and the crude benches, arguing that we could eat with plates and cups in our hands. But this brought a unanimous protest from the two of us who regarded a meal as a real high point in the day's programme.

'In any case, morale on board will collapse if we begin to live like pigs,' stated Norman, as an experienced naval officer.

Our minds were at peace. The air had been cleared, as though by a lightning conductor, and for once there was really room to move about on board without mountaineering. But the wind had not returned.

The next day was equally still, and the next as well. And the next.

We simply lay where we were. It did not look as if we were sinking any more for the time being, but neither were we making any visible progress.

'The statistics say one per cent calm here in May,' said Norman, putting his finger on the navigational chart. 'We have had 100 per cent for a full week.'

We tried to work the long, heavy rowing-oars. No use. But we seemed to be out of immediate danger. We jumped into the sea and enjoyed life. The sun blazed down on us while the Canary Islands and Africa on either side lay hidden in the haze. Cold, fresh water. Norman swam with the duck in tow. Safi hung by her back legs, reaching for the surface of the water. Inviting water. But in heaven's name, could we never get away from those little black oil clots, floating above and below the surface? Madani had actually netted some samples every day since we left. This time we were going to make a more systematic investigation, day by day. Last time we had only noticed the pollution when the water was so filthy that we could not overlook it. But the report and samples we had sent to the Norwegian delegation at the United Nations had aroused so much interest that more thorough observation was clearly worthwhile, now that we had our noses to the surface again. We used the sea from morning to night, as tooth-glass, wash-basin, bidet and bath. Fortunately there was enough space between the clots for us not to bump into them. We ducked under the papyrus bundles. Crystal clear. Masses of fish. Striped pilot fish and spotted pampano waggled about in *Ra II*'s shadow, or kept station close under the papyrus. The papyrus was sleekly firm and sturdy, the whale-belly shape even more stylish than on *Ra I*. Look there, a hulking great grouper, nearly five feet long, deep and fat and heavy. We could not be far from the Canary Islands; these fish do not venture far out to sea. The grouper came right over and poked at Georges' diving mask. An eight-inch, zebra-striped pilot fish came gliding like a little zeppelin towards my fingers. Santiago was right, the fish swam when they were on the surface. But they appeared not to swim, but to fly, free as birds, when seen down in their own watery element. Two extraordinary creatures resembling footless stockings undulated past my nose. And there, a round disc resembling a rubbery jellyfish. With Portuguese men-o'-war fresh in our memories we kept clear of this sort of unknown invertebrate.

'Shark, big shark!'

It was a long way off. Dorsal and tail fins were cutting through the water an uncanny distance apart, so it was really big. It was not bothering about *Ra II*. It continued unperturbed on its course at right angles to our own.

Everyone was in good humour after seeing how perfect *Ra II* looked under water. The tail was as strong and elegant as ever. No list to windward. Not one reed loose. Yuri and Georges even thought the papyrus bundles had lifted themselves out of the water a little in front. Perhaps the tropical sun was steaming off the moisture absorbed above the waterline during the first days' rolling. The day before they had thought that not more than two or three men should be before the masts at one time, to prevent the bow from sinking. Now they agreed to our making seats out of the few materials we had left, to provide us with a cosy dining-room on the foredeck.

For a week we lay idly yawing to the south-east, with feeble puffs of wind from east and west which did not even lift yard and sail free of the mainmast and with the whole sea drifting slowly under us. The sea was moving. Only we could not see it, because sea and boat were drifting at the same rate. Then the air began to follow suit, slowly at first. We began to nourish hopes of getting enough wind to give us steerageway. When we were bathing or diving to play with the tame fish, we always had a long rope looped round our bodies, so that we would be towed along if the boat began to move in the variable breezes. It would be too bad if we lost the boat.

On the last day of calm, Norman, Santiago and Sinbad the duck were all swimming on their ropes when I dived out with mine and swam across underneath the boat before coming up to the rippling surface and lying on my back to drink in the sun. A perfect holiday idyll. Unusual to see the underside of a duck swimming, nothing but a fat belly flanked by paddling feet. I turned over to enjoy the sight of the extraordinary vessel beside us. Noah's Ark. Straw and yellow bamboo. Monkey in the stays, dove on the roof, and two bare feet sticking out of the cabin doorway. What a strange sensation. The sail was bellying slightly. Small ripples round the steering oars, we were really beginning to move. Strange that I could not feel the tug of the rope. What an astonishingly long rope I had. The rope! Where was it? Nowhere. Gone. I had swum out of the loop and was lying sunning myself alone on the Atlantic while *Ra II* sailed on. I felt a stab of panic – I was being left behind. Relax, *Ra II* was still quite close. I was far from being a swimming champion like Georges or Norman, but this I could manage easily. Made it. Jammed my fingers into the tight, thin rope round the smooth papyrus and hoisted myself on board. How safe those sturdy reed bundles felt. Said nothing, but rigged up the bathing net on the lee quarter, a sack-shaped net which I had designed so that we could scramble down into it and bathe overboard as we sailed. We did not know what effect soapsuds would have on the papyrus if we took a shower on board; the soap would remain between the reeds, for there was no planking here to be scrubbed as on an ordinary deck.

We got our wind. With the north-east trade-wind blowing in on the starboard quarter, we pushed the tillers of both rudder-oars across as far as we could and rushed along with the waves without sighting land in any direction. On May 26th Norman came down from the cabin roof with sextant, pencil and paper and breathed a sigh of relief. We must be past Cape Juby. Hurrah, the coastal cliffs, *Ra II*'s most dangerous enemies, were behind us. Now the sea lay free and open before us once again, and this time we faced it with *Ra II*'s tail still curving skyward and with unbroken oarshafts as thick as telegraph poles. Everyone who had seen those exaggeratedly hefty poles before the start had smiled. We could have managed with something much slimmer and lighter, the thin papyrus stems would be torn to pieces a hundred times before such massive logs would snap.

Life was sweeter than we had ever known it on a papyrus deck. From the invisible coasts on both sides of us we had been met by a gaudy aviary which came fluttering wearily out of the sky. One at a time they had settled on the yard-arm, on the cabin roof, on the shaft of the steering-oar, on the papyrus peaks fore and aft. Carlo's fantasy of living in a floating birds' nest had materialized. There were friends from home, a wild dove, tits, swallows, finches and sparrows, a parrot-coloured beauty of a roller with its dazzling blue and green plumage, and a carrier-pigeon with a copper ring on its leg which circled over us, made a half-landing on the mast and sailed down to join the bridge watch under the blue flag of the United Nations. The dove of peace, we all thought. It and the UN flag we were sailing under seemed to belong together. '27773–68A–España', we read on the copper ring. We had become a floating zoo. Mute, wriggling fish of many species kept us company below, and on board twittering birds in bright colours sat everywhere, pecking at water bowls and grain originally intended for the poultry. But as we glided steadily further away from the Canary Islands, without attempting to reach land, the rested birds made their adieux one by one, and left. Only the parrot-coloured beauty queen could do no more and gradually faded away. She was an insect-eater and we had not so much as a fly to offer. But the ring-marked dove took a fancy to Sinbad the duck's grain ration. It grew sleekly fat and tame and had apparently made up its mind to come to America with us.

As the wind returned, *Ra II* seemed to rise a little in the water. It looked as if the mighty, wind-filled sail were lifting the foredeck into the air. We were sailing in a kite a little too heavy to become airborne. And when *Ra II* came to life in the fresh breeze she rapidly began to make up for lost time. At a speed of 60, 70, or 80 sea miles, that is 110, 130, even 150 kilometres a day, she carried us on across the open Atlantic.

The days quickly settled into a routine. Everyone was happy. Song and laughter. Nothing to repair. Easy watches. Good food from earthenware jars. No rationing. Four superb cooks. Any pharaoh would have envied us Georges' spiced Egyptian dishes; no geisha could have bettered Kei's cooking. Madani's piquant recipe for salt meat in onions and oil à la Berber and Carlo's tireless capacity for producing something good when the others had not volunteered, all helped to make us feel we were speeding over the waves on a first-papyrus-class ticket.

When the evening shadow of the sail fell across the boat, seven sunburned, bearded, cheerful men sat round the empty hencoop eating, while the eighth man stood on the steering bridge turning the thick rudder-oar with the setting sun for guide. The compass pointed west. The sun spread its very last rays like a peacock's tail over the sea in front of our own golden paper swan as she forged ahead on the very heels of the immortal *Ra* of past and present. And then the Great Bear with the Pole Star stepped out on the starboard beam. Good friends. Part of our little world. We knew it all so well from the last time.

A fresh night breeze. On with long trousers and jerseys. Madani in his thick Moroccan kaftan with the pointed hood looked like a medieval monk as he settled down on the roof, silhouetted against the tropic sky, and bowed his face to the ground in worship. An uncommonly pleasant and good-natured travelling companion. He had come in Abdullah's place, to represent the coloured men of Africa. He was not quite as raven-black as Abdullah, but he was of the darkest type of Berber. Abdullah was the only man from the *Ra I* team whom we had unfortunately lost on the starting line in Safi, three days before the start. For a year he had been a voluntary refugee from Chad, where a bloody conflict was now in progress between his Mohammedan co-religionists in the north and the Christian African government, supported by the French Foreign Legion. Abdullah felt increasingly uneasy, with a wife here and a wife there, and geographical obstacles in the way of a normal family life. In one hand a photograph of three charming African children in Chad, in the other a telegram to say that now, just now, his latest, favourite wife had borne him a daughter in Cairo. Who was going to sort out these tangles if Abdullah went to sea again on a papyrus boat? Good-bye, Abdullah, we will all miss you. Abdullah was no sooner out of the door than Madani Ait Ouhanni stepped smilingly from behind the cupboard in the hotel where we all lived. Could he come with us? He had just been appointed overseer by the big phosphate factory in Safi, which had recently taken over the hotel. He was carried off from his hotel by seven guests about to set sail, who needed a genuine African on the voyage in Abdullah's place.

We had known Madani for three days. None of us had ever seen Kei before. A Swedish friend of mine was going to Tokyo to negotiate an exchange of television programmes. I had asked him to recommend a Japanese film photographer with a friendly nature and good health. Soon after, stocky little Kei Ohara tumbled in through the hotel doors in Safi, laden with camera equipment, and bursting with *joie de vivre*, music and judo muscles. Experience at sea? One sightseeing trip by water bus in Tokyo Bay. And then, he had been on a film assignment on Lake Titicaca and photographed the Indians in reed boats.

'And you, Madani?' asked Norman, rather anxiously.

'I went on a fishing trip off the jetty once, when I first came down to Safi from Marrakesh, but I was sea-sick and went ashore.'

'Nothing but landlubbers this time too,' said Norman, looking at me in mild despair.

'Then they won't load the papyrus boat as sailors would have loaded an ordinary wooden ship,' I said, referring to last year's catastrophe. 'Safest with those who realize they know nothing about papyrus navigation. A practised ski-jumper is seldom flexible enough to make a good parachute jump.'

Both the first-trip men suffered the fearful torments of the sea-sick for the first two days, while the slender papyrus boat rolled and pitched like an empty bottle in fierce seas. Then Buddha and Allah seemed to hear their prayers for calm, in defiance of all the statistics and the weather chart, and when at last the wind stole up on us again the representatives of Japan and Morocco had slipped quite naturally into the picture. As on *Ra I*, we shared the same trials and the same blessings. Those who were pale turned brown in the sun. Those who were still browner increased their lead, without anyone thinking about family trees, certificates of baptism, membership cards or passports. There was little room on the foredeck, still less on the afterdeck, and only a strip three feet wide along both sides of the thin cabin walls. The basket cabin consisted of a single room too low for standing, except on the roof, and much too narrow to turn over in bed in a curled-up position without putting a knee in one's neighbour's stomach or an elbow in his eye. We knew each other's oaths, snores, table manners and jokes, even if the shrieks and creaks from mast-stays and lashed steering bridge often made it difficult in the darkness to decide who was producing the oddest sounds. Madani was musical even when he slept. After personally locating oriental pipe-notes and wind instruments invisibly housed in his nose, and a veritable workshop of saws, drills and planes operating in the throat of the more practically-inclined Carlo, I went back to sleep with a good conscience, ignoring their accusations that I myself had swallowed a lion. Only Santiago and Georges occasionally asked Yuri for sleeping pills. We might have been at a non-stop party; no room for secrets; at all times of day and in every situation we were all there, at the closest possible range.

If an American and a Russian seldom get properly acquainted, two of them were getting thoroughly familiar with each other now. If Arabs and Jews had been natural enemies, one of them would have disappeared into the waves behind *Ra II*. If the Almighty did not allow Himself to be worshipped under many names, we would have had a religious war on board. We represented a babel of eight different languages, but English, Italian and French were the ones spoken daily, Arabic and Spanish occasionally, Russian, Norwegian and Japanese only in our sleep. We argued, told funny stories and sang in chorus whenever we had leisure, especially after supper, with two or three men sitting at the bottom of the mast ladder and the rest seated round the hencoop, because inside the cabin there was always someone wanting to sleep. We discussed politics, and never pulled our punches.

For here the arguments for East and West were uncensored; no one was standing by with loaded pistols. Hand harpoons, hatchets and fish-hooks were the nearest things to weapons on board. They were used for the common good, for we were all in the same boat. Together, like other people, we mulled over the Palestinian problem, the tribal feuds in Africa, the intervention of the Americans in Vietnam and of the Russians in Czechoslovakia. No one got angry, no one was offended, no one raised his voice. We quite often agreed. We discussed religion and no one felt a holy wrath. Copt and Catholic, Protestant and Mohammedan, Buddhist, atheist, free-thinker and half-Christian Jew, there was no space for a greater mixture on our little ark, where the monkey was Noah and we played the animal roles. We had no religious feuds on board. But – we discussed the ownership of a lost-and-found toothbrush and then we heard yells of rage and angry curses in various tongues. In their inmost hearts human beings are amazingly alike, regardless of geographical location. A toothbrush held close to your nose is bigger than a cannon a thousand miles off. It is easy to find differences between man and man, but still easier to find the highest common factors of mankind. Whether we tried to understand one another or not, we were packed close enough together on board our papyrus ark to see each other as slices cut from the same loaf. We rejoiced and were angry over the same things; we helped each other all we could, because we were helping ourselves. One steered so that others could sleep, cooked so that others could eat, sewed sails and hauled on ropes so that we should all make good progress. We had to keep each other in top form so that we would all be ready for a major effort whenever it was needed to withstand the threat from outside.

Days and nights passed. Weeks passed. A month passed.

'It's getting quite boring,' Carlo complained cheerfully as he picked up his fishing rod. 'Not like *Ra I*; there's nothing to repair, no breaking timber, no ropes to splice.'

> 106. *Ra II*, built by Indians from Lake Titicaca, was perfectly designed and crossed the Atlantic without loss or damage to a single papyrus stem.
> 107. *Madani Ait Ouhanni* from Morocco collected samples of the oil clots floating all over the Atlantic.
> 108. *Kei Ohara* from Japan took most of the films of the *Ra II* expedition.

He sat down in the bow with his feet overboard and hooked on a little flying fish as bait. Plenty of them came sailing on board. We had pampano among the pilot fish underneath us which were quite good and bit at once when we wanted them to. But the coveted dorado, or gold mackerel, the raft sailor's surest prey, was a far from frequent visitor this time, and the tunny fish just flipped their tails or shot into the air at a distance without allowing themselves to be tempted on to the hook. One day Georges swam through a seemingly endless shoal of silver cigars: bonitos. Big whales passed quickly by closer to Africa; perhaps it was the same family as last time. A flat manta ray, big as the whole bridge of *Ra II*, shot itself above the waves in a mighty leap and dropped like a pancake with a shattering crash. Busy, resilient porpoises rolled past us, criss-crossing and leaping for joy, and a fat, lazy eel, as long as a man and thick as a thigh, undulated sleepily away in our wake. One afternoon a pink giant of a squid also appeared from the ropes beneath *Ra II* and climbed, arm over groping arm, from papyrus bundles to steering-oar before it let go, and stretching all ten tentacles above its head, shot backwards down into the depths by built-in jet power.

So there was still some life left in the ocean, but there were far more oil lumps than fish. In the first month there were only three days on which Madani had not spotted any of the drifting black clots, but then the sea had been too choppy for proper observation. On June 16th, one month after the start, the sea was so filthy that it was uncomfortable to wash in. Big and small lumps, from the size of a potato to a pea or a grain of rice, covered the water. Only in the current between Morocco and the Canary Islands had we seen worse on this voyage, but then there had been a flat calm when it was easy to see anything afloat. On May 21st I had noted in the logbook:

'The pollution is shocking. Madani is fishing up tar-like lumps as big as prunes and overgrown with little barnacles. Small crabs, worms and many-legged crustacea are living on some of them. In the afternoon the smooth surface of the sea was covered with enormous

---

109. *Ra II* was ten feet shorter than *Ra I* and had a crew of eight instead of seven men.

110. *In fifty-seven days Ra II* crossed the Atlantic from Safi in Morocco to Barbados in the West Indies. Nightfall, near voyage-end.

quantities of brown and black clots of asphalt, floating in something which looked like soap-suds, and here and there the surface shimmered in all colours as if covered with petrol.'

In the same area a few of the stocking-like coelenterata were swimming. When alive they were taut like sausage-shaped balloons painted orange and green. However, thousands upon thousands of them floated dead among the oil clots, collapsed and flat as punctured toy balloons. For two days we drifted in this muck of oil and dead coelenterata before sailing beyond it. This polluted surface was travelling on the same course, but more slowly, towards America. Later on the voyage, when the seas began to mount up, big clots, big as a fist, would be washed on board and left there when the sea water filtered away through the papyrus stalks as it does through the baleen of a whale. Yet oil pollution was not modern man's only gift to the sea. As we kept a lookout scarcely a day passed without some form of plastic container, beer-can, bottle or more perishable materials such as packing-cases, cork and other rubbish drifting close by *Ra II*'s sides.

We had covered 1,725 sea miles from the starting point and had about 1,525 left to sail when we ran into an absolute plethora of oil pollution for the second time. The next day the wind was strong. The day after that, June 18th, the sea began to pile up in the biggest waves we had seen on either of the *Ra* voyages. The wind which reached us was a moderate gale with fierce squalls approaching full gale strength, but the breakers reared up in parallel ridges, higher and higher, out of proportion to the force of the wind. Perhaps a major storm had passed where they came from in the north-east. At first it was exciting, then one after another we began to feel a little suppressed anxiety, followed by astonishment and a rather dubious relief at how well we were doing. Finally we felt a surge of uninhibited admiration for the masterly way in which our little nut-shell took the towering walls of water. I stood alone on watch on the steering bridge behind the cabin, turning the port oar so that we took the seas directly astern, while the starboard oar-shaft was lashed securely and thus worked only as a keel. It went unbelievably well; the breaking wave-ridges were quite different from breakers in shallow water on a beach. The sloping base of the wave first overtook us from behind, rolled in under the sickle-shaped stern and lifted us high into the air before the crest broke. The comb would usually break while we were perched on top, so that we shot forward in the rush of wind, water and foam, and sped at a mad rate, tail up and nose down, into the deep, blue-green valleys. It was vital then not to swing broadside on.

'Twenty feet, twenty-five feet.'

The men were guessing at the height of the wave crests with a mixture of glee and horror.

'Thirty feet.' Now the wave-tops were towering above the mast-head.

Thirty feet. Madani was struggling with sea-sickness. Thick storm clouds and rain on every side. Everything going like clockwork. *Ra II* took those parallel hills of water with incredible elegance. Just a little spray on deck now and then, nothing to speak of. No problem so long as we could keep our fabulous tail to the pursuing water. Fortunately the waves were regular, well-spaced, just right for *Ra II*'s length and shape, the ranks evenly dressed, one, two, three, lined up behind one another. Best not to turn one's head, to steer straight. Behind, a wall of glass seemed to be toppling forward to bury us as we fled, unable to escape. My companions, off watch, crawled into the cabin turn by turn. There they could stare up at the basket roof and only listen to the deafening noise of the sea in uproar. But Carlo, the mountaineer, went on sitting in the high papyrus bow, his favourite spot, legs dangling as if he were on horseback.

Once again I felt the boat being lifted high in the air, higher than usual, and rushing forward and downward with the wall of water. Then the same crest rose ahead of us again, smooth and white-streaked, as it swept past.

'That was higher than the top of the mast,' yelled Carlo enthusiastically, white teeth flashing in his full red beard.

A little later he unhitched himself from the bows and came teetering aft, dragging his lifeline, to join the others inside. Then he told us that a gulf of a valley had yawned under him in the bows, so deep that when *Ra II* tilted and began to rush down, it looked as if we were plunging headlong into a bottomless watery grave. Better not to look.

The change of watch must be almost due, but I dared not take my attention off the course for a second, the boat must not turn broadside to the waves. It must be nearly four o'clock in the afternoon. From behind came the sound of the next foaming wave-crest, higher above us than any of the others. Every muscle tensed to prevent the oar-blade from being swept round. I felt a tremendous wall of water grip hold of the stern and lift us up, up, up. Eyes fixed to the compass so as not to lose the course. Must lie at right-angles to the wave. Was there no end to the height we would reach this time before the boiling giant passed under us? Then the crest itself came gushing along our beams, seemed to be passing; the foam seethed, we tipped sharply and were about to career forward and down again at breakneck speed, as if on a surf-board equipped with a giant sail. Then it happened. A mighty crack. The harsh sound of thick timber breaking. A shock through oar-shaft and vessel, and *Ra II* was rushing diagonally forward out of control, port side foremost, into the valley of water.

It was like being stunned with a club. I clung to uncertainty for a moment before forcing myself to turn my head and look catastrophe in the face. The rudder-oar! The thick shaft of the rudder-oar I was holding had snapped right across and the broad blade hung loose, dangling on the safety rope. I caught only a glimpse of it before the masses of water broke over us, rushing unimpeded over the whole starboard beam now that the peaked stern was not breaking the waves and lifting us into the air.

'All hands on deck! Port rudder-oar broken! Out with the sea anchor, Yuri!'

Vessel and bridge together buckled savagely under the pressure of water, and I allowed myself to slide sideways down to the lashed oar-shaft on the starboard side, to loosen the ropes there. The roar of water surging against the cabin wall and the thunder of the mainsail twisting and slamming against the straddled mast told the seven men in the cabin more than any call from the bridge, and they came swarming out, silent and dogged, knotting loose lifelines round their middles.

'Which sea anchor?'

'The biggest.'

I had undone the lashing on the undamaged rudder-oar, but the two hardwood forks which held it top and bottom were stuck askew, so that the rudder-shaft could not be moved. Another heavy sea broke over us, and another. The mast creaked ominously, while wind and water flung sail and papyrus boat about at will.

'Lower the mainsail!'

To increase our speed Norman had recently hoisted a little topsail on a bamboo pole. That had already splintered and the topsail was flapping and whipping against the mainsail like a punctured balloon.

'Lower the mainsail before it rips!'

Norman took command on the foredeck and clambered up to the masthead himself to cut down the topsail. Then five men grasped the thick halyard to lower the mainsail and soon the twenty-five-foot yard began to move away from the mast top. But instead of allowing itself to be lowered, the heavy yard was lifted forward and up by the big wind-filled sail and all the men on the foredeck could only hang on with ten outstretched arms and all their united weight to stop the mainsail from flying out like a kite over the waves. Another thunderous sea engulfed us.

'Out with the sea anchor, damn it!'

'The waves have tangled the rope!'

'Then throw out the little one before the seas smash us to bits!'

Another sea right over the boat. And an even bigger one. It was lucky that we happened to be twisted starboard on to the torrents. The cabin had no opening on that side and we had covered the long wall with sail-cloth, against which the sea was now hammering, up to the height of the roof.

'The little one is out,' called Carlo triumphantly.

But the braking power was too little; the small bag we were now streaming in our wake did not hold well enough to turn the stern of the waterlogged papyrus boat back again. Yuri and Carlo stood waist-deep in water on the papyrus aft and regularly disappeared altogether in the tumble of foam as they worked feverishly to sort out the tow rope of the biggest canvas bag, which the waves were continuously tangling up on deck.

'Check your lifelines. Everyone must be tied on!'

Then I managed to get the jammed starboard oar turned a few inches, a little more and still a few more inches. But it was no good. The squalls tossed the bottom edge of the huge sail heavily against the top of the peaked papyrus stem. Wild, uncontrolled uppercuts from right and left, then the sail hooked itself over the slender tip and wrenched the papyrus prow to port. Seas and gale crashed and howled, so that shouts and suggestions from every side had to be intercepted and transmitted from bridge to mast and back again.

'Lower the sail before the whole ship is torn to shreds!' I shouted.

Now it was jerking its way down.

'Stop! Get the sail up again before a wave gets hold of it!' screamed Norman.

'If it falls in the sea we'll never get it on board again,' yelled Georges.

He was absolutely right. Across the bottom the Egyptian sail was the same width as the deck, but at the top, the same sail and the heavy yard holding it were very much wider, so to lower it without the wide upper section being swept up by the wild waves on both sides of the deck was hardly feasible.

A solution offered itself. The sail was lowered a few inches at a time but never touched the deck, because five men stood secured across the boat, rolling it up from below as it came down. The five were struggling all the time to keep their feet against gusts of wind, the rolling boat and surging floods of water. Tugging and banging on the tiller as well as the shaft of the unbroken starboard rudder-oar, I finally forced it to swing by degrees in uneven jerks, but it did not help at all with the course. The men on the sail managed bit by bit to roll up one third and reefed the roll firmly with a series of rope-ends hanging in a line along the sail for this very purpose. It was time to rescue the big loose oar-blade, which was still dangling and skipping wildly in tow, and was regularly flung heavily against the stern by the waves. The safety rope attached to the blade, copied from Egyptian tomb paintings, helped us to pull it in. The shaft had broken across just by the lower fork. Sixteen centimetres thick all the way down, or about six inches, like the average telegraph pole, and made of the strongest heartwood pine, the timber we had all regarded as invulnerable had snapped like a matchstick, though there was no fault in the wood. Not a single papyrus reed was broken, loose or damaged. The papyrus bundles had withstood more than the wooden log, so once again the strength of Goliath had been forced to yield to the dexterity of David. The accident taught us once and for all that we had used too thick a rope to secure the rudder-oar top and bottom. We should have tied it with thinner rope at the bottom so that the rope would snap, like a safety-catch, before the oar-shaft. Only upon our return did we learn that this was precisely what the ancient Egyptians had done, but this detail had been overlooked on the ancient design, since everybody had thought that the difference in thickness of the upper and lower ropes had been a mere coincidence in the artist's reproduction. Yet a re-examination of the old designs showed that this difference in thickness was most consistent.

It was Georges who hauled in the heavy oar-blade, overgrown with edible barnacles. He cut off a bunch of short papyrus stubs which Norman had tied to the blade in order to streamline it on the side where we had bound the thick shaft. He threw the short, mal-treated papyrus ends into the sea and stood expectantly waiting to see what would happen. They sank. He said not a word to a soul, and had no idea that someone else was watching from the bridge, equally perplexed and with the same sinking feeling in the stomach. What was the matter with the papyrus? Had all the air been squeezed out of it? Yuri and Carlo had their backs turned to him. They had quite enough on their hands, sorting out the rope of the big sea anchor. Then it too was in the sea, the little one was shipped, and now the canvas bag held and began to turn the stern slowly back again. But not completely. We were still lying slightly across the wind, taking the sea in huge waves over the starboard quarter, just as on *Ra I.*

The storm raged. The time on board was ten to nine and night was falling when the men on the foredeck managed to reef half the main-sail so that the orange-red sun symbol was left half rolled up from the bottom, like a reflection of the sunset we could see behind the storm clouds. Had we seen it, it would not have been straight ahead today, as we lay drifting at an angle; it would have been far to the left of the crooked bow.

Tragedy. Catastrophe. No reserve logs thick enough or long enough for a new oar-shaft. All heavy hardwood pieces suitable for splicing had been dumped overboard at the Canary Islands. If we lay here long enough, with the sea anchor out to brake our speed, they might come drifting after us! Bad joke. Hopeless situation. No solution. Good-night everybody. We must sleep now and think tomorrow. Useless to steer any more, with half a shaft and no blade, and another which does not work. The sea can thunder on board and out again, the sea anchor will hold our course so that it does not come gushing in through the cabin door. But we must alternate watches through the night, to avoid being run down by ships in the big waves.

It was hopeless trying to sleep that night. We were on *Ra I* again, on those last nights when the sea was gaining the upper hand. Tons of water smacked against the back wall on the starboard side, surging, seething, sucking, gurgling and clucking all round us. A regular river was running to and fro on board, under the cabin floor, in the broad, deep cleft between the two papyrus rolls which kept us afloat. The water surged along the papyrus, chasing wildly along the cracks between the reeds which could have let it out. But the reeds were swelling more and more and closing up all the fissures so that the water never had time to run out before new torrents surged on board and filled the big bathtub to the brim.

I tossed about in my sleeping bag and did not manage to sleep a wink before it was my turn to crawl out and keep watch. Then, I fell asleep like a log, sitting on the bamboo bench, lashed fast, outside the cabin door. I awoke with a shock, ashamed and bewildered, to see a bat, no, it was a night owl, swerving round and round *Ra II* until it came tumbling in between the lines of stays straight towards me. Swooping to the attack, our nocturnal visitor was flying badly, caught a wing on a guy rope, missed me, and staggered before getting its feet safely under it on the bench close beside me. But it was a pigeon! It was our own ringed travelling companion! It had been scared away from the roof by the mad battle of sail and heavy seas, had missed the usual human company on the steering bridge, which was empty and deserted. Frightened by the loneliness of its own basket nest on the roof, it had searched vainly for another dry spot, and now come back exhausted. It continued to sit close beside successive watches in the doorway until day dawned. Round the corner the Atlantic broke on board unimpeded. It poured overboard again on each side of the cabin, so that we on the lee side only had rivulets running back and forth round our feet before they too ran out again into the sea.

Extraordinary vessel. The trouble was that she was beginning to be as watertight as an ordinary boat, so the water no longer ran away fast enough through the hull, which should have had a leaky bottom.

The next day was still an inferno. We were dead tired as we waded in foaming water, moved jars which had to be rescued from the stormy side, threw the cracked ones into the sea, re-secured loose cargo, tightened stays and stitched sails and racked our brains trying to work out how to recover steerageway. Lying as we were, water-logged and at an angle to the waves, the sea's final victory was only a question of time. Wood and reed were only held together with rope which we could expect to snap at any time under this enormous strain. The long spiral rope which held the papyrus together was fourteen millimetres thick, like a man's little finger. The cabin, the feet of the mast and steering bridge were all lashed in place with a much thinner, eight-millimetre rope, plaited in three like a pigtail.

The Indians would not allow anything thicker to pass between the reed bundles. But we danced ahead like a ball. If all the joints of cabin, bridge and mast had not been completely flexible the sea would have torn us apart as violently as it could splinter timber and bend steel. During the early days the sea got nowhere with the reed ball as it bounced away from all the punches. But the sea had another trick. It slowly boarded us and lay there as useless deck cargo, pushing us under. We were beginning once more to sink at frightening speed, partly because of tons of splashing sea water dammed up as a dead weight in the long deep ditch between our two papyrus rolls, and partly because this water, entering from above, was now penetrating the upper half of the papyrus rolls, which had stayed dry and light hitherto. All the papyrus was busy soaking itself full and heavy, from above and from below. We were really sinking at uncanny speed again. We all realized that. There was no sign that anyone was seriously afraid; everyone was doggedly determined that we should weather this. We all made suggestions, which were considered and then unanimously rejected. Madani, who had not seen the sea on board *Ra I*, took me aside and asked warily if it was dangerous. When told that for the time being it was not, he was all smiles from ear to ear again. Kei shook the sea water off his ears and his shining black hair and said with a broad grin that he had had no idea that such waves existed.

Thanks to the sea anchor the stern had turned slightly to meet the waves. If we pulled it in we would be lying broadside on again and get the whole sea over our full breadth. On the other hand, with the sea anchor out we stayed put and made no progress. We were stuck in the middle of the Atlantic, sinking, 1,900 sea miles from the start and about 1,350 sea miles from our goal.

For two days we could do nothing but fight to save ourselves and the cargo. To splice the rudder oar proved impossible. The waves continued to run twenty to twenty-five feet high, with a few thirty to thirty-five foot giants among them. Inside the cabin I cut up the back of a writing block and made a model of the loose oar-blade, the two broken pieces of shaft and the height of the steering bridge, indicating the distance between the two wooden forks which held the slanting rudder shaft in place top and bottom. The model showed that if we tied the upper and longer portion of the shaft to the upper part of the blade, the top of the shaft would just reach the floor of the bridge. That was how we fixed it, evolving by our united efforts a system which

U

allowed the helmsman to stand on the opposite side of the bridge, twisting the starboard rudder-oar with his right hand, while he turned the curtailed shaft on the port side one way by means of a rope tied to his foot, and the other way by means of a long bamboo pole held in his left hand. This was quite an acrobatic performance, and the manoeuvring became still worse because the helmsman also constantly had to haul on the sheets, which were tied to the railing of the bridge, because the reed boat was now lying so deep that the combined effect of two rudder-oars was not always enough. If the boat did not obey the two rudders, it was necessary to steer with the sail as well, to avoid being caught broadside on by wind and wave.

Ra II was lying uncomfortably deep in the water when we were ready to try out the new system late on the second evening. Everyone realized that we had a tough job ahead of us if we were to complete the second half of the voyage. The position improved a little as soon as we got the crippled oar in place. We immediately managed to turn the stern into the seas, ship the sea anchor and speed westward under reefed sail. The day after that we took a chance on unfurling and hoisting the whole mainsail. Once again the big sail seemed to lift us higher out of the water as it drove us forward at a rate of almost three knots, over a hundred kilometres a day. But now the deck was only just above water. Astern the seas continued to wash in one side and out the other. Ahead, heavy seas flung themselves over us at regular intervals if we tried to sit round the hencoop as before, so we all had to squeeze together and eat on the mast-ladder, like birds on a bough.

'We must make a barrier against the worst breakers so that the water on board has time to run out, otherwise we'll sink', said Yuri, and busied himself hanging up a strip of canvas which he stretched forward from the mast stays on the starboard side, and made fast with thick cords top and bottom.

'Relax, Yuri!' Everyone laughed. 'The first wave will rip the sail-cloth.' But the enterprising Yuri went resolutely on.

The next wave came frothing along the starboard cabin wall, lazily pushed Yuri's sail-cloth wall into a little bulge and poured overboard. Only a little water trickled in on the forward deck; the canvas had channelled the rest away. Yuri sat down triumphantly at the hencoop to eat, while the rest of us came down wide-eyed from the mast-ladder with our plates when we saw that the next wave did the same, and the next. There we sat at the table, gazing at Yuri the wizard who could stop the sea by hanging up a cloth. The secret was that the papyrus tail aft took the force of the sea and split the wave in two. The sail-cloth curtain had only to channel overboard that cross-section of the wall of water which came surging along both sides of the boat.

'More sail-cloth!'

With the sheath-knife we cut up all the sail-cloth which covered the front wall of the cabin, so from then on we could see straight through the wickerwork to the hencoop, the masts and the sea. Then we cut up the whole of the spare mainsail. Yuri hung up the pieces and soon we were living behind a veritable screen of burgundy, orange, green and yellow. The waves flowed along the screen, giving it a friendly nudge so that the mast stays swung like clothes-lines in the wind and only a tiny proportion of the torrents of water found its way on board.

'Hippies! Gypsies!' cried Carlo and Georges, roaring with laughter, next time they launched the little three-man rubber raft to film us from outside. We popped our heads up over Yuri's multi-coloured screen and looked at the two of them as they vanished and reappeared behind the wave crests.

'Come back,' I yelled. 'Get yourselves on board a proper ship before you capsize.'

We had inflated the little raft and filmed ourselves before, in a flat calm and later on fine seas, but now we were so used to waves and salt water that everyone was beginning to get reckless.

Days and weeks continued to roll on with the waves. In the course of barely a year, the six of us who had been on *Ra I* would have been sitting on reed rolls together for almost four months. After the accident with the rudder-oar we had to start water rationing, half a litre per man per day, plus nine litres jointly for cooking. Several jars had cracked, some had admitted salt water. That we ourselves had poured the contents of most of the goatskins out into the sea when we were becalmed was a delicate subject which it was better not to broach. What a piece of impetuosity! Carlo was plagued with salt water sores in the groin and Yuri prescribed bathing with fresh water twice a day. Poor Carlo used the contents of one cup; he would not allow himself any more. The duck, the dove and the monkey together tippled as much as one man every day. Georges protested violently at innocent animals being rationed like us men. Santiago was not 100 per cent fit, either. He had been operated on for kidney

307

stones before the start and was not supposed to eat salt meat, nuts, dried vegetables, eggs. These were the dishes which dominated our menu. He was fatigued, but performed all his duties on board without a murmur. As long as he was not neglecting a duty he preferred to lie on his back in the inmost corner of the cabin, where Yuri kept him under observation.

One evening we were all tired. Santiago came out of the cabin opening with a dark face and sat down with the rest of us by the hencoop. He looked from Carlo to Georges.

'I heard some dirty remarks through the cabin wall!'

Carlo blew up! 'Drop that professorial face.'

'Take on a bit more, like the rest of us,' interrupted Georges. 'If you volunteer to relieve a tired helmsman you turn up ten minutes before the watch changes.'

The accusations began to flow. Hard-working Carlo and playboy Georges had had difficulty in understanding each other on the previous trip, but they were the best of friends now and for the moment the quiet professor of anthropology had got under both their skins. He was now informed that he lay in the corner psychoanalysing others while they worked. Moreover, it was his idiotic idea that we should have food and water in jars this time as well, instead of light tins, and water in jerry-cans. On *Ra I* we had proved that it was possible to live without modern food. Why the devil did we have to prove it a second time? And having talked us into bringing more than a hundred ceramic jars this time as well, he as quartermaster should have secured them well enough to prevent them from breaking and forcing us to ration the water.

'The jars are just as light as jerry-cans, and who was it who emptied all the water out of the big goatskins into the sea!'

There was a savage duel of words; angry allegations and all sorts of suppressed irritations poured out and took away the appetite of everyone round the hencoop. Santiago struck out again, from his soapbox on the mast-ladder, but was left sitting almost punch-drunk under the joint assault of the others.

'Carlo,' I said. 'You are a professional mountaineer, an experienced expedition man. You mustn't expect a university professor to be as good as you at knots and weight-lifting. You are like a priest, so perfect that you want other people to do everything as well as you do.'

That was quite the worst thing I could have said. Carlo rose slowly, his face turning redder than his beard, one hand clutching at his bushy hair.

'I, a priest!'

For a moment he stood speechless, swallowing. Then he turned away from me to Santiago and suddenly thrust out an open palm, covered with callouses:

'All right. Let's forget all about it, chaps!'

Everyone leaned across the hencoop and shook hands. Norman ran to fetch harmonicas for himself and Kei, and Madani pulled out his Moroccan drum. When I slipped into bed two hours later I fell asleep to the sound of a festival orchestra and chorus from the foredeck, with a repertoire from seven different quarters of the globe.

The experiment with *Ra I* the year before had been reduced to a mere drift voyage on the very first day at sea, when we broke both rudder-oars. The elements carried us westward in a curve, and we were making straight for Barbados, far south in the West Indian chain, when we broke off the experiment. This time we were still completely seaworthy, and decided to steer for the island to which nature herself would have carried us last time. So, every day, the distance ahead was measured in numbers of sea miles from Barbados. We could not have picked a better course to give us wind and sea dead astern. But it was damnably difficult for the helmsman to prevent the waterlogged reed boat from broaching to and drifting beam on towards Barbados. We were worn out at the end of an average night watch, almost unable to straighten our cramped fingers. And if the boat swung round so that the sail was taken aback and the sea rushed on board, it was as if devils had boarded our ship under cover of the night. Yuri's sail-cloth would be torn and angry curses rained down on the poor helmsman as seven naked men had to put on their life-belts. Naked bodies tumbled out into the darkness, waist-deep in seething water, to heave and haul at the sail, row or back the oars at the stern, and rescue cargo. Some of the men asked as a precaution not to be left responsible for the bridge alone, so we increased the hard night watch from two to three hours, but with two men on the bridge at once.

We had to think of something if we were to avoid wearing ourselves to death with the laborious steering system.

'If only we could move the masts forward,' I mused one night, when Norman and I were keeping watch together on the bridge. 'If the sail were right forward in the bows the boat would steer itself down wind.'

'We can,' said Norman eagerly. And before anyone really knew what was happening next morning we were carrying out an extremely difficult operation. The top of the heavy straddled mast must be tilted to bring the big sail forward.

Norman began chopping at the base of the masts with a hatchet, so that the footplate began to lean forward. Next we cautiously slackened off all the twelve parallel stays which ran aft from the straddled mast to both sides of the reed boat. We could then tilt forward the thirty-foot double mast, which weighed at least 600 lbs. As we pulled the mast-top forward the yard followed, and when we fastened the mast stays again the wind-filled mainsail was hanging in a curve down in front of the high papyrus bow. The steering improved at once, as long as our only desire was to follow the wind, nose first.

Ra II sailed westward at dazzling speed. All further sinking soon stopped when there was enough papyrus under water to counteract the new cargo we had shipped in the form of unwanted sea water on deck. Five weeks after the start we were no longer sinking, but we were lying so low that in calm water the deck was scarcely above the surface, and from now on barnacles began to grow on the papyrus deck along the exposed starboard wall of the cabin. Madani continued to fish up lumps of oil every single day.

On a day of rain and savage squalls the sail caught fast on the slender bow and turned it a little more askew, while the sail-cloth seam along the bottom tore. The sail was next in importance to us after the hull, and after consultation we decided to sacrifice the fine upswept prow. Carlo sat astride in the bow, sawing away at our proud vessel. For safety's sake we tied a rope firmly round the bow so that the whole reed boat would not split when the two important spiral ropes were cut as we sliced off the entire tip of the boat. But our Indian builders had been right. The rope was wedged so tightly in its coils round the little built-in central bundle that, even with our combined efforts, we could not pull it loose. The papyrus reeds were so compressed and swollen that the cross-section in front looked like a giant onion slice when the prow fell to the vandals' saw. *Ra II* at once took on a more sober, modern line, and through the wicker of the cabin wall we could suddenly see the whole horizon ahead under the sail. It was as if the shutters of the ark had been set ajar so that we could begin to look out for land ahead.

Not many days later we decided to saw off the stern peak as well. It had been left standing like a close-hauled sail after the bow had fallen and made the course unsteady, besides which we wanted to reduce unnecessary weight. It was with a distinctly shaky feeling that we removed the fatal bowstring from the tip of the curly tail and moved it down to the flat, broad chicken's tail which was left. But no amount of interference seemed to affect the unrivalled toughness of this vessel. One after another we slipped overboard on a line, emerging relieved and delighted to report to those who had not yet been under the living-room floor and seen for themselves that *Ra II* was unchanged under water, just as rigid, just as firm, just as complete. Not a reed, not a rope had shifted, only now it was covered with living shells, like little black and white mushrooms, with waving yellow gill fringes.

The little amateur radio set came out of its case less often now than on the previous trip. We thought the families at home were feeling more secure and were reluctant to worry them with much more than a simple 'all well on board'. But in the last half of the second month we were sailing so fast and had travelled so far that we could give an approximate time and place for landing. Yvonne packed her bag at once and flew to Barbados with the children.

Not long afterwards Norman made contact with a radio ham on Barbados and we heard Yvonne's voice. She produced six unexpectedly technical questions about the marine life which had joined us under the reed bundles and next explained that the answers were of interest to the head of a marine biology project which the United Nations Development Aid Department had stationed on Barbados for the time being. We were able to report on the faithful escort of small friends swimming with us under the reed floor, a couple of dorados chasing flying fish round us, and large flocks of sea birds from South America circling like drifting clouds over the horizon to south and west, where glittering tunny fish exploded like silver rockets out of the blue sea. Next day the radio ham told us to expect a visit from a UN research vessel.

On June 25th a brown, four-winged dragonfly fluttered on board. Were we so close to land? Or had the big insect hitched a ride on some boat which had passed beyond the horizon? There had been an extraordinary dearth of ships since a couple had almost run us down in the traffic off Africa.

We were now sailing at full speed into the area where we had abandoned *Ra I* after the last dramatic days of last year's voyage. We all shuddered when a shout from the steering bridge drew our attention to a fierce shark which was snapping furiously at the red buoy we were towing in case anyone fell overboard. It was just here that we had met all the sharks last year. But this year's solitary wanderer soon abandoned the red buoy and disappeared northward. The sharks were apparently uninterested in a craft like *Ra II*, which needed no underwater repairs.

On June 26th the seas began to heave violently again and the waves came racing after us, with white combs frothing like spray from a rotary snow plough. Rain gushed down on us from dense clouds. We let the salt wash off our bodies and licked our arms. We could have collected rain water, but we were sailing so fast that the rations would hold out. The duck waddled round on the roof, sipping at the puddles. Safi wanted to crawl into the cabin. The starboard rudder-oar stuck in its forks and we were afraid it would break, but Kei chipped it loose under water. Next day the tame dove had gone. For some time it had seemed restless, flying in big circles over *Ra II*, and yet always fluttering back to the grain bowl on the roof. But on June 27th it took off and was gone for good. The Flood must be nearly over. The Ark had lost its dove. We missed it. Had it got wind of land? The nearest coast was French Guiana to the south. The venturesome dove now bore two rings, one with its Spanish number and another marked '*Ra II*'.

On June 28th the water temperature suddenly rose two degrees and after that we saw no more lumps of oil. Had we passed into another branch of the current? This was strange, for it was just here that we had been wallowing in lumps of oil when we abandoned *Ra I* last year, and the whole sea moves in an incessant round between the continents.

On June 29th we found Safi's chain hanging slackly in the sea. It was empty. Chaos on board. Then Safi, free at the top of the mast, was looking triumphantly down at us. Neither coconut nor honey tempted her down, but when Yuri fetched her favourite toy, an ugly green, squeaking, rubber frog with big red eyes, Safi was down on deck like lightning to recover the frog, while Yuri recovered the monkey. Immediately afterwards there was a yell from Norman in the cabin. He had made direct contact with a radio ham on the UN research vessel *Calamar*, which was quite close, and which had asked us to send up rockets after nightfall so that she could find us in the choppy seas.

That night we were given a fright of a quite unexpected kind. Norman roused me in a low voice for the change of watch on June 30th at 0.30 hours, and I sat up in my sleeping-bag and began to pull on my socks, as the air was raw and cold on the bridge. Then he called again, and this time there was terror in his voice:

'Come quick, quick! Look there!'

I dived out of the opening in the wicker wall with Santiago close at my heels and we hoisted ourselves over the cabin roof where Norman was pointing.

It was like the Day of Judgement. Over the horizon to port, in the north-west, rose a round, livid disc which never completely left the water, but grew and grew like a phantom aluminium-coloured moon rising half-hidden by the rim of sea. Like a compact nebula, brighter than the Milky Way and symmetrically circular, it grew in size like a stemless mushroom, and seemed to be rushing straight towards us as it spread further and further across the sky. The moon was up on the opposite side, in a starry, cloudless sky. I first thought it was a reflection against a veil of humidity from an enormous searchlight over the horizon, or perhaps an atomic cloud caused by human error, or a phenomenon of the northern lights, but the feeling that a scintillating shower of foreign bodies was descending on us from the cosmos persisted, until the disc of light was covering about thirty degrees of sky. Then it suddenly stopped growing, dissolved almost imperceptibly, and disappeared. We were left without an explanation.

We ourselves now began to burn flickering red flares and send up rockets of starry rain to show the *Calamar* our position. That was an extraordinary night, with a bizarre atmosphere. We heard the voice from the *Calamar* on the little set again, but they could not see the rockets and had not been on deck when the disc of light appeared. Next morning we heard through the radio ham on Barbados that the same phenomenon had been observed from several of the West Indian Islands, but in a north-easterly direction. Was it a section of rocket from Cape Kennedy which had exploded and burned out as it fell into the atmosphere? We never knew. But UFO enthusiasts, looking for evidence of flying saucers, confused the phenomenon with two other observations we had made on two successive nights, further out to sea. We had seen small orange lights on the horizon to the north-west. One was a brief flash, with no sign of a ship, the other was drop-shaped and we saw it just as it sailed diagonally down and vanished into the sea. We had warned radio hams on land, in case they were emergency rockets from ships in trouble, but no sos had been sent out so the indications were that they were signals between naval vessels on exercise, perhaps a submarine marking its position on the surface.

While we continued to drive due west, under full sail, the *Calamar* zigzagged about us all night, searching. We were short of rockets, but kept a constant look-out from the mast top. The sun rose, day dawned and Norman, who had his hands full with sextant, abacus and the little hand-powered emergency radio, could constantly report that the *Calamar* must be close by. Now to the north, now to the south. Always hidden behind endless ranks of high waves. We ate lunch. And supper. We gave up the idea that anyone would find us. The tropical sun was about to set again. Local time was only 6 p.m., though our watches stood at 9, because we had adjusted them only once since leaving Africa. It was then that the lookouts on both boats saw each other simultaneously. They reported sighting a sail and we saw an almost invisible green speck on the horizon – behind us. Darkness was about to fall when a ship overtook us from behind. It was a great moment.

The big, fast trawler came close up on our beam and saluted by lowering and raising the blue flag of the United Nations which fluttered from the masthead. Norman hurried over to the straddled mast and replied with our own UN flag. Only two-thirds of it remained: the rest had been ripped away in a storm. We were exultant. We all climbed on to the bridge, the roof, the mast, waving and hallooing and blowing our shrill hunting horn. The whole crew of the UN boat – brown, black and white alike – stood along the railing, waving and hallooing back. The captain was standing on the bridge. He was Chinese. Beside him stood a man with a loud-hailer who yelled in Spanish:

'Welcome to the American side of the ocean!'

When Kei saw the Chinese on the bridge his cup of joy overflowed. He crawled over to me on the roof and held out his hand.

'Thank you for letting me come.'

There was something unreal about the whole meeting: that a UN

314

boat should actually be the first to meet us on the other side. I had never seen a boat flying the UN flag before, apart from our own. Darkness closed over the sea. The brightly lighted boat circled round us a few times, then switched off her engines to drift through the night. Her lights quickly disappeared behind us until we were left alone with the waves and our own feeble paraffin lamp. Snug, but lonely.

Late that night we were reminded that the voyage was not yet over. A powerful squall suddenly rushed down from the north and took the sail completely aback before the watchers on the bridge could pull themselves together. The pressure of wind on the big sail was terrific, forcing the whole ship to heel over to port until the deck was under water. It was an unusual sensation for us in the cabin to tumble out on the lee side and immediately find ourselves thigh-deep in water, water which was no breaker frothing its way overboard, but the actual surface of the sea itself, looking as if it had come to stay. For the first time on any raft I felt that we were now quite definitely on our way to the bottom of the sea. There was no more buoyancy. Yells and shouts and flashing torches. Madani waist-deep in water without his lifeline. Yuri's screen on the lee side torn to ribbons. Then the wind veered back to the east, the direction we were used to, and eight experienced papyrus sailors finally managed to turn the sail back into position. *Ra II* righted herself serenely as the water poured overboard; the deck returned to the level it had maintained for the last part of the voyage. But three of the many jars which had hitherto stood safely in the lee on the port side had been smashed by the masses of water, and wading barefoot I cut my toes on the fragments, so that Yuri had to bandage my foot. The port side had also been infiltrated by a web of the thin, glistening, stinging tentacles of Portuguese men-o'-war, and Georges burned himself while he was answering the call of nature. He had to be bathed with ammonia.

Next morning the *Calamar*, which had switched off her engines, took some time to catch up with us again. No one on board the trawler had expected any great turn of speed from a primitive reed boat. But in spite of our tribulations we had sailed 75 sea miles, or 140 kilometres, in the last twenty-four hours.

The *Calamar* delivered post, ointment to soothe Carlo's sufferings, some bags of delicious Barbados fruit and a big carton of ice-cream which had melted to custard before it reached us in the bobbing rubber boat. The *Calamar* stayed near us for two days, then increased speed and went ahead with fresh greetings for Barbados. Now we were once again in those waters off the West Indies which are the birthplace of the Atlantic hurricanes. The weather was unsettled now, at the beginning of July. Dark walls of rain were falling on all sides, driven over us almost every day by powerful gusts of wind, often at gale force. Again and again we had to stream the sea anchor and struggle to save the sail. But wind and current remained generally in our favour and in the final days we made the best average speed of the voyage, covering up to 81 miles, or 151 kilometres, in a day. We frequently encountered ships now, plying between North and South America.

On July 8th we were only 200 sea miles from Barbados and the island authorities sent a fast little government boat, the *Culpeper*, to welcome us to this little independent corner of the British Empire. Yvonne and our eldest daughter, Anette, were the only passengers on board. If they found us on the basis of our position we should meet late that same night.

The night passed, and the day as well, while the *Culpeper* rolled about, over and among the waves in our immediate neighbourhood, without finding us. The weather was far from perfect and we intercepted reports from the government boat to the land station describing the big waves and reporting that the raft sailor's wife was suffering from sea-sickness but had bravely insisted on carrying on the search. The search still continued for a further two nights and two days. It was near nightfall on the second day and we half expected to reach land before the government boat, for there were barely a hundred sea miles left. Then the *Culpeper* appeared on the wrong horizon, overtaking us from astern. Flat and broad and seaworthy, a real man's boat, she manoeuvred alongside, with two white ladies clinging to the railings, surrounded by a waving black crew. While the two ladies were obviously having difficulty in sorting out all the sunburned shaggy creatures with full beards, waving wildly from the roof of the bamboo cabin, the crew of the *Culpeper* turned their attention to Madani, whom they thought to be a sailor from Barbados. Madani, the landlubber from Marrakesh, impressed the onlookers by throwing out a fish-hook baited with salt sausage and immediately pulling in five pampano and an unknown silver-green fish of the same general type. Georges, the skin-diver, crossed to the *Culpeper* just as the sun was setting to negotiate a morally permissible barter: fresh fish, Egyptian bread and the ever-tasty Moroccan *sello* in exchange for unnecessary but very welcome oranges. He was standing on the afterdeck, about to dive for his swim back to *Ra II* with the *Culpeper*'s searchlight playing on the waves to show him the way, when a black man stopped him and asked him if we on *Ra II* were not afraid of sharks.

'No,' said Georges grandly, but swallowed his boast when the man pointed calmly to a large man-eater, gliding slowly out of the ship's wake into the beam of light. Our own rubber raft was so worn by rubbing against the earthenware jars on board that we did not dare to launch it. Georges had to spend the night on the *Culpeper* and return next morning in a little oarless dinghy let out on tow from the *Culpeper*, and hauled back again empty.

The *Culpeper* stayed on our port quarter all night. The day after, July 12th, such large flocks of seabirds flew out towards us from the west that we knew land must be just over the horizon. It was Sunday, and Norman and I, who had the five to eight watch, were standing on the bridge looking forward to our relief. Soon Carlo and Kei would be scrambling out and unbedding our last eggs from the lime paste to be fried for the occasion: Sunday breakfast. We still had plenty of provisions, especially sacks of Egyptian 'mummy bread' in the chests we slept on, salt sausage and ham hanging under the bamboo roof and jars of *sello*, the honey and almond mixture which contained everything a desert traveller in Morocco needed. We had never gone hungry and were in good form. Then I noticed something and grabbed Norman by the arm.

'Do you get it?' I said, snuffing up the salt sea air. 'Fantastic, a distinct scent of green, fresh-cut grass!'

The two of us stood and sniffed. We had been at sea for fifty-seven days. Santiago, Carlo and the others came out and sniffed with us. The non-smokers among us smelt it distinctly. And blowed if I didn't scent cow-dung, too, the smell of farming. It was pitch dark and we could see nothing. But the movement of the waves was strange, too, a different rhythm, somehow, which must be the effect of backwash from land. We pushed both rudder-oars hard over to starboard, where the wind was coming from, and held a course as close to the north as we could. It was incredible how well the low-lying reed boat was able to sail close-hauled.

Norman, Carlo and Santiago climbed to the masthead in turn all morning, and at 12.15 our time we heard a wild yell from above our heads:

'Hurrah!'

Norman had sighted land. Safi screamed and the duck flapped across the roof. Like flies we swarmed up the steps of the swaying masts, every man-jack of us, for *Ra II* was more stable now that most of the papyrus was under water. The *Culpeper* blew her siren. Then we all saw land, low and flat on the horizon to the north-west. We had steered too far south the day before, trying to counteract the current which swung north just before the islands. We had succeeded only too well. So now we had to turn the mainsail and shove the rudder-oars right over in the opposite direction, otherwise we would sail past Barbados and land somewhere on the dense chain of islands just behind. That was all very well, but family and friends were now waiting for us on Barbados. *Ra II* responded to manoeuvring like a keeled vessel. The straight deep furrow running right along the bottom between the two reed rolls evidently acted as a negative keel. With the wind almost across our beam the red lifebuoy was being towed dead astern, showing that we were moving in the direction the bow was pointing, without any side drift, straight towards the low coastline.

When we sat down round the hencoop for lunch we knew it would be our last meal on board. Late in the afternoon we heard the hum of aircraft. A little private plane circled over us and waggled its wings. Soon after, a bigger, twin-engined plane came out from the islands with the Prime Minister of Barbados, and soon there were four planes circling over our masts. One of them dived so low that the draught threatened to take the mainsail aback. The land mass rose higher and the sun flashed on the glass of distant windows. We saw more and more houses. Dozens of boats were on their way out through the land haze. A speedboat came bucking over the waves with Norman's wife, Mary Ann, and my two youngest daughters, Marian and Bettina, on board. Boats of all sorts. Sea-sick faces, joyful faces, gaping faces. Some were laughing themselves silly, shouting and asking if we had really come from Morocco on 'that thing'. Seen from outside, we were just a wickerwork cabin floating on the water behind a majestic Egyptian sail, with two shorn-off tufts of reed sticking out of the water at either end.

Yuri's motley rag-curtain did not exactly reinforce the impression of an ocean voyager, either. Over fifty vessels of every type and size finally escorted *Ra II* across the finishing line. We were making for Bridgetown, the capital. Sailing boats, speedboats, fishing boats, yachts of many kinds, a catamaran, a trimaran, a police boat, a Hollywood-type full-rigger decorated as a pirate ship and packed with tourists, and our old friend the *Culpeper*, circled round us in a mêlée which made the peace-loving Carlo long for the solitude of the sea. Georges, on the contrary, felt quite at home; he lit our last red flare and installed himself like the Statue of Liberty on the cabin roof.

So ended the *Ra* voyages. Outside Bridgetown harbour we lowered the bleached mainsail with its round solar orb for the last time, and furled it while the crew of the *Culpeper* tossed us a tow-rope.

The harbour area was swarming like an ant-heap. Every street was packed with people. It was five minutes to seven by our watches; we must adjust them to Barbados' time, a long-awaited moment, for we had sailed 3,270 sea miles, or more than 6,100 kilometres, since last we set foot on land.

Before putting into the quay we found an opportunity to shake hands, all eight of us. There was not one of us who failed to realize that it was only thanks to a common effort that we had come safely across the sea.

We threw a last look back at the vanquished ocean. There it lay, seemingly boundless, as in Columbus' day, as in the golden age of mighty Lixus, as in the days of the roving Phoenicians and intrepid Olmecs. How long would whale and fish gambol out there? Would man at the eleventh hour learn to dispose of his modern garbage, would he abandon his war against nature? Would future generations restore early man's respect and veneration for the sea and the earth, humbly worshipped by the Inca as *Mama-Cocha* and *Mama-Alpa*, 'Mother-Sea' and 'Mother-Earth'? If not, it will be of little use to struggle for peace among nations, and still less to wage war, on board our little space-craft.

The ocean is not endless.

We jumped barefoot ashore at the other end.

The ocean current rolled on alone. Fifty-seven days. 5,700 years. Has mankind changed? Nature has not. And man is nature.

Epilogue

DRY FEET. Dry hair. Everything dry. Windows closed. Big trees swaying in the wind outside. But the paper on my desk doesn't flutter, doesn't even move. Nor does my chair. Everything is stable, fixed and firm. I am safe, back in my own work-room. Between the moving branches of the trees, blue water can be seen: the Mediterranean, the highway of early cultures, the link between three continents that enclose it tightly except for a single gap at Gibraltar. There are white caps on the sea, but to hear the surf I must open the window.

It feels unbelievably good to be safe in my study again, with books on every wall. Books and closed windows. I pull down a large roller-map in front of the window that faces the sea. It shows the Atlantic the way the map-makers see it: a flat, lifeless obstacle, dividing a rectangular world in two: Africa to the right, America to the left; North up and South down. What a shocking misconception of the most dynamic, vigorous, never-resting, ever-rushing conveyer that Nature ever set in motion! The map represents it as motionless like the Sahara, petrified like the Alps; and differing from them only in colour – blue, while the land is yellow, brown, green or white.

What a perfect board it would make for a game! Just right for moving small pieces about at the throw of dice. You make your throw, then move your piece on any colour until stopped by blue. If you try to cross blue you are cheating.

But the diffusionists couldn't care less. They cheat. They move on blue in all directions. How amazed the players would be if blue on the board began to move as the ocean moves, rolling in wide bands, throwing their pieces about, sending them from Africa to tropical America, and from tropical America to Asia and back again to North America. If the maps had been made mobile, new rules for the game

320

would have had to be invented. White or black pieces, reaching a square off Morocco, would gain an extra leap to America on the blue band of the Canary Current. Yellow pieces off Indonesia would hit the moving band coming from Polynesia and get sent back home in two throws, by way of the Japan Current and North-West America. Heading in one direction, blue would always mean a long forward jump; in the other direction, the loss of a turn; while green areas would become the new obstacles in this realistic game; so would the yellow desert and the white ice.

I snatch at the string to send my stupid roller-map rocketing up the window. The Mediterranean moves again between the trees like a meadow combed by the wind. I push the window open, listening for the living surf, and let the wind play havoc with all my papers and speculations. To hell with paper! To hell with -isms; diffusionism as well as isolationism!

If only the rumbling sea could speak! Then it would have stories to tell of unrecorded voyages of antiquity matching any of those recorded in medieval times. The men of antiquity were not pieces on a board. Their stupendous creations show that they were dynamic, imaginative, inquisitive, courageous, clever – stronger than the men of the press-button age, and with greater trust in their gods. Sailors from ancient Egypt left the Red Sea to visit Mesopotamia and Asian ports beyond. From the mouth of the Nile they criss-crossed the eastern Mediterranean to collect taxes from remote islands for a distant pharaoh. The people of Egypt and the people of Mesopotamia, affiliated, though speaking different languages and writing different scripts, bred sailors as able as their architects, and caused sea-borne civilizations to blossom, again with different languages and different scripts, on all the distant islands that formed stepping stones north and west.

We do not know when the Egyptian influence on the islands began, but the Phoenicians gradually took over. We know little of the origins of the Phoenicians or of the kind of ships they first constructed. Reed boats were originally used among their nearest neighbours east and south, and even west; for an engraved ring from ancient Crete shows a crescent-shaped reed boat with transverse lashings, mast and cabin. From Phoenician waters, culture spread beyond Gibraltar: to Lixus, for instance, where reed boats survived. No one will ever be able to retrace the routes of all these vessels or reconstruct the relationships between all these diversified civilizations, intimately interlocked and yet clearly different as they were, partly imposed on earlier local cultures, and nourished by different rulers, in different geographical environments. Who will ever identify the mariners of the fourth century BC who carried a jar of gold and copper Mediterranean coins to Corvo Island in the outer Azores, a point nearer to North America than to Gibraltar? Seeking fortune or refuge, thousands of ships left their home ports during antiquity, leaving no written records. As we have seen, royal artists recorded the Egyptian Queen Hatshepsut's great naval expedition in wooden ships down the Red Sea to Punt, but only by chance did the geographer Eratosthenes record the distance between Ceylon and the mouth of the Ganges in terms of the number of sailing days needed by ordinary papyrus boats with Egyptian sail and rigging. No temple was raised in their honour. Only when the noble Hanno personally sailed through the Straits of Gibraltar in the fifth century BC, with sixty ships stocked with provisions and carrying thousands of Phoenician colonists of both sexes, was the event immortalized on an inscribed stele raised in his honour at Carthage. Yet the inscription admits that Hanno was no pioneer, for on the fourth day of coastal sailing beyond Gibraltar his fleet reached the city of Lixus, where he took on local pilots who knew the coast and had names for all the capes for a further twenty-eight days of sailing. With provisions for two months, Hanno turned back only when his fleet had reached well down the coast of equatorial West Africa.

The stele, as later recorded by the Greeks, referred to the population of Lixus as foreigners among whom the explorers sojourned long enough to secure friendship and advice. These ancient voyagers were masters in the art of developing fruitful relations even with hostile, primitive people. According to their own records, before they dared to leave their ships they always sent a tempting gift ashore as a token of friendship, to be picked up by local tribes. The obvious benefits of international collaboration on voyages to foreign lands were fully understood by the men of antiquity, and not least by the Egyptians and Phoenicians. This is why it was quite normal that Egyptians and Phoenicians should have joined hands in the first historically recorded circumnavigation of Africa, nearly two centuries before Hanno's skilfully prepared fleet of emigrants sailed down the already known west coast. In fact, Pharaoh Necho's round-Africa expedition of about 600 BC was an Egyptian enterprise with Phoenician ships and crew; but no king or pharaoh accompanied the three-year venture, so no tomb or stele tells the story. It just happened that Herodotus recorded the event before it was forgotten.

What kind of culture would have begun to blossom among formerly primitive jungle hunters on the other side of the Atlantic if such a mixed expedition of colonists or explorers had been driven there? Something quite new and yet quite similar, with a strong local flavour?

That stupid map with the dead blue area which places Mexico centuries or millennia away from Morocco, instead of a few weeks! A few snatches of sleep for a monkey, a duck, or any other passenger. Mere seconds, when counted within the framework of history. True, the people of America had not seen ribbed ships of wooden planks before the arrival of Columbus, but the people of Morocco and of the entire Mediterranean and of Mesopotamia had seen reed boats, like those that survive in America. I had made a fumbling experiment of building only two such vessels, with the aid of a few lake people, and yet had sailed some 6,000 miles in four months, landing in America on the second trip. By building a hundred, we too, like Hanno, might have learned to sail safely up and down off the dreaded Cape Juby. But in the meantime, how many times would we have run the risk of breaking the rudder and landing in America? And heaven knows *what* kind of culture pattern we from *Ra* would have agreed upon!

I close the window. I grab my pencil and write—

I still don't know. I have no theory, except that a reed boat is seaworthy and the Atlantic is a conveyer. But from now on I shall be of the opinion that it must have been miraculous if some of the countless maritime expeditions during the millennia of antiquity did not break their rudders off Lixus or were not swept off course while struggling to avoid shipwreck in the perilous currents off Cape Juby. Did we drift to America because of unprecedented stupidity in handling woodwork, or because of unprecedented skill in sitting on reeds?

Here I have a theory: perhaps because we sailed on the ocean and not on a map.

INDEX

Abaydar tribe, 90, 91
Abdullah, *see* Djibrine, Abdullah
Adamitullu, 100
Addis Ababa, 82, 92, 99, 100, 110, 281
adobe blocks: use of in building on both sides of Atlantic, 23; in Peru, 121, 247; in Mexico, 122, 247
Africa, Central, 54–78, 236. *See also* Chad, Republic of; Chad, Lake of
Africa, West, Phoenicians trade with, 237
African Neptune, New York, gives fruit to crew, 230, 242
Akapana pyramid, 41, 281
Alaska, first inhabited area of America, 21–2
Aleutian islands, 22
Alexandria, 147, 150; papyrus library at, 240–1
Ali, motor-boat skipper, 90–2, 110–11
Amara, Madame Aicha, 150; packs amphorae, 157; presents monkey to *Ra I*, 158; launches *Ra I*, 151; launches *Ra II*, 282
Amara, Pasha Taieb, 116, 150, 158, 277, 281
America, discovery and re-discovery of, 21–2
American Antiquity (1966), 37
American BOMEX Project, 273
American Peace Corps, 71
American sweet potato, introduced onto Easter Island, 34, 35
amphorae, made on ancient Egyptian pattern, 154, 156

Ankar, Peter, Norwegian Ambassador in Cairo, 108, 109, 134, 151, 158
Arabs, Moroccan, 148, 149; different physical types of, 189
Arctic Asia, settlers from in America, 21–2
Aseffa, acts as interpreter, 93, 95, 96, 99
Asia Minor, *see* Mesopotamia
askam: journey to find reeds for, 47–51; discarded example of, 52–3
Axum, old kingdom of, 85, 86
Axum monolith, 111
Aymara Indians, 42, 117, 281; build *Ra II*, 281, 283–5
Aztecs: collapse of kingdom of, 25; tradition of fair bearded men, 25, 249–50; writing of, 252

Baba, 59, 64; ability of as mechanic, 60–1; disappears with jeep, 77, 78
Bahar Dar, 83
Baja California, 46
Baker, Norman: on *Ra I*, 158–273; illness of, 163–83; as navigator, 184, 207, 213, 232, 245; as member of crew, 202–7, 214–17; humour of, 224; stung by Portuguese man-o'-war, 229; as radio operator, 152, 241–2; diffusionists' argument explained to, 246; sights Shenandoah, 269; unwilling to give up experiment, 272; on *Ra II*, 274–319; sights land, 317–18
balsa log raft, 30, 41; experiments upon, 233. *See also* Kon-Tiki
Barbados, 311; *Ra II* lands at Bridgetown, 318–19

Benhima Ahmed, Moroccan Ambassador to United Nations, 116
Berbers, 148, 149; different physical types of, 189, 243
Bernal, Dr Ignacio, exponent of isolationism, 124–5
berrendo deer, Heyerdahl's encounter with, 48–9
Bible, references to papyrus boats in, 240
bilharzia, dangers from, 62–3, 64, 70, 92, 101–2
bird men: Egyptian tomb paintings of, 20, 27, 250; Easter Island paintings of, 27
black monks, 84; knowledge of boat building, 85–9
Bol, 114, 128, 129, 130, 280; papyrus at, 57, 58; radio telephone at, 57–8, 77; journey to, 59–63; guest house at, 63–4, 71, 72; market day in, 69–70; tom-tom dance at, 73–6
Bolivia, 41, 281
Bravo, Ramon, 45, 47, 118, 153–4
British Museum, 235
Buhumi, Mussa: helps to build *Ra I*, 20, 135–47, 285; builds *kaday*, 68, 71; accepts Heyerdahl's invitation, 76–7; difficulty in obtaining labour contract for, 128–30; passport and medical examination of, 131; journeys to Egypt, 132–5; returns to Chad, 149–50
Buschi, Commendatore Mario, 111; transports reeds for *Ra I*, 115; transports reeds for *Ra II*, 281
Byblos, 235; trades with Egypt, 19, 108

cactus, forest, 44–5

Cairo, 134, 137; Mussa and Omar visit, 140
Cairo Museum, 108, 154, 156
Caitano, 48–50; paddles old *askam*, 53
Calamar, United Nations research vessel, 313, 314–15
California, Gulf of, 46
Canary Current, direction of, 148; *Ra I* enters, 190, 194–5
Canary Islands, 185, 188–90, 237, 243, 251
Cape Juby: dangerous sandbanks near, 181–2, 183, 186–7; second voyage, 275, 280, 292
Cape Verde Islands, 191, 223, 227; poor visibility around, 213–14
cargo, moved to port, 183, 193
Carlo, *see* Mauri, Carlo
Carrasco, German, 45
cenebar: use of for mast, 161; spare mast of, 191
ceramic jars, contents of, 222
Cerro Colorado, similar to Egyptian pyramids, 118, 121
Ceylon, papyrus ships reach, 241
Chad Embassy (Washington), 126
Chad, Lake, 17; floating islands of, 55, 65, 70; reed boats resemble those on Lake Titicaca, 56, 65, 70, 149; reed boats resemble those on Lake Zwai, 94; inaccessible nature of, 57; day spent on, 71; impossible to bring papyrus from, 79; strength of boats, 90, 94; boat builders from, 91, 125; no close contact with antiquity, 281
Chad Republic, 54–78; transport problems in, 55, 57–8; unrest in, 58; unfriendliness of Arab villages in, 60–1; guerrilla warfare in, 150, 202, 211

326

Niger, papyrus boats in, 68

Nile, 16, 56; transport on, 18; calmness of, 19, 20; Heyerdahl follows course of, 80–3; papyrus at source of, 80–1; Upper Nile, reaches of, 56, 82, 149; as means of transport for reeds for building *Ra I*, 111

Nile Valley, stepped pyramids in, 122

Nineveh, stone slab from, depicts two types of reed boats, 235–6, 244, 276

Noi Young You, 263

Norman, *see* Baker, Norman

Norway's National Day, 150

Norwegian Resistance Museum, 112

Nuraghi ruins, 149; Heyerdahl visits, 275–6

obolu: Laki papyrus boat, 101; resembled boats in Mexico, Peru and Chad, 106; need to dry, 107

Ohara, Kei: on *Ra II*, 274–319; cooking of, 293, 317; arrives at Safi, 294

oil clots: Abdullah discovers, 181; reappearance of, 208, 232, 269, 273; Madani takes samples of, 297–8, 310

Olmecs: stone monuments of, 121–2, 251, 279–80; pyramid builders, 124, 248; portraits show two types, 251–2

Omar, *see* M'Bulu, Omar

Ossama, Ex-Colonel Attia, 115

Ouhanni, Madani Ait, on *Ra II*, 274–319; takes samples of oil clots, 297–8, 310; recipes of, 293; joins *Ra II*, 294

Palenque pyramid, 119–24, 255; sun king's tomb, 122–3

pampano, 232, 290, 297

paper boat, 16

papyrus boats: historical precedent for, 17–30, 43; ancient wall paintings of, 17, 26; on ceramic jars in Peru, 26; use of in ancient Egypt, 79–80, 277; black monks hang up to dry, 87, 88; supposed limited life of, 110; need for reeds to be compressed at ends, 234

papyrus lifebelts, 241

Paris, plane from for Chad, 126

Peru, 115; voyages from, 18; acceptance of Spaniards in, 22, 24; culture of, 23–5, 41–3, 247, 255–7; weaving and art, 23–4, 253–4; communications and agriculture, 24; mining, 253; imported culture of, 26; ceramic paintings of reed boats, 26, 27, 30, 256; sun worship in, 27, 247, 250; cultural affinity with ancient Egypt, 28, 34, 37, 38, 236, 247, 279; use of *totora*, 35, 42; reed boats in, 43, 117–18; two types of reed boats, 236; pyramids in, 120, 121; mummies, 255; bearded statues, 244; use of paper, 252–3

petrels, 193

Phoenicians: ships of, 19–20, 108; papyriform, 20; trade with Morocco, 148, 236–8; as navigators, 239–41; use of red dye, 255; probably founded Lixus, 238–9, 279

photographer's boat, 258, 261

Pillars of Hercules, 148

pilot fish, 232, 290, 291, 297

Pizarro, Francisco, 258

'Plumed Serpent', divine symbol of bird and snake, 250

Pole Star, latitude measured by, 169

31–2, 36; in Central America, 41–2; in Central Africa, 56–78; at source of Nile, 79–107; compression produces longevity of, 117

Safi, Pasha of, *see* Amara Taieb

Safi, port of, 116, 145, 148; *Ra I* launched at, 149–51

Safi, ship's monkey, 158, 173, 206, 208–9, 211, 262; fondness for nuts, 222, 264; joins *Ra II*, 289–90, 312–13

Sahara, 15–17, 20, 56, 127; journey through, 60–3; sandstorm in, 139–40; sand from falls in Central America, 228, 273

San Salvador, 22

Santiago, *see* Genoves, Dr Santiago

Sardinia, 149; reed boats in, 236, 275–6; observation towers similar to those in Mexico, 276

Schjelderup, Thorleif, accompanies Heyerdahl to Peru, 117–18

sello, 157, 215, 316

Senkevitch, Yuri Alexandrovich: on *Ra I* as ship's doctor, 152–3, 158–273; his patients, 163, 165, 166–7, 169; keeps diary, 179; skill of, 186, relationship with rest of crew, 202–7, 215–16; stung by Portuguese man-o'-war, 210; humour of, 153, 213, 224; willing to continue experiment, 272–3; on *Ra II*, 274–319; invents sailcloth barrier, 306–7, 318

Seris Indians, 46–53; village of, 46–7; planted reeds for boat building, 51; knowledge of reed boats imported, 51–3

sextant, use of, 169, 195

shafat, near collapse of, 101–2;

similar to boats in Mexico, Peru and Chad, 106; need to dry, 107

Shari river, 68, 77

Shark Island, 48–51

sharks, 228–9, 271, 290–1, 317; attack *Ra I*, 245–6; attack *Ra II*, 312

Shenandoah, 262; radio contact with, 266, 268; comes into view, 269; *Ra I*'s cargo transferred to, 270–1; danger of hurricane to, 271–2

Siberia, 21, 22

Sinbad (I): sparing of, 208–9; broken leg of, 264, 268, 289

Sinbad (II), 291

Skraelings, 39

Smith, Percy, theory of, 28–9, 38

Sonora Desert, 46

Sourial, Georges: knowledge of Nile, 80; deep sea diver, 155–6; on *Ra I*, 158–273; manages steering oar, 184–5; inspects *Ra I*, from below, 197, 199, 212; background of, 202; volunteers as orderly, 204; relationship with rest of crew, 202–7, 214–16; unwell, 211; catches dolphins, 226, 227; teaches Abdullah to write, 229; interest in antiquity, 236, 240; sews *Ra I* together, 261, 264, 271; stung by Portuguese man-o'-war, 267, 315; unwilling to give up experiment, 272; on *Ra II*, 274–319; Egyptian dishes of, 293; argues with Santiago, 307–9; on board *Culpeper*, 316–17

Spanish conquistadores: welcome for, 22–4; settlements of, 258

Sphinx, 115, 135

Stockholm, Ethnographical Museum in, 112

Sudan, unrest in, 82